RICHARD'S BIBLE COMMENTARY

Part 2 - New Testament

BY

Richard Hirsch

authorHOUSE

AuthorHouse™
1663 Liberty Drive
Bloomington, IN 47403
www.authorhouse.com
Phone: 833-262-8899

Published by AuthorHouse 08/31/2020

ISBN: 978-1-7283-5853-6 (sc)
ISBN: 978-1-7283-5852-9 (e)

Print information available on the last page.

This book is printed on acid-free paper.

ACKNOWLEDGEMENTS

My grateful thanks and praise to Almighty God for His mercy and grace in permitting me to honor Him with this writing. Thanks also to the Holy Spirit for restoring my motivation when it waned.

Most heartfelt thanks and appreciation are extended to my beloved wife, HUGUETTE, who did without my company for many hours during the past year, while often giving me the benefit of her superb views on the true meaning of scriptural passages.

In addition I am most grateful for the encouragement given to me by three other sisters in Christ, namely my own daughter NANCY, my cousin and proxy sister, JOAN, and my sister-in-law FRANCOISE. Without the support of all it is doubtful that I would have completed this commentary as written.

Finally without the patient and thoughtful assistance of my Design Consultant ASHLEY and my Book Designer JESSICA at AuthorHouse, on the processing and printing of this commentary, I may have lacked the motivation to have it published. My sincere thanks and appreciation to you, Ashley and Jessica.

RICHARD C. HIRSCH

A WORD TO THE PURCHASERS OF THIS COMMENTARY: Thanks for selecting my commentary to enhance your understanding of the New Testament portion of God's Holy Bible. I hope that you will find it most useful in comprehending the most logical and correct meaning of scripture. I recommend that you use it in conjunction with a good Christian Bible, such as the New American Standard, the New King James Version, the New International Version, or the New Revised Standard.

CORAM DEO—SOLA FIDE—SOLA SCRIPTURA—SOLA GRACIA
—In the presence, by the power, for the glory of God
—By faith alone---By the Scripture alone—By grace alone—

TABLE OF CONTENTS

FOREWORD

In early January 1999, while pondering what New Year's resolutions to make, I decided to attempt a complete reading of the Holy Bible, and forthwith began with the first book of the Old Testament, Genesis, in my large print Bible. For easier reading, I switched to a Bible study program on my personal computer for a regular daily perusal of The Word according to a prescribed schedule.

Immediately, I began to take note of information and hidden meaning in passages of scripture that seemed new, unusual, sometimes complex, and different from my previous understanding. Later in my reading, the idea grew that perhaps I should compile some kind of personal commentary to share with my family, on portions of scripture that seemed special and meaningful. My initial objective was to write commentary on selective content, but not the entire Bible.

After reading through the entire Bible, I received inspiration to devote more time to intense study with a new objective to write commentary on all of it One of my primary working tools was a bible study program on a CD-ROM disk, called "Quick Verse." Yes, 20th century technology was most helpful in making this project possible, by lending motivation to stick with it. Other published textbooks were used to compare all views.

Just as some other Richard had written his Almanac in times past, I decided to use a title equally personal as "Richard's Bible Commentary." This title, to some, may denote a more formal style of writing than I contemplated. Mine would not be a scholarly or theologically thorough writing considered suitable for 'men of the cloth' to use as a reliable reference textbook. It was written to benefit lay readers in normal study of the Bible.

My objective was to share my personal observations and clarifying comments on the most likely or logical meaning of all scripture. As my writing progressed, I was challenged to bring out special meaning on unusual or complex details that aroused my curiosity or impressed me. It would be more typical of a layman's views.

After 6 years of intermittent work to complete Part 1-Old Testament of Richard's Bible Commentary, it was submitted to AuthorHouse in March of 2004 for first publication. Since it was my first attempt as an author, much refinement and editing was required before it was published for general distribution, in February 2005.

The completion of Part 1 inspired me greatly to continue at an accelerated pace on Part 2-New Testament. With a regular work schedule of more hours per day, I completed this writing in a year, to submit it for first publication in March of 2005. The two volumes go hand in hand, with Old Testament prophecy tied in with New Testament revelation.

It is my fervent hope that all who use this commentary will spend much more time in God's Word, with understanding enhanced by my contribution even though it barely scratches the surface of HIS supernaturally composed and preserved Word to us. Most important, may this publication Honor the Lord while it sharpens your own spiritual sensitivity to God's Word.

RICHARD C. HIRSCH

THE BIBLE AS GOD'S WORD

The Bible—what is it—what should it mean to mankind? How can one better understanding it? These are questions that generate a vast variety of answers. The book in itself is remarkable for its longevity and survival throughout the centuries, existing in early history as hidden manuscripts and much later as a completed text.

Any attempt to date the Bible accurately as to the origin of earliest written accounts is an exercise in futility. The same is true of the timing of major biblical events such as creation, the time of the great flood, the exodus from Egypt, and more. The earliest writings of the Bible in manuscript form may have occurred about 3500 years ago, based on the dating of clay tablets inscribed with crude scripts that were discovered in the Euphrates valley. Common belief is that creation and the origin of sin in the garden of Eden took place about 4000 BC., but this appears to be no less speculative than some scholars suggesting a time of 8000-10,000 B.C. (see Unger's Bible Handbook, by Moody Press)

The word "Bible" was formed from a Greek term 'biblos' meaning books in the plural. The modern Christian Bible written and compiled over a span of 1600 years, is composed of 66 separate writings (called books) that are divided into two parts: Part 1 consists of 39 books called the Old Testament; this is followed by Part 2 made up of 27 books known as the New Testament. Numerous translation versions are now available. The first five books of Old Testament (called the Pentateuch), classed as historical, are Genesis, Exodus, Leviticus, Numbers, and Deuteronomy. Popular belief is that they were written by Moses. They are about the origins of the Jewish race and culture from creation to the land of Canaan.

Genesis reveals how life began and how sin and rebellion damaged man's relationship with God. Exodus reveals the birth of Moses and his role in rescuing the Hebrews from slavery in Egypt to move them towards the land of Canaan. Leviticus is about worship laws and communion with the Lord. Numbers speaks of the experiences of the Hebrews as they moved through a time of hostility and grief to their promised inheritance. Deuteronomy gives instructions for the people of Israel about to enter the land of Canaan. Collectively, these books constitute an excellent introduction to the entire bible.

Old testament books are generally classified as historical, poetic, or prophetic. A total of 17 have been classified as historical books, as follows: the 5 books of the Pentateuch, followed by Joshua, Judges, Ruth, I & II Samuel, I & II Kings, I & II Chronicles, Ezra, Nehemiah, and Esther. Poetical books include these 6: Job, Psalms, Proverbs, Ecclesiastes, Song of Solomon, and Lamentations. The remaining 16 classed as prophetic books are: 4

Major— Isaiah, Jeremiah, Ezekiel, Daniel; 12 Minor— Hosea, Joel, Amos, Obadiah, Jonah, Micah, Nahum, Habakkuk, Zephaniah, Haggai, Zechariah, and Malachi.

The New Testament which literally means the 'new covenant" is separated into 4 basic parts. The first 4 books, Matthew, Mark, Luke, and John, commonly called the Gospels, describe the life and ministry of Jesus Christ. Next is the book of ACTS, a history of the beginning of the church and the growth of Christianity. This is followed by 21 letters, from Romans to Jude, of which the apostle Paul wrote as many as 14. They primarily teach Christian doctrine as it applies to life situations. The last book of Revelations describes the endtimes victory of Jesus Christ and His people over a world of sin for eternity.

Books are divided by chapters and verses. There are 1189 chapters in all, with 929 in the Old Testament and 260 in the New Testament. Psalms, with the most chapters totaling 150, also has the longest Bible chapter in Psalms 119 and the shortest chapter of the Bible, Psalms 117, which is also the middle chapter of the Bible.

Some say that the Bible is the greatest of all books and to study it to gain utmost understanding is a noble pursuit of the highest degree. The beginning of understanding requires the simple but often difficult step of opening and reading it with an open and inquiring mind. The reading of it may be selective at first of some of the shorter books, by subject matter, or topics of personal interest, from the historical, poetic, or prophetic books. No matter what the motivation is, one should focus on deriving the most logical understanding possible, and use all cross-references that may clarify or add to the best view.

The objective is always to understand as accurately as possible what the Bible says, without reading into it some hidden or obscure meaning based on personal or church doctrinal beliefs or preferences. A good rule for realistic understanding is: 'when unvarnished words of scripture makes common sense, seek no other sense, but accept every word at its indicated literal meaning unless pertinent cross-references clearly say otherwise.' That was my major objective in the writing of this commentary.

Some of the most interesting facts about the Bible include the following: —it is the world's best seller, translated into more languages than any other book, —it is always a timely message for mankind, and —it is clearly a uniquely divine gift from God Himself.

In depth study confirms that the Bible is truly God's holy word. Although recorded by human authors, they were inspired by God to write what He wanted them to say. Christ is the central theme of the Bible, in prophecy in the Old Testament, and the main personality in the New Testament story of His life and future glory.

Abraham Lincoln said: 'I believe the Bible is the best gift God has ever given to man. All the good from the savior of the world is communicated to us through this book.' Napoleon said: 'The Bible is no mere book, but a Living Creature, with a power that conquers all that oppose it.' Robert E. Lee said: 'In all my perplexities and distresses, the Bible has never failed to give me light and strength.' A multiple Amen to these comments!

The Bible is constructed around the resurrection and life of Christ and His promise of life eternal to all those who know of Him, believe in Him, and follow Him. It is God's word as no other book ever written has been or will be. Everyone who understands it will know that it is a divine presentation of facts pertaining to a meaningful life. Without the Bible there is no real purpose to life's honors.

Published commentaries in existence today emphasize features and details of the book in different ways for separate reasons, depending upon the author's doctrinal views. Readers of this commentary are encouraged to peruse the pages of all the references listed that were used to compile this documentary for more information about the Bible.

It is my heartfelt hope and desire that this commentary will add to the spiritual discernment of all who want to know and understand the Bible to the best to their ability

RICHARD C. HIRSCH

TABLE OF REFERENCES

The following references were used in my study of New Testament books and the language used by other authors, not only to gain understanding, but to confirm my own comprehension of the true or most plausible meaning of the written word. Where different views were presented among several references, my interpretation was based on what seemed most logical to me. My views are by no means presented as the only understanding that one can derive from a study of biblical doctrine and historical narration, but they are what made sense to me.

THE BIBLE READER'S COMPANION- by Lawrence O. Richards
Ottenheimer Publishers, Inc.-1991

RYRIE STUDY BIBLE, New American Standard Bible-1995 update
Charles C Ryrie Expanded Edition, Moody Press

THE NELSON STUDY BIBLE, New King James Version,
Earl D. Radmacher, General Editor, Thomas Nelson Publishers-1982

REVELATION, PAST-PRESENT-FUTURE, by Preston A. Taylor
Blue Line Graphics—1980

UNGER'S BIBLE DICTIONARY- by Merrill F. Unger
Moody Press-1957

HALLEY'S BIBLE HANDBOOK- by Henry H. Halley
Zondervan Publishing House-1965

THE PRE-WRATH RAPTURE OF THE CHURCH
By Marvin Rosenthal, Thomas Nelson Publishers-1990

THE RAPTURE QUESTION ANSWERED
By Robert Van Kampen, Fleming H. Revell Co.-1997

ERDMAN'S HANDBOOK TO THE BIBLE
Wm B. Eerdman's Publishing Co.-1973

QUICK VERSE NEW BIBLE REFERENCE COLLECTION
From a CD Rom disk by Parson Technology-1995—including:
—Matthew Henry's Concise Commentary—
—NRSV- New Revised Standard Bible—
—NIV- New International—
—KJV-King James Bible—
—Holman Bible Dictionary—

INTRODUCTION TO THE NEW TESTAMENT

The main message of the New Testament is the fulfillment of all that the Old Testament promised mankind through prophecy over many centuries It tells of a new dispensation when God sent His only son Jesus Christ in human form to be a better solution for mankind's desperate problem of sin. It tells how <u>Christ became a sacrificial lamb to</u> <u>give mankind a road map to a better relationship with God</u> and eternal life in Christ with the prerequisites of repentance, faith and commitment. Christ's teaching focused on the 'Kingdom of Heaven.'

The New Testament contains clear instructions for living a life that is pleasing to the Lord. As the name implies it literally is a <u>new covenant between God and His beloved children</u> in His own image, with His Son Christ as the Ambassador of Goodwill. Christ is also portrayed as the 'miracle worker,' evidenced by His many miraculous works of healing, exorcising demons, extraordinary demonstrations, and compassion for people of low estate.

Salvation, pure and simple, is the central theme of the New Testament, <u>facilitated by the</u> <u>death and resurrection of Jesus Christ.</u> This is spelled out in the 27 books written by 8-9 authors over a period of about 50 years. The first four books, called the Gospels, describe in detail the genealogy, the life, and the ministry of Jesus Christ. The fifth book of Acts gives a history of the beginning of Christ's Church under the ministry of the 12 disciples, with the spread of Christianity throughout the Greco-Roman world.

This is followed by 21 letters (epistles), Romans through Jude, with the Apostle Paul recognized as the certain author of 13 of them. He may also have authored the book of Hebrews. Other authors were: James, the brother of Jesus, for his book; Peter for I and II Peter; John for I, II, III John, and Revelation; and Jude the half-brother of Jesus, for his book. The letters teach Christian church doctrine.

The last book of Revelations <u>describes the dramatic consequences of God's endtime</u> <u>scenario,</u> with Christ's second coming in triumph over sin to establish His millennial kingdom, after God's Wrath Judgment deals with the worldly wicked.

Over 400 years transpired from the writing of the last book of the Old Testament, Malachi, and the writings of the New Testament. During that time the <u>Old Testament was translated</u> <u>from the Hebrew or Aramaic language</u> into the Greek language, to be named the Septuagint. Fourteen other writings during these years, called the Apocrypha, are not part of the Christian Bible, but 11 of them are in the Roman Catholic Bible. They were not recognized as Scripture by the Jews or by Jesus, or by scholars who compiled the Protestant Bible. Nevertheless, they are interesting to read for their historic content.

This commentary was written in an attempt to ferret out the true basic meaning of New Testament scripture apart from denominational doctrine or injection of theological views. <u>Recognition was given to God's logic in all things,</u> in particular, to His endtimes scenario for the return of Christ as King of all Mankind!

This includes the gathering of the Saints in what is called the 'Rapture.'

GOSPEL OF MATTHEW—BOOK ONE

Just as Genesis is the book of beginnings for the Old Testament, the Gospel of Matthew is the book of beginnings for the New Testament. It sets the stage for a new era in man's relationship with God through His Son Jesus Christ. Matthew has been appropriately called the book of Jesus Christ, where He is presented as the Son of God at least 23 times. It is recognized as authoritative in its emphasis on the teachings of Jesus and His power to command the disciples to spread the gospel throughout the world.

The author of the book is generally recognized as Matthew, the Jewish disciple of Christ, a.k.a. Levi, a tax collector for the Roman administration of that day and a man of intelligence. Most scholars date his writing to the decade of 50-60 AD. Legend has it that he died a martyrs death but this is not revealed in the scriptures.

Matthew identifies Christ more than any other gospel as King of the Jews, with fulfillment of Old Testament prophecy pertaining to the Messiah. As many as 93 quotes from the Old Testament have been identified, more than in any other New Testament book. Although primarily a message to the Jews, the book provides a tie-in of Gentiles into the Jewish culture, initially with the arrival of the wise men from the east searching for the 'King of the Jews.'

The book is basically compiled in seven sections: the beginning, followed by 5 teaching sections, and the ending. Chapter 1 opens with a genealogy confirming the lineage of Jesus from the Old Testament branch of David, and 2-4 continue with details on the childhood days of Jesus. Next is the Sermon on Mount in chapters 5-7, where Jesus emphasizes the important of His commandments, followed by chapters 8-10, where 10 miracles are described that demonstrate His authority over physical defects and earthly elements. Chapters 11-13 relate how Jesus spoke in parables and how people reacted to His words and His teaching in the synagogue. Chapters 14-18 are His teachings in the synagogue in Nazareth and 19-25 tells of His cleansing of the synagogue of commercialism with more teaching to scribes and Pharisees. In 26-28 Matthew recounts the conspiracy which resulted in Christ's execution and subsequent resurrection.

CHAPTER 1:   The first 17 verses enumerate a total of the 42 generations from Abraham through David in an apparent effort to convince the Jews that Jesus Christ had a legal right to be recognized as King of the Jews, or the long awaited Messiah. This is as God had ordained early in human history, as far back as 4000 years. Along with the many men who are identified as fathers of named offspring are 4 Old Testament women named as the mothers, namely Tamar, Rahab, Ruth and Bathsheba in verses 3-6.

In verses 18-2599, the genealogy is traced to Joseph, the husband to be of Mary, who in her own right was not in the royal line of David, although Jesus was born solely of her by divine conception. None of the other women were in the chosen line of Abraham or the royal line of David but they gave birth to children for fathers who were in that line. Even though Joseph was a direct descendant of David he could not be the physical father of Jesus, the son of God, because conception took place before he had intimacy with his betrothed.

When Joseph learned of Mary's pregnancy without his involvement he first wanted to separate from her, but an Angel of the Lord persuaded him to <u>honor his commitment to her by consummating the marriage.</u> He was told that conception was brought about by God's Holy Spirit and God's preselected name for the child was to be Jesus. Joseph complied in a most commendable fashion, even to <u>not having intimacy with Mary before the birth of Jesus.</u> In Hebrew the name Jesus means 'Jehovah saves,' thus explaining His purpose to save sinners of the world. The prophecy of a virgin birth of a sinless Son to be called Immanuel is found in Isaiah 7:14-16. Other prophecy about the coming Messiah is found in Gen. 3:5, 12:3, 17:19, and 49:10; Isaiah 9:7; and Micah 5:2.

CHAPTER 2: In verses 1-12, we are told of the 'Wise men from the East' coming to Jerusalem to find the baby Jesus who they identified as one <u>worthy of worship as the 'King</u> of the Jews.' When their search effort aroused the ruling King Herod the Great, he was concerned over a future contender for his throne, and asked his legal minds for the birthplace of the Child. Based on prophecy in Micah 5:2, they <u>advised him it was Bethlehem,</u> at which he secretly requested of the wise men that they inform him of the Child's location so he too could worship him. His reason appears to be hypocritical!.

The wise men left to follow the guiding star to where it appeared to hover, and there they found the Child with his parents living in a home, presumably <u>months or even a year or</u> <u>more after his birth.</u> After a time of worship and presentation of gifts of gold (symbolizing royalty), frankincense (fragrance of purity), and myrrh (an ointment of death), they left to return to their own country without seeing Herod, having been warned in a divine dream not to go back to him.

Verses 13-18 tell of an angel instructing Joseph in a heavenly dream to take his family to Egypt to escape Herod's efforts to kill the Child. By night they departed and journeyed about 150 miles to Egypt. It is presumed that they may have hired camel transportation using some of the gold they had received; this <u>can be seen as divine provision from God.</u>

Meanwhile, evil Herod, angry over the wise men's disobedience, had all male children up to 2 years of age in Bethlehem and surrounding communities <u>put to death.</u> Since this caused great mourning, some say that this fulfilled prophecy in Jeremiah 31:15, where Rachel mourned the absence of her sons. The 2 year age limit may have been due to a delay of Herod's decision.

After Herod died, an angel spoke again to Joseph in a dream, telling him it was safe to return to Israel; as stated in verses 19-23, the family traveled almost 200 miles <u>returning to Galilee to live in Nazareth.</u> This too has some prophetic relevance; an angel had informed Mary and Joseph that she was to have a child when they lived earlier in Nazareth, and Jesus was to be called a 'Nazarene' (meaning contemptible or despised) as generally described in Isaiah 53:3.

<u>VIEWPOINTS:</u> It is significant that God provided divine intervention 3 times in this chapter; 1st to the wise men to disregard Herod's instructions, and 2nd, to warn Joseph twice for safety reasons, to flee to Egypt and then to return to Israel to live in Nazareth. This points to fulfillment of prophecy as God intended, to further <u>confirm Christ as His Son.</u>

CHAPTER 3: Verses 1-13 describe the ministry of John the Baptist in a desert wasteland west of the Dead Sea. This relates to a prophecy in Isaiah 40:3 of one who was to spiritually prepare the way for Christ's ministry to the Jews. John was dressed as a desert nomad in a camel hide held shut by a belt; he also ate locusts and honey where he found them.

In spite of his unconventional lifestyle, his message of righteousness motivated many people to be baptized as they repented of their sins. This did not include Pharisees and Sadducees, who held views deviant to righteousness as John preached it. He chastised them for their hypocrisy and legalism and warned them that they would be subject to God's judgment if they did not repent and become fruitful in the Lord's service. He announced that one would come (Christ) who in the power of the Holy Spirit would gather those acceptable to Him (the rapture of the saints) and destroy those who are nothing but chaff, the unrepentant (end-times judgment). These events are spoken of as closely sequential!

Jesus heard of John's ministry and came to him requesting baptism also, in verses 13-

17, but John declared that Jesus should properly baptize him. Jesus merely replied that John should 'permit it to be so' for Jesus to be baptized to fulfill all righteousness, meaning that as the epitome of righteousness (without sin) before Almighty God He wanted to identify with sinners who repented and were baptized. Redemption of sinners was to be His mission.

After His baptism, the Holy Spirit descended like a dove from heaven to envelop Him, and a voice from above (God the Father) said, 'This is My beloved Son, in whom I am well-pleased.' This is in agreement with the words of Isaiah 11:1, signifying that Jesus was fully inaugurated into His ministry with His Father's approval. Thus, we have a pact involving the Trinity, a union of the Father, the Holy Spirit, and the Son of God.

CHAPTER 4: Here we read of Christ's 1ˢᵗ temptation by Satan in verses 1-11, to make Him sin and become disqualified as the Redeemer. This happened after Jesus endured a 40 day fast in a nearby wilderness, possibly as a form of spiritual retreat after His anointment by the Holy Spirit and God. Satan tempted Him in His weakness of under-nourishment, by suggesting that Jesus turn stones into bread. Jesus rebutted him with words from Deuteronomy 8:2-3, that one should not rely on bread alone for life, but more importantly heed the Word of God.

Verse 5 says that Satan (the devil) took Jesus to a holy city (unidentified) to stand on a high point of a temple, and taunts Him, 'As the Son of God, jump to the ground, for God will command His angels to keep You from harm,' quoting a part of Psalms 91:11-12 in justification. Jesus quoted Deut. 6:16 in response to say, 'One should not put God to the Test against His will.'

For a 3ʳᵈ time, Satan tempts Jesus after taking Him to a high mountain to show Him the glory and splendor of all the kingdoms that Satan controlled. He offered all of them to Jesus if He would fall on His knees and worship him. Jesus told Satan to beat it, adding from Deut. 6:13-14, that 'You shall worship the Lord your God, and serve Him only.'

After this rebuke, Satan left, and angels came to minister to Jesus, providing for His need, a reward for resisting evil.

After His bout with Satan, Jesus began His ministry in Galilee as told in verses 12-17, to reside in Capernaum, which fulfilled the prophecy of Is. 9:1-2, that people in that region would be enlightened in their faith. Jesus preached, 'Repent, for the Kingdom of Heaven is at hand.' Could this have meant that Jesus was ready to establish His millennial kingdom if the people accepted and yielded to His message of repentance? It is a logical thought!

Jesus begins to assemble His disciples in 18-21, by calling on 4 fishermen to join Him. First, he recruited 2 brothers, Simon Peter and Andrew, and then two other brothers, James and John, with the invitation to 'Follow Me and I will make you fishers of men.' All four left their fishing boats and followed Him. To obey without question may suggest that they had heard enough of Christ's message to have already been convicted in their faith of His cause.

Verses 23-25 tell how Jesus moved everywhere healing people of sickness, diseases, and demonic spirits, gaining much fame and a large following as He moved to other places in Jerusalem, Judea, and east of the Jordan River. He worked hard! A significant ministry inasmuch as there had been none like it for over 400 years.

VIEWPOINTS: How was Satan able to 'take' Jesus to two different places away from the wilderness? This is not easy to understand! The implication is that Satan had the power to do so, but it may be that Jesus willingly went along, knowing what Satan was up to, just to demonstrate how to resist temptation in accordance with God's Word. Bravo!

CHAPTER 5:   This chapter plus 6 & 7 include Christ's teaching known as the Sermon on the Mount, probably because verses 1-2 tell that He first delivered it on the side of a mountain, primarily to his disciples. In verses 3-11, He gives all the good characteristics, or attitudes, which bring spiritual blessings for an improved quality of life.

Among the blessed are the 'poor in spirit, those who mourn, the meek, those who yearn for righteousness, the merciful, the pure in heart, the peacemakers, and those who suffer persecution from insults and false charges because of their faith.'

Basically, good people are cited here! Their rewards include a future in heaven, divine comfort, a good earthly life, spiritual fulfillment, compassion for others, a close relationship with God for which they will be recognized, and a measure of gratitude with happiness to cope with the meanness of the world.

Commendatory remarks given in verses 13-16 include: 'salt of the earth' and 'light of the world.' These may have been addressed primarily to the disciples. As salt of the earth, they were to be a preservative of Christ's teachings; as light of the world, they were to be an example as well as an advocate of righteous living to all men. The spice of their spiritual fervor was to be combined with their illumination of Christ's teachings to enhance the spiritual growth of others.

In 17-20, Jesus assures them that He did not intend to diminish the importance of Old Testament Law or Prophecy; rather, He was to shed new light on applying and fulfilling them. The laws are to be obeyed as always and taught as applicable to a righteous life. Prophecies would be fulfilled sooner or later. All are truth for today and tomorrow if not yet fulfilled! Those who maintain their faith in this regard will reap great rewards when they reached heaven.

Verses 21-48 relate what Jesus said about 6 specific acts or attitudes that relate to bad character, or lead to trouble, i.e.: anger, adultery, marriage and divorce, false witnessing, and retaliation versus charitable love. Hatred and anger should be avoided or tempered to <u>avoid murderous acts;</u> slanderous language such as calling another a 'bird brain or a fool' without justification <u>can produce harmful </u>results. It is better to seek God's help to reconcile differences with others, and to <u>do so before attempting to serve the Lord,</u> lest one be considered a hypocrite.

Not only is the act of adultery forbidden in 27-30, but a man looking upon a woman with sexual lust is deemed <u>guilty of the same sin.</u> Although not a physical involvement, such lust is of the heart, and can lead to the act itself if the emotion is not removed as quickly as possible. The seriousness of this sin and the need for overcoming it is illustrated by destroying an eye or hand if either should <u>contribute to the sinful act or thought.</u> Turning to God in remorse for Him to pluck such feelings out of mind and heart is the best way to cleansing.

The bond of marriage between a man and a woman with conditions for divorce are given clarity in verses 31-32; sexual immorality (adultery, homosexuality, bestiality, etc.) is given as the <u>only specified justification for divorce.</u> Incompatibility is not a good reason in this context.

Verses 33-37 might seem to forbid taking an oath to tell the truth, with 'so help me God.' It more logically <u>prohibits swearing untruthfully in the name of God.</u> An honest 'yes' or 'no' is really all that is necessary, but our legal system regularly incorporates reference to God. This is not a sin in itself if absolute <u>honesty is the basis of the oath.</u>

Jesus seems to cancel out the old covenant retaliatory of 'An eye for an eye, or a tooth for a tooth' in verses 38-42, by <u>advocating greater tolerance and compassion</u> to those who do us harm. While we must sometimes seek legal restitution, our motive should not be vindictive or unduly injurious to an opponent. An effort to overcome evil or animosity with deeds of kindness and understanding can often remove antagonism and <u>contribute to the spiritual needs of others.</u>

In verses 43-48, replacing hate with love, as hard as it may be, can bring <u>greater satisfaction in personal relationships</u>, than to harbor ill feelings towards others. By so doing, we mirror the perfection and compassion of a forgiving God, who helps us to cope with this problem.

CHAPTER 6:   Three demonstrations of piety are discussed in verses 1-18: <u>giving to the poor, public prayer, and fasting.</u> Perhaps most applicable to the Jewish temple leaders, these acts, if done by anyone for self-aggrandizement do not find favor with God. Verses 1-4 admonish charitable works to be a private matter without fanfare or <u>pretentious publicity.</u>

As for prayer, as discussed in 5-15, it should be rendered sincerely and intelligently from the heart to God the Father, <u>without an eloquent use of words</u> to impress nearby listeners. On personal petitions, it is best to pray in private, although <u>group intercessory prayer is acceptable</u> too. Verse 7 cautions against vain repetitions as the heathens do (Gentiles in some translations); one might wonder if this includes speaking in tongues, which is <u>claimed to be a special gift</u> that is often ego related by those who do so.

Jesus gave His disciples what we know as the Lord's Prayer, in verses 9-13, which is now voiced repetitively in many churches. This can be a <u>vain repetition if spoken without heartfelt emotion</u>, but if spoken as one's personal expression to God, it is better than no cogent prayer. In verse 14, Jesus emphasized that the forgiveness of others also <u>brings us God's forgiveness.</u>

The acknowledgment, 'For Yours is the kingdom, the power, and the glory forever' is almost identical with the <u>words of I Chron. 29:11 (OT)</u>.

As stated in 16-18, fasting should also be done without pretentious public demonstration, but as an <u>act of reverence to God</u>. Verses 19-21 admonish that earthly wealth should not have priority over heavenly treasures <u>earned through dedicated Christian living</u>.

Our perception of what is right or wrong, bright or dark, depends on our <u>spiritual vision of God's purpose</u> for our lives as spelled out in verses 25-34. We must choose to serve God in all things, and avoid worldly allegiance. In this way, worry is not a problem <u>as God provides for our needs,</u> just as He does for birds, vegetation, and other living creatures. Basically, we are to live one day at a time, trusting in God, without anxiety or worry about tomorrow.

<u>CHAPTER 7:</u>   Of the 3 chapters on the Sermon on the Mount, this one is the most difficult to understand in a practical sense, perhaps <u>because of its metaphorical language</u>. In 1-5, a speck of sawdust and a beam of wood are used in the matter of judging others; that is to say we should not find fault with <u>small imperfections in others</u> while <u>overlooking our own major flaws</u>. In other words, consider our own faults before judging others for theirs; then be careful to correct ourselves before we try to correct others.

To give something sacred to dogs and to throw pearls in front of pigs, as forbidden in verse 6, may speak of <u>presenting Christian principles to degenerate sinners</u> who would reject them and then denigrate the donor. Don't waste precious spiritual values on unholy people!

Verses 7-12 seems to say that one can receive anything desired just by asking, but verse 11 clarifies that <u>God will give what is good for us</u>, not what is bad in His judgment. The 3 words, ask, seek, and knock can form the acronym—ASK. This is the basis of fervent prayer at the <u>throne of God</u>. Like a loving father who would not give his son a stone or a snake for food, so it is with Almighty God, <u>He gives us according to His wisdom</u> what we need the most. Verse 12 confirms this as 'Give unto others as you would have them give to you.'

Good and bad choices for Christian living are given in verses 12-20, beginning with <u>selecting the narrow gate of spirituality</u> rather than the broad gate of worldly values. Warning is given to be wary of false teachings by those who appear to be benign but their agenda is evil and <u>not in accordance with God's Word</u>. Their influence is to be removed like a non- bearing fruit tree. What they say and do should be evaluated against factual biblical doctrine.

Obedience to the will of God is essential to eternal life in heaven in verse 21. Those who indulge in boastful self-glorification (vs 22-23), lacking a truly righteous nature or dedication in His service are <u>not acceptable to God.</u>

In 24-27, Jesus identifies all who listen and obey His teachings to be wise as one who <u>builds a home on a stable foundation</u>. With such a firm foundation in our spiritual relationship with God, we can withstand the hazards of life (symbolically floods, storms, tornadoes, etc.). Jesus amazed the crowds in verse 28-29; He <u>spoke with divine authority</u>.

<u>CHAPTER 8:</u>   As Jesus came down from the mountain, in verses 1-4, many followed him, including a leper who respectfully <u>submitted to His will for healing</u>. Jesus healed the man and instructed him to visit the temple priest to participate in the <u>cleansing sacrificial</u> <u>ceremony</u> <u>prescribed by Moses</u> in Chapter 14 of the Old Testament Book of Leviticus.

Jesus continues His healing ministry in verses 5-34. A Roman military officer came to Him requesting healing for his paralyzed servant. When Jesus agreed to go with the man, he said that was not necessary; he <u>credited Jesus with the power to heal by only speaking the</u> <u>word</u>, thereby recognizing His authority in the same light as the officer's command authority over his men. Jesus was greatly impressed with the faith of this Gentile man, declaring it <u>greater than that of the Jews</u>. Sadly, many Jews will lose out on their expectation of eternal life.

Verses 11-12 seem to speak of Christ's millennial reign when all <u>believing saints</u>, whether Jewish or Gentile, will join Him at a banquet, but the <u>unbelieving Jews will be</u> <u>relegated to hell</u>. The faith of the Roman officer is contrasted against the skeptical and apostate Jews, called sons of the kingdom. Jesus then tells the officer that his servant was healed according to his faith.

Two acts of healing follow in 14-17, that of Peter's mother-in-law with a fever, and demon possessed and otherwise ill people, thus <u>fulfilling the words of Is. 53:4.</u>

Possibly because of human fatigue, in 18-26, when Jesus beheld the huge crowd before Him, He <u>asked the disciples to take him by boat across the sea</u> of Galilee. Before they could embark, a scribe (writer) offered to follow Jesus anywhere, to which He pointed out that such a commitment <u>would bring deprivation and hardship</u> because He (Son of God) lacked normal creature comforts. Another disciple asked to be excused to bury his deceased father, or to stay at home until his father died, to which Jesus clarified that <u>following Him</u> <u>had a higher priority</u>.

Verses 23-27 tell of a great storm that came upon their boat after departing that almost capsized the vessel. Jesus was awakened from His sleep by the terrified crew <u>begging</u> <u>Him to</u> <u>save the ship from sinking</u>. After rebuking them for their lack of faith, He spoke to the winds and sea, and <u>absolute calmness prevailed.</u> Naturally, the men marveled at this supernatural power.

The chapter ends with the healing of two demon possessed men in verses 28-34. The demons addressed Jesus through their hostage humans, as the 'Son of God,' and accused Him of coming to torment them. Knowing that Jesus had the power to exorcise them from the body of the men, the demons requested that they <u>be allowed to possess a herd of pigs</u> nearby. Jesus merely said 'GO' and they entered the pigs which immediately plunged over a cliff <u>into the</u> <u>sea to drown.</u> The keepers of the pigs fled in terror to tell all in a nearby city. This caused the inhabitants to confront Jesus to <u>demand that He leave their community</u>.

<u>VIEWPOINTS:</u> The faith of the Roman officer may have been the most impressive demonstration of faith that Jesus encountered in His ministry, so much so that He used it as an example of what He wanted to see in his own people, <u>the Jews</u>. The misplaced faith of the pig herders and the city people <u>made them reject Jesus in favor of material possessions</u>. This is a tragic tendency on the part of many people who covet material wealth over spiritual values.

CHAPTER 9: In verses 1-8, a paralytic is brought to Jesus who saw genuine faith in him and his attendants, and quickly told the paralytic to <u>be happy because his sins were forgiven.</u> Scribes who observed this muttered that Jesus was blaspheming. Knowing their mindset, Jesus rebuked them for thinking evil of Him, because <u>forgiving sins was one of His powers</u>

on earth. Then He told the paralytic to rise, and take his cot to his house. The crowds praised God in awe!

While passing by a tax office in 9-13, Jesus saw Matthew and commanded him to 'Follow Me.' Matthew complied and invited Jesus to dine with him at his home in the company of other tax collectors and known sinners. This offended some Pharisees who questioned His disciples why this was so. Jesus rebukes them with an explanation that He was serving His purpose of healing both physical as well as spiritual sickness, according to the existing need. He suggests they learn the meaning of Hosea 6:6, that loyalty is more important than sacrifice.

In 14-17, some disciples of John (the Baptist?) asked Jesus why His disciples did not fast as they did with the Pharisees; John's disciples may have been fasting while mourning over his jailing. Jesus plainly said that mourning was not normal when He (the bridegroom) was still present, but the day would come when He would die and then His followers could fast. His analogy about using new material to patch an old garment, and using old wineskins for new wine appears to means that new things are not compatible with old things. Could this mean that old covenant practices are in conflict with new covenant ways, and should not be interposed on the new?

Six healings take place in verses 18-34. First a local official came to Jesus in 18-26, to ask Him to go to his house to restore his dying daughter. As Jesus and His disciples proceeded on this mission, a woman who had suffered from blood hemorrhaging for 12 years came up behind Jesus. She believed that if she could touch the hem of His garment that healing would come to her. As she did so, Jesus turned and told her, 'Be happy daughter, your faith has made you well.'

When they came to the official's house, Jesus told all the mourners to step aside to let Him pass, because the girl was only sleeping. Ridiculing Him, the people went out; Jesus went in, took the girl by the hand and she arose from her bed. This was widely reported in that area.

In 27-34, as Jesus moved on, 2 blind men cried out to Him, saying 'Son of David, have mercy on us." When Jesus asked them if they really believed that He could heal them, they merely said, "Yes, Lord.' Their vision was restored as Jesus touched them and said, 'As you believe, so let it be.' Even though Jesus told them to keep their healing a secret, they told everyone.

A mute demon-possessed man was brought to Jesus in 32-34. Jesus healed him, the people were awe struck again, and the Pharisees accused Him of doing this by Satan's power.

From there Jesus went to many communities to teach in synagogues, to preach His gospel of the kingdom, and to heal many of sickness and disease. He had compassion on the people who seemed to be weary and distressed. This prompted Him to say to His disciples, 'There is much work to be done, but few workers, so pray for God (Lord) to find more workers to harvest souls.

VIEWPOINTS: Jesus saw the faith of some of the petitioners for healing and commended them for it as healing was given. This impressed the crowds who were ordinary folks, but the scribes and Pharisees, the more educated ones, were the doubters and scoffers. This trait is increasingly evident in the world today; our educational institutions may be contributing to this by their apostate free thinking teachings.

Jesus saw the need for more workers (pastors, missionaries, church folks, etc.) to serve in a spiritual capacity so unbelievers, doubters, and scoffers would be enlightened about their spiritual needs and be rewarded with salvation of their souls for eternity. It is interesting that He asked the disciples to pray to God for more workers in the harvest fields. The harvest may refer to the conversion of lost souls to become part of the Kingdom of God to come in the future.

CHAPTER 10:   Jesus commissions His disciples for their evangelistic mission, in verses 1-15. Now there are 12 of them, sent out in 6 pairs, as follows: Simon Peter with brother Andrew, James with brother John; Philip with Bartholomew, Thomas with Matthew, James with Thaddeus, and Simon with Judas Iscariot (the betrayer). He gave them much power to cast out demons, and to heal all kinds of disease and sickness, much as He had done before.

His instructions to them included the following: go to the lost Jews but avoid the Gentiles and the city of the Samaritans; preach that the kingdom of heaven is at hand. Without expecting compensation, heal the sick, raise the dead, restore lepers, and cast out demons. Take no money or extra clothing, but depend on handouts. Stay at the homes of reputable citizens, bless them if they measure up as friendly and open-minded folks, but when not well received, leave without concern for them.

Jesus warns of persecutions and difficulties in verses 16-20, cautioning them to act like harmless sheep, with the prudence of a snake and the innocence of a dove, when confronted by hateful and vicious men. If subjected to legal action, they were not to worry about what to do or say because the Holy Spirit would enable them.

Verses 21-23 speak of betrayal amongst family members at some future time, even resulting in death, to include hatred towards those who believe in Christ. People will need to flee to other places to escape persecution, but the Son of Man (Christ) will return before one can flee to every city in Israel. This seems to speak of the Great Tribulation of the 70th week of Daniel. Those who endure this time of affliction will be saved to eternal life with the Lord.

Jesus says that a disciple is not greater than his teacher, or a servant above his master, in verses 24-25; but both should be identifiable with their mentor. If the master of a household is named a demon, then so will his subordinates be identified. In any case, don't fear them because their nature will not be hidden.

In 27-33, Jesus speaks of fearing God and allegiance to Him. The disciples are to make His teachings very clear to their audiences, without fear of those who are hostile. They should only fear God, who will shield them even more than sparrows in flight, because He values them to the point of every hair on their head. By confessing Jesus before the world, Jesus will vouch for us before God in heaven. Denying Him will bring His denial when mortal life is over.

Verses 34-39 are somewhat enigmatic since the language seems to say that Christ brings discord into the world figuratively with a sword, even to causing great family strife. This is not His intention but only an illustration of the conflict that develops between persons, including family members, over their different attitudes and beliefs regarding Christ's kingdom message and their allegiance to Him. Conversely, by holding family members or others in greater esteem than Christ, they will lose His divine recognition., as will those who thinks too highly of self. By putting Jesus first in one's life, even to the point of death for Him, <u>eternity in heaven is assured.</u>

The chapter ends with an example of giving and receiving in verses 40-42. Those who honor the message they receive from a disciple of Christ will have a spiritual relationship with Him, and through Him with God the Father. And anyone who gives freely of knowledge, hospitality, or nothing more than a cup of cold water, if given <u>in the name of Jesus or His disciple,</u> will earn a heavenly reward.

<u>VIEWPOINTS:</u>   Of the 12 disciples named, only <u>5 were identified earlier</u> at the time of their calling: Simon Peter, Andrew, James and John in Chapter 4, and Matthew in Chapter 9. Other gospels may shed more light on the other 7 disciples. The marching orders given by Jesus were not without negatives, just as life is <u>unfair and difficult for all believers serving spiritually.</u> One must always keep the promised heavenly rewards in mind to endure and be fruitful for Him.

CHAPTER 11:   More teaching and clarification of His purposes is given in this chapter. In the first 6 verses Jesus gives reassurance to imprisoned John the Baptist that He is the Messiah the prophets of the Old Testament anticipated. John evidently became doubtful when Jesus did not immediately establish His kingdom reign, and sent 2 of his disciples to inquire of Jesus if He was the Expected One. Jesus responded that they <u>should report back</u> to John about all <u>the miracles that He had performed, the restoration of lives, and the gospel</u> that was being <u>preached to all.</u>

Jesus then began to question a crowd in 7-19 about their interest in going to hear John the Baptist, whether it was idle curiosity about the man or his attire. Jesus said if they went to see a prophet, they saw one that was special, as described in Isa. 40:3 and Mal. 3:1, <u>a messenger to prepare the way for His own ministry.</u> Even so, John would not be greater than those who would derive their faith from Christ's fulfilled purpose as the Redeemer.

Unfortunately, John's ministry provoked much violence between supporters and opponents, and regional rulers, even though His <u>message was based on Old Testament prophecy.</u> If the people properly perceived, they would have recognized John as the promised Elijah to come before the endtimes Day of the Lord event (re. Matt. 17:11-12). But Jesus calls them children looking for a good time, not knowing the truth, and prone to call Him and John bad names.

In 20-24, Jesus denounces 3 cities where repentance did not occur in spite of His many miracles, namely: Chorazin, Bethsaida, and Capernaum, and to a lesser degree, Tyre and Sidon. He <u>promised them a sad day of judgment.</u> His disappointment can be easily imagined!

Jesus gives thanks to God in verses 25-26 that the persons of low estate <u>were made to understand His ministry,</u> while those who were more intellectual resisted His message. Then he acknowledges that Father God fully equipped Him for His mission in 27, which God understood, as He understood the Father, and as anyone else <u>would know if they accepted Jesus' teachings.</u>

Verses 28-30 are Christ's personal invitation to all who are burdened with the struggles of life, to come to Him to learn <u>how to find rest,</u> and to <u>become witnesses for</u> Him. He gives assurance that as His nature is gentle and humble, so His Yoke is easy and His burden is light.

VIEWPOINTS: Jesus was probably both discouraged and angry over the lack of acceptance by many people who should have understood His message based on Old Testament prophecy. Yet He thanked God for providing what was needed to carry out His Ministry. His simple invitation to weary people to join with Him to find rest, even though a servant yoke and burden is inherited, is still much easier than to endure life without His presence in our hearts.

CHAPTER 12: The Pharisees find fault with Jesus and His disciples over their activity on the Sabbath in verses 1-14. First, because they picked grain to satisfy their hunger and then when Jesus healed the shriveled hand of a man; the Pharisees charged these actions broke Mosaic Law.

Jesus lectured them sternly, telling them in effect that when one is hungry, especially while serving the Lord, the act of securing food was permissible, citing the priests on duty in the Temple eating the sacred barley or wheat bread left on the altar. He again applies Hosea 6:6, as in 9:13, that mercy comes before sacrifice in His agenda as the Son of Man, the Lord, and that doing good on the Sabbath is an acceptable and commendable thing.

At this point, the Pharisees became more antagonistic towards Jesus and began plotting how to destroy Him. Undoubtedly, we see a definite and irrevocable rejection of Christ's teachings about the new covenant kingdom of heaven amongst the Jewish spiritual leaders, mainly because of their dogmatic adherence to Mosaic law.

Knowing the tide was turning against Him, Jesus moved on in 15-21, with many people following and being healed. He warned them to say nothing about His merciful acts by quoting the words of Is. 42:1-4; this was a prophesy of God's words about the gentle and merciful nature of His Son to come that would be manifested on the Gentiles, because of Jewish rejection.

In 22-37, they became more vicious in their condemnation of Jesus for His healing of a blind mute man who was also demon-possessed. The amazed crowds wondered if He truly was the 'Son of David.' The Pharisees negatively accused Him of casting out demons under the power of Satan.

Knowing their thoughts, Jesus lectured them that nothing can survive if there is division within, including city government, or a family unit. Then He points out that if Satan facilitated the casting out of demons, he would be divided against himself; whereas, by Him casting them out by the Spirit of God, the kingdom of God has been presented in absolute unity of purpose. For this reason, Jesus says that those who are not with Him are against Him and their efforts are futile.

He clarifies the meaning of an unforgivable 'unpardonable sin' as blasphemy against the Holy Spirit, adding that words spoken against Him could be forgiven, but not so with the Spirit. Using the analogy of a fruit tree that is preserved as long as it bears fruit, He calls the Pharisees a 'brood of vipers' whose words betray their evil spirit, for which they would be condemned to hell.

Again in verse 38, the Pharisees confront Jesus, hypocritically addressing Him as 'Teacher', as they ask for a sign or miracle from Him. Jesus tells them in 39-42 that no immediate sign would be given because of their wicked motives; but a sign figuratively like that of Jonah's 3 days in the belly of a whale would soon come to one greater than Jonah, namely the Son of

God, who would spend 3 days & nights in the grave. He speaks of the people of Nineveh and a queen from the south (Sheba), all Gentiles, who would fare better for their response <u>than the unrepentant Jews.</u>

In 43-45, Jesus speaks of what an evil spirit (demon) does, when removed from a person who <u>does not acquire a new spirit from God;</u> the demon looks in other places for a home but finding none decides to return to his former victim, bringing 7 more demons with him. The poor man would be worse off than at first, and so it would be <u>with the wicked</u> <u>generation of Jesus' day</u>.

The final verses 46-49 tell of the mother and brothers of Jesus trying to speak to Him. When told of this, Jesus asks, '<u>Who is My mother and My brothers</u>?' He then turns to His disciples to claim them as His mother and brothers, because they were doing the will of God. Thus, He seemed to remove Himself further from His earthly family as time neared for His <u>return to sit at the right hand of God the Father.</u>

VIEWPOINTS: In this chapter, Jesus seems to recognize the coming eventual rejection by the Jews, as characterized by the Pharisees, and twice alludes to a future time <u>when the Gentiles would be favored for their repentance and faithfulness</u> to Him, God the Father, and the Holy Spirit. First He calls the Pharisees 'vipers' and in the end the people a 'wicked generation.'

CHAPTER 13: Jesus teaches the multitudes in parables for 52 out of 58 verses in this chapter. In 1-9, while <u>sitting in a boat on the sea shore,</u> He spoke the mysterious parable of the sower, a farmer who planted grain using the broadcast method. Some seed fell on a path, to be quickly consumed by birds, and some fell in rocky places with no depth of soil, to sprout quickly but to wither away from the sun's heat because the roots had no nourishment. Some fell amongst thorns, which choked out the sprouts, but <u>more seed fell on good soil</u> <u>to produce up to 100 times</u> the seeds that were sown. To this, Jesus said, 'Listen up, all you who have ears to hear!'

In 10-17, His disciples asked why He was teaching in parables, to which Jesus replied that while they understood 'mysteries* (truths) of the heavenly kingdom' many others did not, mainly the close-minded unbelievers. Those who understand, gain more perception; but those who are skeptical, become more ignorant. (*See Bible Mysteries, at end of Book of Romans)

Therefore He <u>preferred to speak in parables for the benefit of the wise</u> so as not to waste words on those who would ultimately reject His teachings. By doing so, Jesus fulfilled the prophecy of Isaiah. 6:9-10 about those who were <u>blind to the truth of God's Word</u> and would not listen or try to understand. He then commended the disciples for their level of perception.

Jesus explained the parable of the sower in 18-23, as meaning that God's Holy Word would be preached throughout the world <u>by servants of the Lord</u> The response to it will vary greatly according to soil quality of the culture that it reaches. His Word will not produce new believers in many places where evil, false teachings, and <u>lack of perception exist,</u> but where learning wisdom and common sense prevail in depth, many will become a harvest of believers <u>committed to the words of the kingdom</u> (Christ's teachings).

Parable No. 2, in verses 24-30 and 36-43, is about wheat and tares (weeds). Jesus compares the kingdom of heaven to a farmer who sowed good seed in his field, and while he slept, some evil men came and <u>scattered weed seeds over his wheat field</u>. Both sprouted and grew up together. When his field hands asked where the weeds came from, the farmer said it was done by an enemy. His helpers wanted to trample the field to pull up the weeds, but the farmer instructed them to wait until harvest time when the weeds would be harvested separately and destroyed before the <u>wheat was gathered into his granary</u>.

When the disciples asked what this parable meant, Jesus told them in 36-43, that the farmer who sowed the seed was He, the Son of God, and the <u>field was the world.</u> The good wheat represented sons of the kingdom (believers) and the weeds are sons of Satan (unbelievers) germinated into the world by him. Most important, harvest time represents the 'end of the age' and the <u>farm hands will be God's angels.</u>

The weeds (unsaved) would be destroyed at the 'end of the age' by God's angels, who will cast them <u>into hell for eternal weeping and grinding of teeth</u>. The righteous however, will be gathered into God's kingdom to become new creatures <u>reflecting the glory of the Father</u>.

Back to verses 31-35, Jesus spoke 2 more parables: one, that a small mustard seed is like the kingdom of heaven, which when sown <u>grows quickly and becomes more prolific</u> than other spiritual movements; and two, He compares the kingdom of heaven to yeast which when embedded in a growth mixture <u>results in rapid expansion to great size</u>. Both seem to say that from a small beginning against rejection by the Jews, the kingdom of heaven will nevertheless <u>flourish to become the greatest</u> as Christ's church proliferates in a Gentile populace.

In 34-35, Jesus said He spoke in parables to fulfill the words of Ps. 78:2, to reveal answers to secrets of old to those <u>who hear, understand, and accept His teachings</u>.

Three parables follow in verses 44-52. The kingdom of heaven is compared to a hidden treasure which when found becomes the <u>means for acquiring greater spiritual values</u>. Then it is compared to a beautiful precious pearl which brings great pleasure <u>and appreciation of value.</u> Last, comparison is made to a dragnet (fishing net) used to catch both good and undesirable creatures of the sea, <u>requiring evaluation to keep the good and cast away the bad.</u> This speaks of God's endtimes judgment to save the righteous and destroy the wicked.

As the disciples said they understood these parables, Jesus told them that they would be like a homeowner who had collected great treasure, both antique and new, <u>to share with others.</u>

Jesus then returned to Nazareth in 53-58, to teach in the synagogue but encountered much opposition by way of deprecation, questioning His authority, former occupation, and family genealogy. Jesus more or less shrugged off their rejection with the comment that <u>a prophet is only without honor in his community</u>, where he is best known. He did very little to help them!

<u>VIEWPOINTS:</u> Perhaps the most significant point of relevancy in this chapter is the oft repeated use of the words 'end of the age,' as a time when there will be a separation by God's angels of the <u>righteous for eternal salvation</u> and the <u>wicked for eternal damnation.</u> This is spoken of as the 'harvest' time of souls according to their spiritual relationship to Christ. Until that time, the good and the bad are pictured as existing together in this world. If this is taken literally, it means that all humanity will have to endure the time of tribulation prophesied so often in the Old Testament, and that the 'harvest of the good' will take place <u>separately from</u>

the destruction of the weeds, the bad. This seems to refute the pre-tribulation rapture concept embraced by many clergy and lay persons of today.

CHAPTER 14:   In 1-12, Jesus receives the bad news about the death of John the Baptist, who had earlier condemned Herod for seducing his brother's wife Herodias, to then take her as his wife. For this reason John was imprisoned. When the daughter of Herodias pleased Herod with a sensual dance for his birthday, he told her she could have anything she wanted as a reward.

Prompted by her mother, she asked for John's head on a platter. Herod had him executed and his head was taken by her to Herodias. After burying his body, John's disciples reported the matter to Jesus. As Herod heard of His ministry, he thought He was a resurrected John the Baptist.

Jesus tried to get away in 13-21 to grieve by Himself but as usual a large crowd followed Him; with compassion He healed the sick until that evening. Then the disciples suggested that the people be sent back to their homes for the evening and some food. Jesus said 'No, let them stay and give them food,' to which they replied that they only had 5 loaves and 2 fish.

Jesus asked for this food, told the people (5000 men plus women and children) to sit down on the grass, and after blessing the food He broke the loaves into pieces and ordered the disciples to feed the crowd. All ate their fill; there was an abundance of food to go around, so much so that 12 baskets were left over. Another spectacular one-of-a-kind miracle by Jesus.

Then Jesus and the disciples departed in 22-33, the disciples sailed off in a boat to the other side, while Jesus went into nearby mountains to pray. In the early hours of morning, Jesus walked out on the sea to join the disciples who were dealing with a dangerous storm. When they saw Him, they were both astonished and fearful, thinking He was a ghost. To allay their fears, Jesus told them to be brave, not to fear, adding 'It is I.' Apparently not sure of His identity, Peter asked Jesus to command him to walk out to Him on the water, if He truly was Jesus.

When Jesus said 'Come' Peter stepped out of the boat and began walking on the water until he took his eyes off of Jesus and saw the danger of the wind and rough sea; then he lost his nerve and called to Jesus to save him as he began to sink. Jesus grabbed his hand, lifted him up, chided him for his weak faith, and both walked on the water to climb aboard. The storm ceased and all disciples worshipped Jesus, as the 'Son of God.'

VIEWPOINTS: Feeding more than 5000 men plus wives and children with 5 loaves and 2 fish was evidence of the miraculous power Jesus possessed, to provide basic necessities. This miracle is also told in the gospels of Mark, Luke, and John with minor differences; it must be accepted at face value without attempts to explain it away in temporal terms.

The endless supply of food miracle is similar to what the prophet Elijah did in I Kings 17:12-16, providing an abundance of flour and oil, and what Elisha did in II Kings 4:1-

7, to supply much oil. In both instances the supply was made possible by God through His prophets to help a needy person who had faith in Him.

The miracle of walking on water, as recorded only in the gospel of Matthew, clearly testifies to the fact that mankind can do the impossible if endowed with unwavering faith in divine power. Lack of adequate faith often afflicts the believer, with negative results, when confronted with difficult or dangerous situations. Natural emotions and forces divert our attention from the source of the greatest power in the universe, that of our triune God. For optimum achievement, we must always focus on the never ending facility emanating from our Creator-Godhead.

CHAPTER 15:   Scribes and Pharisees resumed their harassment of Jesus in 1-9, accusing His disciples of violating traditional ceremonial practice by not washing their hands before eating. Jesus responded with a gross example of their own transgression of condoning a practice whereby a son could dishonor his parents by breaking the commandment to 'Honor your father and your mother.' Then He calls them hypocrites in the order of prophecy spoken by Isaiah in Is. 29:13.

In 10-16, Jesus speaks words of wisdom to a crowd of people and to His disciples. To the crowd, He merely says that what comes out of one's mouth can pollute the speaker much more than what is put in the mouth. The disciples informed Him that this remark had offended the Pharisees. He said it meant that they were like plants without God's roots, and not to pay attention to them because they were blind leaders leading the blind off the track into a ditch.

Puzzled, Peter asked for an explanation, to which Jesus asked if he lacked understanding too. He stated that after food is eaten it passes through to be eliminated and discarded, a natural process that does not defile a person's character; on the other hand, the evil that comes out of a mouth is from an evil heart. This pollutes one's character just as evil thoughts of other sins are 'out of the heart'. Eating with unwashed hands however does not defile a person.

Jesus does more healing in 21-28. Having gone on to the region of Tyre and Sidon, a Canaanite woman (a Gentile) pleads to Him as the 'Son of David,' for mercy to heal her demon-possessed daughter. He did not respond until the disciples asked that He send her away; then He said that He was on earth to minister to the Israelites, not the Gentiles.

When the woman persisted in a worship mode, asking for help, Jesus spoke a provoking comment that 'It was bad to take food from children (Jews) to give to dogs (Gentiles).' She agreed but added that 'the dogs still were allowed to eat crumbs that fell off the master's table.' To this, Jesus complimented her for her reasoning faith, and her daughter was healed instantly.

Jesus moved back to a mountain near the Sea of Galilee for what may have been a rest, but a crowd of people converged on Him bringing many afflicted persons to be healed. The people, amazed as Jesus healed many of diverse ailments, praised the God of Israel.

Verses 32-39 tells of another mass feeding miracle after crowds kept Jesus and His disciples company for 3 days. Jesus had compassion on them, knowing they were in need of food, and wanted to feed them. When the disciples told Him they only had 7 loaves of bread and a few small fish, Jesus told the crowd to sit down, gave a word of thanks, and broke the food into pieces for the disciples to pass out to the people. Not counting woman and children who were present, a total of 4000 men were fed all they wanted and 7 baskets of fragments remained. Jesus then sent them home before getting into a boat headed for another region. This is the 2nd time that Jesus fed a huge number of people with an insignificant food reserve, also as done in chapter 14.

VIEWPOINTS: The term 'of the heart' with respect to human thoughts and actions is somewhat paradoxical. Anatomically, the heart does no thinking as it mechanically pumps blood, the vital fluid of life, through a human body. In the Bible, the heart is spoken of as the center of the physical, mental, and spiritual life of humans, and as such, it refers to a person as a whole. To call to heart (mind) something means to recall something. Although being functions of the mind, feelings and affections of a person are connected with the heart in biblical language. Emotions such as joy are said to originate in the heart (see Ps. 4:7; Is 65:14); this includes sadness, depression, envy, compassion, love and its opposite, hate.

In Scripture, the heart is spoken of as the center of the moral and spiritual life, with the conscience associated with it. Spiritually, it is where God does His work in the individual. His commandments are "written in our hearts," with conscience as the proof of this (Rom. 2:15). As the seat of emotion, the love of God, the Holy Spirit, and Christ dwells in our hearts, according to our spiritual faith and commitment. (Mark 12:30, 2 Cor. 1:22, Eph. 3:17, Rom. 5:5).

CHAPTER 16:   Jesus is disturbed by another request from Pharisees and Sadducees for a sign from heaven in 1-12. He chides them for not knowing the signs of the times of His existence as the Messiah, from Old Testament prophecy, even though they were expert at predicting weather conditions. Again, He stated that only the sign of Jonah would be made known, a reference to His resurrection after 3 days in a tomb.

Evidently with disgust, He left them and sailed off again to the east side of the Sea of Galilee into Gentile territory. When the disciples realized that they lacked food, Jesus uttered a strange warning, 'Watch out and beware of the leaven of the Pharisees and Sadducees.' He chided them for lack of faith in not recalling how much bread was obtained on two previous occasions to feed many, but added that He was not speaking of bread when He gave His warning. Then they understood that He meant to beware of the false teachings of the Pharisees and Sadducees.

In 13-20, Jesus brought forth a contrast between the people at large and the disciples as to His identity. From the disciples He heard that the people identified Him as John the Baptist, Elijah, Jeremiah, or another prophet. When He asked what their view was, Simon Peter said, 'You are Christ, Son of the living God.' Jesus was pleased and blessed him as Simon, the son of Jonah, for knowing the truth as a revelation from God.

Then, addressing him as Peter, Jesus declares that He would 'build His church on the rock' of such faith as Peter had demonstrated, and Satan would not be able to destroy it. He adds that He would give the disciples the keys (power) to the 'kingdom of heaven' with divine authority to establish and launch His church, a growing body of believers, consisting of both Gentile and Jew. Since Jewish leaders had already rejected Him, He warned them not to reveal his true identity to anyone.

Verses 21-28 focus on Christ's realization that His death was more impending, and His determination to prepare His disciples for this sad event. Peter, impulsive as usual, rejected this idea and rebuked Jesus for saying it, because God would not permit it. Jesus sharply rebuked him, as if he were Satan, for replacing God's purposes with man's.

Jesus then clarifies to the disciples what their role would be: involving sacrifice and danger, possible loss of life, a strong spiritual commitment, <u>an enduring faith of His return</u>, and of judgment to come with rewards for the faithful, or condemnation for the unfaithful. He adds a final statement that some of them would live to see Him coming in glory into His kingdom, seemingly a manifestation of his <u>second coming known as the transfiguration in</u> <u>Chapter 17.</u>

CHAPTER 17:   A week later, in verses 1-13, Jesus took 3 disciples, Peter, James and John to the top of a mountain, possibly Mt. Hermon, where a startling change in His appearance took place. He was transfigured, <u>literally recreated for a short time,</u> as His face became bright as the sun, and His clothing became white as sparkling snow. Moses and Elijah appeared talking to Him. Peter blurted out a rather foolish proposal that he make three shelters, one for each of them.

Before Jesus could respond, a bright cloud enveloped them and a voice spoke from it, saying, 'This is My beloved Son, with whom I am well-pleased; <u>listen to Him</u>!' (Except for the last 3 words, this is the same statement that God spoke after John the Baptist baptized Jesus in chapter 3:17.) Hearing this, the <u>disciples fell face down in fear</u> until Jesus touched them and told them to rise and not be afraid. They opened their eyes to see only Jesus, who then told them to say nothing of this event <u>until after His resurrection from death.</u>

Overlooking the remark about His death, they were curious about why scribes claimed that Elijah would come before the Messiah. Jesus explained that Elijah had figuratively already come in the being of John the Baptist, to prepare the way for Him, but that <u>both would</u> <u>suffer</u> <u>death at the hands of those who did not recognize them.</u> The disciples understood this!

In verses 14-21, Jesus learns of a breakdown in faith healing by the disciples, when a man begged Him to heal his lunatic son, because <u>the disciples could not do so earlier.</u> With some disgust, Jesus asked how much longer would He have to put up with such weakness of faith, and then healed the boy. When the disciples asked why they could not do so, Jesus bluntly told them they lacked faith, but <u>if they had possessed as little faith as a mustard</u> <u>seed</u> they would have had <u>the power to do so.</u> With prayer and fasting, they could have commanded a mountain (a difficult task) to get out of the way, and it would have done so.

Jesus grieved the disciples by again predicting His <u>death and resurrection</u> in verses 22-23. Then in Capernaum, temple tax-collectors asked if Jesus would pay a tax, to which He said, 'Yes,' so as not to offend them. Then He told Peter to go catch a fish which would have money in its mouth, so that he could pay taxes to the temple men. Jesus did not want to violate a custom even though <u>He legitimately was not obligated to pay a tax.</u>

CHAPTER 18:   Much of Jesus' teachings in this chapter speaks of humility and forgiveness. The first 6 verses portrays the greatness found in an innocent naïve child that <u>a worldly</u> <u>person</u> <u>lacks.</u> The disciples ask, 'Who is the greatest in the kingdom of heaven?,' Jesus used a child to illustrate that a new believer is like a spiritual babe that must be open to new concepts of learning, <u>with humbleness and trust.</u> This is a quality that leads to spiritual greatness, which if accepted <u>brings one closer to Him.</u> He adds a warning that one who leads such a child astray will suffer <u>consequences equal to being thrown into the sea</u> with a millstone around the neck.

In verses 7-9, Jesus denounces the world for its abundant sinfulness, as well as the person who causes others to sin. In terms of resisting or avoiding sin, Jesus compared it to a lame foot, or a roaming eye (viewing pornography?), which leads to sin. This could mean that to put sin aside, one may suffer an experience equal to amputation of a leg or blindness; yet it is better to suffer such deprivation than to continue on to suffer eternal damnation. As a parable, it is not likely that His words on physical removal should be taken literally.

Again in the example of a child as a 'little one,' or a new believer, in verses 10-14, Jesus warns that they should not be treated with disrespect, because they too have guardian angels looking after them as God requires to safeguard the 'newly saved.' His guardianship is like that of a shepherd who leaves 99 sheep in a secure place to look for one that is lost.

Finding the lost brings more joy than He feels for those in safe haven. His will is that no one should be lost!

How to deal with a wayward church member or fellow Christian is the theme of 15-20. Speaking of a believer whose obvious sin is disturbing to a fellow believer, Jesus gives a 3 phase procedure to help the sinner overcome and get back on track. First, the initial observer should personally speak to the offender in a kind and considerate manner, 2nd, if he refuses to listen, then 1-2 more discerning people should be included in a direct confrontation, and 3rd, if no positive reaction is seen, the concerned church congregation should speak to the culprit. If no favorable response is received before the church, it should disassociate from the offender as from an atheist or a 'tax collector.' (Tax-collectors were viewed as evil types by the Jews)

Then Jesus clarifies that whatever is forbidden on earth is forbidden in heaven, and conversely, whatever is allowed on earth is allowed in heaven, (provided that all is in accord with God's Word). Verses 19-20 seem to say that if 2 or more persons agree on something in prayer to God, that He will grant them their desire; this should be construed to essentially mean if they are acting in accord in the name of Jesus, and He is in agreement with them. This promise should not be taken as a blank check unconditional approval for anything that is desired, because it logically requires a Will of God endorsement for cashing in.

In 21-35, Jesus answers Peter's question, 'If my brother repeatedly does me wrong, how many times should I forgive him, up to 7 times?' Jesus tells him to forgive 70x7 times (490 times?), basically an unlimited number. He then illustrates this with a parable about a servant who owed his master a huge sum of money (some say $10 million); when he could not repay this sum, his master moved to sell him as a slave along with his family to obtain some repayment. Falling at the master's feet, he begged for more time so effectively and sincerely that the master forgave him the entire debt. The master had a big heart!

As the beneficiary of such great forgiveness, this slave then collared another slave who owed him a small amount, said to be only $17 value, demanding immediate repayment. When the debtor slave begged for more time, the first slave had him thrown in prison. When this injustice was told to the master by other slaves, he called the offender on the carpet and severely upbraided him for his lack of generosity and mercy as he had received from his master, and handed him over to torturers until he could repay his original indebtedness. Jesus ended by saying God would not forgive them, if they would not forgive another The point is made that we should treat others as we would have them treat us, including forgiveness for failure or wrongdoing.

VIEWPOINTS: In the last parable on forgiveness of indebtedness, it is hard to understand how one could repay a debt if confined in prison, with no assets to begin with. Also, it is inconceivable that a slave could owe as much as $10 million to his master. Perhaps the real point in this story is that what we forgive of others is minuscule to the multitudinous sins that God may forgive a person during a lifetime. It may also tell us that compassion for others who are in difficult straits is pleasing to God and may often bring equal or greater compassion to those who are forgiving in the first place.

In a democratic society, the act of filing for bankruptcy brings a form of forgiveness of debt, even though the debtor may have foolishly accrued insolvency. In reality, this form of relief can be a gross injustice to lenders who may have been misled in their initial trust of the debtor. Honesty is a most important ingredient in debt situations, and when dishonesty is involved it would seem proper justice to impose penalties on the debtor to force restitution of some kind. Perhaps other passages of scripture will clarify this point in a logical fashion.

Godly people should be more forgiving than the ungodly who are often motivated by greed in their transactions with others. It is easier for a righteous person to forgive because they most likely equate the countless times when God forgave their own errors and failures.

CHAPTER 19:   Jesus moved on, in verses 1-12, to the region of Judea east of the Jordan River, healing many in the crowd that followed Him. Some Pharisees asked Him if it was legal for a man to divorce his wife for just any reason, hoping that He would take a position that they could use against Him. Jesus merely gave 3 reasons why a husband and wife should stay together. The 1st was because God made man and woman (Adam & Eve) to be as one; 2nd, when married they are no longer bound to their birth family. The 3rd reason was that what God had put together, should not be disjoined by anyone.

To this, the Pharisees asked why Moses gave permission for a husband to put a wife aside with a certificate of divorce, without good reason (Deut. 24:1-4). Jesus tells them it was because of the lack of love in the man's heart at that time, but it was not in accord with God's Will. Then He allows only one reason for divorce, that of immorality on the part of the wife. Surely this must include immorality on the part of a husband.

The disciples expressed their view that it may be best not to marry, so as to avoid divorce. Jesus told them that this was not applicable except for those who either choose a life of celibacy, or are unable to fulfill the reproductive purposes of a marriage as in the case of a 'eunuch,' a male deprived of the testes or external genitals. If a man elects to become a eunuch 'for the sake of the kingdom of heaven' He may be more useful in kingdom work.

In 13-15, when little children were brought to Him, to which the disciples objected, Jesus instructed that they be allowed to come to Him because they had equal rights in the kingdom of heaven. He blessed them and moved on again.

Then a young Jew asked Him in 16-26, what good deed he should do to obtain eternal life. Jesus replied that God was the authority on 'good deeds' and obedience to His Commandments was a worthy action. When asked, 'Which Ones?' Jesus named 6 of those given in the Ten

<u>Commandments of Ex. 20:1-16</u>, including murder, adultery, stealing, lying, honoring parents, and being a good and forgiving neighbor.

Saying he had honored these from his youth the young man asked: 'What do I still lack?' Jesus told him to be perfect, he should sell or give to the poor all of his possessions and become His disciple. Being rich, and <u>not willing to part with his wealth</u>, the young man sorrowfully left.

Jesus explained to His disciples that it was most difficult for a wealthy man to enter the kingdom of heaven, mainly because he would hold his wealth above God. When Jesus said that it was easier for a camel to pass through the eye of a needle, they asked, 'Who then can be saved?' possibly thinking that wealth was a God given blessing. Jesus replied that salvation is possible only by God's mercy! Wealth has nothing to do with the reward of salvation for righteousness!

After all this, Peter observed that all the disciples had forsaken their earthly possessions to follow Jesus, and asked, 'What's in it for us?' Jesus gave them the good news, that they would be <u>like kings on separate thrones,</u> in God's endtimes plan for Christ's millennial reign, each having jurisdiction over one of the original 12 tribes of Israel. Even more, they would inherit eternal life and be <u>rewarded many times over what they once had</u>. Concluding His remarks, Jesus said that many at the top on earth would be at a lower level in His kingdom, and many now at the bottom shall be first.

<u>VIEWPOINTS:</u>   Divorce was so common among the Jews in the time of Jesus that it caused division among the Pharisees as to the valid basis for divorce. The option of divorce was solely that of the husband; the wife could leave her husband, but she could not divorce him. Now in this world, <u>a wife has equal rights with the husband</u> in the matter of divorce.

Jesus did not approve of divorce; he clearly stressed the consequences of it. Biblically, a divorce <u>should not occur between a Christian man and a Christian woman.</u> God's intention from creation is that a marriage should be permanent. How to deal with current laws on marriage and divorce is a <u>most difficult matter in today's world.</u>

CHAPTER 20:   Verses 1-16 are a parable Jesus recited about the compensation given to workers in a vineyard, to illustrate <u>more about the kingdom of heaven.</u> An owner of the vineyard agreed with the workers that they would receive a Roman silver coin (said to be worth $20) per day of labor. He found idle men at 9 a.m., at noon, at 3 p.m. and at 5 p.m. who wanted to work, so he sent them into the vineyard with the same promise of pay.

That evening when work ended, the owner paid each worker one equal value silver coin regardless of the hours worked, <u>starting with the last ones that went to work</u> for him. Those hired earlier expected to receive more for their additional hours, and complained when they received nothing more than one silver coin. The owner told them he had done no wrong because <u>he kept his word on the agreed upon wage</u>, adding that he would give what he wished. Jesus added that the last would be first, and the first would be last, but <u>few would be chosen</u>.

Jesus again predicts His death in verses 17-19, saying He would be betrayed and condemned to death by <u>crucifixion at the hands of the Romans</u> (Gentiles), but on the 3rd day He would rise again from death.

In 20-28, the mother of James and John ambitiously asked Jesus to allow each of her sons the privilege <u>to sit at His side in His Kingdom.</u> Jesus told her that she was ignorant in her question of what would be required of them for this honor, and then asked the two men if they were prepared to endure what was ahead for Him. Again, without knowing what was involved, they said, 'We are able.' Jesus said they would indeed share in His suffering, but it was <u>not His right to say who would sit beside Him,</u> because it was God's decision.

The other 10 disciples were displeased with their 2 brothers over this request, so Jesus had to clarify the matter with them; He emphasized that the <u>greatest on earth could</u> <u>well be the least in Heaven,</u> and the best way to receive high honors would be to serve others as a slave might, <u>just as He came to serve and to give His life for many.</u>

As they left Jericho, Jesus performed another miracle in 29-34, by healing 2 blind men who were sitting along the roadside; they asked mercy of Him as the 'Son of David' and in compassion <u>He gave back their sight.</u> They followed Him, confirming their spiritual insight.

<u>VIEWPOINTS:</u>   In these modern times, compensation is closely tied to hours, days, or weeks worked, and any deviation from this formula would bring strong objection and legal action in the courts. The parable was intended to show that compensation in God's domain is pegged more <u>on the quality of service rendered than the time factor.</u> Service to others, the needy, the handicapped, the weak and weary, and especially fellow believers, is what God wants of His own.

CHAPTER 21:   Apparently knowing that His time of ministry was drawing to a close, Jesus <u>decided to visit Jerusalem</u> in verses 1-11. Nearing the Mount of Olives, He sent 2 disciples ahead to borrow a donkey, with a colt, from a friendly owner who would gladly lend them to the Lord.

When the donkey and colt were in hand the disciples laid their coats on them where Jesus sat; he possibly rode on the donkey with his feet on the colt along side. A huge crowd following Him also <u>laid their coats or tree branches on the road</u> before Him. They shouted a praise, 'Hosanna (meaning, Save, we beg of you) to the Son of David, who comes in the name of God, the highest;' and identified Jesus to the city folks as a prophet from Nazareth. This entry was foretold in the O.T. book of Zechariah 9:9.

In 12-17, He confronted the priests in the temple for their corrupt money exchange and marketing practices, <u>driving the violators out and upsetting their counters.</u> He told them that the temple was to be a house of prayers, not a robber's den (see Is. 56:7 & Jer. 7:11). Then He healed blind and sick people in the temple which angered the scribes and chief priests even more.

When children hailed Him as Son of David, the temple officials asked if He heard them, as if they wanted a correction of this title. Jesus said it was all right because <u>perfect</u> <u>recognition can come from the mouth of little ones.</u> Then He and his disciples went to Bethany for the night.

Next morning, in 18-22, on the way back to Jerusalem, He became hungry and found an in-season fig tree; finding no figs, He placed a <u>curse on it to be forever fruitless.</u> The disciples were amazed as it withered immediately. Jesus then lectured them on their faith, that if it was sufficient they could do the same thing to a fig tree or even cause a mountain to slip into the sea, <u>provided they prayed with complete faith</u>. Some say that Israel represents the fruitless fig tree, and removing the mountain speaks of <u>overcoming obstacles to carry the gospel to the Gentiles.</u>

As He entered the temple again, in 23-27, the chief priests and other temple officials challenged His authority to teach in the temple. Jesus proposed that they answer a question from Him, before He answered them, and <u>asked them from where came John the Baptist's authority</u> to baptize people. They feared to say 'from heaven' or from the people themselves, so they admitted they didn't know the answer. That was all the reason Jesus needed to say that <u>He would not reveal His authority to them.</u>

In 28-32, Jesus continues with a parable about two sons who were asked by their father to <u>work in his vineyard</u>. The 1ˢᵗ son refused but regretted it and went to work, but the 2ⁿᵈ son said okay and then <u>failed to do the work.</u> Jesus asked which one obeyed his father, and they (the temple officials) <u>logically chose the 1ˢᵗ son</u>. Jesus told them that repentant tax collectors and prostitutes would enter the kingdom of heaven before any of them, because they refused to believe in John while the <u>named sinners did,</u> nor did they believe after they witnessed their conversion. (None of my reference texts correlated the parable with the rebuke Jesus gave to the responders to His question; regrettably, with my limited perception, I'm not able to do so either.)

A parable in 33-45 portrays evil vine dressers who leased a well-equipped vineyard from the owner, and <u>then killed his servants</u> when they came to collect the grape harvest. Twice they killed servants and <u>finally the owner's son</u>, thinking they could seize his inheritance. When Jesus asked the temple officials what the owner should do to these wicked vine dressers, they said to <u>execute them and lease the vineyard to honest ones</u>. (The vineyard could be looked upon as the ideal kingdom of God, the owner as God, the vine dressers as the nation of Israel, and the servants as God's messengers, whose prophecy was rejected by the Jewish leaders.)

Jesus asked them if they had read Ps. 118:22-23, about a stone (the Messiah), that builder's rejected, which then <u>became a cornerstone for something greater</u> (the kingdom of heaven). The stone would become the foundation for a multitude of people (comprising the Gentile church) who would be <u>more fruitful and willingly share of their fruit.</u> Those who stumble over the stone will receive no fruit; if the stone falls on them, they would be marked for destruction.

The Pharisees and temple officials realized that Jesus had spoken of their wickedness and in anger would have seized him except for the crowds <u>who considered Him to be a prophet.</u>

CHAPTER 22: The chapter begins with a parable about a wedding feast in verses 1-14. Jesus compares the kingdom of heaven to a king who had much food prepared for a wedding banquet to honor his son. He sent servants out twice with <u>invitations to those on a selected list</u> but they declined to come for various reasons. When some seized his servants and killed them, the king was furious and sent his military out to <u>kill the murderers and to burn their cities.</u> Still, with all preparations thoroughly made, there were no guests present. If those on the selected list (the Israelites) refused to come, then why not open the door to all others, including Gentiles?

That is what the king did, by sending more servants out to invite just anybody off the streets, good and bad; so many responded that the wedding hall was filled. However, when the king entered to greet them, he found one man not wearing the garment (cloak) that was provided, and asked why this was so. The man had no answer, so the king ordered his servants to tie him up like so much trash and to toss him out into the night. Then Jesus adds, 'For many are called, but few are chosen,' identical to His remark in chapter 20:16.

VIEWPOINTS: Much can be read into this parable. The chosen prospective guests who declined to accept the invitation parallel the Jews who rejected prophecy of Christ as the Messiah, being more concerned with their earthly matters. Death of the servants equates to Christ's crucifixion, and the burning of the cities may relate to the future burning of Jerusalem in 70 A.D.

Gathering people from the streets seems to imply that God would open the door to messianic Jews of the future and the Gentile world to become part of the kingdom of Heaven. The wedding garment might be likened to the 'cloak of righteousness' every true believer should wear; as opposed to professing believers who live in disobedience to God's commandments.

With respect to the many who are called (invited) to accept Jesus as the Messiah, few of the Jews in His day did so, and in terms of total earthly population until the endtimes, relatively few may be chosen as children of God, with their names in His 'Book of Life.'

The remainder of the chapter tells of more harassment of Jesus by temple and political figures. In verses 15-22, He is accosted by representatives of the Pharisees and some Herodians (Jews loyal to the Romans), who asked Him in flattering terms was it legal to pay taxes to Caesar. Jesus called them hypocrites, knowing they asked a proper question for evil purposes. He then asked for a Roman coin. Given a silver denarius coin, He asked them whose image and inscription appeared on it. When they said, 'Caesar's,' He told them to 'pay unto Caesar what was his, and to God the things that are His.' His answer baffled them, and they left in frustration.

Later that day, in 23-33, Sadducees who disbelieved in resurrections, addressed Him as Teacher, to ask whose wife a woman would be in heaven, if her first husband died, and in succession she married a 1st, 2nd, and on to a 7th brother (each of them died), in accordance with Mosaic law in Deut. 25:5-6. Jesus told them they were mistaken in their understanding of Scriptures, for after resurrection to heaven there would be no marriage since all would be like God's angels.

Then, referring to resurrection of the dead, Jesus pointed out the words of God to Moses, in Ex 3:6 & 15, 'I AM the God of Abraham, Isaac, and Jacob,' who were no longer alive. By using the verb 'AM' He clearly meant they had been resurrected to eternal life with Him. Thus, He is God of the living, and not the dead! This astonished the listening crowd.

Next, the Pharisees in 34-40, have one of their lawyers ask a trick question of Jesus, 'What is the great commandment in the Law of Moses?' Jesus concisely responded, 'The first is to love the Lord with all your heart, soul, and mind, and next is to love your neighbor as yourself, for on these two the Law and prophecy are dependent.' By keeping these two, all the other commandments will be respected and obeyed, as they should be, without legalism.

In 41-45, Jesus turns the tables on the Pharisees with a question, 'What do you think of

Christ, and whose Son is He? To their answer, 'The Son of David' Jesus asked, 'How was it then that David, <u>when inspired by the Holy Spirit, called Him Lord</u>?' If David calls Him Lord, how could Christ be David's son? Unable to answer that, the Pharisees stopped questioning Him. For more enlightenment on this point, see Ps. 2:7, Ps. 110:1.

CHAPTER 23: In this chapter, Jesus expressed His total disgust and loss of respect for the <u>scribes and Pharisees of the temple</u>. It is clear that differences between them had become irreconcilable. He pronounced a 'woe' (misery and pain) on them 8 times, as hypocrites, and finally called them snakes and a brood of vipers.

In the first 12 verses, He acknowledged to the disciples and the crowd that as teachers of the Mosaic Law, the Pharisees <u>generally advised temple worshipers correctly</u> and therefore they should be obeyed. But, He cautioned worshipers not to do as the Pharisees because they <u>failed to live up to a huge number of conditions and rules</u> that they prescribed for others.

He denounced them for all they did to draw attention to themselves, such as wearing large scripture boxes on their foreheads and long tassels on their garments, demanding special honors when seated at banquets and in the synagogues, being called Rabbi (teacher) in public places, and <u>to be recognized as superior above all others</u>. Because their ego was a dominant characteristic, Jesus emphasized that they should be like brothers to others and not lord it over them under titles of superiority. Jesus declared that He is the only true teacher of God's word, and that for greatness and exaltation by others, <u>a person should be a servant who humbles himself</u>.

With 2 'woes to you' in verses 13-15, Jesus called the scribes and Pharisees hypocrites for <u>falsely presenting the kingdom of heaven to others</u>, and after going to great effort to convert them to their ways, they corrupted them afterwards to be twice more a devil as themselves. They unjustly acquired the estates of widows, while voicing fairness and equity in long public prayers.

With a 'woe' to them as blind guides, in 16-22, He chastised them for blind use of false swearing, which if based on gold of the temple, the altar or the temple itself; <u>would not be valid or considered evidence of truth.</u> He stated that sworn oaths are to be made only in the name of God.

With 3 more 'woes to you hypocrites' in 23-28, Jesus criticized the scribes and Pharisees for neglecting to show justice, mercy, and faithfulness in their ministry while they gave liberally of their resources. They blindly <u>focused on minor sins while committing the major ones</u>.

He denounced them for portraying themselves as pure and holy when they were <u>filled with greed and self-serving</u>. In terms of washing dishes, He compared their character to the washing of the outside of a dish and saucer while leaving the inside dirty; and says that they should clean the inside to be clean on the outside. He likened them to whitewashed tombs that are beautiful on the outside, but are filled with rot and stench on the inside; they did this to make themselves appear most righteous to others, while being <u>filled with hypocrisy and evil</u>.

With a final 'woe to you hypocrites' in 29-32, Jesus says that even though they built tombs for the prophets and decorated graves for the righteous, that if they had lived in the days of their own ancestors, but now claimed they would not have murdered such good men, they falsely testified against themselves and <u>inherited the sins of their forefathers</u>.

In 33-36, calling them snakes and vipers that would not escape from being condemned to hell, Jesus said that He would send prophets and wise man <u>to try to save them.</u> He predicted that they would kill some, crucify others, and be covered with the righteous blood of those they put to death. Jesus cried out in verses 37-39 to the people and Jerusalem with longing and love in His heart, as if He were a mother hen gathering her chicks under her wings with great care. Calling the temple and Jerusalem spiritually barren and desolate, He tells a crowd that <u>they would not see Him again until they would bless Him as the Messiah</u> they had hoped to see.

CHAPTER 24: Behold, the Olivet Discourse! This chapter and chapter 25 present the Olivet Discourse, by Jesus on the Mount of Olives, telling about His Second coming as part of God's endtimes plan. Much of it is difficult to understand, because it contains apocalyptic, symbolic, and visionary language that does not relate to today's world. Warning is given against misplaced belief in deceptive signs which truly do not portend the end of the world. Also, diverse viewpoints exist among biblical scholars and various denominations of Christians as to the interpretation and application of the discourse, <u>whether it be solely for</u> the Jews as God's <u>chosen people, or to all Christian (Jesus) believers of Jewish or Gentile</u> extraction.

A contentious interpretation revolves around the timing of the 'rapture' within the 70th week of Daniel, also known as the 7 years of tribulation. Some believe that Christ will gather His own, believers of all walks of life, <u>shortly before the tribulation years begin,</u> and then return with His bride, the church, after 7 years of tribulation, to establish His Messianic role with converted Jews as part of His millennial kingdom. Others contend that the rapture will take place in the last half of the tribulation <u>years immediately prior to God's Great Wrath judgment</u> against antichrist forces, including all who have rejected Christ and God, both Jew and Gentile.

In this commentary, every effort will be made to arrive at logical conclusions that make sense, based on scripture apart from denominational doctrine that exists today. Believing that God is emblematic of logic, as creatures of His design, <u>our human logic coupled with His spiritual direction</u> should produce a reasonable understanding of the Olivet Discourse.

In verses 1-2, Jesus left the temple, when His disciples offer to show him more of the surrounding buildings. He declined saying that <u>all of the structures would be totally destroyed</u>, so why bother to view them. (in 70 AD the Roman army reduced them to rubble).

After relocating to the Mount of Olives, the disciples asked 2 questions: <u>'When would this happen?'</u> and 'What will be the sign of Your coming, and the end of the age?' His answer follows in verses 4-51, under several topics, after warning against deceivers representing themselves as 'the Christ,' a manifestation that is evident in our present age!

The first signs given in 6-14, will be wars, rumors of wars, strife between nations and governments, along with famines, disease epidemics, and earthquakes, all part of the beginning of 'sorrows', a preliminary time of minor trouble before a more intense tribulation time arrives. <u>Christians and Jews will be hated, persecuted, betrayed and killed,</u> as apostasy grows under the influence of false prophets. Lawlessness will increase as brotherly love wanes, even though the message of the gospels concerning the kingdom of God will be preached worldwide. Those who survive these troublesome times, living a Godly life, will be <u>saved as God's chosen ones</u>.

Verses 15-28 describe a worsening spiritual situation as an 'abomination of desolation' appears in a holy place, presumably a temple in Jerusalem. This is understood to be an evil man of great persuasion <u>who will persecute Christ's followers</u>, causing many to flee in great fear to the shelter of mountains. Jesus includes advice that no one should tarry, if working on a house top leave personal possessions, if working in the field forget about clean clothes, and sadly, pregnant or nursing mothers may not make it to safety. All should pray for an escape in summer rather than in winter, or on the Lord's Day.

Tribulation will be the worst ever in history, but this <u>time will be shortened</u> for the sake of the 'elect,' those who have faithfully held to their belief in God and His Son Jesus Christ, <u>including both Jews and Gentiles;</u> they will steadfastly resist false teachings from false prophets. Then Christ will come again in a spectacular fashion, like lighting flashing across the heavens, with God's judgment leaving multitudes of the wicked ungodly dead for the vultures to eat as He destroys the antichrist forces. <u>Everyone will know that Jesus has returned openly as never before!</u>

More details are given by Jesus in 29-31, concerning His second coming as the greatest tribulation in history ends <u>with heavenly phenomena occurring</u>. There will be loss of sunshine and moonlight, falling stars, and cosmic disturbances in the universe. He will appear in the sky descending on clouds, as His entourage of angels are <u>dispatched with a loud trumpet signal</u> to gather 'His elect,' all the believers throughout the world, regardless of ethnicity.

Just as the green leaves appear on a fig tree to signal the arrival of summer, in 32-36, so <u>will Jesus appear as the above signs occur</u>. The generation living at that time will witness this event as surely as God's word has survived for centuries.

Conditions on earth preceding Christ's return will be much like in the days of Noah according to verses 36-41; <u>none will be concerned about their destiny</u>, they will be living it up for personal pleasure. They will not understand what is to happen until Christ appears, at a time that <u>only God will decide</u>. Separation of the righteous and the ungodly in all places and activities will take place as Christ returns, some will be 'taken up' and the <u>remainder will face judgment.</u>

Jesus cautioned that all believers should be constantly vigilant in 42-51, to be ready and <u>acceptable for the unknown time of Christ's appearance;</u> no predictive guesses will be allowed. A parable of a faithful and reliable slave is given as an illustration of readiness, for which the master (God) blesses with greater benefits. Conversely, an evil slave did much harm to others since he did not expect his master to return soon to evaluate and punish him.

<u>VIEWPOINTS:</u>   This chapter gives no indication that Christ's 2nd coming will be in 2 stages, <u>before the tribulation to gather up His saints</u>, and then at the end of the tribulation to begin His millennial reign. Verse 22 implies that He will gather his saints as the Great Tribulation time is <u>shortened to preserve them.</u> Verses 29-30 says that His coming will be at the end of the tribulation after dramatic celestial disturbances take place; verse 31 says that a trumpet will sound <u>to put angels to work gathering His elect,</u> the believers of all walks of life.

Verses 40-41 speak of the 'rapture' after all the signs for the end of the tribulation take place. Language in verse 13 implies that spiritual survival will be the <u>reward for those</u> <u>who</u> <u>endure the tribulation years</u> without loss of faith in God and Jesus Christ. Verse 34 seems to say that the Jewish nation will survive to see all of the above take place; there is <u>no</u> <u>language</u> <u>which says that believers of the Gentile nations will be spared the tribulation years,</u> by an early departure from earth, as purported by those believing in the 'pre-trib' rapture.

CHAPTER 25:   Jesus presents 2 parables in this chapter about preparedness for Christ's return for the kingdom of heaven, and the <u>approved use of God-given talents in His service.</u> The first in verses 1-13 is about 10 virgins (bridesmaids), 5 who were vigilant and 5 who were careless and indifferent. All 10, representing all humanity, took their lamps (evidence of their spiritual illumination) to guide them to a rendezvous with the bridegroom (the Messiah Jesus). Of the 10, only 5 were gifted with sufficient wisdom and foresight to take along an added supply of oil (belief in their mission), while the other 5 <u>took no extra oil (they lacked</u> <u>conviction).</u> During a time delay waiting for the bridegroom, all 10 of them rested and slept.

At the hour of midnight, when least expected, a cry was heard (a trumpet?) that he had arrived and <u>they were to welcome him.</u> All 10 immediately adjusted their lamps for good illumination, but the time delay used up all the oil in the lamps of the 5 foolish women; they tried to beg some off of the 5 well-prepared women, who declined to give of their supply for fear this would cause a shortage for all of them.

The 5 foolish women were told to go to dealers to buy more oil, but <u>the bridegroom</u> <u>came</u> <u>while they were away.</u> The 5 who were prepared entered into the banquet hall and the door closed behind them. When the 5 unprepared ones returned, it was too late for them, as they were told by the bridegroom that <u>he did not recognize them as worthy</u> to enter. They lacked the spiritual preparedness to be welcome at the bridegroom's wedding, <u>just as</u> <u>insincere professors</u> <u>of faith</u> in the triune God will be rejected when Christ returns to claim His own (all believers).

A parable about talents (God-given gifts), as related in verses 14-30, is about a master (figuratively, the Lord Jesus) who gave his 3 servants a sum of money (8000 talents, figuratively God's gifts), each according to their dominant abilities, to invest for him during his absence <u>for an indefinite time.</u> When he returned, he found that his most able—1st servant had doubled the value of his 5000 talent allotment, the next—2nd servant had also doubled his 2000 talent allotment, but the 3rd one had hidden his 1000 talents in a pit and had no profit to return to his master.

The master praised the 2 servants that had doubled their allotment and <u>blessed them</u> <u>with</u> <u>new tasks for their enjoyment.</u> The deadbeat servant rudely accused the master of being a hard man that would take away any profit earned, and so he was <u>only returning what</u> <u>he had</u> <u>received.</u> This angered his master, who called him wicked and lazy, took away the 1000 talents and gave it to the 1st servant, and fired the useless servant to suffer his fate. The point of the story is that those who do well with their God-given spiritual talents in His service reap great blessings, but the <u>unfruitful will lose what little they had</u> when the final accounting is taken.

Verses 31-46 are an account of the God's judgment near the end of the tribulation time <u>when Christ returns in glory</u> with heaven's angels to establish His 1000 year reign. This will be the time when all mankind, from Israel and all Gentile nations, will be <u>gathered</u> <u>and divided</u>

into 2 categories. All righteous believers (sheep) who faithfully and generously served God during their lifetime and through the tribulation years will be assembled to Christ's right in a place of honor for eternity. The rest, the wicked non-believers (goats), will be moved to His left for consignment to an everlasting punishment of fire with Satan and his angels.

As part of the judgment, when each group asks why they are treated in this manner, Jesus said that what they did or did not do to one of the least of His faithful was done to Him during His earthly life. He described their actions and deeds as provision of food and water, housing, clothing, and visitation during difficult times.

VIEWPOINTS: The parable of the virgins implies that we should vigilantly maintain a Godly relationship at all times, because the time of our death is unknown, as is the time of Christ's return. The parable of talents suggests that rewards or punishment are doled out by God, at the time of Christ's 2nd coming, according to what we have done with God-given talents or gifts that should be used to fulfill kingdom of heaven requirements.

The language of verses 31-46 adds more support to the understanding that the rapture of all believers, both Jew and Gentile, will occur as phase 1 near the end of the tribulation in conjunction with Christ's 2nd coming, followed immediately by phase 2, condemnation and relegation of the wicked to eternal hell.

CHAPTER 26:   Commentary on this chapter of 75 verses is segmented according to related events, rather than in the order the scripture is recorded. Scripture will be discussed as follows:

  a. The Plot against Jesus, verses 1-5 and His betrayal by Judas, verses 14-16
  b. Special anointing in Bethany, verses 6-13
  c. Celebrating the Passover and Instituting the Lord's Supper, verses 17-30
  d. Peter's denial foretold and consummated, verses 31-35, and 69-75
  e. Prayer, betrayal, and arrest in the Garden of Gethsemane, verses 36-56
  f. Trial before the Sanhedrin, verses 57-68

As Jesus completed His teaching in Ch. 25, He startled His disciples in verses 1-5 with the statement, 'In 2 days we will celebrate the Passover and I, the Son of Man, will be taken to be crucified.' At that moment, synagogue leaders were plotting to take Him by trickery and kill Him.

Conveniently, for them to succeed, disciple Judas came to them later, in 14-16, offering to betray Jesus for a price; they gave him 30 pieces of silver, the cost of a slave in those days, and Judas looked for an opportunity to do his dirty work.

In verses 6-13, Jesus spent a night and day in Bethany at the home of Simon, a leper He may have healed. There an unnamed woman came to Him with a flask of expensive perfume which she poured on His Head. Some disciples, critical of this act, deplored the waste of a product that could have been sold for assistance to the poor.

Jesus reproached them, saying she had done a good thing that honored Him, because He would soon be gone, while the poor would always be present. The perfume was a sacrifice symbolizing His death, an act that would be remembered as His gospel was preached worldwide. It signified the value of Christ's gift to sinful mankind far more than the cost of His betrayal.

The next day, in verses 17-30, the first day of the Feast of Unleavened Bread, when the disciples asked where Jesus wanted to eat the Passover, He instructed them to go into Jerusalem to advise a man that they would observe it at his home. That evening, as Jesus dined with His disciples, He suddenly said that one of them would betray Him. With sadness, they asked who it would be, and Jesus said it would be one who dipped his bread with Him in a dish of broth they were eating, and it would have been better if that man had never been born.

Judas then asked, 'Rabbi, is it I?' to which Jesus replied, 'You are the one.' Nothing is said here of any reaction by Judas. It may be a safe assumption that he then left the group and did not participate in the next group activity, the Lord's Supper, which Jesus inaugurated.

He took bread, blessed it, gave some to each disciple and said, 'Take eat, this is My body.' Then He took a cup of wine, gave thanks, and passed it around for them to sip from it, saying, "Drink of My blood of the New Covenant, which is shed for many (not all), for the remission (exoneration) of their sins. Then, concluding the ceremony, He stated that He would not join them in this observance again until His second coming and millennial reign. They sang a hymn and went together to the Mount of Olives.

In verses 31-35, Jesus told the disciples that they would all desert Him that night, like sheep of a flock being scattered, as prophesied in Zech. 13:7, but He would meet them in Galilee after being restored. Peter quickly denied that he would desert Jesus, to which Jesus said, 'You will deny Me 3 times, before you hear a rooster crowing.' Peter with the other disciples said that they would die before they would deny Jesus.

Later, in 69-75, after Jesus was tried, Peter was accused 3 times, by a servant girl, another girl at a gate, and a group of bystanders, for being a follower of Jesus. Each time, he denied that he even knew Jesus, and even cursed them for their accusations. Suddenly, when he hears a rooster crowing, realizing that he had in fact denied Christ, he ran off weeping bitterly in remorse.

Now back to verses 36-56, Jesus takes Peter, James and John with him to pray apart from the others who were told to sit and wait at a spot in the Garden of Gethsemane. Jesus expressed great sorrow to the 3 disciples, and asked them to keep watch while He prayed to God, asking to be spared the agony of what was ahead, provided that it was God's will.

Returning to the 3, He found them asleep, waking them He chided Peter and the other 2 for their failure to be watchful and in prayer to avoid temptations to come. Twice more Jesus prayed apart from them, asking for strength to endure what God willed. Returning to the disciples, He woke them with the declaration that the time had come for His betrayal.

As He spoke, in verses 47-56, Judas appeared with a crowd armed with clubs and swords, all sent by the synagogue leaders to find Jesus. Judas went up to Jesus, said, 'Greetings, Rabbi' and kissed Him; this was the sign that Judas had given that would identify Jesus. Strangely, Jesus said, 'Friend, do what you came for!'

As Jesus was seized, a disciple (Peter) cut off the ear of one aggressor with a sword. Jesus told him to put the sword away because those who use a sword will die by one. He added that He could have obtained protection from 12 legions (72,000) angels if He had asked God for them, but this would have negated prophecy of His death. Turning to the captor crowd, He chided them for coming as armed robbers to take Him. He reminded them of the times He had taught them in the temple, and concluded that <u>this moment was what the prophets had predicted</u>.

Yes, at this point all the disciples fled to abandon him.

The mob led Jesus away to the Sanhedrin in 57-68, where high priest Caiaphas and other officials <u>began their interrogation of Him.</u> (Peter returned to see what would happen.) Determined to obtain incriminating evidence that would justify putting Jesus to death, they <u>listened to many false witnesses</u>. Then 2 witnessed that Jesus said that He could destroy the temple of God and rebuild it in 3 days. Caiaphas demanded that Jesus explain Himself on this charge, but <u>Jesus kept silent.</u>

Caiaphas then charged Jesus under the power of God to answer his question, '<u>Are You the Christ, the Son of God.</u>?' Jesus admitted that He was and added that at a future time He would be seated at the right hand of God, and would be seen <u>returning on a cloud.</u> This response energized Caiaphas to tear his robe and proclaim that Jesus had spoken blasphemously, to which all the officials <u>shouted their judgment of death for Him.</u> They spit in His face, beat and slapped Him, and then asked Him to identify who had hit Him, evidently after they had blindfolded Him.

This action conclusively confirmed their total rejection of Jesus as their Messiah, as predicted in Isaiah. 50:6 and 53:3.

VIEWPOINTS: The Blood of the New Covenant that Jesus spoke of at the end of the Lord's Supper, implies that a <u>new arrangement was coming into being</u> between God and all mankind, in which Jesus becomes a key factor to replace the O.T. covenant with the Israelites.

Jeremiah portrayed God's promise of a new covenant in 32:40 and 50:5, a covenant whose obligations would be deeply rooted in the hearts of believers to give them willpower to obey. Forgiveness through the atoning blood of Jesus would <u>characterize God's relationship</u> to the <u>new covenant people</u>. Jesus used the Last Supper to interpret His ministry, and particularly His death, as <u>fulfillment of Jeremiah's new covenant prophecy</u>.

It is questionable that the oath Caiaphas imposed on Jesus under the power of God was administered to Him in a normal fashion that required Him to accept it. He appeared to have given His answer willingly knowing that His fate was sealed.

CHAPTER 27:   Early on Friday morning the temple leaders decided that Jesus should die and <u>turned him over to Pilate, the Roman governor</u>. In 3-10, when Judas learned of this, he was remorseful over his sin of betraying an innocent man, and returned the 30 pieces of silver to the temple leaders, who shrugged off his guilt as no problem of theirs. Judas threw the money into the temple and left to hang himself.

The top priests picked up the money and used it to buy a potters 'Field of Blood' for the burial of visiting strangers. This was <u>fulfillment of a prophecy credited to the prophet Jeremiah,</u> as recorded in Zech. 11:12-13, for some strange reason.

In verses 11-26, Jesus is interrogated by Pilate, whose 1st question was 'Are you King of the Jews?'—a title furnished by the temple leaders. <u>Jesus affirmed this</u> and then remained silent as the temple leaders levied their charges against Him. When Pilate asked Him what He had to say about the charges, Jesus remained silent, thus amazing the governor.

Pilate resorted to a practice of asking the crowd what prisoner they would like released, a common crook named Barabbas, or Jesus Christ. While the temple leaders were urging the crowd to ask for Barabbas, Pilate's wife sent him a message not to a get involved because of a bad dream she had about Him. When the crowd demanded Barabbas be released, Pilate then asked what should be done to Jesus and they shouted, 'Crucify Him.' Pilate asked why should this be for one who had done no wrong, but the unruly crowd angrily demanded His crucifixion Seeing that their mind was made up and he could not change it, Pilate washed his hands before them, proclaiming his innocence of this unjust action. To this, the people agreed that 'His blood will be on us and our children.' Pilate released Barabbas and turned Jesus over to his soldiers for flogging.

In 27-31, the soldiers took Jesus to Pilate's headquarters area to be stripped, covered with a scarlet robe, crowned with a wreath of thorns, and given a stick in His right hand. The entire garrison of men mocked him on bended knee, saying 'Hail, King of the Jews.' After spitting on Him, they beat him over the head with the stick, replaced the robe with His own clothes, and led him away to be crucified.

Being weakened by the brutality inflicted on Him by the soldiers, and unable to carry the cross as was usually required, in 32-44, a Cyrenean Jew named Simon was compelled to carry the cross to Golgotha (Place of a Skull). After refusing a drink of pain-numbing sour wine with gall, He was hung on the cross, under a sign reading 'THIS IS JESUS, KING OF THE JEWS.'

Fulfilling Ps. 22:18, the soldiers drew lots to divide up His clothes, and sat down to watch Him and 2 robbers crucified along side die a slow tortuous death. People passing by, the chief priests, and the 2 robbers, all taunted Him for not saving Himself, if He was the Son of God. (See Luke 23:40-43 for more on this story) They reviled Him further, saying, "He saved many, but can't save Himself. He trusts God, let God save Him, if He is God's Son, as He said of Himself.'

Verses 45-56 tell of a darkness like night settling over the area from noon on Friday to about 3 p.m. when Jesus cried out in great agony, 'My God, My God, why have You forsaken Me?' Bystanders thought He was calling out for Elijah, and one offered Him a sponge soaked with wine which He accepted, before He cried out again and yielded up 'His Spirit.'

Immediately, the temple veil was ripped from top to bottom, an earthquake split rocks, and tombs opened for many dead saints to rise alive to witness before others in the city. When the OIC and his soldiers saw this, they fearfully admitted that Jesus was the Son of God. Three faithful women who also witnessed these supernatural events were: Mary Magdalene, Mary the mother of James and Joses, and Salome the mother of disciples James and John.

In 57-61, a wealthy man named Joseph, a follower of Jesus, received permission from Pilate to remove His body from the cross. After wrapping it in clean linen, he buried Jesus in his own unused tomb, closed it with a large stone, and left. Mary Magdalene and the other Mary witnessed the entombment as they sat nearby.

The next day, a Saturday, Pilate had the entrance stone sealed in place and posted a round-the-clock guard detail by the tomb to prevent anyone from entering the tomb and stealing the body of Jesus. This was done after the temple officers and Pharisees warned him that Jesus had said He would rise alive in 3 days.

VIEWPOINTS: When assessing guilt for the decision to crucify Christ, the chief priests of the Sanhedrin were the chief instigators who persuaded the common people, supporters of Jesus all along, to turn away from Him. The Sanhedrin was not allowed to initiate capital punishment; only the Romans could do so, hence they shared the guilt.

The entire procedure included scourging with a whip, having pieces of metal or bone attached, until the blood flowed, mockery and degradation, carrying the cross or the crossbeam to the site, and the crucifixion in which the body was either tied or spiked to the wooden beams. Brutality is hardly an adequate word to describe the horrendous suffering imposed on the victim.

As Christ 'yielded up His Spirit' He voluntarily surrendered life in human form, knowing that He had fulfilled God's requirement to be a living sacrifice to atone for the sins of all who embraced His teachings about the Kingdom of Heaven and accepted Him as the Messiah. He died much earlier than most victims exposed to this form of execution.

In the O.T., atonement is the process God established whereby humans could make an offering to God to restore fellowship with Him. Offerings, including both live and dead animals, incense, and money, were required to remove the damage of human sin. In His atoning work Christ is a substitute offering, meaning that in Christ, God Himself bears the consequences of human sin.

Over time, Satan, the head of evil forces and archenemy of God, achieved much power over humanity. Christ, as the Warrior of God, enters the battle, and by His death and resurrection, He defeated Satan and his minions, and opened a door of redemption for repentant sinners. Christ's death is called a "sacrifice for sins" (Heb. 10:12), a "sacrifice to God" (Eph. 5:2), and a sacrifice to initiate the New Covenant for all humanity, Jews and Gentiles.

A mystery surrounds the resurrection of saints from their graves, as to the characteristics of their bodies, and their fate after their appearance in Jerusalem. Did they live out their lives as a type of restored Lazarus, or were they translated later to heaven with Christ? Were they God's confirmation in limited number of the raising of the dead at His endtimes gathering?

The tearing asunder of the temple curtain removed the need of an intermediary between mankind and God, such as priests. Direct access to God is now available for help through prayer, truly believing in His divine provision.

CHAPTER 28:   The resurrection of Christ from death is confirmed initially by 2 woman of 27:56, Mary Magdalene and Mary, followed by the security guards, and later by His disciples, as related in verses 1-10, and 18. The two women waited until Sunday, the 3rd day after His burial, to pay their respects, but before they arrived at the tomb, an earthquake and angels rolled away the stone to open the entrance.

An angel in great heavenly brilliance was seated on the stone, causing the guards to faint away. He invited the 2 women to inspect the tomb to verify that Jesus was no longer there, and told them to inform the disciples to rendezvous with Him at a mountain in Galilee.

In 11-15, more evidence of the duplicity of the Sanhedrin leaders is seen as the guards report all that happened after they recovered from their shock. The guards were paid a large sum of money and given <u>instructions to say that the disciples had stolen Christ's body</u> at night as they slept. The leaders promised the guards that they would stand up for them if this news reached Pilate's ears; the guards were <u>in danger of a death penalty</u> if they admitted falling asleep on duty.

Finally, in 16-20, Jesus met with the 11 disciples (and possibly with a tagalong crowd) at the prescribed place in Galilee; most worshipped Him, but some were skeptical. His <u>primary message to them</u> was that He had been given all authority on earth and in Heaven to direct evangelistic efforts in the world. Then He gave them what is known as the Great Commission, to preach the gospel to convert sinners to become righteous believers, baptize them in the name of the Father, the Son, and the Holy Spirit (a triune unity), and to teach them to obey all of His commandments. He closed with this, 'Lo, I am with you always, even to the end of the age.'

<u>VIEWPOINTS:</u>   The phony alibi proposed by the Sanhedrin leaders is as full of holes as a sieve. How could the guards have seen anyone removing the body of Jesus if they were asleep? Dereliction of duty was subject to a death penalty, so if they admitted falling asleep, they would be <u>signing their own their death. warrant.</u> Nevertheless, this big lie was planted in the minds of many in Matthew's day, <u>to explain away the disappearance of His</u> <u>body.</u>

In His statement of being with the disciples always, and to the end of the age, Jesus made a long time <u>commitment of leadership to all believers,</u> providing strength to avoid sin and endurance through tribulations of life. The term 'end of the age' most logically refers to the end of the Great Tribulation of the 70th week of Daniel, when His saints of all nations would be gathered in <u>close proximity to God's Wrath judgment</u> on antichrist and all the unsaved of the world. No language here indicates a pre-tribulation rapture of Gentile Christians!

SUMMARY: This book confirms the divine power of Jesus to command His disciples to spread His gospel throughout all the world. When Jesus assured His disciples that He would be with them always and even to the ends of the earth, the disciples must have understood that He included <u>all people in His purposes for an indefinite period of time.</u>

Matthew often stated that forgiveness of sins comes through the <u>death of the divine</u> <u>Son</u> <u>of God.</u> His proxy father, Joseph, was told that Jesus would "save His people from their sins." Jesus assured His disciples that His destiny was "to give his life as a ransom for many." He left a continuing reminder of His role in the forgiveness of sins <u>by instituting</u> <u>the Lord's Supper.</u>

While the resurrection of Jesus involved His physical body; His new existence was a new kind of <u>life called into being by God.</u> Because of His resurrection, we have absolute assurance of the resurrection of all persons—some to eternal salvation and some to eternal damnation. This is how He defeated physical and spiritual death. <u>He provided a future, either</u> <u>good or</u> <u>bad,</u> after life on this earth is over.

With this introduction to the Gospels, students of the Bible should focus on the amplification or variation of details as narrated by the gospels of Mark, Luke, and John, remembering that <u>all</u> <u>4 authors may not have been present</u> to witness each event about Jesus. The following Gospel Cross-Reference Index is provided as an aid to better understanding.

GOSPEL CROSS-REFERENCE INDEX

	MATTHEW	MARK	LUKE	JOHN
Ch.	1:1-17		3:23-28	
	1:18-24		2:1-7	
Ch.	2:19-23		2:39	
Ch.	3:1-12	1:2-8	3:1-20	
	3:13-17	1:9-11	3:21	1:29-34
Ch	4:1-1	11:12-13	4:1-13	
	4:12-17	1:14	4:14-15	
	4:18-22	1:16-20	5:1-11	
	4:23-25	1:35-39	4:44, 6:17-19	
Ch	5:3-11		6:20-26	
	5:13-16	9:50	14:34-35	
	5:21-26		12:57-59	
	5:31-37	10:11-12	16:18	
	5:38-42		6:29-31	
	5:43-48		6:27-28, 32-36	
Ch	6:5-14		11:2-4	
	6:19-21		12:33-34	
	6:22-23		11:34-36	
	6:25-34		12:22-31	
Ch.	7:1-6		6:37-42	
	7:7-12		11:9-13	
	7:13-14		13:24	
	7:15-20		6:43-45	
	7:21-23		6:46, 13:26-27	
	7:24-27		6:47-49	
Ch.	8:2-4	1:40-45	5:12-16	
	8:5-12		7:1-10	
	8:14-15	1:29-31	4:38-39	
	8:18-22		9:57-62	
	8:23-27	4:35-41	8:22-25	
	8:28-34	5:1-20	8:36-39	
Ch	9:2-8	2:1-12	5:17-26	
	9:9-13	2:13-17	5:27-32	
	9:14-17	2:18-22		
	9:18-25	5:21-42	8:40-56	
	9:36-38		10:2-3	
Ch.	10:1-4	3:13-19	6:12-16	

	MATTHEW	MARK	LUKE	JOHN
	10:5-15	6:7-13	9:1-	
	10:16-26	13:9-13	21:12-17	
	10:27-31		12:3-7	
Ch.	10:32-33		12:8-9	
	10:34-39		12:51-53, 14:26-27	
	10:40-42	9:41		
Ch.	11:2-19		7:18-35	
	11:20-24		10:13-15	
	11:25-30		10:21-22	
Ch.	12:1-8	2:23-28	6:1-5	
	12:9-14	3:1-6	6:6-11	
	12:22-30	3:22-27	11:14-23	
	12:31:32	3:28-30		
	12:33-37	7:15-20		
	12:38-42		11:29-32	
	12:43-45		11:24-26	
	12:46-50	3:31-35	8:19-21	
Ch.	13:3-9	4:1-9	8:4-8	
	13:10-17	4:10-12	8:9-10	
	13:18-23	4:13-20	8:11-15	
	13:31-32	4:30-32	13:18-19	
	13:33		13:20-21	
	13:53-57	6:1-6	4:16-30	
Ch.	14:1-12	6:14-29	9:7-9	
	14:13-21	6:30-44	9:10-17	6:1-14
	14:22-33	6:45-52		6:15-21
	14:34-36	6:53-56		
Ch.	15:1-20	7:1-23		
	15:21-28	7:24-30		
	15:29-31	7:31-37		
	15:32-39	8:1-10		
Ch.	16:1-4	8:11-13	12:54-56	
	16:5-12	8:14-21		
	16:13-20	8:27-30	9:18-20	
	16:21-23	8:31-33	9:21-22	
	16:24-27	8:34-38	9:23-27	
	16:28	9:1-13	9:28-36	
Ch.	17:1-13	"	"	

	MATTHEW	MARK	LUKE	JOHN
	17:14-21	9:14-29	9:37-42	
	17:22-23	9:30-32	9:43-45	
Ch.	18:1-5	9:33-37	9:46-48	
	18:6-9	9:42-48	17:1-4	
	18:10-14		15:1-7	
Ch.	19:1-10	10:1-12		
	19:13-15	10:13-16	18:15-17	
	19:16-27	10:17-22	18:18-23	
	19:23-30	10:23-31	18:24-3	
Ch.	20:17-19	10:32-34	18:31-34	
	20:20-28	10:35-45		
	20:29-34	10:46-53	18:35-43	
Ch.	21:1-11	11:1-10	19:28-40	12:12-19
	21:12-16	11:15-19	19:45-48	2:13-22
	21:18-19	11:12-14		
	21:20-22	11:20-24		
	21:23-27	11:27-33	20:1-8	
	21:33-46	12:1-12	20:9-19	
Ch.	22:1-14		14:15-24	
	22:15-22	12:13-17	20:20-26	
	22:23-33	12:18-27	20:27-40	
	22:34-40	12:28-34	10:25-28	
	23:41-46	12:35-37	20:41-44	
Ch.	23:1-36	12:38-40	20:45-47	
	23:37-39		13:34-35	
Ch.	24:1-2	13:1-2	21:5-6	
	24:3-14	13:3-13	21:17-19	
	24:15-28	13:14-23	17:23-24, 37, 21:20-24	
	24:29-31	13:24-27	21:25-28	
	24:32-35	13:28-31	21:29-33	
	24:36-44	13:32-37	17:26-27, 34-35, 21:34-36	
	24:45-51		12:41-48	
Ch.	25:14-30		19:11-27	
Ch.	26:1-5	14:1-2	22:1-2	11:45-53
	26:6-13	14:3-9	12:1-8	
	26:14-16	14:10-11	22:3-6	

	MATTHEW	MARK	LUKE	JOHN
	26:17-25	14:12-21	22:7-13	
	26:26-30	14:22-36	22:14-23	
	26:31-35	14:27-31	22:31-34	13:36-38
	26:36-46	14:32-42	22:39-46	
	26:47-56	14:43-52	22:47-53	18:1-11
	26:57-68	14:53-65	22:66-71	18:12-14, 19-24
	26:69-75	14:66-72	22:54-62	18:15-18, 25-2
Ch.	27:1-2	15:1	23:11	8:28
	27:11-14	15:2-52	3:2-5	18:29-38
	27:15-26	15:6-15	23:13-25	18:39-40
	27:27-31	15:16-20		
	27:32-44	15:21-32	23:26-43	19:17-27
	27:45-56	15:33-41	23:44-49	19:28-30
	27:57-61	15:42-47	23:50-56	19:38-42
Ch.	28:1-8	16:1-8	24:1-12	20:1-10
	28:16-20	16:14-18	24:36-49	20:19-23

Compiled with the aid of The Nelson Study Bible, New King James Version.

GOSPEL OF MARK—BOOK TWO

The Gospel of Mark (gospel of action) is the briefest of the 4 gospels, consisting of only 16 action packed chapters, with little of the lengthy discourses by Jesus as in the Gospel of Matthew. Portraying Jesus as a Man of Action, Mark's account of His movements is characterized as 'immediate.' Written primarily to the Roman Christian Gentiles, historically an active people, Mark's writings accented the ministry of Jesus in terms of energetic activity.

Although the author of this gospel, about 64 to 68 A.D., Mark (Roman name) was not a disciple of Christ; he became an early missionary interpreter for the disciple Peter in Rome, preserving his teachings to Roman Christians shortly before the apostle's death (see 1 Pet. 5:13). As the son of a Mary, in whose home the Jerusalem believers met to pray when Peter was imprisoned by Herod Agrippa I (Acts 12:12), Mark was known by his Jewish name, John.

He learned much from his cousin Barnabas, and the Apostle Paul on several missionary journeys. He emphasized the messianic suffering of Jesus (the Servant) as if to inspire Christians to follow a similar path of spiritual servanthood; this was applicable to Roman believers suffering much under Nero's persecutions. His favorite title for Jesus was 'Son of Man,' identifying Him with humanity as a Man possessed of every human emotion, i.e. moved by compassion, anger, frustration, mercy, and sorrow.

In this gospel, Christ's great promise to those who have repented, with their sins forgiven, is that they will be baptized with the Holy Ghost; be purified by His graces, and refreshed by His comforts. Jesus came to give His life as a living sacrifice in order that humanity could be saved.

Frequent references are made to the Gospel of Matthew in this commentary on Mark.

CHAPTER 1: Without genealogy or information about the childhood days of Jesus, Mark opened his narration in verses 1-8 with a 'good news' salute to Him as the Son of God; he also referred to prophecy in Is. 40:3 and Mal. 3:1, which speaks of John the Baptist as a forerunner to lay the groundwork for the gospel of Jesus Christ. John's appearance and ministry are briefly described in verses 4-8, in which he credits Jesus as a coming divine power who would baptize and bestow the Holy Spirit on those who accepted His message. (See Matt. 3:1-17 & 4:1-11)

In 9-13, Mark tells of Christ's baptism followed by 40 days of wilderness temptation by Satan. At His baptism, God made known His approval with these words, 'You are My beloved Son, in whom I am well pleased.' Immediately, the Holy Spirit motivated Him to spend 40 days of desolate solitude in preparation for His earthly ministry, dependent on angels for safety and sustenance. There He resisted the tempting by Satan, which gave Him greater spiritual strength.

His ministry began in Galilee after John was imprisoned, as stated in 14-20, with an introductory statement that, 'The time has come for the kingdom of God to be offered, for sinners to repent and believe. He recruited His 1st disciples, all fishermen, Simon and Andrew, and brothers James and John, with this invitation, 'Follow Me and I will make you fishers of men." So it is with any believer, we must forsake every thing that is against our allegiance to Christ, and that can be harmful to our souls, serving according to His will and our talents.

In 21-29, while teaching in a synagogue in Capernaum, Jesus amazed the listeners with His profound knowledge, and aroused an evil spirit in a man who challenged Him. Amazingly, the <u>demon addressed Jesus as the Holy One of God</u> as he tried to distance himself from Him. In short order, Jesus told him to shut up and leave the man, which he did as <u>the man suffered convulsions.</u> The onlookers were more amazed at this display of authority and spread the news about in the area. Jesus then left to visit the home of Simon and Andrew. (See Matt. 4:12-22 for the above)

Finding Simon's mother-in-law sick in bed in 30-31, Jesus healed her completely so she was able to serve them. Verses 32-34 tell of many sick and demon possessed people coming that evening; He <u>healed them all without allowing demons to identify him as before.</u> (Matt. 8:14-15)

The next morning, in 35-38, Jesus sought a secluded spot where He could pray in private, but Simon and companions found Him and said that many more people were looking for Him. To this, Jesus said that He <u>wished to move on to other places to preach,</u> as this was His real purpose.

Verses 39-45 tell more of his preaching and healing ministry throughout Galilee. When a leper beseeched Him for healing, Jesus compassionately healed him and requested that he say nothing to the people but <u>go to a priest for a cleansing ceremony as prescribed by</u> Mosaic law.

The leper disobeyed and told the news far and wide so that Jesus was besieged by so many people that He could not enter the city but stayed in surrounding areas. Jesus <u>did not</u> <u>want to be known only as a miracle man,</u> He wanted to preach the gospel of the kingdom. Today is a different matter, believers are to witness about healing, physically and spiritually, so that <u>unbelievers will be influenced to seek a true spiritual relationship with Christ.</u> (See Matt. 4:23-25 & 8:2-4 for the above)

CHAPTER 2:   In this chapter, Jesus is back in His home town of Capernaum. In 1-12, while speaking to an overflow crowd in someone's home, 4 men brought a paralyzed young man for healing, but due to the congestion, they carried him to the roof and lowered him through a hole they had cut. When Jesus <u>saw their great faith as demonstrated by this act,</u> He told the young man that his sins were forgiven. (See Matt. 9:2-8 for the above and 9-9-25 for the following)

Some scribes present considered that Jesus had blasphemed God because in their view only God had authority to forgive sins. With His clairvoyance, Jesus discerned their thoughts and asked them what was easier to do, <u>tell someone their sins were forgiven,</u> or to <u>say they were healed</u> and to get up and walk. Then, identifying Himself as the Son of Man with authority to forgive sins and also heal, He told the young man to get off his mat, and carry it with him. <u>Christ proved His power to forgive sin,</u> by also showing His power to heal. As the young man got up and walked out, the people praised God for a demonstration they had never seen before.

Jesus recruits His 5th disciple in 13-17, a man named Levi (Matthew of the Gospel), who was sitting at a tax collector's booth. Responding to a curt 'Follow Me' from Jesus, Matthew <u>left his place of business to escort Jesus to his home.</u> Having a meal there with many other tax collectors (considered to be sinners by the Jewish people), some scribes and Pharisees indignantly asked His disciples why He was eating in such company. Jesus informed them

His primary <u>purpose was to minister to sinners, not those who were spiritually</u> <u>healthy,</u> so He ate with them.

In 18-22, Jesus deals with the subject of fasting, which Pharisees and disciples of John the Baptist were doing. They asked why His disciples were not fasting with them. Profoundly, Jesus told them this was <u>not proper when the bridegroom (Himself) was present,</u> but after He was taken away, they should mourn and fast. He then used 2 metaphors to indicate that O.T. rules on fasting were out-dated by New Covenant standards. First, a patch of new material should not be used to repair an old garment, and 2nd, new wine should not be put into old wineskins (which would burst as the wine fermented and all would be lost). <u>New wine goes</u> <u>into new wineskins!</u>

On a Sabbath day, Jesus and his disciples were picking heads of grain in verses 23-27 (Matt. 12:1-8). Again, Pharisees <u>challenged them for breaking Sabbath rules.</u> Jesus reminded them that David of old and his band entered God's temple to eat consecrated bread that only priests were allowed to eat. He added that the Sabbath was made for man, <u>not man for the</u> <u>Sabbath,</u> and as the Son of Man **He was Lord over that day**.

The Sabbath was instituted for the good of mankind; <u>God never intended it to be a</u> <u>burden</u> <u>to us,</u> therefore we must not make it so to ourselves. The Hebrew word shabbat, means "<u>to</u> <u>cease or desist,</u>' primarily the cessation from all work, and recreation which **interferes with** **proper worship of the Lord.**

<u>VIEWPOINTS:</u>   Just as the Sabbath was not intended to hamstring the faithful to neglect basic necessities, <u>so too is Sunday for the Christian believers.</u> The act of plucking heads of wheat to eat was an allowable act in Deut. 23:25, but because it was done on the Sabbath, the Pharisees hypocritically alleged that this was work which should be avoided on the Lord's day.

CHAPTER 3:   More controversy over what Jesus did on the Sabbath is related in verses 1-6, as in Matt. 12:9-14, when <u>He healed the withered hand of a man</u> in the synagogue. Knowing that the Pharisees were maliciously watching His actions, Jesus asked them a very pertinent question, 'What is right on the Sabbath, <u>to do good or to do evil</u>? Is it right to save a life or to cause a death?'

In spite of the hardness of their hearts, they refused to answer for fear of implicating themselves. After an angry and disgusted look at them, Jesus told the man to extend his hand, which was healed as he did so. True to their Machiavellian nature, the Pharisees left to plot with Herodians for the death of Jesus.

At this point in His ministry, many people followed Jesus and His disciples in 7-12, as they moved to the sea of Galilee, where He healed many, and <u>cast out demons who knew</u> <u>Him</u> <u>as the Son of God;</u> He sternly warned them not to identity Him, no doubt because He did not want evil beings to witness the good that He did, which <u>might confuse the innocent.</u>

Verses 13-19 (Matt. 10:1-4) briefly name the last 7 disciples, Philip, Bartholomew, Thomas, another James, Thaddaeus, Simon, and Judas Iscariot, in <u>addition to the 5 already</u> <u>recruited:</u> Simon, now renamed Peter, Andrew, brothers James and John, and Matthew. He commissioned them as His apostles to <u>preach His message and to cast out demons.</u> All were Galileans except Judas Iscariot.

Returning to the house where He was staying, in 20-27 (see Matt. 12:22-30), the crowds converged on Him in such number that eating was impossible, so some friends and family members decided to rescue Him, <u>thinking that He had overdone things in His ministry</u>. Scribes were saying that He cast out demons because He was Beelzebub (meaning Lord of the Flies), another name for Satan.

To this, Jesus used a parable, with a question, 'How can Satan cast out Satan?' He contrasted unity with disunity by pointing out that if a kingdom, or lesser group, or Satan himself, is divided or is combative against itself, <u>then it cannot survive</u>. Because the scribes accused Him of being a leader of evil spirits, Jesus gave them the verdict that blasphemies against the Holy Spirit are unforgivable, and they <u>bring eternal damnation to the violator.</u>

In 31-35, as in Matt. 12:48-50, when people told Him that His mother and some brothers were asking for Him, Jesus said to the disciples around Him that <u>they were His mother and brothers because they were doing the will of God.</u> By this Jesus may have revealed His own disappointment over the lack of understanding on the part of His own family as to His mission. He meant that eternal spiritual relationships surpass <u>earthly temporary ones.</u>

CHAPTER 4:   This is a teaching chapter in which Jesus uses 3 parables, which were riddles to some, and prefaced His remarks with an admonishment to 'Listen up' in verses 3,

9, and 23. Located at seaside in a boat, in verses 1-9, (Matt. 13:3-9) He delivered a parable to a crowd about the sower, as in Matt. 13:3-9. Briefly, seed that fell on a road, rocky ground, and among thorns, <u>did not produce a crop, or bear fruit.</u> Only seed that fell on good soil with adequate moisture produced a bountiful crop. Jesus wanted them to understand this teaching, which emphasizes the condition or quality of one's spiritual relationship with God.

Figuratively, the Sower is Jesus Christ and the seed is the Word of God that is spread throughout the world. While many will hear it, few will receive and <u>nourish it in their hearts,</u> because they are not attuned to spiritual matters, being more attached to material concerns. Other reasons for no spiritual fruit are indifference, shallowness, and insincerity.

Satan does his best to keep seed from falling on open ears, responsive hearts, and willing spirits. By God's grace <u>our hearts can become fertile ground</u> to bear the fruit of good results in our lives through Jesus Christ, thus giving praise and glory to God the Father.

In 10-20, as in Matt. 13:10-23, Jesus explained this parable to the disciples who asked for clarification. He tells them that this is His way to teach them about the kingdom of God, while the <u>truth is a mystery* to those who are not receptive</u> to spiritual matters. The seed of God's Word is most productive in good receptive soil (hearts), but produces no fruit in hardened unbelievers. (*See Bible Mysteries, at end of Book of Romans)

In 21-25, He speaks about the usefulness of a lamp to illuminate what one can see, and relates it to the <u>importance of receiving spiritual insight</u> by first hearing God's Good news, receiving it as truth for living, and <u>applying it to bear fruit.</u> Having this spiritual value, one will grow and become more effective as a servant to the Lord.

Jesus tells the parable of a growing seed in verses 26-29 (exclusive to Mark). If planted in fertile soil it grows without much care from the sower or <u>understanding of how it grows.</u> In the church domain, if the word of Christ is firmly embedded in one's soul, it will show itself in a good conversation, witnessing, and works. The growth in spiritual effectiveness is slow but sure: first the blade (conviction); then the ear (learning); after that the full corn on the cob (productive ministry). The work of grace in the soul becomes increasingly effective in God's purposes.

The parable of the mustard seed, as told in Matt. 13:31-31, is related in 30-32, to picture how the growth of Christianity can grow from very small beginnings. The relatively little impact of Christ's teaching with the Jews would be compounded greatly when shared with the Gentiles. Verses 33-34 says that Jesus spoke to the people with many parables which He explained privately to his disciples. They received the benefit of total understanding missed by unbelievers.

The stormy boat ride on the sea of Galilee, as told in Matt. 8:23-27, is repeated in verses 35-41, again revealing human weariness that must have prompted Him to escape from the crowd by boat, but also the power that Jesus had over earthly elements,. Most significantly, Jesus chided the disciples for the fear they felt over the storm, rather than be confidant in their faith that they were in safe hands with Him. Undoubtedly, they should have remained calm and let Him sleep.

Sometimes, when our fickle hearts are restless like a stormy sea, or our passions are out of control, we should heed the words of Christ, saying, 'Be silent, be calm. Why are you so fearful?' There may be cause for some fear at times, but we should always keep our trust in God to overcome it!

CHAPTER 5:   This is a chapter of 3 miracles by Jesus on the eastern shore of the Sea of Galilee. In verses 1-20 a more detailed account is given, than in Matt. 8:24-34, of a demon possessed man made whole by Jesus. This man was beset with so many demons that he could no longer function as a normal human being, but the demons within him recognized Jesus as the Son of the Most High God, as they pleaded to be left alone.

Without hesitation, Jesus ordered the demons collectively as an unclean spirit to "Come out of the man' and then asked for a name. The evil spirit spokesman said, "Legion, for we are many.' In the Roman army, a legion of soldiers totaled as many as 6000 men; but the number of demons, however many, were not necessarily this number but all were enemies of God and to this poor man.

When the demons asked that they be allowed to enter the bodies of many swine nearby (about 2000), Jesus gave them permission to do so. As the evil spirits entered the swine, the entire herd ran amuck down a steep bank into the sea to drown. The herdsmen ran to inform the owners and their neighbors of this great loss. When the people heard of this, they demonstrated their dislike of Jesus by asking him to leave their area. They were more concerned over their material loss than over the merciful act by Jesus to free a man of demons.

Contrary to previous cases, where Jesus asked that His healing not be mentioned, He instructed this man to spread the word far and wide among his friends, which he did. This may have been because He was unknown in this particular region, and crowds were smaller.

Crossing over the sea to the western side in 21-34, He was met by a huge crowd, including an official of the local synagogue named Jairus, (see Matt. 918:26) who asked Jesus to come to his home to <u>heal his young daughter who was near death.</u>

Jesus agreed to go with him and the crowd followed, including a woman who had suffered from hemorrhages for over 12 years. Along the way, she managed to get close enough to Jesus to touch the hem of His garment, <u>believing that this alone would heal her,</u> based on all that she had heard about His power to heal. She was healed instantly, and Jesus became <u>aware of healing power flowing from Him.</u> He stopped and asked who had touched Him, and the frightened woman confessed that she had. Jesus magnanimously said, 'Daughter, your faith has healed you, so now go in peace with no worry.' Her faith was in Jesus as the healer, and thus she had <u>reason to resume a normal life</u> knowing that her ailment was part of her past.

Now back to the daughter of Jairus in verses 35-43, word came that the girl had died, but Jesus <u>urged him not to fear,</u> that this was not so. Taking with him only 3 disciples, Peter, James and John, Jesus approached the home of Jairus to find many mourners wailing and weeping. When He told them that the child was not dead, just sleeping, <u>they ridiculed Him.</u>

Entering the home with His disciples and the parents, He spoke to the 12 year old girl, 'Little One, get up on your feet', and she <u>arose immediately and walked.</u> Her parents were amazed, but Jesus requested that they say nothing of her restoration, but to feed her. Again, faith is the only remedy against grief and fear at such a time.

CHAPTER 6: Jesus and His disciples returned to Nazareth, His childhood home, in verses 1-6, as related in Matt. 13-58. When He taught in the synagogue on the Sabbath, <u>people were impressed but also prejudiced</u> as they saw Him as the human son of Joseph and Mary, with 4 brothers, James, Joses, Judas, and Simon, plus 2 or more sisters. (James authored the Book of James, and Judas is said to have written the Book of Jude)

Jesus saw their unbelief and remarked to them that a "Prophet is not without honor except among His own people.' and <u>limited His teaching to surrounding villages</u> Sadly, the Nazarenes lost much by obstinate prejudices against Jesus! May people of this age be delivered from such blind unbelief, so they may see Christ as the savior of the soul.

As in Matt. 10: 5-15, Jesus commissions His 12 disciples in verses 7-13, to go out as 6 pairs of 2 <u>to minister and exorcise evil spirits.</u> They were told to go without any provisions and to depend on the populace for their needs. He gave them strict orders not to waste any time where they were <u>not welcomed and given courteous treatment.</u> They obeyed most effectively, telling the people to repent of their sins, and turn to God. Servants of Christ today have this commission also to <u>help unbelievers obtain spiritual healing</u> by the power of the Holy Spirit.

Verses 14-29, as in Matt. 14:1-12, repeat the details of Herod's beheading of John the Baptist. Nothing new is contained in Mark's account of this sad incident. One may wonder why God permitted John's execution for such fallacious reasons. While His ways are unfathomable, believe that He is <u>constant in repaying His servants</u> for what they endure or lose for his sake.

Another miracle, that of feeding the 5000 men (undoubtedly many women and children also), is described in verses 30-44, very much like the account in Matt. 14:13:21. Christ <u>generously shared the good news of the gospel with the people</u>, and then abundantly provided all the food they needed at the time. At the end of the mealtime, He taught that food should not be wasted, just as man should not be careless about any of His blessings, and be willing to share leftovers with those in need. Someday we may need the fragments that we now throw away.

In verses 45-52, as in Matt. 14:22-33, Jesus walked on the sea of Galilee out to the boat in which His disciples were rowing with all their might against a strong head wind. In this account, Mark omitted the part about Peter walking on the water to meet Christ. In like manner as Jesus was a comfort to His disciples under duress, He is so for Christians today.

Verses 53-56 tell of many people being healed, even by touching His garment.

CHAPTER 7:   The matter of defilement as seen by the Pharisees and scribes is contrasted by Jesus to God's view in verses 1-23, as also related in Matt. 15:1-20. The Pharisees found fault with the disciples for omitting a ceremonial washing of their hands before eating, as was traditional with them and earlier generations. Jesus denounced them as hypocrites for following manmade practices not required by Old Testament laws while ignoring the real commandments of God. Christ on more than one occasion set aside ceremonial law; where men embellished the law beyond what God intended. Mark explains this as if informing non-Jewish readers.

In verses 11, Jesus uses the word 'Corban' (a gift designated for God's purposes) to describe a practice by some Jews to avoid helping the needy by declaring their resources as gifts intended for God's use. This was His example of failure to honor one's father or mother, thus neglecting obedience of God's commandments.

Jesus emphasizes that defilement comes more from the heart in the form of sin, than from hands that were not subjected to a ceremonial washing. Having a spiritual understanding of the law of God, and a sense of the defilement of sin, will cause a man to strive for the grace of the Holy Spirit, to as to avoid evil thoughts and actions as much as possible.

Evidently to get away from crowds and harassment, Jesus went north about 60 miles to the non-Jewish area of Tyre and Sidon in verses 24-30, where He healed the demon- possessed daughter of a Syrian born Phoenician woman, as also related in Matt. 15:21-28. He did not command the demon to leave, nor did He see the girl; His power was effective long-distance to remove the demon.

Then, in verses 31-37, (see Matt. 15:39-31) Jesus traveled a considerable distance southeast (as much as 80 miles) to the region of Decapolis, again avoiding Jewish communities. People there had heard of His healing powers and brought a deaf man with speech difficulties to Him, begging that He would lay a hand on him. With more symbolic action Jesus took the man aside, put His fingers in the man's ears, spit on the man's tongue, and looking up to heaven, said 'Be opened.' Immediately, the man's hearing was restored and his speech problem was gone.

Here again, Jesus requested that this miracle not be told about, but to no avail, it was broadcast, and the people marveled over His powers of healing. Jesus used considerably more visible actions in this cure than usual, possibly to draw attention to His power to cure the man, but also to encourage his faith, and of those that brought him.

CHAPTER 8: As told in Matt. 15:32-39, Mark tells of the feeding of 4000 people (Matt. says men, plus women and children) in verses 1-9, with disciples questioning again how this could be done, <u>having forgotten how Jesus fed the 5000</u> (see 6:30-44). The leftovers from this feeding were much greater than from the previous one. By repeating this miracle, Christ demonstrated His readiness to meet our desires and needs, <u>in spite of our weakness</u> of faith.

In 11-12, the Pharisees tested Jesus again when they asked for a sign of His divine power as in Matt. 16:1-4. Christ <u>denied their demand</u> knowing they were insincere and would not be convinced! Sadly, lukewarm Christians of today may often forget past blessings, unexplained survival from danger, and miraculous experiences, <u>and want more of God.</u>

Jesus left by boat to cross over the sea, no doubt disgusted with the unbelieving Pharisees, in verses 13-21 (See Matt. 16:5-12), and once again <u>the disciples failed to take</u> <u>sufficient food</u> <u>with them.</u> When Jesus cautioned them to be wary of the leaven (worldly hypocrisy) of the Pharisees, they thought He was referring to their failure. Jesus chided them for their lack of understanding, asked if their hearts were hardened, or their eyes, ears, and memories had gone bad, and <u>reminded them of the surplus of bread after the feeding of the 5000.</u> They failed to meet His expectation of understanding. Spiritual blindness likewise needs the light of His grace!

Unique to Mark is the description of a blind man healed in verses 22-26. As in 7:31-37, Jesus took this man away from the people, spit on his eyes, laid hands on him and then asked if he saw anything. Saying that he saw what looked like trees walking, <u>Jesus put His hands</u> <u>on the man's eyes and asked him to look upward.</u> This restored his vision, and Jesus urged him to be silent.

On the road again, in 27-30, Jesus asked who people said He was, as in Matt. 16:13-20. When they said John the Baptist, Elijah, or a prophet, He asked who they thought He was. <u>Peter quickly answered,</u> 'The Christ.' Again, Jesus asked that they not voice this about.

Verses 31-33 (Matt. 16:21-23) tell of His clear prediction, as the Son of Man, of His <u>imminent death and resurrection after 3 days.</u> When Peter disputed this. Jesus rebuked him for yielding to thoughts provoked by Satan, rather than focusing on the will of God. Just as Peter did not rightly understand the nature of Christ's agenda, mankind's attempt to limit divine direction bespeaks human foolishness

In the final verses of 34-38 (as in Matt. 16:24-27) Jesus addresses the people and His disciples to set forth a scale of values, comparing earthly ambitions with spiritual objectives, which He <u>summed up as taking up a cross to follow Him.</u> The prospect for eternal happiness in heaven with Christ has far greater value than material gains of the world or personal victories that <u>preclude a personal relationship with Him.</u> We should always keep in mind that the day is coming when we will have to give an accounting of our earthly achievements, and <u>admit</u> <u>our shortcomings against God's standards.</u>

CHAPTER 9: A most amazing episode is described in verses 1-13, as in Matt. 16:28-17:13, of the transfiguration of Jesus on an unnamed mountain near the Sea of Galilee, 6 days after Jesus told His disciples in verses 1, that some of them would live <u>to see a mighty</u> <u>demonstration of heavenly power.</u> This was seen by 3 disciples that Jesus selected: Peter,

James and John Elijah and Moses appeared with Jesus; (Malachi 4:5-6 predicted Elijah as a prominent figure in the future coming of Jesus.) Jesus said that John the Baptist was a representation of Elijah. This episode was a preview of Christ's endtimes kingdom, and how wonderful the homecoming will be <u>with a glorified Christ and all His saints</u>.

Verses 14-20 tell of the healing of a demon-possessed boy by Jesus, as also told in Matt. 17:14-21. Being a <u>case where the disciples were not able to help</u>, Jesus chided them as a 'faithless generation,' requiring more prayer and fasting to focus on such dire needs.

Briefly, in 30-37, Jesus again predicts His death and resurrection, as in Matt. 17:22-23, <u>which the disciples failed to understand completely</u>. Instead of asking for clarification, they argued amongst themselves as to who would be the greatest in His future kingdom (see Matt. 18:1-5). Christ emphasized that service to others in His name was the way to greatness.

Verses 38-50, are teachings of Jesus to His disciples, as in Matt. 10: 40-42 and 18:6-9. He identifies favorably with others who perform miracles or do good works in His name. He cautions against the sin of causing a newly converted believer to stumble spiritually, and figuratively says that if a hand, foot or eye causes sin, they should be removed, meaning that <u>strong spiritual surgery of heart and mind is sometimes necessary</u> to break the bonds of sin.

Concluding His remarks, Jesus speaks of salt as a preservative of both good and bad characteristics, meaning that <u>indwelling of the Holy Spirit is necessary for eternal life with Him,</u> while those without it will be subjected to God's judgmental seasoning in eternal hell. If one is salted with the Holy Spirit, afflictions can be endured and put in proper perspective, and His grace will be <u>manifested in a Christian example of living to please God.</u>

CHAPTER 10: As in Matt. 19:1-9, Jesus clarifies what God intended for marriage and divorce in verses 1-12, in answer to a crafty question from the Pharisees. Having created man and woman to be together; <u>God intended the marriage bond to not be lightly untied.</u> Those who are inclined to put aside their spouse, husband or wife, should consider what would be their lot if God would deal with them in like manner. The only reason Mosaic law provided for divorce was because of the <u>hardness of heart making a marriage most unpleasant</u> and difficult.

In 13-16, as in Matt. 19:13-15, Jesus is displeased when little children are kept from him by the disciples and <u>makes it clear that He welcomed them.</u> They are to be taught about Jesus as early in childhood as they are able to understand what He is about. Jesus implied that all mankind must accept and believe in the kingdom of God with the <u>naiveté of little children,</u> obediently with sincerity and humble faith.

Jesus gives the ultimate requirement to the rich young man for inheriting eternal life in verses 17-22, as in Matt. 19:16-22. Knowing the love of wealth to be in his heart, Jesus told him to sell, or give away, all of his wealth, and to follow Him and share His burdens. No doubt, with much sorrow, the young man <u>decided not be a follower of Christ</u> on such extreme terms; he chose to forego eternal life to keep his worldly possessions.

Explaining why it is more difficult for the wealthy to enter the kingdom of God in verses 23-31, as in Matt. 19:23-30, Jesus makes clear that when wealthy people seek the wealth of the world, <u>they rarely put God first in their life.</u> To be content with much less, and even part with all we have in Christ's service, is a more certain way to inherit eternal richness in His kingdom.

For the 3rd time in this book, in verses 32-34, as in Matt. 20:17-19, Jesus speaks of His death and resurrection to His disciples. Then in 35-45, as in Matt. 20:20-28, He clarifies to James and John that He could not promise them a place of honor by His side in heaven, because that was God's business to decide what rewards they would receive.

As humans, these two disciples typified the vain ambition for special recognition that prevails in the world. Our desire, in wisdom and grace, should be to know how to suffer the tribulations of life with complete trust in God to provide relief on earth with eternal glory later.

One of His last acts of healing is recounted in verses 46-52, as in Matt. 20:29-

34, where Jesus heals the blindness of a man named Bartimaeus near the city of Jericho, who addressed Him respectfully as 'Rabboni,' meaning master or teacher in the Aramaic language. Afterwards, the man followed Jesus for a while.

This demonstrates that we should follow Jesus diligently when we receive healing, whether physical or spiritual; thus we honor Him and are in line to be blessed more abundantly. With spiritual vision, one can see the beauty of Christ as a powerful inducement to follow Him.

CHAPTER 11: As Jesus and His disciples neared Jerusalem at the Mount of Olives, He instructed 2 of them to enter a nearby village to procure a colt (donkey) that had never been broken for riding. In verses 1-11, as in Matt. 21:1-11, they were to inform the owner that the 'Lord had need of it.' They did as commanded and brought the colt to Jesus where they covered it with extra clothes on which He sat. His power over animal nature was demonstrated when He apparently rode an untrained donkey without difficulty. Mark made no mention of a second young colt, as in the Matthew narration.

Other people spread their clothes, or leafy branches, on the road over which He rode; many of them honored Him with praise language. He entered Jerusalem and directly visited the temple for a quick inspection before returning to Bethany for the night. He did this boldly without evidence of fear from temple leaders who were hostile to Him; this must have been encouragement to the disciples who were filled with fear.

Verses 12-14, as in Matt. 21:18-19, tell of Jesus coming out of Bethany the next morning to pass a leafy fig tree without fruit for which He may have hungered. Finding nothing, He pronounced a curse on it to never have fruit again. The next day, in verses 20-24 (Matt. 21:20-

22), as He and the disciples passed by it, they saw that it had died. To this, Jesus gave them instruction on faith, using the tree as an example of lack of spiritual fruit in the people of that day and the doom to come upon the Jewish church in which He found no fruit of the Spirit. Christ told them to pray in faith that God would provide as they had needs.

Again in Jerusalem, in verses 15-19 (Matt. 21:12-17), Jesus returns to the temple where He drove out the vendors, overturned money changer tables, and the benches of dove sellers. He allowed no sales items to enter the place. He declared the temple to be a house of prayer for all nations (including Gentiles?), and that it was off-limits to crooked merchandisers. This angered temple officials while the people were awed.

In 25-26 (Matt. 6:14-15), Jesus admonished them to have a charitable heart towards others when praying, without malice, <u>to receive God's blessings</u>. Forgiveness of others is a prerequisite to forgiveness of one's own sins, and to remove mountains of problems.

When Jesus' authority to cleanse the temple is questioned by the temple officials in 27-33, as in Matt. 21:23-27, He agreed to tell them <u>if they first answered His question</u> of them. His question was, 'Was the baptism authority of John from heaven or from men?' Fearing to answer in any way, they said, 'We don't know!' Jesus then told them <u>He would not answer their question</u>. Factually, He had no reason to tell them, for the works He had done was sufficient evidence that His authority came from God.

CHAPTER 12:   The parable of the wicked vineyard workers, as told in Matt. 21:33-46, is repeated in verses 1-12, as given by Jesus to the temple officials. The workers, <u>representing the Israelites,</u> were literally punished when the Romans invaded Jerusalem and destroyed the temple in 70 AD. Giving the vineyard to others signified a shift in God's ministry to the Gentiles.

Again, as related in Matt. 22:15-22, the Pharisees with Herodians tried to entrap Jesus in verses 13-17, about the <u>matter of paying taxes to Caesar</u>. Jesus avoided the snare, by turning their words against them, causing the people to marvel over His great wisdom.

Sadducees pose a trick question to Jesus in verses 18-27 (Matt. 22:23-33) about <u>whose wife a woman would be in heaven if she married a series of 7 brothers</u> in accordance with Mosaic law. This question was to discredit the doctrine of resurrection, which the Sadducees rejected.

Christ put the objection of the Sadducees aside, by explaining the future state of husbands and wives in heaven <u>in terms of angels who do not marry or procreate</u>. He tells them that God will raise the dead because He is the God of Abraham, Isaac, and Jacob, as if they were still alive.

Jesus is asked 'Which is the first, or greatest commandment of all?' by a scribe, in verses 28-34, as in Matt. 22:34-40. The 1st is to <u>love God with all your hearts, soul, mind, and strength.</u> A 2nd one is to 'Love a neighbor as yourself.' No other commandments are greater than these two! When the scribe agreed with this, Jesus declared him close to Christianity. Making these a ruling principle in the soul, will draw us into God's pleasure zone.

In 35-37, Jesus refers to Himself as the Son of David, being a descendent of David, yet <u>of divine origin as the Son of God</u> (see Matt. 22:41-46. Jesus warns against phony teachers of law in 38-40, as in Matt. 23-1-7, as being self-centered and avaricious.

Jesus commends a widow who gives of her meager funds in 41-44, as being more generous <u>than those who give from their abundance</u>. The modest efforts of the poor to honor the Lord will be rewarded in the day of judgment, while the benevolent self-aggrandizement giving of unbelievers may be looked upon with contempt.

CHAPTER 13:   The 1st 2 verses are a repeat of Matt. 24:1-2, in which Jesus tells His disciples that the beauty and splendor of the temple would be totally destroyed, which it was, in 70 AD <u>by the army of Roman General Titus.</u>

As in Matt. 24:3-14, Jesus informed 4 disciples, Peter, James, John, and Andrew in verses 3-14, about the <u>signs connected with the End of the Age</u> (part of the Olivet Discourse). He warned of false prophets or impersonators of Himself, rampant warfare, conflict between nations, earthquakes and famines, as a time of sorrows, for the first half of Daniel's 70th We ek. God's messengers would suffer persecution, but the Holy Spirit would enable them to say and do the right thing. Conflict and betrayal will prevail in family circles. Those who endure such conditions, with God's help to the end of their time, will be saved forever. Enduring to the end includes service in the Lord's ministry to carry the gospel to all the world.

The Great Tribulation is discussed in 14-23, as in Matt. 24:15-28, (according to the prophecy of Daniel 9:26-27, 11:36-45, and 12:1-13). Some say this was fulfilled in 70 AD by the Romans, but more realistically this is a prediction of such destruction and desolation, not really found in any historic documentation, that it has to be a future occurrence.

In 24-37, as in Matt. 24-44, Jesus gave information on His 2nd coming as the Son of Man, with great power and glory, with His angels gathering all of His believers, Jews and Gentiles, the dead first and then the living. Based on the sequence of Christ's prophecy, His coming to gather His own (the rapture) and the day of God's Wrath Judgment, will occur near the end of Daniel's 70th Week, as the Great Tribulation days are cut short. Those alive at that time, who know and believe in God's word, will recognize these signs and be ready.

Jesus made clear that no one knows the exact time when these climactic endtimes events will occur, so it is important to always be prepared for Christ's return. It could happen when we are young, middle aged, or an old-timer; whenever our Lord comes, let Him find us active in His service, mindful and wary of worldly sins, and dedicated to living a blameless life. We should always be prepared, watchful, and faithful, to end of our days, or to end of His days!

CHAPTER 14: While Jesus rested at a home in Bethany, in verses 1-11, as recorded in Matt. 26: 1-16, with the Passover and the feast of Unleavened Bread at hand, the chief priests and scribes plotted to somehow seize and kill Him without arousing crowd objection. As Jesus sat at a table, a woman (said to be Mary of Bethany, the sister of Martha and Lazarus) broke open an alabaster flask of expensive perfume and anointed Him by pouring it on His head.

Some disciples were critical of this act, Judas believed to be one of them, with the premise that it could have been sold to help the poor. Jesus defended and commended her act as an anointment of His body for burial, a matter to be remembered. At this point Judas contacted the chief priests to enter into an agreement to betray Jesus; he may have coveted wealth which Satan used as temptation to yield to this grave sin. Compare the beauty of a loving gift of expensive perfume with the lust for material gain which brought eternal condemnation to the betrayer.

In verses 12-26, as in Matt. 26:17-29, Jesus celebrates the Passover and institutes the Lord's Supper with His disciples in a large upper room of a house in Jerusalem, that Jesus pre-selected. Some scholars speculate the home may have belonged to Mark's father.

The Lord's Supper (Eucharist, meaning Thanksgiving) was to become a memorial ceremony of Christ's sacrificial death within the fellowship of believers until His 2nd coming. It is also a reminder of the spiritual dividends His death provided for redeemed sinners. It is to be observed only by those who have a right relationship with Christ, with sins forgiven

Afterwards, at the Mount of Olives in the Garden of Gethsemane, as related in verses

27-41, and Matt. 26:31-46, Jesus predicts that the disciples will desert him that coming night. They denied this would happen, Peter most emphatically, even when Jesus said he would do so 3 times before a rooster crowed twice. (Matthew says before a rooster crowed once.)

Jesus, in His human nature prayed repeatedly to God that He be spared the agony of death, but only if it were God's will. No doubt, He did not relish the coming brutality and crucifixion, most of all the thought of becoming a curse for the sins of man. Meanwhile, as He agonized and prayed, with 3 disciples nearby (Peter, James, and John), He found them asleep 3 times as He returned to them; this grieved and disappointed Him.

Jesus then tells the 3 disciples to wake up and rise in 42-62 (as in Matt. 26:47-56) as He discerns that Judas is about to betray Him. With a large troop of men armed with swords and clubs, Judas appears and identifies Jesus with a kiss. Mark tells of a disciple, believed to be Peter, drawing his sword to cut off the ear of one of the troop, but says nothing about Jesus restoring the ear or chiding Peter for becoming violent. At this point, the disciples fled the scene.

Oddly, 51-52 tell of a young man following Jesus, wearing only a loin cloth, who fled naked when some other young men took hold of him. Since this is not in other gospel accounts, it would appear that this may have been Mark, who did not flee with the disciples.

Jesus is taken before the Sanhedrin, in 53-65, as in Matt. 26:57-68, with Peter following at a safe distance to sit by a fire in the high priest's courtyard. Witnesses are called to speak against Jesus, falsely in most cases, but without the necessary consistency to support a binding charge for condemnation to death. When the high priest Caiaphas asked Him if He was Christ, the Son of God, Jesus admitted that He was the Son of Man who would sit at God's right hand and come again on clouds of heaven. This infuriated the high priest who demanded a verdict from the others; they all said that Jesus deserved to be put to death. The abuse and beatings followed.

Back to Peter, in 66-72, as in Matt. 26:69-75, Peter is confronted twice by a servant girl and again by others, all identifying him as a follower of Jesus, which he denied vehemently, using some foul language against his accusers. Mark says that the rooster crowed after his 1st denial, and the 2nd time after his 3rd denial; Peter then remembered the words of Jesus and wept with grief at his weakness and lack of courage. Repentance is not without grief! In Peter's case this may have fortified him for a more effective ministry later which required him to be more faithful.

VIEWPOINTS: The scribes, high priests, and other community leaders, realized that the people were largely supportive of Jesus and His ministry, no doubt due to the many miracles of healing and demon exorcism that He had performed. For this reason, they feared taking action during normal daylight hours to bring charges for a death penalty and did their dirty work during hours of darkness, seizing Him after He prayed in the Garden of Gethsaemane late on a Thursday evening, and immediately bringing Him before the Sanhedrin for a mock trial. Early Friday morning they delivered Him to Pilate, the Roman governor, for ratification of their charges, thus placing the onus of His arrest on an authority above them, which the people dared not challenge.

CHAPTER 15:   Verses 1-15 tells of Jesus before Pilate for interrogation and an official decision to allow capital punishment, a legal matter reserved for the Roman governor. In 1-5, as in Matt. 27:1-2 and 11-14, Pilate asks Jesus 'Are you King of the Jews' to which Jesus said 'It is as you say.' <u>Claiming to be a king</u> over the people went against Roman law and was <u>punishable by death.</u>

To the charges by the chief priests, Jesus said nothing, which puzzled Pilate. Going further, in 6-15, as in Matt. 27:15-26, Pilate then is faced with the practice of releasing one prisoner to the Jews, so he asked if Jesus should be the fortunate one, but the crowd with the chief priests urging <u>asked for a cold-blooded murderer named Barabbas</u> to be released. When Pilate asked what should be done with Jesus, they cried out repeatedly, 'Crucify Him.' Pilate <u>chose to yield to the crowd</u> and after soldiers scourged Jesus, He was prepared for crucifixion.

By giving up Jesus to die for no justified reason, the Jews were <u>turning their backs on the kingdom of God,</u> which was to be given to the Gentile world, as the disciple's mission after His translation to heaven. The jealousy of the temple priests to bring this about led to this abhorrent evil deed, that cost the Jewish people at large a <u>precious opportunity to be</u> <u>world leaders</u> for God's purposes of evangelizing all mankind. A tragedy many do not yet understand or regret!

In the hands of the Roman soldiers, in 16-20 (Matt. 27:27-31), Jesus is mocked and beaten, crowned with a thorny headpiece, spat upon, and ridiculed while wearing a purple (or scarlet hue) robe. After restoring His customary clothes, <u>He was escorted to the crucifixion site.</u> Jesus wore a crown of thorns which we deserve much more for our sins, so that we may put on a crown of glory, <u>that He merited much more.</u> He suffered shame and contempt to deliver us from sin.

In verses 21-32, as in Matt. 27:32-44, Jesus is taken to a hill called Golgotha (Place of the Skull, or Calvary in Latin). Having lost blood at the hands of the soldiers, Jesus <u>lacked the strength to carry the crossbeam</u> as was customary, so a man named Simon was forced to carry it

Before He was nailed to the cross a sedative drink of wine with myrrh was offered, but <u>He refused it.</u> At 9 AM on a Friday morning, He was crucified, and His garments were divided out by lottery to the soldiers (see Ps. 22:18).

Under an overhead plaque, reading 'THE KING OF THE JEWS, Jesus hung between 2 common thieves, fulfilling prophecy that He <u>would be numbered with transgressors</u> (Is. 53:9 & 12). The people with the high priests mocked and challenged Him to save Himself from the cross. Mark says that the two thieves also reviled Him, but see Luke 23:40-43 for another story.

He dies on the cross as related in verses 33-41, and in Matt. 27:45-56, 6 hours after being hung on the cross, at 3 PM that Friday, after crying out to God, '**My God, My God, why have You forsaken me.!**' At that moment daylight was replaced by darkness like night, signifying the burden which the human soul of Christ was under, as <u>He became a sacrificial</u> <u>offering for mankind's sin, thus opening a new door into the kingdom of God.</u>

The temple veil was torn in two from top to bottom, signifying a <u>new open door for all humanity to approach God in prayer or repentance,</u> without the necessity of an intervening agent. A centurion who saw Christ yield His life in just 6 hours, rather than linger a day or two, declared that <u>Jesus was truly the Son of God.</u> The horrible scene was viewed by many women who had loved and served Jesus, including Mary Magdalene, one named Mary, and another named Salome.

As related in Matt. 27:57-61, verses 42-47 relate how Jesus was buried in the private tomb of a man called Joseph of Arimathea, a more pious member of the Sanhedrin, who obtained Pilate's permission to do so after His death was verified. He had the body wrapped in fine linen, and laid in the tomb which was tightly closed with a large circular stone across the entrance. This considerate man was divinely motivated to do this to honor the memory of Jesus, not knowing what was to happen to Him later. Mary Magdalene and the other Mary observed the entombment.

CHAPTER 16:   The first 8 verses are not as complete in detail as Matt. 28:1-8, which mentioned an earthquake in conjunction with the movement of the stone to open the tomb, and speaks of the Roman guards fainting from fright. It tells of Mary Magdalene and another Mary coming to the tomb on Sunday, after the Jewish Sabbath, to anoint the body of Jesus with spices.

They wondered how they could remove the stone from the tomb entrance, not realizing that divine providence would do the task. It can be said that if we are diligent in serving the Lord, He will remove obstacles in unexpected ways. Mark does not identify the young man in white as an angel, but does name Peter as one to be informed of Christ's resurrection, and His desire to meet with His disciples in Galilee. Mark also says in verse 8 that the women fled in fright and said nothing to anyone, contrary to what Matthew's version tells us. Mark just didn't know!

There is a question as to the authorship of verses 9-20 according to biblical references which state that they were not included in two 4th century manuscripts; however without them, verse 8 would not be a proper ending to Mark's gospel. We should accept these verses as God's will at work in providing them, and as a truthful conclusion.

Verse 9-12, as well as Matt. 28:9-10, tells that Jesus first appeared to the 2 women who went immediately to tell the disciples (but evidently no one else), but they would not believe and continued mourning. Jesus appeared to 2 unnamed disciples who were out walking; the other disciples did not believe their account either. In a sense, their caution in accepting such reports may have added greater conviction to their ministry later, based on Christ's appearance in person.

Later, in verses 14-18 (Matt. 28:16-20) after an undetermined time interval, Jesus appeared to the 11 disciples as they sat at a table eating a meal. He chided them for not believing reports of His resurrection, and immediately instructed them to begin a world ministry (The Great Commission) to carry the gospel of redemption from sin to all mankind.

While reestablishing His personal relationship with the 11, and commissioning them into a lifetime of service to bring others into the kingdom of God, Jesus mentions some signs of believer spirituality, some being evident in the early Christian church, i.e., casting out demons, speaking in tongues, handling serpents, and healing the sick. Drinking poison without physical consequences is mentioned in verse 18, but this is not confirmed elsewhere in New Testament accounts. It may have been a hypothetical illustration of God's infinite power to <u>save us from any peril.</u>

Very briefly, Mark states in 19-20, that Christ ascended into heaven to sit at the right side of God, while the disciples <u>went to work preaching everywhere</u> with God's power through them confirmed by given signs, and other miracles.

Christ's workers of today need not have miracles or supernatural signs to prove their message to unbelievers; the written <u>Word of divine origin is sufficient to convict</u> those who reject it or neglect to give adequate consideration to understand it. Hearing and realizing the validity of God's message can and does lead to believing, repentance and obedience of His commandments.

<u>SUMMARY:</u> Clearly, Mark presented Jesus as a man of action, moving considerable distances from region to region, as if <u>to promulgate His ministry to reach as many people as possible.</u> Mark gave some added emphasis to His gestures, change of attitude and emotions, and chiding of the disciples by Jesus.

Another salient aspect of His ministry was to cleanse the Temple of commercialism with the objective of <u>restoring it</u> as a 'house of prayer' for the people of Jerusalem, and giving it <u>as an example for all places of worship</u> in the world. In a sense His curse on the non-productive fig tree symbolized His displeasure over the lack of spiritual fruit from the religious leaders of the Temple. Purifying the Temple provided a divine standard for proper usage of any house of God, of any denomination, but it <u>also contributed to His own death.</u>

Noticeable also, was Jesus' attempt to conceal His identity, when He healed or removed demons, by instructing those who were blessed by His restoration, and His disciples, to not spread the word, but to be silent. He mainly did not want it known that demons recognized Him, and <u>He wished to conserve time for more teaching.</u>

Mark's account confirms the deity of Jesus, from the divine voice announcing it from heaven at His baptism, demons screaming it in agony, Peter professing it boldly, and at His death, <u>when a Roman soldier acknowledged,</u> "Truly, this man was the Son of God!" (15:39).

PARABLES OF JESUS CHRIST—GOSPEL CROSS REFERENCE INDEX

TOPIC	IN MATTHEW	IN MARK	IN LUKE	IN JOHN
Lamp under Bowl	5:14-16	4:21-22	8:16-18	—
Blind Guides	7:3-5	—	6:41-42	—
Wise-foolish Builders	7:24-29	—	6:47-49	—
Patches &	9:16-17	2:21-22	5:36-39	—
Marketplace Children	11:16-17	—	7:31-32	—
Empty House-Evil Spirit	12:43-45	—	11:24-26	—
Sower, Seed & Soils	13:3-9, 18-23	4:1-9, 13-20	8:4-8, 11-15	—
Wheat & Weeds	13:24-30, 36-45	—	—	—
Kingdom-Growing Seed	—	4:26-29	—	—
Mustard Seed	13:31-32	4:30-32	13:18-19	—
Kingdom like Yeast	13:33	—	13:20-21	—
Hidden Treasure	13:44	—	—	—
Pearl of Great Price	13:45-46	—	—	—
Kingdom like a Dragnet	13:47-50	—	—	—
Lost Sheep Found	18:10-14	—	15:1-7	—
Unforgiving Servant	18:21-35	—	7:41-43, 17:4	—
Workers in the Vineyard	20:1-16	—	—	—
Vineyard Work-2 Sons	21:28-31	—	—	—
Tenants in the Vineyard	21:33-45	12:1-12	20:9-19	—

Wedding Banquet	22:1-14	—	14:16-24	—
Good Samaritan	22:34-40	12:28-34	10:30-37	—
Seating-Wedding Feast	23:12	—	14:7-11	—
Fig Tree Endtimes Sign	24:32-34	13:28-31	21:29-33	—
Absent Householder	24:36, 42-44	13:33-37		
Wise-Foolish Virgins	25:1-13	—	—	—
Talents to Servants	25:14-30	—	19:11-27	—
Sheep-Goat Judgment	25:31-36	—	—	10:26-29
Persistent Friend Knocks	—	—	11:5-10	—
Rich Fool	—	—	12:16-21	—
Watchful Servants	25:45-51	—	12:35-40,42-48	—
Fruitless Fig Tree	—	—	13:6-9	—
Warring King	—	—	14:31-33	—
Lost Coin-Sinner Found	—	—	15:8-10	—
Prodigal Son Returns	—	—	15:11-32	—
Self-serving Manager	—	—	16:1-13	—
Rich Man & Lazarus	—	—	16:19-31	—
Unworthy Slave	—	—	17:7-10	—
Persistent Widow- Judge	—	—	18:1-88	—
Pharisee &Tax Collector	—	—	18:9-14	—
True Shepherd	—	—	—	10:1-18

GOSPEL OF LUKE—BOOK THREE

Historical records adequately confirm that Luke was the author of this gospel, most likely written about 60 AD while he was in Caesarea, the Roman ruled capital of Palestine, and the Apostle Paul was there awaiting trial. As a close friend of Paul's and possibly one of his converts, Luke is believed to have accompanied Paul and Mark on several missionary trips. Paul identified him as a physician of non-Jewish lineage, and several sources identify him as a Greek Gentile.

Luke was not a disciple of Jesus Christ, but apparently became a follower and coworker evangelist through the ministry of Paul and the disciples who helped organize the early churches. Nothing is known of his medical training or practice; more is known of his talent for recording facts about the life of Jesus and the growth of the early church. Evidence exists that he never married and died at age 84.

He stated that his reason for writing the gospel was to inform his dear friend named Theophilus (meaning 'friend of God'), of all that he had learned about Jesus and His purpose as the Son of God. It is commonly believed that Theophilus was a Roman Gentile who was most interested in the new Christian faith, and that his conversion may have been brought about by Luke's writings to him.

Scholars credit Luke with writing the most beautiful story of God's love in Christ, based on his intimate contact with Paul, Mark, and disciples James and John. He stressed the universal redemption available to all through Christ. Luke also stressed the humanity of Jesus from His compassion for the afflicted, and concern for several women He encountered in His ministry.

Luke's account gives more details than the other gospels on a variety of miracles, some parables, teachings, and the ascension of Christ. His gospel stresses that God's plan of salvation is for the entire world, all races and denominations, which accept and live by it. Reference will be made to the Gospel of Matthew where appropriate on similar accounts.

CHAPTER 1:   In the 1st 4 verses, Luke gives as his reason for writing this gospel his desire to acquaint his friend Theophillus (an official of some kind) with the total truth about the birth of Jesus as the Messiah, as he personally was able to determine after thorough investigation and consultation with eyewitnesses. No doubt, his understanding was perfected by divine insight.

The birth of John the Baptist is made known to his father, a priest named Zacharias, in verses 5-25, by God's special angel Gabriel. As in the O.T. story of Abraham and Sarah, who were given a son by God in their old age, Zacharias and his wife Elizabeth were seniors without a child, somewhat of a disgrace in the Jewish culture.

As Zacharias was tending to his priestly duties in the temple, Gabriel put the fear of God in him by suddenly appearing next to an altar. When Gabriel assured him that he had nothing to fear, because his wife would conceive and bear a son, to be named John, Zacharias expressed doubt because of their advanced years and asked for a sign.

Gabriel may have been indignant when he informed Zacharias that as a representative of

God, who sent him to convey the good news, he should not have doubted and because he did, his ability to speak would be put on hold. This kept him from speaking more words of doubt.

Earnest prayers for which answers are not received as we hope for, can be answered in God's own time even when age or other reasons might seem to be limiting factors. God's patience with us is much greater than our patience with Him. We should be thankful for this sweet mercy. When even the righteous dishonor God with unbelief of abnormal circumstances, out of confusion and uncertainty, their voice of witnessing may be silenced until joy and gratitude returns.

In his description of John, the child to be, Gabriel gave a glowing report of his future as a source of joy and happiness, of God's high esteem for him, his abstinence from alcoholic drink, being filled with the Holy Spirit from day one, and his ability to evangelize many Jewish people to prepare the way for Messiah's ministry. This was also fulfillment of prophecy that a type of Elijah would lead the way. (see Malachi 3:1 & 4:5)

When Zacharias came out of the temple holy place speechless, he tried to communicate with the people with gestures; they concluded that he had been shocked by a vision. After he returned to his home, Elizabeth did conceive and in silent gratitude remained in seclusion for over 5 months, giving praise to God for His blessing.

Once again, God's angel Gabriel communicates with a human in verses 26-38, about another birth to take place. This was to a young virgin girl in Nazareth named Mary (a cousin of Elizabeth), who was betrothed to a man named Joseph, a descendant of the line of David.

He informed her that she was highly esteemed by God and had been selected to conceive and give birth to a son, whose name would be Jesus, to have an endless kingdom. as the Son of God. When she asked how this was possible since she had not had intimacy with a man, Gabriel told her that conception would be brought about by the Holy Spirit of God. (see Is. 7:14)

At the same time, he told her of Elizabeth's pregnancy of 6 months in her old age, as another case of the impossible being possible with God. To this, Mary conceded her willingness to be of service to God in this capacity, in total faith, without asking for a sign as Zacharias did.

Verses 39-45 tell of Mary's visit to Elizabeth, whose unborn child stirred vigorously in her womb, as Mary arrived. Elizabeth thus was given discernment of the divine nature of Mary's pregnancy and voiced praise and blessing that she, as the mother of the Lord, came to visit her.

In verses 46-55, Mary expresses her joy and gratitude over her divinely ordained role, in words that describe God's magnificence, in a song now commonly called the Magnificat. About 3 months later, she returned to her own home, shortly before John was born.

Friends and relatives rejoiced with Zacharias and Elizabeth as John is born in verses 57-66. At his circumcision rite 8 day's later, they wanted to name the boy Zacharias after his father, but Elizabeth said it would be John. When they asked Zacharias about it, He wrote on a pad, 'His name is John.' Marvelously, his speech ability returned and he praised God and prophesied about John's future role in verses 67-79, in words of a song now called the 'Benedictus.' Verse 80 states that John grew up strong in spirituality, while living quietly in the countryside.

VIEWPOINTS: Mary's singular experience as the mother of Jesus does not justify calling her 'the Mother of God' as done in some Christian circles. She is to be admired as a fitting example of faith and commitment to God's purposes, but <u>she should not be a subject of worship</u>. Her words of praise and thanksgiving reveal her knowledge of the O.T. to which she referred about 15 times, mostly to passages in Psalms.

When Zacharias confirmed in writing that the name of his son would be John, he also showed his faith in God's purposes for him; this simple <u>act of faith was reason enough</u> for <u>God to restore his speech ability</u> to forcefully preach the word about John's role in God's plan.

CHAPTER 2:   Luke gives an historical tie to the timing of the birth of Jesus in verses 1-7 (Matt. 1:18-25) which <u>most authorities set at 5-4 BC</u>. While in Bethlehem registering for a census, Mary gave birth to Him, her firstborn son, fulfilling the prophecy of Micah 5:2. With an overcrowded town, this took place in a stable or cave with a feeding manger for His bed.

While the Christian church celebrates His birth on December 25th, verses 8-20 suggest that the time of year for <u>His birth may have been the summer months</u> when shepherds lived on the field with their herds. Some in a nearby field were awed when God's angel informed them of Christ's birth and the location where He could be seen, as other angels voiced the refrain, 'Glory to God in the highest, and on earth peace, goodwill toward men!' This clearly spoke of God's intention for His son to be a source of <u>peace and goodwill, for those</u> <u>who accepted Him</u>.

The shepherds found Jesus and His parents and immediately recognized Him as the Savior, Christ, and Lord as the angels had told them. <u>This they made known throughout</u> the area. Verse 21 interjects the comment that He was circumcised after 8 days and named Jesus; 32 days later, as stated in 22-24, Mary underwent a purification ceremony and He was presented in the temple <u>for dedication to the Lord</u> with the sacrifice of only 2 pigeons (a sign of their poverty). Christian parents in some churches present their children to the Lord in some kind of ceremony after birth, as a form of dedication to God, asking Him to keep them from sin, holy to Himself.

When presented in the temple, a priest named Simeon was given divine perception to recognize Jesus as the long awaited Messiah, as described in verses 25-35. He blessed the child and <u>thanked God for permitting him to see Christ before his own death</u>, clearly demonstrating great faith in salvation through Him. Simeon also blessed Joseph and Mary but warned her of a time of great sorrow in the future, <u>over His rejection and crucifixion.</u>

Before leaving the temple, as stated in 36-40, an old (possibly 100 years of age) priestess named Anna gave thanks for Christ's arrival and shared the salvation message to others thereafter. Returning to Nazareth, Jesus became spiritually strong with wisdom and grace in His youth.

In His 12th year, during a 7 day visit to Jerusalem for the Passover in 41-50, without His parents knowledge <u>Jesus stayed behind as they returned home</u>. After a day's journey, they returned to find Him in the temple conversing with teachers over scriptural doctrine. Mary chided Him for causing them anguish over His disappearance. He baffled them with his reply that they need not have found Him, because <u>He had to take care of His Father's business.</u> Was this disobedience to His parents, or giving precedence to God's calling?

This can be a lesson for all Christians—that we should attend to God's purposes, with all <u>other concerns giving way to His business.</u> In obedience, Jesus then returned home with

Mom and Dad, continuing to grow in wisdom and standing with God, His parents, and His neighbors. Though He was already the Son of God, He had to remain subject to earthly parents for a time.

CHAPTER 3: As in Matthew 3:1-17, verses 1-22 recount the ministry of John the Baptist shortly <u>before Jesus began his ministry,</u> as confirmed by Luke's historic sketch which includes Pontius Pilate as governor of Judea, and Caiaphas as high priest in the temple at Jerusalem.

John preached that repentance was necessary for the remission of sins, followed by water baptism of water as an outward sign of inward cleansing and renewal of heart. He fulfilled prophecy of Isa. 40:3-5, preaching boldly against the hypocrisy of mankind, which he called vipers, with a mandate to <u>change one's way of life to avoid the ax of God's wrath.</u>

Three groups of people sought his advice, the people at large, tax collectors, and the military men. In the order listed, he told them to share with the needy, to collect only what was due, and to <u>treat civilians fairly and not to augment their pay by acts of extortion.</u>

He was so dynamic that some thought he was the Messiah, but John the Baptist disowned himself as the Christ, confirming that He would appear soon <u>with far greater</u> <u>authority than his</u>. He compared his simple baptism with water to that of the Messiah who would baptize with the Holy Spirit and ultimately with God's involvement at some future time, <u>after redeeming the good,</u> He would destroy the bad by fire.

Luke briefly states that Jesus was baptized by John and while He prayed, (probably praising God because He had no sin to confess) <u>God spoke from heaven</u> to say, 'You are My beloved Son, in You I am well pleased.'

Then Herod put John in prison for rebuking him for wickedness and his immorality with a niece, after divorcing his wife. John boldly condemned sin at all levels.

In verses 23-38, Luke presents a most amazing genealogy of Jesus Christ, as He began His ministry at age 30, <u>in which he names 76 men,</u> beginning with His adoptive father Joseph back through David, Abraham, Noah, Methuselah, all the way to Adam, called the son of God by creation.

The genealogy in Matt. 1:2-16, begins with Abraham and moves forward to Jesus through the line of kings which followed David, but Luke traces it through Mary's line. Both are consistent with each other, and accomplish the same purpose to show <u>that Jesus was both the son of Adam and the Son of God,</u> a proper linkage between God and created mankind.

Descendants of Adam without God in their lives will wither and die, but those who inherit the Holy Spirit through Jesus, the 2nd Adam, will <u>reap eternal joy with God</u> and His angels. How wonderful!

VIEWPOINTS: How Luke obtained the detailed chronology covering several millennia of Christ's ancestry is a mystery in itself. Did he obtain it from Mary or her father? Approximately 15 of the 76 fathers named lived to be considerably more than 100 years of age, with Methuselah living to age 969. By extrapolation, allowing an average of 100 years for each generation, <u>a total time span of over 7600 years could have elapsed from Adam's creation to Christ's birth.</u>

Most biblical accounts choose to ignore the matter of time from creation; some place it at

4000-5000 BC; but <u>some suggest a date of 8000-10,000 BC</u> (Unger's Bible Handbook, 1967 edition). This greater time span seems to be more accurate based on Luke's genealogy, and the above age calculation.

CHAPTER 4:   As in Matt. 4:1-13, the temptation of Jesus by Satan is recounted in verses 1-13, after first being <u>led by the Holy Spirit into the wilderness for 40 days</u> of fasting and testing. Using the advantage of having Jesus alone and very hungry, without helpful disciples, Satan's 1st temptation was to invite Him to deal with a bodily need for food; his 2nd was to give (limited) authority over nations of the world to Jesus if He would worship him (sell His soul); and his 3rd was for Jesus to demonstrate His divine nature by attempting a suicide that angels would thwart (a test of the Spirit). <u>Christ resisted on the strength of God's word</u>, being victorious in His own right, but also on our behalf. Though defeated, Satan would no doubt try again as he does with humanity, coming often during times of stress and weakness of spirit.

Luke introduced the beginning of Christ's spirit filled ministry in just 2 verses, 14-15, as compared to Matt. 4:12-17, in the region of Galilee <u>with effective synagogue teaching</u>. Then in verses 16-30, (as in Matt. 13:54-58), Jesus returns to His hometown of Nazareth where He read from Is. 61:1-2 (only half of vs. 2), in the synagogue on the Sabbath.

When He told the audience that He was the fulfillment of the prophetic passage they had just heard, <u>they became indignant</u>, seeing Him merely as 'Joseph's 31 year old son' rather than as the Messiah. Sensing their rejection, He gives them examples of rejection that allude to the fact that God would favor the Gentiles because of the <u>Jew's rejection of His Son.</u> This so angered the crowd that they escorted Him to a nearby hill intending to throw Him to His death. Jesus foiled their plans by boldly, <u>with poise and confidence, walking away.</u>

Verses 32-41 tell of 3 healings by Jesus in His favorite town of Capernaum, where the people were <u>in awe of His teaching and supernatural acts.</u> The 1st healing was of a demon possessed man, after the demon recognized Him as 'Jesus of Nazareth.' The 2nd was to remove a fever that afflicted Simon's mother-in-law, as told in Matt. 8:14-15. The 3rd was of many people who were diseased or demon possessed that came late in the day for healing (Matt. 8:16-17)

The chapter ends with verses 42-44 (as in Matt. 4:23-25) telling of Jesus moving on the next day to preach in the synagogues of Galilee, as was <u>His God given purpose.</u> Today, all people of all nations are subject to God's purpose of revealing through His Word and Spirit the message of forgiveness from sin, by acknowledging Christ as His Son, and our redeemer.

CHAPTER 5:   Jesus calls His 1st disciples, 3 Sea of Galilee fishermen in verses 1-11 (Matt. 4:18-22) named Simon Peter, James and John. <u>Jesus performed a miracle for them,</u> by coaching them to cast their nets for a huge catch during daylight hours, after they had caught nothing all night. This so awed Peter that he felt he was unworthy to be in the presence of Christ's holiness. Jesus reassured him with this statement, 'Do not be afraid, for you will now catch men." All 3 left their boats and became ordained followers of Jesus.

Sometimes man will quit a career when desired success is not achieved. At other times, a change is made when spiritual prompting suggests a better way to serve the Lord. These fishermen forsook all when they experienced a prosperous moment that Christ willed for them. They recognized the divine source of their rich increase, and chose to serve their benefactor.

A leprous man is quickly healed in 12-16, as also told in Matt. 8:1-4, when Jesus recognized great faith and humility in the man. This increased His popularity with many others who came for healing, causing Jesus to escape to secluded places for relaxation through prayer. Today, He wearies not when believers bring others to Him for spiritual healing.

Another healing took place in verses 17-26 (Matt. 9:2-8) of a paralytic who was lowered before Jesus, through an opening in the roof of a house where He was teaching a group. When Jesus first forgave the man his sins, scribes and Pharisees had critical views of this divine act by a human. After chastising them for their thoughts, Jesus healed the man and sent him home.

Taking the drastic step of opening the roof was evidence of great faith, always pleasing to God, as it was to Christ. We should strive for the same kind of faith with respect to God's ability and willingness to pardon our sins. Believing in His power to cleanse our souls will enhance our ability and commitment to cheerfully keep on doing what pleases Him.

In 27-32, as in Matt. 9:9-13, Jesus recruits His 4th disciple, a tax collector named Levi, otherwise known as Matthew, who gave up a lucrative practice to follow a more noble agenda. While hosting Jesus at his house with other tax collectors, Jesus again came under question for keeping company with such men, considered to be gross sinners by the scribes and Pharisees. Jesus clarified that His mission was to call sinners to repentance, hence His association with them.

The same trouble makers questioned Jesus in verses 33-39 (Matt. 9:14-17) about His disciples not fasting as they did twice a week, and on other special occasions, as a form of spiritual rededication. He compared his presence to that of friends celebrating the marriage of a bridegroom, when fasting would be totally out of place, but added that fasting would be in order if the bridegroom were removed as if by death. Christ used the parable about new patches on old garments and new wine in old wineskins, to point out the incompatibility of His critics with His New Testament message of redemption.

CHAPTER 6: In the first 11 verses, as in Matt. 12:1-14, the scribes and Pharisees accuse Jesus of violating Old Testament rules for observing the Sabbath. In the first case (vs. 1-5) they accused Him and the disciples of working when they plucked some heads of grain to eat. Christ justified this action as a necessity to satisfy their hunger. He declared that the Sabbath was His Day, that believers should remember and honor in worship and thanks to Him.

The 2nd case was when He healed a man's hand while teaching in the synagogue, which enraged His critics. As Christ was neither ashamed nor afraid to exercise His power of grace for others, Christians should not shirk their obligation to be helpful in the face of any opposition where justice is important.

Verses 12-16 tell of Christ's naming of the 12 apostles after a night of prayer, as in Matt. 10:1-4. Important decisions are best made after talking them out with God. After this, He and the disciples spent time in ministry, healing many of disease and unclean spirits (Matt. 4:24-25)

As in Matt. 5:1-12, Luke gives a brief version of the Sermon on the Mount, as given to the disciples. In addition, in verses 24-26, <u>woes are pronounced against prosperous sinners</u> <u>as miserable people</u>, even though the world envies them.

Christ continued teaching His disciples in 27-36 about loving enemies, as in Matt. 5:38-48. These are hard lessons for humanity, but a <u>thorough grounding in the faith</u> of Christ's <u>love makes it much easier to conform to His love concept.</u> If one knows and appreciates the greatness of His mercy and the love, it produces an inclination to be merciful towards others.

Christ teaches about not judging others in 37-42, as in Matt. 7:1-5, lest the <u>judging</u> comes <u>against those who judge unfairly</u>. Care is necessary when blaming others; for no one is perfect. By being understanding and forgiving, we may <u>reap greater benefits in the help</u> we give. Jesus used the parable of the blind leading the blind and a speck in a brother's eye to illustrate His point.

Using the identification of a tree by the fruit it bears, in verses 43-45 (Matt. 7:15- 20), He makes the point that <u>one is known by actions of the heart more than words,</u> for what is spoken is based on the heart condition. If the word of Christ is well grafted into our hearts, we may be more fruitful in both word and deeds.

Jesus concludes His teaching session in 46-49, as in Matt. 7:21-27, about greater stability in life against setbacks when we have our house of <u>faith built on a strong foundation</u>, which is found in Christ's teachings. He is the Rock of Ages, no greater can man find than this. With such a foundation, man can endure tribulation and death, while being kept <u>by the</u> <u>power of</u> <u>Christ through faith</u> unto salvation for eternal life with Him.

CHAPTER 7:   Jesus continues His ministry of healing in verses 1-10, in this case the <u>servant of a Roman army officer</u> (centurion), as told in Matt. 8:5-13. Luke's version has the officer sending some Jewish friends to Jesus to request restoration of the servant who was near death. They implored Jesus to honor the request <u>out of gratitude to the officer</u> for his goodness to them.

Other friends conveyed the officer's belief that a word of healing from Jesus was all that was necessary, without coming to his house. Jesus was <u>pleased and marveled over the</u> <u>officer's</u> <u>faith that honored His power</u> and compassion. He made the servant well again immediately.

In verses 11-15, Luke gives an exclusive report of Christ's first restoration of life to the <u>son of a poor widow</u> in the town of Nain in Galilee. He saw the body being carried out for burial and had compassion on the weeping mother. Telling her to not weep, He touched the open coffin and told the young man to get up; he rose up speaking and was <u>restored to his</u> <u>mother</u>. All people, especially the young, should heed God's call for spiritual renewal out of sin, and then <u>witness accordingly with joy and gratitude</u> over their future reward of eternal life with Christ.

In verses 16-35, Luke says that the people became fearful over Christ's power but they <u>praised Him as a great prophet of God.</u> His works were widely reported, even to John the Baptist (probably in prison), who then sent 2 of his followers to ask Jesus <u>if He really was</u> <u>the</u> <u>King of the Jews</u>, as prophesied in Zech. 9:9, and as told in Matt. 11:2-19.

While they were with Jesus, He was busy healing many of afflictions and unclean spirits, and then told John's messengers to <u>give him an account of all these miracles</u> they had seen, that fulfilled the prophecies of healing in Is. 35:5-6. Jesus then questioned the crowd as to why they went to hear John's preaching, and to emphasize that John was important in God's plan, He <u>identified him as the messenger spoken of in Malachi 3:1</u> to pave the way for the Messiah's coming.

All who had been baptized by John acknowledged God's will in this regard, but the <u>scribes and Pharisees did not.</u> For this reason, Jesus compared then to little children who <u>could not enjoy each other's company</u> without finding fault. Such is the problem in the world today, millions of people spend time finding fault with others, without for one minute becoming serious over <u>their own spiritual condition and destiny of their souls.</u> All should wisely explore and heed God's Word, and find great <u>pleasure in sharing the Good News of Christ's salvation message.</u>

Jesus accepted the invitation of a Pharisee named Simon to dine with him, as related in verses 36-50, where a woman, who had no doubt been convicted of her sin by His or John's ministry, showed her love and gratitude to Jesus in an unusual manner. She <u>washed His feet with her tears,</u> wiped them with her hair, and then kissed and anointed them with alabaster oil.

The Pharisee, being critical in his thoughts, felt that a prophet of God should know that the woman was a sinner, and <u>not allow her touching.</u> Jesus used the parable of 2 debtors to illustrate which had the greatest love when forgiven of their debt. Simon rightly said the one who had been forgiven the most, to which Jesus compared all that the woman had done to the little that the Pharisee had done to make Him comfortable and welcome.

This episode was ended by Jesus telling the woman that she should go in peace, and her sins were forgiven because of her great faith. The Pharisee, engrossed in her previous character based on his own vanity, <u>could not appreciate the quality of her faith</u> and her expression of love with thankfulness for the forgiveness of her sins.

CHAPTER 8: Just as Jesus ministered to the people at large, preaching the gospel of the kingdom of God, so too 3 women are named in verses 1-3 who <u>ministered to Him from their own resources,</u> as they accompanied Him and the disciples. This allowed Jesus to devote more time to His mission, no doubt with humble gratitude to the women for their help. His spiritual wealth was supplemented by needed material resources for human achievement.

Luke also recounts the parable of the sower with an explanation of it's purpose, in verses 4-15, very much as in Matt. 13:1-23, where adequate commentary is applicable to Luke's account. It is a matter of hearing and heeding God's Word, to profit from it, and to understand the mysteries* of His kingdom; that Christ expects of His followers, <u>as good seed growing in good soil.</u> By growing productively through the wisdom of Holy Scripture, mankind reaps a rich eternal inheritance. (*See Bible Mysteries at end of Book of Romans)

A parable of revealed light is given in verses 16-18, in which Jesus compares His teaching to light <u>which should be shared with others,</u> rather than hidden to be without value to anyone. And in 19-21, as in Matt. 12:46-50, He declared that those who hear and do the will of God are more <u>family to Him in a spiritual sense</u> than His own mother and blood brothers, who came to visit Him. Nothing is said about a time of visitation with them in this account, but it may be a safe assumption that He spent some time with them in love and appreciation of their interest in Him.

As related in Matt. 8:23-27, Luke also tells of the stormy boat ride across the Sea of Galilee, in verses 22-25, when Jesus went to sleep, and was <u>awakened by the disciples</u> <u>fearful of dying at sea.</u> This story illustrates that as mankind sails the seas of life, dangerous storms will arise to put fear in the heart, thus giving <u>ample reason to call on the Lord (out</u> of weakness) <u>for deliverance.</u> When problems pass, we may also marvel over His divine providence, and be thankful for it.

In verses 26-39, Luke tells of one demon-possessed man being healed as in Matt.

8:28-9:1, where two men are so inflicted. The unclean <u>demons were allowed to enter the bodies of 'unclean' swine,</u> owned by Gentile farmers who feared further losses and asked Jesus to leave. Their material interests were greater than their spiritual needs.

Verses 40-55 give a double-header account of a healing and a restoration of life, as in Matt. 9:18-26. A woman with a chronic blood loss problem was <u>healed by touching the</u> <u>garment that Jesus wore,</u> and the daughter of the chief elder (Jairus) of a local synagogue was <u>restored to life as Jesus said 'Little girl, arise!'</u>

VIEWPOINTS: Many persons are healed or restored spiritually by Christ, <u>without anyone else's knowledge,</u> but there will be times when the Lord will draw public attention to such miracles for the purpose of stirring hearts over His divine grace, which strengthens faith in Him. There should be no fear in calling on God for such restoration, but the greater one fears, <u>the less likely is one's faith in God's response.</u> A plea with confidence is more likely to earn His grace and mercy! As Jesus said to Jairus, 'Fear not, only believe!' Replacing fear with trust produces extra dividends, in terms of blessings and assistance when needed.

CHAPTER 9:   As in Matt. 10:5-15, Jesus prepares the 12 disciples in verses 1-6 to carry on His mission after He is gone, by giving them power to heal and cast out demons <u>as they preached the gospel of the kingdom of God to the people.</u> As with most full-time servants of the Lord, they were to be totally dependent on those to whom they ministered, for their personal needs. God cares for those who <u>give of themselves totally in His service,</u> just as Jesus gave totally of Himself on behalf of humanity. His generosity is without limits when believers give freely of themselves in His service.

The wide-spread ministry by Christ and His 12 helpers came to the attention of the Roman ruler, Herod, in 7-9 (see Matt. 14:1-12) who became apprehensive when others told him that <u>Jesus was a resurrected John the Baptist.</u> He wanted to see Jesus but did nothing at this time.

The feeding of the 5000 men (plus uncounted women and children) near the city of Bethsaida is recounted in verses 10-17, as is told in Matt. 14:13-21, when Jesus supernaturally <u>multiplied 5 loaves of bread and 2 fish into enough food</u> to feed them, with 12 baskets left over.

Even though many in the crowd may have been unworthy of Christ's provisions, His <u>compassion over their need covered them</u> like an umbrella. He blessed them with enough to eat and His blessing overflowed with a surplus remaining; just as God's provisions to His flock goes beyond <u>their individual needs to bless others.</u> We do not have a stingy God!

In a time of communication with His disciples in verses 18-27, as in Matt. 16:13-28,

Jesus first asks them how the crowds identified Him. After receiving answers that He was John the Baptist, Elijah, or a prophet of old, Jesus strangely <u>asked them for their views.</u> Peter came through with the right answer, 'The Christ of God." Christ then predicts his death and resurrection, with admonishment that they should not make this generally known, because this went <u>contrary to common expectations of the Messiah's role and destiny.</u>

He concluded his remarks to them about taking up a cross to follow Him, in essence describing His own crucifixion. In reality, He made clear that their <u>faithfulness to God's purposes would not be easy,</u> for it would entail much sacrifice and hardship, even death. He declared that some of them would see the glory of God's kingdom soon <u>before their own</u> <u>death.</u>

That moment came about 8 days later, as related in verses 28-36 (also Matt. 17:1-9), when Jesus took Peter, John, and James, his most experienced and dedicated disciples, to a nearby mountain for prayer. While in prayer, a transformation came over Jesus, as He took on a heavenly image like an angel, and then <u>spoke about His own death to heavenly images</u> of <u>Moses and Elijah,</u> who also appeared in a glorified state.

The 3 disciples missed part of this spectacular scene when they fell asleep as Jesus prayed, but they <u>awoke in time to see the three heavenly figures.</u> Peter then made the ridiculous suggestion that he prepare a separate shelter for each of the three, probably hoping that all 3 would <u>remain for a while as they appeared then.</u>

God put a stop to that idea by bringing a glory cloud down on all of them, from which He spoke these words, 'This is My beloved Son, Hear Him.' When the cloud lifted, Jesus stood alone before them, and <u>they were awed to silence,</u> not knowing that they had seen a preview of Christ's 2nd coming on a cloud.

In 37-45, as in Matt. 17:14-23, Jesus healed a boy, (possibly an epileptic), who suffered convulsions as caused by demons of that day. <u>Everyone marveled over this display of divine</u> <u>power.</u> Then Jesus told His disciples to be aware that He was about to be betrayed into the hands of hostile men. They <u>failed to understand such a contradiction to their concept</u> of Christ's mission, and they feared to ask for clarification.

Thinking of their own destiny, an argument arose amongst them in 46-48 (Matt. 18:1-5), as to which of them <u>would be the greatest in Christ's earthly kingdom,</u> believing still that He would fulfill that leadership role. Christ sat an innocent and naive child by His side, and told them that by accepting the child in His name, they in effect accepted Him, and <u>thereby</u> <u>accepted God the Father,</u> meaning that a child as the least in ability could still serve a great purpose in God's domain.

Verses 48-50 briefly tell of the concern that John had over an unknown person casting out demons in Christ's name; Jesus told him not to interfere because the man was an ally, under the principle that <u>he was not acting as an opponent.</u> Could this apply to professed Christian denominations who find fault with others not of their own group, for frivolous reasons, or doctrinal differences?

Verses 51-56, unique to the gospel of Luke, tells of Christ's decision to go to Jerusalem, by way of a route through the town of Samaria. Sending an advance party there, perhaps to arrange for overnight accommodations, <u>resistance was encountered</u> from <u>unfriendly</u> <u>Samaritans.</u> James and John wanted to take lethal action against them, for which Jesus rebuked them, saying that His mission was to save mankind, not destroy them. So they went to another village. The 2 disciples did not realize that the Samaritan rejection was based more on ethnic prejudices than opposition to God's word and worship.

The chapter ends with Christ's rejection in 57-62 (Matt. 8:18-22) of followers who did not comprehend the cost of being His disciple. To 3 volunteers, He said in effect that one could not bear the deprivation of such a life; to another, that service to God was a higher priority than being present at a father's death, and to the 3rd, if one is concerned about the welfare of those left behind, he would not be able to properly serve the Lord. In following Jesus in life and service, there must be no compromise or hesitation. Those who are called into God's service must be resolved to continue or nothing of lasting value will be accomplished.

CHAPTER 10: Perhaps the above discourse on the cost of serving God occurred as Jesus proceeded to select 70 missionary men, as related only by Luke, in verses 1-12, to go as pairs into the land to prepare the way for His own evangelical efforts. He deplored the lack of workers when the harvest for conversion of souls was so great.

Again, Jesus instructs these men to live off the economy, depending on those who responded positively to their message, and not to waste time where they received no hospitality. Those who rejected them would fare worse at God's ultimate day of judgment than the condemned of Sodom.

In 13-16, as in Matt. 11:20-24, Jesus pronounced woe to 2 areas, Chorazin and Bethsaida, where He had been rejected in earlier forays of preaching and healing. They too would face a more severe judgment by God in His endtimes cleanup of evil and wickedness. This would be true also for those who despised His 70 faithful ministers; they would be reckoned as despisers of God and Christ and punished accordingly.

The 70 men returned from their missionary assignment with great joy in verses 17-24; they reported their success in casting out demons in Christ's name. Jesus saw this as an ultimate defeat of Satan who would be exiled out of heaven, through the power of God. Lest these men be filled with vain pride over their achievements, Jesus reminds them that their real blessing was to have their names written in God's book of life.

Jesus is filled with Holy Spirit Joy in 21-24, as in Matt. 11:25-27, and gave thanks to God the Father, for divine power to bring about the salvation of souls, which could be given to the least of mankind. That moment of joy was much deserved as Jesus had so few of them, being known as a man of sorrows. He said to know God, one must first know Jesus spiritually.

Verses 25-37 give the story of Christ's conversation with a lawyer in which He used the parable about a Samaritan helping a Jewish man, to convey the proper principle of compassion for others regardless of status, somewhat similar to the content of Matt. 22:34-40. The lawyer asked what he should do to inherit eternal life, to which Jesus asked him to go by God's word (Deut. 6:5); he correctly shared that it is to love God totally and a neighbor as one's self. But then, the lawyer became legalistic, and asked 'Who is my neighbor?

Jesus then told him about a Jewish man who had been waylaid and beaten by robbers and left to die on a rocky road. Two Jewish men, a priest and a Levite, saw him as they passed by without enough compassion to help the man. Then a Gentile Samaritan came by and was filled with such great compassion that he stopped, tended to the man's wounds, and transported him on his donkey to a nearby inn where he <u>contracted to pay for additional</u> care.

In answer to Jesus' question, which of the three men was truly a compassionate neighbor, the lawyer naturally picked the Samaritan, to which Jesus said, '<u>Go and do the same.</u>' The wounded man received no help from those who should have helped, but received it <u>from one who had a measure of divine love in his heart</u>, even towards Jews who looked down upon Samaritans as 'low class types.' This is what a Christian should possess, a love for others comparable to the love of God for mankind, to help when and where needed in dire circumstances to the best of one's ability, <u>without reservation over ethnicity, social class, or religious beliefs.</u>

The chapter ends with a side note in verses 38-42 about two women, Mary and Martha, who helped Jesus in His ministry by <u>adding to His comfort</u>. Martha welcomed Him into her home and as a good hostess, prepared for His stay by providing good food and creature comforts, while her sister Mary, just <u>sat at Jesus feet to listen to His words</u>. When Martha complained and asked Jesus to order Mary to help her, He made it clear that the attention Mary was giving Him had a higher priority than all that Martha proposed doing.

By sitting at Jesus' feet, Mary's attention signified interest in His words, a desire to learn from them, and a <u>willingness to be yielded to His wise counsel</u>. This is a fine example of Christian devotion to the word of God, signifying total yielding to divine instruction.

<u>CHAPTER 11:</u> In verse 1, the disciples asked Jesus to teach them to pray, after witnessing His time of prayer. In 2-4, Luke gives a <u>shortened version of the 'Lord's Prayer</u>, as given more fully in Matt. 6:9-15. The use of the personal pronoun 'us' indicates that this is a prayer suitable for congregational use to honor God, yield to His will, and to ask for sustenance, forgiveness of sins, a charitable heart towards others, and spiritual protection to avoid evil.

Although called the Lord's Prayer, it is here more appropriately a 'disciple's prayer,' but as such it is a <u>believer's basic prayer</u>, on which to develop a more profound dialogue with God. Jesus prayed often to 'God the Father' for strength and His will, but not for forgiveness of sin; in His humanity, Jesus may have needed spiritual strengthening, but <u>in prayer He was an example.</u>

Luke slips in an example of true caring friendship in verses 5-8, citing that <u>boldness and persistence in asking brings results,</u> as it did for the man asking his neighbor for bread to feed a guest. When God delays answers to our prayers, we should continue with submission to His will.

More is said about persistence in prayer in verses 9-13, as in Matt. 7:7-11, <u>under the acronym ASK</u> (ask, seek, & knock), to receive what God deems most beneficial or appropriate, with anointing by the Holy Spirit.

In verses 14-26, Jesus responds to blasphemous charges that He removed demons <u>by the power of 'Beelzebub,'</u> (Jewish epithet for Satan), as also given in Matt. 12:22-30. Jesus refuted this charge very simply by pointing out that if Satan allowed the removal of demons in his name, he would be <u>working against his own interests,</u> thus a house divided against itself cannot stand. Jesus asked under what power His disciples cast out demons, if not done under God's power.

The general term 'demons' might include human vices, such as the use of harmful drugs, alcoholism, gluttony, unbridled passions, or wicked lust for power. Such are used by Satan to diminish primary allegiance to God in all things physically and spiritually healthy. Man can become content with such a life, unless a strong concern for God's quality of life standards provokes one into self-evaluation and a desire to meet His standards. This may come about as a soul is converted to God, restoring the soul to freely recover interest in what is God's best.

If a soul is momentarily swept clean of sin, but not washed clean by the blood of Jesus, for the heart to be indwelled by the Holy Spirit, those 'demons' can return in great number (Matt. 12:43-45). Without the whole armor of God, wicked spirits feel welcome to enter easily, to stay and do their dirty work for an indefinite time. Earnest prayer to be delivered from this predicament is needed!

In 27-28, to a woman's word of blessing to His mother, Jesus said it was more blessed to hear God's word and to obey it. Then in 29-32, as in Matt. 12:28-42, Jesus denounced the people as an evil generation, always seeking new signs as a basis for believing, rather than maintaining faith based on the example of Jonah, the Queen of Sheba, the wisdom of Solomon, and the repentance of Nineveh.

Using a lamp for proper illumination in verses 33-36, as in Matt. 6:22-23, Jesus equated it to the light of understanding that comes from seeing what is spiritually good for the soul. Being fully illuminated spiritually, the soul is like the bright light of a good lamp for all to see.

Verses 37-54, unique to Luke, gives a diatribe by Jesus against the Pharisees and lawyers (scribes), after some of them were critical because He did not wash His hands before sitting down to eat at the table of a host Pharisee. He told them that this practice of theirs was like washing the outside of a cup and plate clean, without concern for inner cleansing; in their case they were full of greed, vanity, wickedness, hypocrisy, and lacking in mercy and compassion for others.

When a lawyer said Jesus insulted them, He pronounced woe upon them for all of their sins from the death of Abel to that of Zechariah. Angrily, they all plotted to destroy Him.

CHAPTER 12: Speaking primarily to His disciples in verses 1-12, but with a crowd listening, Jesus warns of hypocrisy in spiritual matters, fear of witnessing of faith in God, and the unpardonable sin of blasphemy against the Holy Spirit (similar to Matt. 10:26-33).

Hypocrisy is the false teaching (leaven-yeast) of Pharisee types, whether given openly or secretly, which will be made known when God judges and punishes the culprits. Therefore, it is always best to fear God most in all circumstances, even when faced with death by evil persecutors of God's people, because He determines who will be consigned to hell for their sins. A faithful believer is secured for eternal salvation with God even more than two tiny sparrows!

The most important achievement in Christ's view is to faithfully witness of His validity as the Son of God, because this earns His approval before the heavenly hosts of angels. Anyone who speaks ignorantly against Jesus can be forgiven, but not so if vile and blasphemous words are spoken against the Holy Spirit, from a hardened heart yielded to Satan's agenda. It is important to seek guidance from the Holy Spirit when subjected to persecution.

In verses 13-34, Jesus uses the parable of a rich fool to warn against the sin of covetousness, the selfish striving for material wealth. Abundance of things often does not add up to genuine happiness and contentment, or satisfy the desires of the soul. Earthly wealth often equates to spiritual poverty, with loss of eternal Godly values.

Jesus advised His followers not to worry about living necessities but to trust in God for help to provide more, as one does their best with what they have. (Matt. 6:19-21 & 25-

34 give similar advice) Just as He provides for ravens of the field, or lilies of the gardens, even more God will give much more within His kingdom of heaven, as we keep the faith. At the end of life, we are not able to take any earthly possessions to our eternal destination.

Therefore, we gain much more in our lifetime, by giving of our surplus to others in need, and for this God adds to our blessings after life on earth.

Jesus spoke a parable in verses 35-48, as in Matt. 24:42-51, about a master of many servants returning from a wedding, expecting his servants to have been on guard to protect his domain, so that he would be pleased with their trustworthy vigilance. In like manner, all of His faithful are to be ever watchful for His 2nd coming, at an unexpected and unannounced time.

When Peter asked if this advice was just for the disciples, or for all the people, Jesus figuratively said it was for all mankind, to do their best as servants before God to measure up to His expectations, without doing harm to others who strive to excel. For violators, discipline can be expected according to the degree of their failure, or ignorance of right and wrong.

Christ admits that He regrets that His role will be to bring judgment (division of the good and the wicked) like fire at some future time, in verses 49-53 (Matt. 10:34-39), which He pictures as similar to the breakup of a family unit. Because of rejection at His 1st coming, dissension will reign within families (and nations) until His 2nd coming. He adds in verses 54-59 (Matt. 16:1-4) that the people were hypocrites because they were not aware of what God was doing and would do through Him, although they could discern weather changes. He adjures all people to take stock of their failures, and make amends before facing final judgment with the danger of having to pay a final heavy price. Christ wants all humanity to be wise in the concerns of their souls, and to make peace with God before it is too late. His purpose was and always will be to reconcile the world to Himself, as His gift to God the Father.

VIEWPOINTS: Language in this chapter suggests that all of God's faithful, who are expectant of Christ's 2nd coming, should be spiritually steadfast as servants of the Lord. This can be done by readily seeking forgiveness of sin, and being diligent in witnessing to others about the consequences of unforgiven sins. Girded with Holy Spirit commitment to withstand evil of all kinds, including persecution for their faith, they will receive eternal life with Him for their endurance under duress.

CHAPTER 13:   What Luke narrated in verse 1-17 is not found in any other gospel. In 1-5, Jesus responds to some who told him about Galileans that had been killed in the temple earlier by Pilate for some reason. The Jews commonly thought that violent death of this kind was due to sin and wickedness of the victims. Jesus also referred to the death of 18 persons when the tower of Siloam fell on them, when He clarified that sin need not be the reason for violent death. He warns that without repentance everyone will suffer a terrible unredeemed (spiritual) death.

Verses 6-9 refer to the nation of Israel as a fig tree, that <u>did not bear fruit after more than 3 years,</u> (coinciding with Christ's time of ministry?), for which the owner (God) would have it cut down. Yet Jesus as the keeper of the orchard prevailed to <u>allow more time for revitalization</u> (perhaps up to His 2nd coming) so the tree (Israel) would yield some fruit. More time and effort is needed for many so-called Christian churches of today to bear more fruit by way of redeemed souls.

In 10-17, Jesus rubbed the masters of the synagogue the wrong way again when he <u>healed a crippled woman there on the Sabbath.</u> She had suffered such disability for 18 years, and when Jesus saw her, His compassion was so great that He healed her without any request from her. She came to learn from Him and was blessed with a cure. What a great example of Christ's grace!.

The synagogue chiefs were critical that this was done on the Sabbath, rather than on 6 other days <u>when healing should take place.</u> Addressing them as hypocrites, Jesus said that if it was OK to untie a donkey and lead it to water on the Sabbath, than surely this woman, a daughter of Abraham, who had been bound by Satan for 18 years, <u>deserved to be healed that day.</u> The critics were put to shame and the crowds rejoiced over Christ's great works. In today's world, many works of necessity or mercy are maintained on Sunday, such as hospitals, law enforcement and fire stations. It is <u>questionable if merchandising and transportation services fall in that category.</u>

Two quick parables are recounted in verses 18-21, as in Matt. 13:31-33, about the <u>growth of a tiny mustard seed</u> into a tree, and the swelling of a batch of <u>flour when seasoned with yeast.</u> This was to illustrate the growth of the kingdom of God from small beginnings then and to come.

Jesus talks about the narrow way for entry into God's kingdom, in 22-33 (Matt. 7:13-14) after someone asks if many would be saved. Entry is on God's terms, not man's! Acceptance of Jesus <u>with repentance in the heart for past sins is the prerequisite,</u> to be accomplished as early as possible in life before the gate is closed, since the time of one's death is unknown. Everyone should strive for this worthy goal of entry through God's heavenly gate.

At God's final judgment, those who have not qualified for their visa to heaven <u>will be turned away,</u> to their great sorrow, as they see people of all walks of life assembled world-wide to sit at His feet. Some who were nothing on earth in the eyes of others will be there, and some who may have been highly esteemed may not be there, all according to their true relationship with God.

After Jesus concluded this teaching, He was warned to depart because Herod the king of that region <u>wanted to kill Him.</u> Jesus brushed off this threat from the 'fox' by requesting that Herod be told that He had a mission to accomplish for more days, until the day would come <u>when He would be perfected</u> (crucified and resurrected) in Jerusalem. In like manner, Christians should strive to nobly serve the Lord in their remaining days, so they may be perfected in Him when death overtakes them.

In 34-35, as in Matt. 23:37-39, Jesus mourns over the <u>apostasy of Jerusalem for</u> <u>rejecting</u> <u>Him when His</u> love for them was like that of a mother hen for her chicks. Their spiritual house would stand empty until He returned and was <u>recognized as the Messiah,</u> when they will say 'Blessed is He who comes in the name of the Lord' (Ps. 118:26).

CHAPTER 14: Jesus was dining in the home of a ruling Pharisee on the Sabbath in verses 1-14, as only Luke relates, where He <u>sees a man across the table greatly swollen</u> by fluid retention. He then asked the critical legal guests if it was lawful to heal on the Sabbath, because He knew they interpreted healing as <u>work done in violation of the 4th commandment</u> When they remained silent, He healed the man and then asked the observers who of them would not recover a donkey or an ox from a pit on the Sabbath. None answered as they all would have done so, and no doubt understood the point Jesus made that <u>a human body was</u> <u>much more</u> <u>worth healing.</u>

In 7-11, from the identity and seating of the guests, Jesus must have discerned a <u>snobbish</u> <u>concern amongst them for seating nearest the host,</u> or someone they considered to be important. He used a parable about an invitation to a wedding feast, to convey that humility is a nobler character trait than exaltation by association. Being humble in our own view earns greater esteem in God's eyes.

Then in 12-15, Jesus voices approval of a host inviting many who are not important in his eyes, or who are not in a position to return the favor, <u>rather than focusing on invitations</u> <u>to the</u> <u>wealthy or influential.</u> Charitable hospitality is better than gatherings for self- aggrandizement. Doing good to the poor and underprivileged in the spirit of God's love brings greater rewards. A comment by one of the guests that 'A man is blessed to dine in God's kingdom' may have been meant to deflate Jesus' view: While true, this comment missed the point!

Jesus responds with a parable of a Great Banquet in 16-24 (Matt. 22:1-14), to which the host invited many, but when the servants gave the call to come to the table, <u>all who had</u> <u>been</u> <u>invited declined</u> for one reason or another. In anger, vowing that none who were first invited would ever dine with him again, the host ordered his servants to bring in the poor, the crippled, beggars and the homeless, which filled his banquet hall.

In a sense, the rejection by the first to be invited correlates with the <u>Jewish nation</u> <u>rejecting</u> <u>Christ as the Messiah,</u> and the invitation to the substitute guests represents the <u>gospel being</u> <u>extended to the Gentile world.</u> In the kingdom of God, the poor and lowly of the world are as welcome as the rich and great; and many times the Christian churches are more successful and productive when supported by those who covet God's approval and blessing to enhance life.

Jesus moves on in the company of a large crowd to which He conveyed a true meaning of discipleship, in verses 25-33, as in Matt. 10:34 -39, which is to <u>give first priority in</u> <u>allegiance to Christ,</u> over family, career ambitions, competition against bad odds, or material possessions. Duty to Him can be as difficult as bearing a cross as Jesus did, when dangers and temptations add to personal tribulation. Maintaining peace with God is a greater advantage than compromising over conflicts in life.

In verses 34-35 (Matt 5:13), Jesus identifies a good disciple (believer, righteous one, effective Christian) as salt, or seasoning to the unsaved, but if zeal to be salt is lost, <u>then one</u>

is nothing more than a professing Christian without much value in the Lord's service. Such a one is 'not worth his salt' as a member of the kingdom of God. Although saved, that one will rank with the least before the throne of God when heavenly rewards are passed out.

CHAPTER 15:   With tax collectors and sinners gathered around to hear the teachings of Jesus, the scribes and Pharisees complained about the company He kept, and Jesus sets them straight with a parable of one lost sheep out of a flock of 100, in verses 1-7, as in Matt.

18:10-14. The lost sheep may represent an apostate believer separated from God by sin, or an unsaved sinner, whom the shepherd (Jesus) seeks to restore to the flock. Finding the weary sheep (sinner), the shepherd provides help to bring it home (fellowship with God), for which friends and family rejoice (angels of heaven). Christ, through the Holy Spirit, has a multitude of ways to find the lost.

Luke added another parable spoken by Jesus in 8-10 about a woman losing one silver coin out of 10 that she owned. She searches for it, finds it, and shares her joy with others over it, just as Jesus searches for those who are lost in sin and angels rejoice over each one found and redeemed.

Verses 11-31 recount another parable by Jesus which illustrates the same point as the two preceding examples, that of God's quickness to forgive, and to welcome home the lost. In this case, the younger of two sons asked his father to advance his inheritance so he could strike out on his own, not being content with the good life that he had. Dad gave it to him, and he departed into the world, to spend it in the bright lights of sinful indulgences, until he had nothing left for food and lodging. To survive, he took a lowly job to feed 'unclean' swine, a despicable task for a Jew.

Coming to his senses, realizing how foolishly he had left a good life with Dad, the boy decided to return home in humility to repent and beg forgiveness with the hope that Dad would be merciful and welcome him back as a hired hand. No doubt he was surprised when Dad saw him coming down the road, ran out to embrace him with great joy, as the boy confessed his sins. Dad gave no words of reproach, and restored this son, who was lost but now is found, into the family.

This illustrates the nature of repentance, and God's readiness to welcome and bless all who return to him with genuine regret over past sins. A sinful life is a waste of God given talent, with time and energy misapplied without thought for needs of the soul. It generally leads to a realization of what is lacking and a return to common sense with the Lord's forgiveness.

Sadly, the oldest son, in the manner of a Pharisee, found fault with Dad's royal treatment of his younger brother, and complained bitterly without sharing joy over his brother's return. With a self-righteous attitude, older son accused his Dad of not appreciating his years of loyal service at home while his brother squandered his inheritance with immoral women. Lovingly, Dad reminded older son that the remainder of his estate would be his someday, so there was no reason why he should not rejoice over his brother's return.

Some people misunderstand God's love for His children, and resent the mercy He shows to someone they disrespect for what they have done or been. Every believer should be as forgiving and merciful at Father God in welcoming unbelievers, or wayward believers, back into the kingdom of God.

CHAPTER 16:   All of this chapter is unique to Luke's gospel; one must wonder about the sources of his account of Christ's words which appear to be <u>contradictory to some degree.</u> In verses 1-13, Jesus spoke to His disciples, with Pharisees nearby listening in, to share a parable about a dishonest servant (manager, steward, etc.) who cheated his rich boss. When confronted and told to account for his dishonesty, before being terminated, the manager decided to go a step further to dishonestly <u>provide for his own welfare after becoming</u> <u>unemployed.</u>

He contacted debtors of his boss and arbitrarily reduced their indebtedness to garner their gratitude for his own benefit later, <u>believing they would help him materially.</u> When his boss learned of this action, even though it was fraudulent, he was impressed with the manager's clever act to insure his survival, but he was <u>not necessarily pleased</u> with the dishonestly involved.

Jesus uses this story to illustrate that honesty is the best policy when one is responsible for property belonging to others, and there is <u>no justification for fraudulently misappropriating</u> it for one's own benefit, no matter how ingenious the concept may be for doing so. On the other hand, taking steps to provide for a secure future is commendable, even sometimes when using money tainted by others, as it passes through our hands. Above all, <u>material resources</u> <u>should not be used solely for self,</u> but according to the need of others wealth should be shared generously.

Jesus appears to have said that the selfish use of wealth is not the best use of it, since all that man has comes from His supply, and therefore <u>should be used wisely to help others</u> <u>less fortunate.</u> The rich man may have amassed his wealth in much the same manner as his manager dishonestly dealt with it before his dismissal, and for this reason, the boss <u>admired</u> <u>the shrewdness of the manager's actions</u> to benefit himself.

Seemingly, Jesus said that such shrewdness is OK for believers to apply when managing what God provides, <u>but in keeping with His righteousness.</u> True riches are most surely associated with spiritual blessings received from God for faithful stewardship of what He entrusts to us, and from it <u>treasure in heaven should be a reward.</u> Above all, the love of money and the misuse of it should not replace faithful service <u>in heartfelt love to God and Jesus Christ.</u>

In 14-31, Jesus chided the Pharisees who heard these words and derided Him. He told them what they esteemed highly was an abomination to God, because their <u>justification was based</u> <u>on Old Testament law</u> rather than on the new covenant of God's kingdom as He preached it to them. Somewhat unrelated, Jesus reminds them that breaking the bond of marriage can lead to adultery, contrary to their loose interpretation of Deuteronomy 24, where Moses allowed divorce merely because of hardness of heart between spouses.

The chapter ends with a story in verses 19-31, somewhat like a parable, about an unnamed rich man and a poor man named Lazarus. The rich man lived sumptuously but Lazarus survived on the <u>crumbs falling from the rich man's table.</u> Lazarus died and was welcomed into God's reception hall but the rich man went to Hades, <u>God's holding station for the wicked</u> on their death.

The story says that the rich man in torment could see Lazarus in the company of Abraham, to whom he <u>pleaded for relief from his suffering</u>. Abraham reminded the man that he deserved his fate just as Lazarus deserved his blessing, and nothing could be done to change things because an <u>impassable gulf now existed</u> between them.

The ex-rich man then asked for an angelic emissary to be sent to his 5 surviving brothers in the hope that they would be <u>converted into God's kingdom.</u> Abraham again said no, because they had the Old Testament messages from Moses and the prophets to learn from, and if they didn't get the truth from that, <u>neither would they heed a voice from the dead.</u> A messenger from heaven could say no more than what is said in the Scriptures.

Perhaps the real sin of the rich man was in providing for himself only; nothing is said about care he may have given to Lazarus. In any case, he could not obtain any relief for his pain in the company of the wicked, because <u>his fate was sealed eternally</u>. In a vague way, he may have been repentant of his sinful past, and felt compassion for his 5 brothers who still had a chance to experience true repentance. This was true without special help, for they could receive the special grace of God's forgiveness <u>if they would but heed His word as</u> <u>provided to them.</u>

CHAPTER 17:   Jesus warns His disciples of harm that small offenses can do in verses 1-4, as in Matt. 18:6-7. Offenses will happen to anyone and the <u>one who brings them unto a</u> <u>new child of God</u> is worthy of being thrown into the sea with a millstone around his neck. Difficult as it may be to do so, we are to forgive a brother who offends us, provided he is <u>repentant</u> <u>and apologetic</u> for it after we rebuke him. This kind of reconciliation is to take place as many times as it happens.

Admitting how difficult it is to forgive sometimes, the disciples ask for more faith in 5-10, as in Matt. 17:19-21. Jesus makes it clear that <u>only a little faith is needed</u>, when it is applied with humility out of consideration for others, and in accordance with God's will. Whatever man does in faith should be done as a matter of conscientious duty.

Exclusive to Luke's gospel is the story of 10 lepers in verses 11-17, who pleaded at a distance for Jesus to have mercy on them as He passed through a village on His way to Jerusalem. All He said was to 'Go show yourselves to the temple priests,' a Mosaic Law requirement of Leviticus 14:2-7, which Jesus also prescribed in Luke 5:14. In faith, they turned towards the temple in obedience and were immediately healed.

One of them, a Samaritan, turned back with praises to God, and prostrated himself before Jesus with words of thanks. Jesus commented on the fact that 9 of them did not return with thanks to God, while this 'despised foreigner' did so, and <u>sent him off with a</u> <u>commendatory</u> <u>blessing.</u>

In 20-37, Jesus gives a lengthy discourse to the Pharisee's question, 'When would the kingdom of God begin?' They may have expected great signs such as related in Joel 2:1-

11. Jesus clarified that the kingdom of God is more a spiritual relationship of hearts in tune with God, than an identifiable form of government. In a sense, <u>it included their acceptance</u> <u>of Jesus and the disciples</u> who were preaching the new covenant doctrine of the kingdom of God for all mankind.

Speaking to His disciples, Jesus then expounded how it would be when He, as the Son of Man rejected by the Jews at His 1ˢᵗ coming, would return to earth again with the speed of lightning at some far distant time, when least expected by sinful man. He compares the <u>world's complacency and lack of spirituality at His 2ⁿᵈ coming</u> to the days of Noah and Sodom and Gemorrah, to also be accompanied by dreadful destruction of the wicked, after securing those who pass His test of righteousness in God.

The saving of the righteous is illustrated as if one of 2 men in bed or in the field, or one of 2 women making flour, <u>are taken away suddenly,</u> while the other remains (see Matt. 24:40-41). When the disciples asked, 'Where Lord?' they may have wanted to know where the taken ones would go, or where <u>God's judgment would take place</u>. In His reply that it would be where the dead bodies are eaten by vultures, Jesus seemingly is saying that those who remain will be the wicked who will be subjected to His judgment, perhaps including the battle of Armageddon. This then infers that <u>those taken away will escape judgment in a secure place with God.</u>

<u>VIEWPOINTS:</u>   Christ's description of the His 2ⁿᵈ coming in verses 26-36 brings the salvation of the righteous and the judgment upon the wicked into view as a sudden and <u>rapid unfolding approximating a simultaneous event.</u> The taking up of some, apparently the righteous, correlates with the understanding of Matt. 24:36-41, that the 'rapture' will occur immediately prior to the unfolding of God's judgment against the wicked. There is no indication in this passage that the rapture will occur about 7 years earlier as some believe.

CHAPTER 18:   In verses 1-14, Luke gives an exclusive account of Jesus teaching about prayer to God. In the 1ˢᵗ example, in parable form, He tells of a stressed widow who asked a secular judge for justice from a person who was giving her trouble. At first the judge ignored her repeated pleas but her persistence <u>made him yield mainly to get her out of his hair.</u>

Jesus contrasted this uncaring judge's response to that of a caring God, saying that if the judge would provide help rather than be punitive, how much more would God surely be pleased and <u>respond to the continual prayer of a faithful believer</u>. He then skeptically or doubtfully asks if He will find such faithful prayer warriors on earth at His 2ⁿᵈ coming.

In the 2ⁿᵈ example on prayer, Jesus gave a parable about a Pharisee and a tax collector to some Pharisee type listeners. This was to contrast the <u>Pharisee's arrogant self-glorification prayer</u> to the tax collector's <u>prayer rendered with humility and dependence</u> on God's mercy and grace. While exalting the tax collector for his prayer, He said the Pharisee would be humbled. God's grace flows freely to the humble and repentant, but is withheld from the proud and vain.

As in Matt. 19:13-15, Jesus instructed the disciples not to keep children away from Him since they <u>typify the simple faith and trust of a new believer</u> who joins God's kingdom. Man must accept God's kingdom as naively as children, as if it were a gift.

Jesus follows this with advice to a rich young ruler in verses 18-30, as in Matt. 19:16-22, on how to qualify for eternal life. Emphasizing that God is the chief representative of what is 'good,' Jesus gave <u>obedience of the 10 commandments as a requirement,</u> and then told the young man to divest himself of all his possessions and become a disciple.

This was too much for the young man because his love for his riches was greater than his willingness to <u>part with it on God's terms</u>. This is true of many wealthy persons in this modern age, possessions which satisfy their ambitions have higher priority than their appetite for a divine authority which they cannot comprehend or appreciate. They want to serve both God and mammon, but if they must choose, they consider their <u>wealth to be a more tangible</u> benefit.

Seeing the young man's sorrow as he left, Jesus describes the difficulty of a rich man entering heaven like the impossibility of a <u>camel passing through the eye of a needle.</u> When listeners asked, 'then who can be saved?' Jesus said that what is impossible in man's eyes is <u>possible with God, and reassured His disciples that their rewards</u> would surpass the sacrifices they made to follow Him.

Again, Jesus predicts His death and resurrection to the disciples in verses 31-34, as in Matt. 20:17-19, to occur in Jerusalem as prophesied (Ps. 22). <u>They could not understand</u> why He had to face such suffering, as the glorified Son of God.

Moving on towards Jerusalem through Jericho, in verses 35-43, as in Matt. 20:29-34, Jesus passes by a blind man who addressed him as the Son of David as he cried out for healing mercy. Jesus <u>gave him sight and commended him for his faith.</u> For this, the man followed Jesus with words of praise and thanks to God, which caused the crowd to praise God also. When sinner's spiritual eyes are opened, they should thankfully acknowledge God's mercy without reservation and <u>help others to reap the same blessing</u>. He is deserving of praise at all times!

CHAPTER 19:   Luke gives an exclusive account in verses 1-10, about a short man named Zacchaeus, the head tax collector for the Jericho area, climbing a tree to see Jesus as He passed through the city. When Jesus saw him, He told him to quickly <u>climb down and take</u> Him to <u>his home,</u> as a self invited guest. Zacchaeus was happy about this but other observers were not because they hated tax collectors, and <u>thought Jesus had made a bad choice of</u> company.

Jesus was pleased that Zacchaeus made such a pronounced effort to see Him, and more so that he gave <u>evidence of his conversion by renouncing his past dishonesty</u> with tax collections and committed to repay what was wrongfully collected. Restitution combined with repentance is the formula for true conversion to <u>right and proper conduct.</u> Christ saw the good in this man and gifted salvation to him, just as He wishes to do for all those who are lost in sin.

As Jesus and His followers neared Jerusalem, knowing that they expected a sudden arrival of the kingdom of God, He gave a parable <u>to dispel this misconception</u> in verses 11-27 (as in Matt. 25:14-30). He spoke of a nobleman (figuratively Himself) going into a far country (back to heaven) to return later as a royal king over his people (His 2nd coming), even though the people rejected him. Before leaving, the nobleman gave 10 servants (his followers) the same sum of money to invest to the best of their ability until <u>such time as he</u> returned as king.

When he returned as king, he called on the 10 servants to give an account of their success. The story tells of 3 servants reporting: the <u>1st had produced a gain of 900%,</u> the 2nd had a 400% gain, but the 3rd had no gain, returning only the original sum with an excuse that he feared the nobleman as a ruthless collector of profits. The 2 servants with a gain were rewarded with all the money they had returned and given authority to rule over 10 and 5 cities respectively in the nobleman's kingdom; but the worthless servant received no reward and had the <u>original loan amount taken from him,</u> which was given to the 1st place servant.

All believers are given talents and resources by which to serve faithfully to the best of their ability <u>in the Lord's ministry on earth.</u> They will be rewarded for their effectiveness when Christ returns to reign in His millennium kingdom, 1ˢᵗ <u>by being taken up to be a part</u> of <u>it,</u> and 2ⁿᵈ by receiving special awards and recognition.

Moving on to enter Jerusalem in verses 28-40, as in Matt 21:1-11, Jesus sent 2 disciples ahead to borrow a colt (donkey) for Him to ride on into the city. The owner was to be told that Jesus had need of it; having dominion over all creatures, He <u>could use them as He pleased.</u> When the colt arrived, personal garments were put on the colt where Jesus sat, and on the roads over which he rode; something <u>like rolling out the red carpet for a dignitary in the</u> <u>modern world.</u>

As they neared the Mount of Olives, the disciples and other followers began to sing praises unto God for Jesus as the King of Peace. The Pharisees demanded that He rebuke this action by the crowd, but Jesus told them 'no way' because if He did that, the stones in the road would begin cheering. This was hardly a triumphal entry into Jerusalem, as Jesus Himself was sorrowful.

As Jesus saw Jerusalem in verses 41-44, He wept in the knowledge that the city would be destroyed in the future because the authorities with popular support <u>would reject Him as</u> <u>the Messiah.</u> He described that destruction as it happened when Titus of Rome besieged the city in 586 BC. As much as Christ cares for mankind, they too will be destroyed if they reject Him as Savior.

He entered the temple in 45-48 (Matt. 21:12-17) to drive out all the merchandisers with the declaration that they had <u>made a house of prayer into a den of thieves.</u> As He continued to teach daily, leaders of the temple and other factions plotted to do away with Him.

CHAPTER 20:   One day while Jesus preached the gospel to people in the temple, in verses 1-8, as in Matthew 21:23-27, chief priests, scribes and other prominent leaders challenged his authority for what he was doing. He responded with a question of his own, asking them <u>by</u> <u>what authority John baptized Him,</u> whether it was from heaven or from men.

They knew it was from heaven, but they realized they could not answer His question without giving Him the recognition He deserved, so they said they did not know the answer. Jesus then told them that He <u>had no reason to tell them</u> by what authority He was ministering. Those who deny knowledge they have, deserve no edification!

Then He gave a parable about wicked vine dressers to the people in verses 9-19 (Matthew 21: 33-46). A man (God) planted a vineyard (new covenant) and rented it to vine dressers, (nation of Israel). The <u>owner went away for a considerable time,</u> but during each season he would send a servant (prophets of old) to the vine dressers to collect some of the grape harvest. Each of the three times that a servant was sent, the vine dressers <u>beat him and send him away</u> <u>empty handed.</u>

Finally the owner (God) decided to send his own beloved son (Jesus), hoping he would be <u>properly treated and respected.</u> When the vine dressers saw him they contrived to kill him thinking that they would then inherit his estate. Jesus concluded this parable by asking if the owner of the vineyard (God) should return and destroy the vine dressers and then <u>give the</u> <u>vineyard to someone else</u> (the Gentiles). The people responded, 'Definitely not.'

Those who refuse to render unto the Son an honest return, and reject Him to embrace spiritual death, deserve God's severest judgment. Yet, those who persevere in sinful ways cannot bear to think of appropriate punishment for their misdeeds.

Jesus then used Psalms 118:22 about a stone (Jesus) builders had rejected that later became the main cornerstone, adding that anyone who opposed the stone would suffer great harm and later on if the stone fell on them they would be destroyed (judgment of the wicked) as if ground to powder. The chief priests and scribes wanted more than ever to do away with Jesus because this parable was spoken against them. They continued to spy on him and harass him with complex questions.

With flattering words in verses 20-26 (Matt. 22: 15-22) they asked him, is it lawful for us to pay taxes to Caesar or not? Knowing they were trying to trap him, Jesus asked them to show him a Roman coin and to tell whose image and inscription was on it. When they replied 'Caesar's,' Jesus then said, 'Give unto Caesar what is his and to God what belongs to Him.' They were stumped into silence by this response.

Divine wisdom enables all who teach the truths of God to avoid the snares laid for them by wicked men; and clearly sets forth duties to God, to earthly rulers, and to all mankind, that the opposition cannot dispute.

Then some Sadducees, who did not believe in the resurrection of life, posed a complicated and ludicrous example in verses 27-40, as in Matt. 22: 23-33, to suggest that resurrection was impossible. On the basis of Deuteronomy 25:5 and Ruth 4:1-12, they asked whose wife a widow would be in heaven if she married seven brothers consecutively as each husband died.

Jesus quickly made it clear that men and women do not marry in heaven because they are like God's Angels. Then he referred to Exodus 3:1-3,15, where Moses referred to the Lord as the God of Abraham, Isaac, and Jacob, as if they were still living, meaning that they would someday be resurrected. The Sadducees admitted that he had given a good explanation. Most assuredly, believers shall be resurrected from death to enter into the joy of God's domain; where perfection in holiness will remove all reasons for earthly conduct and custom.

Then in verse 41-44, as in Matthew 22: 41-46, Jesus clarified that He was the Son of David as well as the Son of God. He concluded with a warning to the people in 45-47 (Matthew 23: 1-7) that they should be wary of the scribes who were hypocritical in presenting themselves as great people while they took homes away from widows.

CHAPTER 21: In verses 1-4 (Matt. 12:41-44) Jesus observed that a poor widow giving back to the Lord of her meager resources, was far more generous than the wealthy who gave of their surplus. God is pleased most of all with gifts from the heart.

Jesus then predicted the destruction of the beautiful temple in Jerusalem in verses 5-6 (Matt. 24:1-2), as done in 70 AD at the hands of the Roman army. The question arose in verse 7 about when such havoc would occur and what signs of imminence would be given. Jesus expounded at length in verses 8-19 (Matt. 24:3-14) about timely signs leading up to God's endtimes scenario, before getting specific about the destruction of the temple and Jerusalem in verses 20-24 (Matt. 24:15-28).

Signs and events over time before Christ's 2nd coming will include: wars and great tragedies, international hostility between nations, earthquakes, famines, and pestilence, persecution of believers by the wicked in power, and some cosmic disturbances. Despite all of the difficulties to come, Jesus said that believers are not to worry, but patiently keep the faith and be confident that the <u>Holy Spirit will enable them to endure</u>, in spite of betrayals by family and friends, even to death.

Getting back to the destruction of Jerusalem, the main sign of imminence was encirclement by the Roman army to impose a siege, at which time, it would be better to <u>flee</u> <u>to the mountains,</u> sadly most difficult for women with or expecting a child. Many would be killed or taken captive, as Jerusalem came under Gentile control, and would remain so <u>until</u> <u>the nation of Israel was restored</u> in June of 1967.

Next, in verses 25-38, as in Matt. 24:29-44, Jesus spoke of His 2nd coming as the Son of Man, with signs in the heavens, <u>distress of nations,</u> and turmoil on the seas of the world. Then mankind will witness His return in a cloud, with divine power and glory. As He returns, <u>with judgment upon the world in mind,</u> He will first redeem (rapture) all that are His from tribulation and the wrath of God to follow upon the wicked.

He gave the parable of a fig tree in 29-33, as a confirmation of His coming, with the <u>signs described appearing as buds to bear fruit.</u> His actual coming will take place quickly so that all <u>those living at that time will know it.</u>

The chapter ends with verses 34-38, which contain Christ's admonition to be ever prayerfully watchful for the predicted signs to take place, and <u>not be distracted by pleasures and sins of the world,</u> so as to be worthy of eternal life with the Son of Man. The danger all mankind faces is to be unprepared when the day of death and of judgment comes. Believers should live each day according to Christ's word, obeying His precepts, and following His example, so that we may <u>be found vigilant on the day of His return.</u> After this discourse, Jesus continued His daily temple teachings with nightly rests on Mount Olivet.

<u>CHAPTER 22:</u> A few days before the Passover Feast of Unleavened Bread was to be celebrated, as related in verses 1-6 (Matt. 26: 1-5) temple chiefs and scribes pondered how <u>to kill Jesus without arousing the people to anger.</u> Satan played into their hands by causing Judas to offer them an opportunity to seize Jesus at an opportune moment, <u>for a price they</u> <u>agreed to pay him.</u> Why Judas was motivated to do this is a mystery; perhaps he felt inferior to the other disciples in the eyes of Jesus.

In verses 7-23, as In Matt. 26:17-30, Jesus ordered Peter and John to prepare the Passover meal at a place they were to find in Jerusalem, by following a man carrying a pitcher of water, a <u>task mostly performed by women</u> of that day. They accomplished this task as instructed, and as they sat down together to partake of the food, Jesus informed them that He would not eat it again with them on earth; the <u>next time would be in God's kingdom.</u>

As He divided wine and bread with them, He explained that the bread represented His body, that would be sacrificed for them and all mankind, and the <u>wine represented the life blood of His new covenant</u> for the salvation of mankind. Before partaking of these symbolic items, He announced that His betrayer (Judas) was also sitting at the table, and would <u>suffer for his heinous act of betrayal.</u> Verse 23 says that the disciples began to wonder who would be the betrayer, but undoubtedly <u>Judas was identified as he left them.</u>

Then for another strange reason, the disciples argued over who would be the greatest in the kingdom of God, for which <u>Jesus gave them clarification,</u> as stated in verses 24-30. Jesus made it clear that a worldly ambition of being the greatest with power is not as lofty as one who serves others, just as He had served them, <u>even as He would humble Himself to</u> <u>endure</u> <u>death</u> on the cross in atonement for man's sins. He also told the 11 disciples that they would be given authority to rule over the 12 tribes of Israel <u>in His future kingdom.</u>

In 31-34 (Matt. 26:31-35) Jesus informed Simon Peter that He had prayed for his faith to be strong enough to become an effective witness<u>, after denying association with Jesus 3</u> <u>times,</u> when accused by worldly people.

Jesus then instructed them in 35-38 on preparations and precautions they should take for their future ministry, <u>after His death.</u> They were told to arm themselves with a sword, meaning the a <u>spiritual sword of trust in God,</u> but they understood Him literally.

Jesus and the disciples went to the Mount of Olives for prayer time in verses 39-53, as in Matt. 26:36-53. Before withdrawing to a private place, Jesus told them to pray that they resist temptation. His own prayer to God was <u>for mercy to be spared the agony of death,</u> only if it was in God's will. An angel came to strengthen Him. In great agony, He prayed so fervently that <u>sweat like drops of blood fell</u> from his face.

Returning to the disciples, He found them asleep and woke them with a warning that they would yield to temptations <u>unless they prayed for spiritual strength.</u> As he spoke, a company of temple priests, scribes, and other local leaders arrived with Judas at the forefront. As Judas kissed Jesus, He <u>rebuked him for betraying with a kiss.</u>

When a disciple (Simon Peter) cut off the right ear of a high priest's servant, Jesus <u>mercifully touched and healed the ear.</u> Then Jesus chided the leaders for coming under darkness to seize Him when they could have <u>taken Him anytime in the temple.</u>

Verses 54-62 (Matt. 26:69-75) tell how Peter denied Jesus 3 times. After the rooster crowed, and Jesus looked at him with sad eyes, Peter <u>departed weeping bitterly.</u> This was his turning back to Jesus in repentance under God's divine grace.

Jesus is blindfolded and subjected to blasphemous mocking, beatings, and questioning in 63-71, as in Matt. 26:57-68, by Roman soldiers, <u>chief priests and other local leaders.</u> When asked if He was the Christ, He told them <u>they wouldn't believe anything He said,</u> or answer His questions, or release Him. He did say, 'The Son of Man will sit on the right hand of the power of God.'

This provoked their question, 'Are You the Son of God?' When Jesus admitted to this identity, they concluded that He had committed blasphemy by claiming a false relationship to God, and this was <u>sufficient evidence for a punishment of death.</u> With their eyes blinded to the truth, they yielded to their human antagonism, and thus became the greatest of blasphemers.

CHAPTER 23:   In 1-12, as in Matt. 27:1-2 & 11-14, Jesus faces the local Roman ruler Pilate and King Herod in turn on the charges brought by the Jewish temple crowd. Rather than charge blasphemy against God which would be of no concern to the Romans, they <u>charged Jesus</u> <u>with political violations of local laws,</u> including disturbing the peace, opposing payment of taxes, and calling Himself a King. Jesus admitted to Pilate that He considered Himself to be King of the Jews only.

Initially, Pilate found no fault in Him, but the <u>mob fiercely accused Jesus</u> of stirring up trouble in all places including Galilee. Since Herod was King of the area including Galilee, and was in Jerusalem at the time, Pilate <u>sent Jesus as a Galilean</u> to him for further interrogation.

Herod was delighted to see Jesus because of his curiosity over miracles by Jesus that had been reported to him; he <u>hoped Jesus would do some for him.</u> To Herod's many questions, Jesus said nothing, so his soldiers joined him in ridiculing and mocking Him. With a fancy robe on Him, <u>Herod sent Jesus back to Pilate</u>.

Calling the temple mob before him, Pilate told them for the 2nd time that both He and Herod <u>found no fault in Jesus.</u>, and proposed that He be whipped and released. The mob protested and demanded that a criminal named Barabbas be released in the place of Jesus, in accordance with traditional custom at that time.

For the 3rd time, Pilate again confronted them, declaring that <u>Jesus did nothing to deserve death.</u> They angrily demanded that Jesus be crucified and Barabbas be released. Fearing their protest would reach Herod's ears to his own detriment, <u>Pilate yielded to their demands</u>. Jesus was immediately given over for crucifixion without appeal rights.

As Jesus is consigned to crucifixion, in verses 26-43 (Matt. 27:32-44), a Cyrenian named Simon was drafted to carry His cross, because of His <u>weakened condition from earlier beatings.</u> To some women who followed along weeping loudly over His plight, Jesus told them to <u>weep more for themselves and their children</u> than for Him, because they would have to suffer through much tribulation at some time ahead.

The bitter sufferings of Jesus should put all Christians in awe over God's justice standard. The best of saints when compared to Christ, are like dry trees; for as He suffered, so <u>too believers must suffer as God ordains.</u>

At Calvary (Golgotha), when Jesus was hung on a cross between 2 criminals <u>on identical crosses,</u> He uttered a simple prayer, 'Father, forgive them, they do not know what they are doing.' The soldiers cast lots to take away His garments. The conniving temple leaders and attending soldiers jeered Him for not saving Himself, as a <u>chosen Son of God.</u> They also ridiculed a sign which read, 'THIS IS THE KING OF THE JEWS.'

One criminal joined in this mockery but the other opined that Jesus <u>was an innocent man,</u> and said to Him, Lord, remember me when You come into Your Kingdom.' Jesus responded, 'Yes, you will be with me in Paradise today." By this act of grace one should understand that Jesus Christ died to give access to the kingdom of heaven to <u>all penitent, obedient believers.</u> While true repentance is never too late, late repentance is not always certain if <u>not from the heart.</u> Man cannot be sure that sufficient time will be given to repent before death!

At the 6th hour after being hung on the cross, as related in 44-56 (Matt. 27:45 -61), the day darkened, the temple veil was torn apart from top to bottom, and Jesus yielded up His spirit after saying, 'Father, into Your hands I commit myself.' (Many victims would survive for as long as 2 days before dying). A centurion who witnessed His death <u>declared that Jesus certainly was a righteous person.</u>

Most of the crowd left, with some beating their breasts in grief, but <u>women and other</u>

followers from Galilee stood by at a distance. A Jewish temple member named Joseph, from the city of Arimathea, who had no part in putting Jesus to death, petitioned and received permission from Pilate to remove and bury the body of Jesus. He wrapped His body in linen and placed it in an unused rock tomb late on a Friday afternoon before the Jewish Sabbath began. The women from Galilee observed this and resolved to return after the Sabbath to anoint His body with spices and oils. Clearly, they did not expect His resurrection.

CHAPTER 24:   The women from Galilee returned on Sunday morning, as stated in verses 1-12 (Matt. 28:1-10), to anoint the body of Jesus, and found the entrance stone rolled away from the tomb entrance. The heavy stone slab may have been moved by an earthquake, or God's angels.

Going inside, they found no body, but saw two male angels in shining garments that put fear in their hearts. One said, 'Why are you looking for His body here, He is risen to life just as He said He would do on the 3rd day after His death.'

With their memories refreshed, the women returned to the 11 disciples and others to share this experience. Mary Magdalene, Joanna, and Mary, the mother of James, were the 3 main witnesses to say that Jesus was risen. Their report was skeptically received and Peter quickly went to check the tomb, where he saw only the linen burial cloths.

In verses 13-32, Luke gives an exclusive detailed account of Jesus encountering 2 of his followers that same day, returning to the village of Emmaus, about 7 miles from Jerusalem. They were discussing all that had happened when He joined them to ask, 'What are you talking about that makes you so sad?' One named Cleopas questioned why Jesus didn't know what things had happened. Jesus asked, 'What things?' as if to keep His identity hidden.

They confided in Him all about His ministry, and the crucifixion brought about by the religious leaders, His burial, and lastly, the disappearance of His body from the tomb. Jesus chided them for not remembering prophecy that He had to suffer death and then rise gloriously to return to heaven. He reviewed prophecy all the way back to Moses. He relied on scripture and fulfillment of prophecy, to confirm His presence.

As they entered Emmaus, the 2 men persuaded Jesus to remain with them for the night. While eating their evening meal, Jesus blessed and broke some bread in the same manner as He had done at the Last Supper, which made them realize who He was, but He immediately vanished. Marveling over His words, they wasted no time returning to Jerusalem, to tell the 11 disciples and other followers all about this experience, only to hear from them that Jesus had appeared also to Simon Peter.

In an account not given in Matthew, Jesus appeared to all of them in verses 36-49, saying, 'Peace to you.' Because they were frightened by what they saw as a vision, Jesus assured them by showing His wounded hands and feet that He was Christ indeed, and then asked for food to eat. That was convincing enough to them that He was a live being, not an hallucination.

Jesus then reminded them of His earlier predictions of His fate as prophesied by scripture, that had now been fulfilled. This removed lingering doubts and opened their understanding greatly. He emphasized that all that had happened was part of God's plan to provide a better way for the salvation of sinners. He told them to preach the word about repentance and remission of sins to all the world, <u>beginning with Jerusalem.</u> This was to be done under the power of the holy Spirit which He promised to provide later during their preparations in Jerusalem to <u>embark on their Great Commission from God.</u>

Jesus then led these followers to Bethany, near the Mount of Olives, where He had prayed before His betrayal by Judas. There, He raised His hands to heaven, blessed them and <u>was raised up to heaven before their eyes.</u> They had not witnessed His resurrection, but they saw His ascension, and they believed in His holiness more than ever.

Feeling greatly blessed, they paused for worship of Jesus before returning to Jerusalem, where with great joy they spent time <u>in the temple praising and honoring God.</u>

SUMMARY: As evidence of Luke's genius for careful research to ferret out details on the ministry of Jesus and the disciples, scholars have noted that <u>some 500 verses in his account give information not found in the other gospels.</u> Over 130 exclusive verses are found in Chapters 1 & 2, mostly pertaining to the birth of John the Baptist and Christ.

Other exclusives include the following: the genealogy of Jesus through His mother's family line in 3:29-38; <u>Christ's first restoration of life</u> to the son of a widow in 7:11-15; the 2 parables about a lost coin and a lost son in 15:8-21; and in Chapter 16, a parable about a dishonest steward and another about a rich man and a poor Lazarus. Chapter 18 includes a parable about a persistent widow, one about a Pharisee and one on a tax collector.

Finally, and most important, Luke gives more information in Chapter 24 of Christ's encounter with the 11 disciples and other followers, who are to be instrumental in the initial ministry <u>to carry out the Great Commission</u> to the world.

Luke contributed another vital portion to the New Testament by authoring the Book of Acts, which describes the <u>early church evangelization</u> efforts of the disciples.

GOSPEL OF JOHN—BOOK FOUR

John focused more on what Jesus said than what He did, differing from the other 3 Gospels on the sequence of His ministry, His language, and the day of His crucifixion. John mentions as 'signs' only 8 of the 35 miracles of Christ, and <u>6 of these are unique to this Gospel</u>. He told nothing of Jesus' birth in Bethlehem, healing of lepers, demon exorcism is not mentioned, and there is no Sermon on the Mount discourse.

An estimated 92% of this Gospel is exclusive from the other 3 Synoptic Gospels which collectively present a similar general view. <u>It was the last to be written</u>—about 90 AD—probably in Ephesus where John lived in his later years.

John and James, both sons of Zebedee, were in the first group of disciples called into service by Jesus. Both were first cousins of Jesus, and John identified himself as the 'one whom Jesus loved.' He was one of the 'inner 3', including James and Peter, who were <u>with Jesus on most special occasions</u>. He and brother James, were also known as the 'Sons of Thunder.' He was given responsibility for Jesus' mother from the cross.

John's account gives a distinctive account of the 'signs' (miracles), words, and ministry of Jesus, <u>with a twofold purpose</u>: to call believers to live and mature by their faith, and for new believers to publicly confess Jesus as the Christ and then join a Christian fellowship. He told of Christ using 'I AM' 7 times to identify as the Son of God.

Most scholarly authorities. attribute this Gospel, the 3 Epistles of John, and the Book of Revelation to John's authorship.

CHAPTER 1:   In Genesis, the words 'In the beginning' open an account of God's creation of all life on earth and more. In this Gospel by John, the same words in verses 1-5 open <u>the door to the identity of Jesus</u> (The Word) as an integral part of the creation process, of being there from the beginning, <u>as God's right hand presence</u>. He coexisted with the Father, and <u>with His participation all creation took place,</u> from the host of angels to the lowliest worm on earth.

Jesus is the sum and substance of all physical life, plus the spiritual life of mankind, giving great illumination <u>to having reasoning ability and common sense</u> to know that He enables us in all that we do. In His light, we should be totally dependent on Him.

Jesus came to earth in human form, to be a Light to a sinful world, but humanity has <u>difficulty seeing Him as the eternal Word of God</u>, because darkness (sin) obscures light. This was most true of the God's chosen people of Israel. If the spiritual eyes of believers are open to behold this Light, and they walk in it, they will <u>be made wise unto salvation, by</u> faith in Jesus Christ.

Reference is made to John the Baptist in verses 6-13, to bear witness of the Light to the Jewish people, as well as all mankind, so they could believe in His divine mission to open a door to spiritual salvation, <u>leading to eternal life in God's presence.</u>

Verses 14-18 speak of Christ (the Word) coming to earth in human form, not lacking in eternal grace and glory, with total integrity, <u>to which John the Baptist attested.</u> By seeing Jesus in a spiritual light as the Son of God, <u>mankind sees God in effect.</u> As a committed believer in Jesus, man can sense a solid relationship with God, and receive His mercy and grace, plus recognition and rewards for faithful service.

John the Baptist identified himself and witnessed about Christ in verses 19-28, as in Matt. 3:1-12. He made clear that he was not Christ, Elijah, or a prophet of God. When pressed by the Jewish leaders, he only admitted to being the forerunner of the Messiah to come, as prophesied in Isaiah 40:3. When asked by what authority he baptized new converts, he said he baptized by water only as an introduction to one far greater than he that they did not know, but who was soon to appear.

John saw his earthly cousin Jesus approaching the next day, in verses 29-34 (Matt. 3:13-17), and is inspired by the Holy Spirit to announce to the world that He is 'the Lamb of God, who takes away the sin of the world.' He made clear that Jesus was the Messiah that he had spoken of earlier to the Jewish leaders, and admitted that he did not know this to be true until he saw the Holy Spirit descend from heaven like a dove when he baptized Jesus. God himself bore witness at that event that Jesus is the Son of God

In verses 35-51, John told how several men came to be disciples of Jesus. When John the Baptist said 'Behold the Lamb of God' 2 of his own disciples began to follow Jesus; one was named Andrew and common belief is that the other was John, the author of this Gospel.

When Jesus asked them what they wanted, they asked where He was staying that day. He invited them to follow and see for themselves, and so they did. Andrew then found his brother Simon Peter, informed him of the Messiah's location, and brought him to Jesus. Jesus recognized him but gave him a new name 'Cephas' meaning a stone.

When Jesus decided to go to Galilee the following day, He recruited another disciple named Philip, who invited a man named Nathanael to meet Jesus, as a person of interest. Nathanael was skeptical that anyone great could come from Nazareth but went to Jesus, who identified him as an Israelite without deceit. Being a sincere person, he was impressed and asked Jesus how He was able to knew his character.

Jesus admitted that He had seen Nathanael meditating under a fig tree earlier. Nathanael then acknowledged that he knew Jesus was the Son of God, and King of Israel. Jesus assured him that greater things would be made known to him through heaven's gate, as angels of God moved with Him. He may have become a disciple of Jesus. Just as Christ knew this man and mankind in general, all people should desire to know Him.

VIEWPOINTS: John gave Jesus 10 different titles in this chapter, as follows: Word and God-vs. 1, Creator-v. 3, Light-vs. 7, only begotten God-vs. 18, Lamb of God-vs. 29 & 36, Son of God-vs. 34 & 49, Messiah-vs. 41, King of Israel-vs. 49, and Son of Man-vs. 51. Undoubtedly, John saw Jesus as the incarnate embodiment of Almighty God.

CHAPTER 2: The 1st of the 'signs' in John's account of Jesus' ministry is described in verses 1-11, that of turning water into wine at a wedding celebration. Jesus, His disciples, and Mary the mother of Jesus were in attendance. When the wine supply ran out, His mother told Jesus about it.

He gave a rather strange response that her 'woman' concern was not His, because His time had not yet come. This should not be taken as disrespect, because the use of the term 'woman' was equal to 'lady,' implying respect in those days. One might properly assume that He used a jocular tone of voice to say that it wasn't time for Him to do some of the work, or that it was too soon for Him to do miracles.

Mary seemed to understand that Jesus was not refusing to help and thus instructed the servants to assist Him in gathering large containers and filling them with water. Jesus then instructed the servants to draw out some of the liquid for the wine master to taste. He thought the bridegroom had provided it and complimented him for serving the best wine last, after the inferior wine had been consumed.

This 'sign' miracle by Jesus evidenced His glory. Although He condoned the drinking of wine for this festive occasion, taken in moderation, it should be remembered that He warned against overindulgence and drunkenness in other teachings, since this impaired common sense.

Some folks interpret the changing of water into wine as symbolic of the new covenant of the kingdom of God replacing the old Mosaic covenant. This supports the adage that 'the best, or the new, is always the last, or better than the old.'

As told in verses 12-24 (Matt: 21:12-17), after a short rest in Capernaum with His family members and the disciples, Jesus moved on to Jerusalem for the Jewish Passover. His first public act there was to angrily chase the venders and money changers out of the temple with a cord whip, saying, 'Don't make My Father's house a market place!'

From this, the disciples remembered Psalm 69:9—'Zeal for Your house has eaten Me up!' In today's world, church leaders still use church facilities for marketing activities; this is especially true in ancient massive cathedrals in Europe which market regularly to tourists.

The Jewish leaders asked for some 'sign' that Jesus had authority to do such things. Jesus replied, 'Destroy this temple, and in 3 days I will raise it up.' In confusion, they asked how He could rebuild the temple structure in 3 days, when it had taken 46 years to build.

In truth, Jesus was foretelling His own death at their hands, and His resurrection by His divine power in 3 days. Later, after He had risen from death, His disciples remembered these words and their faith was strengthened by His words.

During the remainder of the Passover days, Jesus won general approval for His miracles that benefited the people, but He did not accept them as true believers, because He discerned the shallowness of their faith and their lack of genuine commitment to Him.

CHAPTER 3: John gives a unique account in verses 1-21 of a conversation between Jesus and a Sanhedrin Pharisee named Nicodemus, who came at night so as not to arouse questions or antagonism from other Pharisees. He acknowledged that Jesus was a God anointed being because of all the miracles He had performed. He was concerned over his own soul and salvation, and what being 'born again' really meant, since Jesus said this was the only way to become a part of the kingdom of God.

Jesus spoke of the necessity and nature of regeneration or the new birth, and directed Nicodemus to the Holy Spirit as the source of holiness of the heart. This brings about a new spiritual quality to life, with a new nature, higher principles, better affections, and an aim to please God in all things.

By the power of the Holy Spirit, a new something is born within us, and for us, which we cannot do for ourselves. In addition to one's physical birth (breaking of water), or baptism by water to attest to a new spiritual belief, a spiritual rebirth is essential to inherit a godly agenda that assures one of eternal life with God.

Nicodemus had difficulty understanding these words from Jesus, just as many humans have had over the ages. Jesus chided him, as well as other Pharisees (humanity in general) for this lack of perception. Nevertheless, He continued to instruct with a comparison of the 'rebirth' principal to the time of Moses as he held up a bronze snake on a pole so that the Israelites in the wilderness could live. In the same sense, Jesus on the cross for all to see before His resurrection took place was an offer of salvation to all.

Having come down from heaven, and having to return there, Jesus, as the Son of Man, was God's gift and ambassador to mankind as a light in the darkness of this world. He made possible a better way through spiritual regeneration to become part of God's kingdom, and not be subject to His endtimes wrath filled with condemnation. Believing in Jesus as the Son of God is an uppermost requirement for spiritual rebirth.

In verses 22-36, Jesus moved on to Judea where he ministered and baptized, just as John the Baptist had been doing. Some Jews protested to John that Jesus was doing the same as he had done, and many people were turning to Him. Knowing that Jesus came from heaven as the Son of God, while he as mortal man could only speak about the basics of religion, John said that Jesus was as a bridegroom in the public eye; as such, He had much more to offer as the voice of God, being His beloved Son and spokesman.

In typing Jesus as the bridegroom, His bride can be understood to be the people that Christ ministered to, and John was thus the bridegroom's friend, whose mission to introduce Jesus as the Messiah was now completed. Jesus was now the key messenger of God's agenda for the salvation of mankind, under the full power of the Holy Spirit.

VIEWPOINTS: "Conversion' is another term for 'rebirth' in Christ, when one encounters God's reality or purpose and responds to it in personal faith and commitment. It can be described as turning 'from darkness to light,' or from 'vanities of the world' towards the living God of heaven, turning from sin to righteousness.

When Jesus had meaningful encounters with concerned persons that resulted in their acknowledging Him as the Christ, they experienced radical changes in their lives, away from evil towards good. While such changes are personal and inward in nature, they do result in a public and outward change of the mind, emotions, and will.

Being born again can be understood as 'born from above,' because our sovereign God brings about an experience of 'regeneration,' through the work of the Holy Spirit. The Holy Spirit takes the truth of the gospel message of salvation through Christ, and makes it comprehensible to the hearer who is seeking the truth, giving birth to a personal commitment as a human response.

CHAPTER 4:   All of this chapter is unique to this gospel. Jesus has an encounter and conversation with a Samaritan woman in verses 1-26, in the region of Samaria. While He rested by a water well that Jacob had dug on land that Joseph inherited, a Samaritan woman came to draw water. When Jesus said, 'Give Me a drink,' she queried why He, a Jew, contrary to Jewish customs, asked her, a Samarian woman, for water.

Jesus told her that she would have asked Him for 'living water' if she had <u>known who He was</u> and the gift of salvation that He offered from God. With no container in hand to obtain water from a deep well, she asked how He could get that 'living water.' Obviously, she was not aware of the spiritual message He was giving her.

Jesus told her that water from the well would quench her thirst for a short time, but drinking <u>the water of the Holy Spirit</u> that He offered her would slake her thirst forever. In this world, drinking the waters of comfort falls far short of the comforts of God's Holy Word, made <u>manifest by the water of the Spirit of grace</u>, which satisfies abundantly.

Understanding Jesus in a literal sense, the woman asked for some of 'this water' so she would not need to draw anymore water. Jesus then used his divine perception to reveal <u>what He knew of her past</u>, by asking her to bring her husband to the well. When she said she had no husband, Jesus then told her that she had been married 5 times and was now living unmarried with a man. This was His way of turning her attention away from earthly matters to that <u>of her spiritual condition.</u>

This revelation so impressed the woman that she declared that Jesus was a prophet, and then oddly asked <u>was it necessary to worship in Jerusalem</u>, since the Samaritan place of worship was Mount Gerizim. Jesus told her a time would come when majoring on a worship place would cease, because the <u>object of true spiritual worship would be the Father</u>, for the salvation offered the Jews would be for all.

When the woman said that she knew the Messiah would come and reveal all things, Jesus abruptly said, "I am He, speaking to you now!" His disciples arrived as the woman swiftly departed to her city to tell some men <u>about her encounter with a Man who could be</u> the Christ, because He knew all about her past. Her view of Him had progressed from Jew, to prophet, and finally to the Messiah. The men left the city to come to Him.

At this point, in verses 27-38, the disciples urged Jesus to eat, but He told them He had food that they did not know about; they thought someone else had brought some. Jesus then declared that <u>His food was to do the will of God</u>, which was to finish sowing the seed of the salvation message, for a harvest to come.

He directed their attention to the situation in Samaria where many souls were ready for the harvest of spiritual rebirth, which would be cause for joy to all. Those who reaped a harvest (leading the unsaved to Christ) would be rewarded and rejoice. He <u>charged them with the task of reaping the harvest</u> that grew from the seed planted by the prophets, John the Baptist, and Himself. The time of His ministry was like a season, requiring a timely harvest of souls.

In 39-42, John tells of a great revival amongst the Samaritans who persuaded Jesus to stay with them for 2 days. <u>Many believed that He was the Christ</u>, the Savior of the world, because they had now seen and heard Him. Amazingly, through His teaching to one poor woman, the salvation story was <u>spread to an entire town.</u>

Jesus moved on to Galilee in verses 43-54 where He was well received for what He had done in Jerusalem at the Passover. A nobleman came to Him pleading for the healing of his dying son, and Jesus <u>performed His 2nd 'sign' by remote control</u> as He told the nobleman to return home to his restored son. Nobility is no security from sickness and death, and like the poor, the greatest men must seek help from God, even to the point of <u>being beggars for</u> His mercy.

When the nobleman neared home, servants informed him the boy was on the mend, and a check of time confirmed that his healing began at the moment Jesus spoke it. This act <u>made believers out of the man's entire household,</u> including his servants. Once again, the power of one word of Christ produced a miracle of both physical and spiritual healing.

CHAPTER 5:   Jesus went to Jerusalem during a Jewish feast festival, in verses 1-16, and stopped by a large pool of water at Bethesda where many crippled and disabled people hoped to receive healing, if <u>they could be the first to enter the pool</u> after an angel stirred up the waters. Jesus singled out one man who had been crippled for 38 years to ask him if he wanted to be healed. The man did not say yes or no, but <u>implied that was his wish</u> by sadly telling Jesus that he was unable to be first into the pool without help.

Without hesitation, Jesus performed his 3rd 'sign' act in John to heal the man with the command, '<u>Get up, take up your mat and walk.</u>' This aroused the ire of Jewish critics because they felt that healing on the Sabbath was a violation of God's laws. When they expressed this view, the man said he merely obeyed his healer. They asked who was the healer; he could not say because <u>Jesus had not identified Himself.</u>

Later in the temple, the man met Jesus, who told him to sin no more, thus <u>offering a spiritual healing too,</u> so as not to miss eternal life in heaven. Later, the man told the critics that it was Jesus who healed him, and they proceeded to harass and plot to kill Jesus. It is doubtful the man identified Jesus spitefully or ungratefully, but he may have done so to <u>avoid trouble from the Jewish authorities.</u>

In verse 17, Jesus defends His action with a terse statement that, 'My Father doesn't take time out doing good, and so it is with me.' By <u>equating Himself with God,</u> He infuriated the critics even more, and He then gave a lengthy discourse in verses 18-47 about honoring God and recognizing His Son as God's right hand executive officer.

He made it clear that none of His doings were independent of God, for out of love God gave Him the power to act <u>according to His own capacity.</u> This included resurrection of the dead, or spiritual rebirth, and ultimate judgment of all mankind for good or bad results. Thus, all should honor Him as the Son of God, in <u>like manner as God is honored.</u>

Jesus gave assurance that all who heard His words and believed in God would not come under a wrathful judgment but <u>would inherit eternal life.</u> This would encompass a conversion from a life of sin to a new spiritual relationship with Him, as endowed by the Holy Spirit, and after physical death, an <u>ultimate resurrection into the kingdom of God.</u> Above all, Jesus acknowledged that He acted only in God's will.

Jesus then admitted that under Jewish law, His own testimony of His status and power was not to be accepted without corroboration by other witnesses. He names John the Baptist as a bright light in this regard, and He <u>cites the many God given miracles that they had</u> <u>witnessed,</u> plus God's voice from heaven at the time of His baptism by John.

Jesus chided them for disbelief in the prophecy of the Scriptures which pointed to Him., and accused them of <u>rejecting Him because they lacked the love of God</u> in their hearts, which were filled with selfish pride, ambition, and worldly desires. Going back to early times, even Moses accused them of spiritual infidelity, and they obviously put no more stock in his words than in the words of Jesus. They were however vulnerable to the acceptance of a false Messiah, just as <u>people will accept the antichrist in God's endtimes.</u>

Jesus felt that the way to eternal life was revealed to them in the Scriptures, as they should have known because <u>the word of God was in their hands</u>. Although very studious in the study of Old Testament Scriptures, they were regrettably strangers to its truth and power. This is a <u>common deficiency in the lives of many professing Christians of today,</u> who also concoct Gospel Scripture meanings that serve their wishful thinking preferences.

CHAPTER 6: In this chapter, John describes the 4ᵗʰ & 5ᵗʰ miracle 'sign' performed by Jesus. The first is the feeding of the 5000 men, plus women and children, as related in all 4 gospels, and the second is that of <u>Jesus walking on the Sea</u> of Galilee.

In verses 1-15, as in Matt. 14:13-21, Jesus takes the 5 barley loaves and 2 small fish that a small boy had with him, and divides them in such a way that the entire multitude of people were adequately fed and much was left over. This demonstration of His supernatural deity so impressed the men that they proclaimed Jesus to be a Prophet, and <u>considered forcing Him to be their political king</u>. Since this was not His purpose, Jesus quickly and perhaps surreptitiously left them to be alone on a mountain.

Later that evening, his regular disciples decided to sail across the sea to Capernaum as stated in verses 16-21, and in Matt. 14:22-23. After rowing out about 3-4 miles, darkness set in and <u>a wind storm stirred up rough waters</u>. Suddenly they saw Jesus walking on the sea towards them and they became fearful, perhaps not recognizing Him. As He drew near, <u>He identified Himself and told them not to be afraid.</u> John ends this episode as the boat suddenly reaches shore (another miracle?) shortly after Jesus got on board; he said nothing of Peter walking on the water to meet Jesus, as Matthew related.

In verses 22-40, the people who had been left behind after being fed by Jesus noted that the disciples had sailed off in the only available boat without Jesus, so they began to look for Him, possibly hoping for another miraculous feeding. Not finding Him, they arranged to <u>have other nearby boaters take them to Capernaum,</u> to see if the disciples knew what happened to Him. He was there as they arrived, and in amazement, they <u>asked when He had arrived there</u>.

Strangely, without answering their question, Jesus accused them of finding Him just to obtain more food, and told them not to strive for physical food, but seek (SPIRITUAL) food <u>that would give them eternal life</u>. This food was available to them through Him, the Son of Man, because God had willed this for Him.

They asked how they could do this and Jesus told them to just believe in Him. Then they asked for a sign from Him, in the manner that Moses had obtained bread (manna) from heaven to keep their foregathers alive in the wilderness, <u>so they would have ample reason to believe.</u>

Jesus set them straight by declaring that it was His Father, God, who provided manna, and was <u>now offering the world a new kind of bread</u> (spiritual) to give eternal life. They asked for this bread, still thinking of it literally as something to eat. Jesus tried to tell them that He was the 'bread of life' which they should accept and believe in, to be fulfilled spiritually, without hunger or thirst for more. As earthly bread is to the physical body, He is to the soul, to nourish and support spiritual growth and health.

Jesus emphasized that His visit to earth was what God willed for Him, and as He would be resurrected on the last (third) day, so would all believers be resurrected to everlasting life at the endtimes of God's patience with the wickedness of the world. His ultimate purpose is to hold unto all believers and raise them up in the last days.

In 41-59, Jesus continued with His teaching after the Jews complained over His claim to be bread from heaven; they saw Him only as the son of Joseph and Mary. Jesus persisted in telling them that He was the Bread (nourishment) given by God to be food to the souls of mankind. However, to overcome their literal understanding, they would have to learn this truth from God, sight unseen, through His inward power upon their minds, from His word, and the ministers sent by Him, before they would be attracted to His Son.

By trusting in Jesus and coalescing with Him as the Bread of Heaven, man can receive eternal life. Christ's life is the bread which He sacrificed to the Father in exchange for all things pertaining to a godly life, above all the forgiveness of all repentant sinners. Giving Himself as Bread for mankind to accept, opened an avenue for eternal life to a sinful world which otherwise would face eternal damnation.

Jesus in effect was attempting to bond His miracles of feeding over 5000 from next to nothing and the turning of water into wine, to His spiritual nature for mankind to absorb, to satisfy and alleviate spiritual hunger and thirst. Jesus called His body real food and His blood real drink. Eating His flesh and drinking His blood figuratively means to believe in Him, followed by submitting to Him body and soul for enlightenment by the Holy Spirit for obedience to God's Word, and then to partake of all God given benefits.

The Jews missed His spiritual connotation because they could not understand this somewhat cannibalistic concept, or may have related it to pagan human sacrifice rites. They were not spiritually minded! They were inclined to accept the worst interpretation of Christ's words, surely under persuasion by Satan. This weakness of perception is even more a common failing in today's world.

Jesus repeated the words 'I will raise them (you) to life on the last day' in 4 verses: 39, 40, 44, and 54, emphasizing that this was God's will for His Son to accomplish, for all who yielded to the urging of the Holy Spirit to accept and believe in Jesus. One must understand that this refers to the taking up of the dead and the living believers (the rapture) at the end of the tribulation times before God exerts His wrath upon the wicked, as implied in Christ's synagogue message at Capernaum.

When His disciples admitted this was difficult to understand and hard to accept, in verses 60-71, Jesus asked what they would think if they saw Him return to Heaven. Would they understand that only God's spirit gives eternal life? He clearly said that all who are physically born without a later spiritual renewal would not receive such a gift. Sensing that many continued in disbelief, He reminded them that none would accept His words unless they yielded to an inner conviction received from God.

After this, many followers turned away to go their own way, and Jesus asked His 12 disciples <u>if they were going to do the same</u>. Simon Peter negated this, asserting that they had no better place to go, because they believed in Him as the Son of God. Jesus curtly said that He had chosen all of them, but one was a devil, namely Judas the betrayer. This episode ends with rejection by many, in place of an earlier desire to make Him their king.

CHAPTER 7: Jesus continued his ministry in Galilee, not wanting to enter Judea because of Jewish leaders intent on killing him. His <u>brothers however sardonically urged Him to go there,</u> in verses 1-13, to demonstrate His powers through miracles to the people gathered for the Feast of Tabernacles. They said 'if you are who you say you are, then show yourself to the world.' This may have been sarcasm or evidence of skepticism.

Jesus responded by acknowledging that they were free to go whenever they wished, without concern over the attitude of others, but His time had not yet come, partly because of the <u>hatred of His opposition that He felt</u>. After His brothers left for Judea, Christ also went there, keeping His presence secret as people spoke good and evil of Him.

In 14-29, Jesus made his presence known by entering the temple to eloquently preach to those in attendance. Some of His listeners marveled at His words, noting that He had never gone to college. Jesus informed them that <u>His doctrine came from God,</u> and if they turned to God they would know this for a fact. Speaking from His own knowledge would be for self glorification, but speaking to glorify the Father is <u>evidence of genuine truth in righteousness</u>. His authority for teaching as He did was from His Father God.

Jesus then asked why the temple leaders sought to kill him and thereby break a law that Moses had given them. The people thought He was demon possessed to say such a thing, because they <u>did not know that the leaders plotted His death.</u> Again referring to the objections of the leaders over His healing of a man on the Sabbath, He points out that they circumcised males on the Sabbath which did not violate a law of Moses. On this basis, <u>restoring health to the afflicted was equally justified</u> on the Sabbath as that rite.

People continued to speculate on who Jesus was, many believing that He was not the Christ because they knew He came from Joseph's family in Nazareth. In frustration, Jesus cried out that even though they knew of his earthly family ties, they did not know God and for that reason, <u>did not realize that He was put on earth by God</u> to do His Will.

This provoked some of the people in verses 30-44 to seize Him but the Holy Spirit restrained them; other people believed He was the Messiah because of all His miracles. Hearing these speculations, the <u>Pharisees and temple leaders sent guards to arrest Him.</u> When Jesus spoke sincerely about His temporary stay before going to heaven where they could not reach Him., the people and the guards were puzzled.

Jesus continued to preach His message until the last day of the feast, when the temple priests drew water and poured it out before the Lord. Using this as an allegory, Jesus said that they should <u>come to Him if thirsty and drink of the truth of His divinity,</u> so their lives would spiritually become as energetic and forceful as a river of real water. This depicted the gift of the Holy Spirit to come after His time on earth, to work innermost in believers as running water, to produce other streams of righteousness to cool and cleanse wayward passions and to be a source of great enlightenment to others.

Confusion reigned in the minds of the people as some said He was a prophet, and others saw him as Christ. With this kind of division amongst them, none dared to lay hands on Him. The temple guards returned to their superiors without Him, saying that no man ever spoke words like Jesus spoke to them. The Pharisees accused them of being easily deceived and accursed along with the crowds.

One leader named Nicodemus, who had an earlier private conversation with Jesus (Ch. 3:1-9), opined that Jewish law should not judge a man before hearing him out to understand his purposes. The Pharisees asked him if he was from Galilee, and falsely added that no prophets had ever come from there. Jonah, Nathum, and Hosea came from Galilee, and some think Elijah, Elisha, and Amos may also have been from that area.

VIEWPOINTS: John used an expression in this chapter, sometimes quoting the words of Jesus, as seen in verses 6, 8, 30, and 33, to the effect that 'his (my) time has not yet come. This gives the impression that Jesus was aware of all that would occur to bring Him to His final moment on the cross. He avoided capture up to a point so as to bring God's ordained agenda for His earthly ministry to a conclusion at a chosen time. Humanly speaking, one could say that He had a premonition, but it must have been more than that.

CHAPTER 8:   Sadly, lacking the hospitality of a follower offering Him a bed, but perhaps by choice, Jesus spent the night after the feast on the Mount of Olives, where He often prayed for strength to endure. In verses 1-11, after He returned to the temple early the next morning, scribes and Pharisee brought a woman before Him that had been apprehended in the sin of adultery. Their objective was to entrap Him regarding Moses' law for this sin, that the violator be stoned to death. Strangely, but perhaps deliberately, they did not present the man, the other party to this sin, for His judgment.

Jesus said nothing but stooped to the ground to write something in the dirt, for the only time recorded in the Gospels. Some think He wrote 2 of the 10 commandments, that condemned adultery and bearing false witness as sins, but this is conjecture. After verbal harassment from the accusers, He arose and merely said, 'Whoever amongst you that has not sinned, go ahead—throw the first stone!'

He returned to writing on the ground, while the men in total silence, one by one, old and young, melted away into the crowd, convicted by their own conscience. They may have been guilty of the same sin, and thus were not qualified to judge the woman. An important principle is that all who choose to find fault with others, must first be concerned with judging themselves, that they too keep themselves without unforgiven sin.

When Jesus and the woman saw that her accusers had dropped her case, He told her to go on with her life without this sin, for which He would not condemn her. He gave her a 2nd chance to go straight, not voicing His forgiveness or requiring her penitence. His mercy towards her was evident in His caution to avoid sin for the saving of her soul.

Returning to His discourse with standby Pharisees in verses 12-30, Jesus defends His witnessing of self and speaks of His impending return to heaven. The Pharisees claimed that His word alone as to His identity and purpose was insufficient, since 2 unrelated witnesses were usually needed to establish fact under Jewish law.

Jesus contended that witnessing of Himself was true evidence because He knew where He came from and where He would return, a fact they knew not based on their human view. In addition, since the Father who sent Him also bore witness of Him, the requirement for 2 witnesses was met. To this, the Pharisees asked 'Where is Your Father?' Curtly, Jesus told them they would not know His Father, since they didn't recognize Him.

For this testy exchange, they had in mind seizing Him but were restrained for 'His time had not yet come.' Jesus continued with His rebuke of them, telling them they would not be able to find Him after His departure, and without Him in their lives they would die in their sin. They did not understand what He said, but wondered if He was speaking of self- destruction, and just who was He.

Many finally believed in Him, when He told them that they would realize who He was when they lifted Him up (crucifixion), and realized that He had been sent by God to do His will. Then He told them in verses 31-34, they would know the truth, as if they were His disciples, by believing His word, and thereby be set free from the slavery of sin. Apart from Christ, a sinful person has no contact with spiritual reality, and is in the wilderness of disbelief and skepticism.

In 37-59, Jesus lectured the Pharisees as Abraham's descendants on their rejection of His teachings and their animosity towards Him. When they claimed Abraham as their father, He refuted this because of their hateful spirit to Him, contrary to Abraham's views. Then they claimed God as their true father, with a snide denial of a fornication birth, thereby implying that Jesus was conceived out of wedlock, as alleged by malicious gossips. Jesus ignored this remark, to tell them they would love Him if God was really their father.

They were unable to hear and understand His words because Satan was their father, who had their ears tuned only for his lies, to the exclusion of truth as God provides. As the author of all lies, Satan calls evil good, and good evil, and promises freedom in sin.

The Jews charged Jesus with being a demon possessed Samaritan, which He denied. He rebuked them for dishonoring Him when His objective was to honor Father God. Those who were so vile would be judged and punished by God, but they still could accept and obey the teachings of Jesus and be saved from spiritual damnation. It was their choice!

The Jews continued to badger Jesus, labeling Him a demon for claiming to be greater than their dead ancestral father Abraham; saying He could keep someone from a physical death, as they understood it. Jesus repeated the statement that He was glorified by His Father, who they claimed as their God, but in reality did not know Him as Jesus did. By saying otherwise, they would see Him to be a liar like them.

When Jesus said that their father Abraham was delighted that he would see Jesus coming as the Messiah, they reacted indignantly that this was impossible because Jesus was not old enough to have known Abraham personally. To this, Jesus said, 'before Abraham, I AM!' That was the last straw to them, His remark was blasphemy to their ears, and they picked up stones to pelt Him. He miraculously escaped from the temple by passing through them in a way that kept Him from harm.

VIEWPOINTS: By identifying Himself as 'I AM' Jesus timed His existence to be before Abraham, to the time of creation, and from eternity past, as stated in Ch. 1:1-2. Recognition that Jesus is one in word and action with His Father was confirmed when He was <u>resurrected to life from death after His crucifixion</u>. The Jews evidently understood His statement 'before Abraham was, I AM' as a divine claim, which they could not accept. This triggered their violent reaction to stone Him for making a presumptive blasphemous claim.

CHAPTER 9: In this scripture, unique to John's Gospel, Jesus performs the 6th 'sign' miracle recorded by John, <u>by healing a blind man</u> in verses 1-12. When first seen by the disciples, they asked if his blindness was because of sin by him or his parents, a common view in those days. Denying this, Jesus declared that God would work a miracle of healing through Him, because as a light to the world, <u>He must do good during His remaining days.</u> Departing from His usual method of merely speaking words of healing, Jesus mixed spit with fine dirt to make a <u>mud patty which He applied to the man's eyes,</u> and then told him to wash it off in the Pool of Siloam. The man obeyed, presumably being led by a companion to the pool, and presto, his sight was restored.

While the man could not see Christ, nor did he have knowledge of His presence, Christ saw him and his need and chose to restore sight, although <u>requiring an act of obedience</u>. To receive healing, physically and spiritually, man must submit in faith to God.

People who were acquainted with the man were puzzled by his ability to see, thinking he might be a look-alike. When assured that he was the man they knew, they <u>wanted to know how it happened.</u> He explained, but could not tell where Jesus went.

In verses 12-34, the poor man was badgered by the Pharisees because he had been healed on the Sabbath. My, my, how many spiritually blind eyes have been opened by the preaching of the gospel on the Lord's day! While they could not deny the miracle of restored sight, they <u>persisted in viewing it as a sinful act</u>, done by an ungodly person. They wanted to know how it happened, who did it, and who He was. The man told them what he knew and that he believed Jesus was a prophet.

Thinking that the man may not have been blind, the Pharisees inquired of his parents who confirmed their son was born blind, <u>but they denied knowledge of his healing</u>, saying he could speak for himself. Calling the man back again, they made him swear to tell the truth, because they felt that Jesus was a sinner. The man told them that he could not say if Jesus was a sinner, but could only tell of his healing by Him.

They requested another accounting of the healing, to which the man said in exasperation, '<u>You got the whole story but won't listen and believe</u>, do you want to become His disciple?' Feeling insulted by this question, they accused him of being a follower of Jesus, as opposed to being a follower of Moses as they professed to be. They could not bear to think of Jesus as the Messiah, because His conduct and doctrine was <u>contrary to their</u> <u>expectations of kingly pomp and ceremony.</u>

At this point, the man spoke boldly to tell the leaders they were blind to the truth, that Jesus could not <u>heal unless He came from God with this power.</u> Having experienced the power and grace of the Lord Jesus, the man seemed to wonder at their willful rejection of Him. In anger, the leaders called the man a sinner, not qualified to teach them anything, and therefore <u>banned him from their places of assembly.</u>

As living evidence of Christ's glory, the man evidently wished to lend credence to His grace to all who desired the same conviction, but the disbelief of the Pharisees was frustrating to him. In verses 35-41, Jesus hears about the man's harassment, finds him, and asks, '**Do you believe in the Son of Man?**' The man said he would, if He knew more about Him. Jesus told him, '**You are looking at Him, talking with you!**' The man believed and worshipped Jesus. True faith through the Holy Spirit comes like the wind, without sound, without a sense of direction, and in a most compelling manner.

Jesus ends this episode by telling the man that He came to judge the people of the world, to give spiritual sight to those who needed and accepted it, but to leave those who were blind to the truth with their own earthly views.

Hearing this also, the Pharisees resented being called blind, so Jesus told them they would be innocent if truly blind to the truth, but as long as they rejected the truth which should have been apparent to them, they were guilty of sin. Their self-conceit and misguided self-confidence remained steadfast as they rejected Christ's mission of mercy, making the degree and guilt of their sin unpardoned, and the power of it unbroken. This is a manifestation of many in the world today, who yield to Satan's distortions of truth.

CHAPTER 10: Unique to John's Gospel is Jesus' discourse in verses 1-21 about sheep, a sheepfold, and the shepherd who cared for the sheep, in which He presents Himself to the Pharisees as the true and good spiritual Shepherd. The sheep are the people that Christ came to save, at that point the Jews, but later the Gentiles are included.

The sheepfold, as the church of the new covenant, to ultimately include Jews and Gentiles, is subject to invasion by false prophets who attempt to steal away members of the flock with deceptive teachings for their own gain. Jesus is God's Shepherd charged with the provision of a safe environment for spiritual growth and integrity.

Jesus told how sheep can and do recognize their shepherd apart from strangers, making it possible to lead them to pasture (spiritual nourishment) and back to safety from a dangerous world. He leads both ways through the gateway of life, thus being the door through which His followers should travel.

When the Jews failed to understand this allegory, Jesus amplified by telling them they were the thieves and robbers trying to invade the sheepfold without going through the proper door, meaning Himself. As the true Shepherd for His church, Jesus was willing to give His life for His sheep, whereas a hired hand would abandon them when threatened with danger by evil trespassers, which He called wolves.

Just as God and Christ are one, with intimate knowledge between them, so is Christ with His sheep, if they have recognized Him as their Shepherd. Jesus said it was also His objective to gather other sheep into His church, if they were lost and wandering about. He loved all sheep and would die for them, whether secure in His flock, or in need of a sanctuary. Just as His Father God loved Him for His willingness to die as an offering to open a gateway to forgiveness of the sins of His sheep, His restoration to life became their gateway to eternal life with Him, as willed by God.

The Jews and their leaders could not understand this word of truth from Jesus. Some said He was 'nuts' or demon possessed, not to be listened to, but others felt that He was neither because He made a blind man to see. Satan ruins many souls by putting blinders over their spiritual eyes, to obscure the truth of God's word with a mantle of self-conceit and stubbornness. The wisdom of man is often foolishness to God!

In verses 22-38, John speaks of more harassment that Jesus endured in Jerusalem a few months later, at the Feast of Dedication celebrated in December. While in the temple on Solomon's Porch, Jews demanded that He tell them clearly if He was Christ.

His reply was, 'I've told you through my works done in God's name, but you refuse to believe because you are not sheep of My flock.' He said they would heed His words if they were His sheep, and they would follow Him to receive eternal life, a gift from God, because He and God were united in securing all who will hear and obey.

These words so enflamed the Jews they were ready to stone Jesus, for the blasphemy of presenting Himself as God, in their judgment. Jesus pointed out that Old Testament scripture referred to men who represented God in some capacity (perhaps as judges), as 'gods.' (See Ps. 82:6) Since such scripture was still authoritative in their lives, Jesus said He could not be guilty of blasphemy because His works of miracles were divinely founded in God, making He and the Father as one.

As with many professing believers of today, these Jews were the real blasphemers, because they misapplied the scripture that justified and confirmed His identity as 'the Christ.' They should have seen this truth as dependent on scripture and accepted Him in true faith.

In 39-42, the Jews decided to seize Him, but He escaped again in His own way. His time had not yet come! Returning to Jordan, many converts of John the Baptist came to Him in true faith. Christ's gospel will prevail somewhere always.

CHAPTER 11:   John records the 7th and last 'sign' miracles that Jesus accomplished, in verses 1-44, the resurrection of Lazarus, the brother of Mary and Martha, all beloved friends of Jesus. When the news came from Judea of Lazarus' illness, Jesus said that it was not to end in death but it was to glorify Him and God. After 2 days, He proposed heading back to Judea but the disciples warned of the people's intention to kill Him. Even though He delayed for 2 days, His intentions were good, because He had a right time in mind.

Jesus remarked that in 12 hours of daylight, anyone could walk without stumbling, but if they walked at night, they would stumble. This odd remark seems to be speaking of traveling on the road of life in God's will, with the illumination of the Holy Spirit, to avoid temptations and pitfalls of sin. It may have been His way of saying that He knew when to return to Lazarus in the light of God's will.

When He added that Lazarus was just sleeping, so He could wake him up, the disciples assumed that recovery was under way, perhaps thinking that returning was unnecessary. Jesus then clarified that Lazarus was dead, for which He was glad, because the disciples would now see a more marvelous miracle to strengthen their belief in Him. As they began their return, disciple Thomas said, 'Lets go along and die with our Lord.'

Jesus found Lazarus after 4 days in the tomb, for which Martha somewhat chided Him by saying that her brother would not have died if Jesus had come sooner; yet she expressed some faith in Him. When Jesus said, 'Your brother will rise again,' she agreed that he <u>would rise in</u> <u>the last days (the rapture of the dead)</u>. Jesus asked her if she believed that all who believed in Him as the resurrection and the life would have eternal life.

After admitting only that she believed that He was the Christ, the Son of God who was in her presence, she <u>returned to sister Mary to say that Jesus was waiting for her</u>. Mary went to him and with sobs of grief voiced the same complaint that Lazarus would not have died if Jesus has come sooner.

Seeing her grief and that of friends with her, Jesus was deeply moved and asked where her brother lay in death. They agreed to show Him. Verse 35, said to be the shortest verse in the Bible, says that, 'Jesus wept.' Even though all saw how grief stricken He was, some still questioned <u>if He could have kept Lazarus from dying</u>.

At the tomb, Jesus asked others to remove the entrance stone, to which Martha commented that after 4 days, the dead body would smell badly. Jesus told her to have faith in the glory of God and with eyes uplifted to heaven, He thanked God for always hearing Him for the sake of those standing by, and then loudly called out, 'Lazarus, come out!' Lo and behold, <u>Lazarus</u> <u>came out still bedecked in grave clothes,</u> which Jesus ordered removed so he could go to his family.

Verses 45-57 (as in Matt. 26:1-5) tell of the reaction of the Jews who witnessed this event. Some believed even more in Him, but some complained to the chief priests and Pharisees who were more determined than ever to do away with Jesus, for <u>fear He would</u> <u>undermine their</u> <u>authority under Roman rule.</u> One high priest, named Caiaphas, strangely predicted Christ's atoning death for all humanity when he opined that it was 'better for Jesus to die for the people, rather than for the nation of Israel to be destroyed.'

Jesus went into hiding with His disciples in the remote village of Ephraim, to avoid the wrath of the Jews. This did not stop people from <u>wondering if He would appear at the</u> <u>Passover</u> <u>festival</u> in Jerusalem, in the face of a Pharisee order to report Him if seen.

CHAPTER 12:   On the 6th day before Christ's crucifixion, Jesus and the disciples came to Bethany to the home of Mary, Martha, and their resurrected brother Lazarus, as related in verses 1-11 (Matt. 26:6-13). Martha in her best capacity served a supper meal to all of them, while <u>Lazarus reclined at the table with Jesus.</u>

The affectionate and caring Mary demonstrated her love for Jesus by anointing His feet with a pound of very <u>expensive and fragrant perfumed oil</u>. It may have been her coveted long term savings! Using her lovely head of hair to wipe His feet, she thus anointed God's Anointed <u>to honor Him as her Anointed Savior.</u>

Judas, the betrayer disciple, protested this use of valuable oil, saying it should have been sold to put money for the poor in the cash box, from which he filched funds. Jesus mildly and lovingly said that <u>it was Okay for Mary to do what she did</u> in preparation for His burial (less than a week away); furthermore taking care of the poor was a never ending concern.

Later in the week, Jewish leaders heard of His presence in the area and came to see Him and the living Lazarus, thinking to kill him also, because his <u>resurrection turned many Jews</u>

to Jesus. Such enmity is hard to explain other than to acknowledge the anger of the wicked leads to utter folly and blind malice.

In 12-19, as in Matt. 21:1-11, many people met Jesus as He and the disciples entered Jerusalem about midweek, to lay palm branches across the road over which He passed, riding on a donkey as prophesied in Zech. 9:9. The people acclaimed Him for having brought Lazarus back to life, to which he had personally witnessed to them. The Pharisees were most jealous of this glorification of Jesus, and their anger was intensified.

Strangely, in 20-26, some Gentile Greeks came to worship at the forthcoming Passover, and having heard of Jesus asked disciple Philip if it was possible to see Him. Philip asked Andrew and the two then asked Jesus. Divine persuasion may have brought these Gentiles to further magnify Jesus as the Redeemer of all mankind, because of Jewish rejection. It is not clear if Jesus spoke directly to the Greeks or through the disciples.

Saying that His time for glorification was near, He used the allegory of a grain of wheat dying when planted to produce a harvest later; which equates to His death that can produce a harvest of spiritual blessings, including eternal life, to those who serve Him. This was for the Jews and the Gentiles to understand, believe in, and to embrace.

Emotionally troubled, Jesus continues in 27-36 to speak of His own death to come on the cross, asking if He should pray to God to spare Him, or suffer it to glorify God. From heaven, God said, 'I have been glorified by your submission, and will be again.' This came across as thunder to some, and as angels speaking to others. God recognized Jesus for yielding to an ordeal that would open the gate to heaven for a sinful world, by breaking the power of sin, condemning Satan as the great deceiver, and being a mighty power to draw souls into the kingdom of heaven.

Jesus told the people that God really spoke on their behalf, not His, although His saving grace would extend to all people as He returned to heaven. Thinking that Jesus as the Messiah would remain on earth forever, the people asked for clarification. Jesus identifies Himself as the light in their midst for a little while, to believe in Him, and to walk in His light to become His light. Then He quickly removed Himself from their presence.

John used Is. 53:1 and 6:9-10, in verses 37-42, to explain that the unbelief of most of the people was predicted and now was being fulfilled. Continued rejection of Jesus put hardness in their hearts. Many believers there, being more concerned with pleasing their contemporaries than God, did not express their faith in Jesus for fear of being ex- communicated from the synagogue.

In another effort to draw more believers to Himself and to God, Jesus cried out in verses 44-50, to declare that belief in Him was equivalent to belief in God who sent Him. Such belief gives the light of understanding to take one out of spiritual darkness. Rejection of Jesus on the other hand, puts unbelievers under the judgment of God.

By seeing the light of God's glory through Jesus, mankind learns to trust, obey and love both God and His Son. This brings freedom from the darkness of sin, clouded by ignorance, indifference, mistakes, and the miseries of life. Jesus closed this brief discourse emphasizing that all that He did and spoke was as God commanded Him to do, for the purpose of bringing everlasting life to all believers.

CHAPTER 13:   Jesus assumes the status of a servant in verses 1-17, to <u>wash the feet of</u> His <u>disciples</u>. He felt great love for them, in the knowledge that His earthly time was nearly over. To prepare them for their future role as divinely appointed servants of the Lord ministering to mankind, Jesus used the customary foot washing after a sandal walk over dusty roads, to teach them humility for greater effectiveness in service. This also <u>demonstrated the value of spiritual washing</u> (regeneration) to cleanse the soul from the pollution of sin.

He replaced His outer garment with a towel wrapped around his waist, thus appearing as a servant or a slave, who normally rendered this courtesy, and used the towel to wipe the feet. Simon Peter was <u>reluctant to have Jesus do such a menial task</u>, until Jesus told him he could no longer fellowship with Him, if he did not submit. Then Peter quickly yielded and offered his whole body for washing, perhaps realizing that Jesus was speaking of a spiritual cleansing through His purifying grace.

Jesus confirmed this precept by telling him that once totally bathed (regenerated by forgiveness of sin), foot washing was <u>symbolic of necessary spiritual maintenance,</u> to remove the dirt of sins incurred from the walk of life in an evil world. He declared that all but one of His disciples were spiritually clean.

After donning His outer garment, He told them that as He had done to them, they <u>should do to one another</u>. Humility is a mutual grace, when we give help to our fellow believers just as readily as we accept it from them; helping and being helped is a two way street to a richer and more fulfilling fellowship with one another, and blessings from the Lord.

Jesus identifies Judas as His betrayer in verses 18-30 (Matt. 26:21-25), not by name but <u>by the act of giving Judas a piece of bread</u> after dipping it in some kind of sauce. Jesus felt much grief as Judas took the bread, and said to him, 'Do what you do quickly.' Judas departed quickly into the night, stepping into spiritual darkness, apparently with no regret. He was under Satan's total control at that time, <u>completely separated from the love of Jesus.</u>

After this, in verses 31-38, Jesus gave the 11 disciples a preview of what was ahead, in which He would be glorified through His suffering in a way that would also glorify God, by satisfying Him through atonement for the sins of man.

Said to be the only time, Jesus addressed them as 'Little Children' to inform them that He would leave them shortly, but <u>they could not accompany Him.</u> He gave them a new commandment, that they should <u>love each other to the same degree that He had loved them.</u> By doing so, they would be a proper example of love in action, to all under their ministry.

Peter evidently did not take these words to heart because he wanted to know where Jesus was going. Jesus did not clarify this point, but merely told Peter that <u>he would follow after living out his life.</u> Peter persisted in his desire to leave with Jesus, saying he would give his life to do so. Jesus then left Peter speechless, by telling him <u>that he would deny Him 3 times before a rooster crowed.</u>

CHAPTER 14:   Jesus continued in this chapter to comfort and assure His disciples of a secure spiritual future for them, including a heavenly home, a closer relationship with God, and the help of the Holy Spirit <u>to cope with the remainder of their earthly days</u>. In verses 1-6, by believing in Him, Jesus assured them of a home in heaven which He would prepare before returning <u>to take his believers there</u>. (the Rapture). When Thomas asked for directions to His destination, Jesus merely responded with a truthful revelation that He was the only way to God.

In verses 7-11, accepting Christ as a mediator between God and man, brings comfort and joy to all forgiven sinners. By knowing Christ in a loving relationship, <u>man knows the Father in like manner</u>. Philip asked a human question—to be shown the Father, to which Jesus chided him for not realizing that <u>He was the manifestation of God in all ways</u>, by word and deed (his miracles), a fact that Philip should have known and believed after all the time they had been together.

Then in verses 12-18, Jesus assured them that in His name, their prayers to God would be answered, and a special helper, the Holy Spirit, would be provided to be in their hearts to <u>pave the way for their great works of ministry</u>. With the Holy Spirit lighting the way, the teachings of Jesus through them would <u>reveal God as the source of enlightenment</u>, holiness, and great power. As the gift of the Holy Ghost was given to the disciples, so it is <u>now given to God's own, all dedicated believers,</u> as an eternal source of righteousness and happiness. Again, Jesus promised to return for His children, and <u>not leave them as orphans</u> in this world.

In 19-31, Christ informed them that they would not see him after His ascension, but at a later time He would return from Heaven to receive all of His sheep. The world of <u>unbelievers would not see Him</u> at that time When asked why this was to be, Jesus emphasized that a future relationship with Him depended on sincere love of Him in one's heart, obedience to the word of God, and daily communication through the Holy Spirit with Him and the Father. Love of Christ and God begets obedience to serve diligently on earth <u>to add others</u> to the church.

Christ bestowed a special gift of peace on the disciples, <u>to overcome fear</u>, when life would bring conflict, or tribulation at the hands of Satan. The love they would maintain for Him and for God, as is true of all mankind, would sustain them, and give them joy as Satan is <u>defeated in his goals as prince of this world</u>. Jesus commanded the disciples, and in reality all believers, to rise up and do what God's wills through them in using their divinely endowed talents.

CHAPTER 15:   In this chapter, John related more of the farewell discourse of Jesus to His disciples, in which He spoke of 3 relationships: that of <u>fruitful believers with Him</u> and God, that of <u>friends filled with His love</u> showing their love for others, and <u>the relationship of faithful believers with unbelievers,</u> those under the influence of Satan.

In verses 1-8, the relationship of the believers with Christ is compared to that of a grapevine, or other fruit bearing vine, in which Christ is the root and central trunk, and the <u>believers are the fruit bearing branches.</u> The caretaker is God the Father who removes the dead or non-fruit bearing branches, and prunes back the fruit-bearing branches seasonally, so that the entire vine can be more fruitful.

The principle demonstrated by this metaphoric picture is that through Christ, human and divine natures are merged, as the root sap of the Holy Spirit nourishes the spiritual life of the believers, or branches of the church, for the whole <u>to become fruitful and productive in all ways.</u> For best results, dead or unfruitful members must be revived or removed, and constant pruning or refining of the fruitful (cleansing from sin) must be maintained. Nourishment (fellowship) between the branches and the trunk is necessary <u>for strength and vigor in overall service.</u>

Just as the caretaker seeks a good crop, God looks to Christians for productivity in His service, while they <u>demonstrate a disposition and lifestyle that Honors Him.</u> Faithfully abiding in Him produces more fruit, to enrich life with added joy and goodness.

Christ gave the key to an abiding relationship with Him, as 'obedience,' and between fellow believers it is 'love,' as stated in verses 9-17, with <u>the believer's love to be as God loved Christ.</u> Faithful obedience to God's commandments begets greater love for others, even to giving one's life for them. Jesus told the disciples that He looked upon them more as friends, rather than servants, <u>because they were His chosen ones</u> to bear fruit out of love for Him and one another. Loving one another was His firm command.

Christ spoke of the world's hatred for Him and His followers in 18-25, a hatred rooted in the failure of the world to recognize God, especially when He is revealed in truth. The world's ignorance is the foundation of its hatred against all disciples of Jesus, the doctrine of salvation, and <u>spiritual realities of life.</u> In His time, all Jews who rejected Him, His miracles, and His teachings, had no excuse for their sin, but they were fulfilling God's indictment as stated in Ps. 69:4, '<u>They hated me without cause.</u>'

In 26-27, Jesus promised that the Holy Spirit (Helper) to come after His departure, would be a powerful witness of <u>His stated purpose and mission under God's divine plan</u> for mankind. The disciples in turn would be more effective in their testimony and witness of Him. Believers who are baptized in the name of God the Father, Christ the Son, and the Holy Spirit must live accordingly in obedience, suffer if necessary, and die under God's umbrella of comfort and assurance,<u> to reap an inheritance of eternal life.</u>

CHAPTER 16:   Jesus continued His instructions to the 11 disciples, with warnings in verses 1-4 of dangers and persecutions ahead, rendered by <u>non-believers hostile to God's plan</u> for mankind. Some will bring suffering and isolation on the disciples in the name of God, therefore without justification for their acts. Believers are warned of such trouble as fulfillment of scriptural prophecy.

In 5-15, Jesus spoke of His imminent departure after which the Holy Spirit would take His place in the lives of the disciples, and all other believers, until His 2nd coming. He recognized their sorrow and assured them that it was really for their good that He would leave.

<u>The Holy Spirit would come to deal with the sins of the entire world</u>, but more importantly to reside in the being of all believers, thereby having a universal presence while Christ as a human was limited to one place at a time.

The Holy Spirit will confirm that all mankind is guilty of sins before God, <u>based on the righteousness of Christ.</u> Through the witness of believers and servants of the Lord, the Holy Spirit will open the eyes of many unbelievers to the truth of Christ's righteousness, convicting them of their sin of unbelief, so they will accept God's gift of forgiveness and salvation. All who reject this divine opportunity will be subjected to the <u>same judgment that Satan will receive.</u>

When Jesus told the disciples in verse 16, that He would shortly leave them to return to the throne of God, but then in <u>a short time they would see Him again</u>, they were puzzled and asked how this could be. Jesus discerned their bewilderment, and explained in 17-22, that when He died on the cross, they would be sorrowful while unbelievers would be pleased, but after His resurrection, <u>they would be most joyful</u>, as a mother is after enduring the pain of childbirth. With the Holy Spirit as the Comforter for the believer, joy will overcome the hostility of mankind and Satan, pain and sufferings of life, and the agony of death.

In 23-33, Jesus said that the day was coming (after His resurrection) when His enigmatic words would make sense, and they would know that He and God were united in love for them. His followers would then also know <u>they deserved no special favors from God,</u> so they would pray to Him in Christ's name, depending on His intercession before God. This helped the disciples to understand because they gained discernment of the divine mission of Christ.

Christ's final words were to warn the 11 that they would soon be scattered, leaving Him alone, and then they would suffer tribulation as they ministered in the world, but they were to <u>remain happy in the knowledge that He had won the victory over Satan.</u>

<u>VIEWPOINTS:</u>   The term 'a little while' in verses 16-19 can be misunderstood in terms of a time factor. It appears to mean that the disciples would not see Jesus for a short time after his arrest and crucifixion, but after His resurrection <u>they would see Him again for</u> a few days. It could also infer they would spiritually see Him after His ascension, in the power of the Holy Spirit. The term does not appear to have any connection to Christ's 2nd coming.

CHAPTER 17:   A 'high priestly prayer' is spoken by Jesus in this chapter, in 3 parts; for <u>His own glorification,</u> for the <u>safety and sanctification of His disciples,</u> and finally, for the <u>unity and glorification of all believers to come.</u>

For His own glorification, in verses 1-5, Jesus asked God to restore the heavenly glory He had before coming to earth, and that the disciples and all other believers resulting from His ministry, be <u>given eternal life and thereby glorify God the Father</u>. Praying as a mediator for His followers, Jesus presented them to the Father as <u>fulfillment of His mission</u> on earth, and as glorification to both He and the Father.

In verses 6-19, Jesus prayed specifically for the 11 disciples who remained loyal to Him, naturally excluding Judas, the betrayer. Declaring them to be <u>His own as a gift from God,</u> but equally belonging to God, Jesus asked for their safety in the world, from sin, from evil corruption by the world, and added strength and resolve in their ministerial efforts.

Being thoroughly indoctrinated in God's plan of salvation for mankind and prepared for service to reach the lost, Jesus presented His disciples to God for <u>sanctification in the truth of God's word and purpose.</u> As the Father and Son are one, Jesus prayed for unity among them within the body of Christ, to demonstrate to the world <u>the truth of God's word,</u> which stands in opposition to the evil spirits of the world. As Christ sanctified Himself in God's service, He asked for the disciples to be sanctified for the mission they would carry out.

Finally, in verses 20-25, Jesus prayed for all believers to come, from the preaching of God's word which He had given to the disciples, that <u>they would be united as one body,</u> through their faith and trust in Christ, the Father, with the Holy Spirit indwelled in them. Thus, all believers could serve to convince the world of the truth of God's word, of His love for mankind, and how they could <u>enjoy sweet communion with God and his saints</u>.

VIEWPOINTS: When speaking of Christ's true believers being united in one body, comprising the Church, one must wonder <u>why so many denominations exist</u> that fragment the main body. In Christ's prayer for unity in the body of believers, it appears that He was speaking of a single body of believers.

In the world today, many churches profess to being Christ centered, but their worship patterns seem to <u>focus more on other personalities,</u> such as the Virgin Mary, or a Saint. Some almost give total preference to the Holy Ghost, as an empowering factor in their spiritual lives, and their <u>benefactor of special gifts of the Spirit</u>.

Early churches were organized as a body in Christ with a mission to accomplish, under the leading of the Holy Spirit, but with <u>worship demonstrating the lordship of Christ.</u> The preeminent characteristic of a church under God's design, will demonstrate total devotion to Jesus Christ as Lord. For He established the church and laid the foundation for its existence by His redeeming <u>death and resurrection under the grace of God's power</u>.

One must assume that God, as the final judge, will filter through all the denominations to bring together those that are truly righteous in Christ's name, and cast aside those that have been polluted by Satan. Christ must be glorified as He reigns in glory over His Church.

CHAPTER 18: Verses 1-11 are an account of the betrayal of Christ by Judas and His arrest in the Garden of Gethsemane, as also told in Matt. 26:47-56. After His prayer above, Jesus went to the garden, where He often rested with His disciples. Knowing this, Judas <u>guided a group of armed Roman soldiers and temple officials</u> to the place at night. Since they carried torches and lanterns, Jesus saw them coming and as they arrived, He stepped in front of them to ask who they were seeking. To their reply "Jesus of Nazareth, He said, 'I am He.'

For some reason, perhaps surprise at His bold and ready admission, they quickly <u>stepped back and some fell to the ground</u>. Christ asked them again who they wanted; to their same reply, He again admitted His identity but asked them to let the disciples go their way. Then Simon Peter drew his sword and cut off the right ear of a high priest's servant, named Malchus. Jesus ordered him to sheath his sword, because <u>this was His ordeal to endure</u>. Nothing is said here about Judas identifying Jesus with a kiss, or Jesus restoring the ear, as stated in Luke 22:51.

In a composite of verses 12-14 and 19-24, Jesus is taken, bound, and brought before Annas, the father-in-law assistant of the official high priest Caiaphas, <u>for questioning about</u> His <u>doctrine and followers</u>. Jesus told them that He had nothing more to say than what they had heard Him say in the synagogues and temples, to which others could testify. A guard slapped Him, and rebuked Him for speaking rudely to the official.

Jesus asked why He was stricken for speaking the truth, rather than evil. Annas then sent him to Caiaphas for further interrogation. Christ was an example of meekness under duress <u>with His way of submission to God's will</u> in this case.

By bringing verses 15-18 and 25-27 together, a full account of Peter's denial of any association with Jesus is given, as also related in Matt. 26:69-75. Evidently the disciples were allowed to go their own way when Jesus was taken; two of them, Simon Peter, and another thought to be John, <u>followed as Jesus was led away</u> to the high priest's courtyard.

When a servant girl asked if he was a Jesus disciple, Peter denied it. Later, while warming himself by a bonfire, he was <u>asked again about his disciple status,</u> and for the 2nd time denied it. Then, a servant relative of Malchus, asked if he was the one he had seen in the garden with Jesus, and for the 3rd time Peter denied this, and the rooster crowed. Nothing more is said here of Peter's sorrowful departure.

Caiaphas sent Jesus to the Roman governor Pilate for further examination and sentencing, in verses 28-40 (Matt. 27:1-2, 11-14), under the <u>charge of being an evildoer.</u> Pilate tried to pass the buck back to the Jewish officials, but they rightly claimed this was a case out of their jurisdiction, for it could call for the death penalty.

Pilate asked Jesus if he was the King of the Jews, to which Jesus asked if this is what was told to him by the Jews. Going further, Pilate asked what offense Jesus had committed. Jesus answered indirectly that <u>He had done nothing wrong</u> because His kingdom was not of this world, but if it had been, His servants would have shielded him from the Jews.

Persisting, Pilate asked again if He was a king, to which <u>Jesus replied affirmatively</u> that He was born to be sovereign, and came into the world to be a witness to the truth of His mission, which believers would hear and accept. In frustration perhaps, Pilate said, 'What is truth?' and told the Jews that <u>He could find nothing wrong with Jesus.</u>

Under a strange custom of law, Pilate then offered to release Jesus to them in honor of the Passover. This was a <u>compromise solution that he preferred</u> rather than insult them by freeing Jesus unconditionally. As in Matt. 27:15-23, the Jews demanded that Pilate release a common robber named Barabbas, in place of Jesus, <u>who they wanted crucified.</u> Pilate was inclined to yield to the Jews; being governed more by worldly expediency than by fair rules of justice.

<u>CHAPTER 19:</u> In verses 1-15, yielding to the demand of the Jews, Pilate had Jesus brutally flogged by the Roman soldiers, who also implanted a crown of thorns on His head, and adorned Him with a purple robe, <u>so they could mock Him</u> as 'K ing of the Jews.' They also slapped him.

Pilate brought Jesus before the Jewish officials with the comment, 'Behold the Man!' The officials reacted with loud cries to 'Crucify Him.' To this, Pilate, told them to <u>do it</u> <u>themselves because he had no reason to do so.</u>

The Jews responded by citing a law of theirs which prescribed the death penalty if someone falsely <u>claimed to be the Son of God.</u> This bothered Pilate and he again asked Jesus where He came from, but Jesus remained silent. When Pilate pointed out to Jesus that he had the power to either crucify or release Him, Jesus said that <u>he really had no power over Him,</u> but the one (Judas or Caiaphas) who delivered Him to Pilate had committed the greater sin. Pilate continued to try to release Jesus, but the Jewish officials threatened him by saying that he <u>would not find favor with Caesar,</u> if Jesus were released when He claimed to be a king.

The Jews blasphemed God by saying they had no king except Caesar. Reluctantly, but thinking of his own welfare, Pilate conceded and <u>had Jesus led away to be crucified</u> in verses 16-37, as also related in Matt. 27:32-56. John said that Jesus carried the cross to Golgatha, the

Place of a Skull (see Mark 15:21-22). He was <u>hung on a cross with two common criminals,</u> one on each side of Him. Pilate put a sign over His cross reading, 'JESUS OF NAZARETH, THE KING OF THE JEWS.'

Naturally, some Jews protested over this sign, saying it should be changed to, '<u>He said, I am the King of the Jews.</u>' Pilate told them it would stay as written, thereby confirming in a sense that Jesus really was King of the Jews. Roman soldiers divided His outer garment 4 ways for each to have a part, and <u>drew lots to decide who would get the inner tunic,</u> thereby fulfilling David's prophecy in Ps. 22:18.

At the foot of His cross, stood His mother Mary, her sister, and Mary Magdalene, <u>with disciple John.</u> Jesus told His mother to behold John as her son, and <u>told him to behold his mother.</u> John became the substitute caring son of Mary. What an example this was, to honor parents in life and death; to provide for their needs, and to <u>promote their comfort by every means possible.</u>

When Jesus said that He was thirsty, the soldiers offered Him sour wine on a sponge; after sipping of it, He suddenly said, 'It is finished,' and <u>bowed His head in death.</u> Since He suffered for the sins of both Jews and Gentiles, it was germane that the Jews should first propose His death, and the Gentiles bring it about. Equal fault!

Not only was His suffering finished, both physical and spiritual, but the atonement for <u>man's redemption and salvation was now completed.</u> Freely, He gave His life for a paid up insurance policy, to wipe out mankind's sin indebtedness, and to provide <u>a passport to eternal life with Him.</u> All that remains for the sinner to receive this gift of redemption, is to sign the application willingly!

With a pre-Sabbath sunset time deadline, the Jews asked Pilate to break the legs of the cross victims <u>to quickly bring on death.</u> This was done to both of the criminals first, but not to Jesus when they realized He was already dead, after a soldier pierced His side with a spear <u>to produce a discharge of blood and water.</u> John verified that this was a true account because he personally witnessed it.

Two prophetic scriptures were fulfilled in this instance: 1st, 'Not one of His bones shall be broken' per Num. 9:12 and Ps. 34:20; and 2nd, 'They shall look on Him whom they pierced,' per Zech. 12:10 and Rev. 1:7. The discharge of blood and water signified <u>2 wonderful benefits all believers receive through Christ,</u> atonement for sin, and purification into righteousness.

Verses 38-42 (Matt. 27:57-61) relate how Jesus was removed from the cross and buried in a tomb. A secret follower of Jesus, a wealthy Joseph of Arimathea, asked for and received permission from Pilate to remove His body, and with the help of Nicodemus (see John 3:1-9, & 7:50), <u>they embalmed His body with spices wrapped within strips of linen</u> and placed it in Joseph's personal unused tomb. This fulfilled the prophecy of Is. 53:9, that Jesus was rich in His death and burial. No shroud was described in His burial as some religious authorities suggest!

These two men valued Christ's person and teachings so much, that the crucifixion could not lessen their devotion. Burial alone in a new unused tomb also removed the possibility for some to say that another person was resurrected.

CHAPTER 20:   The tomb is found empty on an early Sunday morning, before daylight, as told in verses 1-10, and in Matt. 28:1-10. John's account is that Mary Magdalene went alone to the tomb and when she saw the stone rolled back from the tomb entrance, she went to Simon Peter and the disciple John (beloved of Jesus), to report that <u>someone had stolen the body from the tomb</u>. This may have been her assumption, because nothing is said here about her looking into the tomb to verify that Jesus was missing, as in other gospels. Also, John said nothing of any other women accompanying her to the tomb. There are other gospel differences on this.

John relates that it was Peter and John who first discovered the tomb was empty, John being the first to enter the tomb. Both saw the <u>linen cloths lying in an orderly fashion</u> with the head cloth neatly folded and laid separately, giving the appearance that they were carefully and deliberately removed from Christ's body.

John says that the 2 disciples then left, returning to their homes in 11-18, while Mary Magdalene remained outside the tomb weeping, before she <u>stooped down and looked into</u> it. That is when she saw 2 seated angels in white, one at the head and the other at the foot location where <u>Jesus' body had laid in the tomb</u>.

<u>VIEWPOINTS:</u>   Some believe that Jesus supernaturally removed Himself from the linen strips, leaving them in the hollow shape of His body. If that were so, why would the angels have been part of the scene? It is my belief that the 2 angels were ordered by God to do the task, and they were instrumental in restoring life to Jesus, as they <u>removed the linen cloths, the bonds of death.</u> Their seated positions at the head and foot locations seems to symbolize this involvement. This resurrection differed from that of Lazarus, who was able to walk out still garbed in burial cloth, that others had to remove.

*****

When asked why she wept, Mary complained that someone had removed His body to an unknown place. Turning around, she saw Jesus, but thought He was a gardener, and <u>asked if He had taken the body so she could retrieve it</u>. Jesus shocked her back to reality with a single word, her name, 'Mary!'

With one word, 'Rabboni' (Teacher), she acknowledged Him, and evidently wrapped her arms around him, because He asked her to release him and go <u>tell the disciples that He would ascend to be with his Father God</u>, who was also theirs.

That Sunday evening, while in their abode behind locked doors for fear of the Jews, Jesus <u>suddenly appeared before them</u> in verses 19-25, saying, 'Peace be with you.' To ascertain recognition, He showed His nail pierced hands and the spear belly wound. <u>They were amazed and joyful</u>. No doors can shut out Christ's presence!

Jesus repeated His words of peace, saying as the Father sent Him, He would also send them, meaning <u>to carry on His ministry to the world</u>. He then imparted the Holy Spirit on them, as if exhaling a breath of fresh air, to give them spiritual authority to reveal how others could <u>receive forgiveness of their sins.</u> Jesus must have disappeared after this episode.

In 24-29, along comes Thomas (the Doubter) 8 days later, who was <u>not present when Jesus appeared earlier</u>. When told that they had seen Jesus, he expressed doubt as to the identity of

Jesus, unless he could thoroughly <u>examine His hand and side wounds</u>. With no doors opened, Jesus supernaturally appeared as before, with the same message, 'Peace to you.'

Jesus instructed Thomas to probe His wounds, and to believe. Thomas said, 'My Lord and my God,' to which Jesus said, 'You have believed because you have seen me; blessed are all who believe in me without seeing me first.' This blessing is for all sinners who would repent and <u>believe in Jesus as their spiritual redeemer.</u>

Jesus performed other miracles before the disciples that John does not describe. In conclusion, John clearly stated his purpose in writing his gospel was to provide convincing evidence that Jesus is the Messiah who fulfilled God's promises to Israel, and subsequently to the Gentile world, so that <u>all who believe will inherit eternal life.</u>

CHAPTER 21: Some time later, at the Sea of Galilee, Jesus appeared again, in the presence of Simon, John, and 5 other disciples, in verses 1-14. For some reason, Peter had decided to go fishing at night, and the other 6 joined him. They caught nothing, and in the morning they saw <u>a man standing on the nearby shore</u>, who called out, 'Friends, have you any fish,' to which they replied, 'None.'

Jesus told them to throw their net out to the right side of the boat. They did so, and lo and behold, the net was laden so full of fish they <u>could not retrieve it</u>. John recognized Jesus and told Peter, 'It is the Lord.' In great excitement, Peter replaced his outer garment and jumped into the sea to swim ashore. The others rowed to shore <u>dragging the full net in the water.</u> This was the 3rd appearance of Jesus told by John.

Arriving on shore, they saw that Jesus had prepared some fish over a fire. He asked them to bring more fish, which they did, out of the <u>total catch of 153 fish.</u> Jesus invited them to eat breakfast with Him, and served them fish and bread. Without a doubt, they knew He was their Jesus!

Then in a strange way, Jesus interrogates Simon Peter, to restore his relationship with Him, and to perhaps <u>remove the sting of Peter's earlier 3 denials</u>. Jesus asks him 3 times if he loved Him, which Peter said, 'Yes Lord, you know that I do.' To Peter's replies Jesus said, 'Feed My sheep,' then 'Tend My sheep,' and again, 'Feed My sheep.'

He continued by telling Peter that while he was younger he walked where he wanted to, but when he would be older, someone would bind him and <u>take him where he did not want to go</u>. This was a prediction of the manner in which Peter would die, crucified upside down. Then Jesus told him, 'Follow me.'

Peter then asked about John's future, to which Jesus said, 'If I want him to remain alive until I return, what business is it of yours. You just follow me!' The other disciples misunderstood this to mean that John would not die, but that was not what Jesus meant.

John's final remark was that there were many other things that he could have written about Jesus but if he had, the world would not have had room for all of it.

SUMMARY: Chapters 14-17 are most significant in John's Gospel, for the intense indoctrination Jesus gave his disciples to prepare them for their role under God's Great Commission <u>to plant the Christian Church in the world.</u> Jesus taught His disciples that as

His followers, they were to be involved in a movement that would continue to grow, after His Ascension. Although the disciples found it difficult to witness to non-Jews, this was done effectively by the Hellenistic Jewish Christians, who were the returned <u>Jews from the dispersion that were converted at Pentecost.</u>

Many parts of John's Gospel are unique for content, with little or no similar detail in the other 3 gospels. Chapter 21, for example, is the sole account of Jesus enjoying a final appearance on the shore of the Sea of Galilee, and His reconciliation dialogue with Simon Peter. Readers are encouraged to read the separate accounts listed on the Gospel Cross-Reference Index, for a complete picture of all activities.

*****

SPREADING THE GOSPEL

The Gospel accounts of the life and ministry of Jesus Christ is followed by the Book of Acts, written by Luke, to document the beginning of the Great Commission effort by the disciples (to become known as Apostles), to carry Christ's message of salvation to the entire world, including interested Jews and all the Gentiles. It is a fascinating story of Old Testament prophecy fulfillment and Christ's predictions on the creation of the Christian Church.

ACTS—BOOK FIVE

This is the 2nd book written by Luke; in combination with the Gospel of Luke, it constitutes the largest portion by a single author for the New Testament. It is believed to have been written about 63 AD, covering about 30 years of early church history, from the Day of Pentecost to the end of Paul's imprisonment at Rome.

In the manner of an historian, Luke's purpose in writing the book was to give an orderly account of the spread of Christianity from the Jewish community in Jerusalem to the Roman world. As a traveling companion in the ministry of the Apostle Paul, he was able to witness much of the achievemants by the disciples continuing the work of their Messiah, Jesus Christ. His writing mainly identifies with themes and emphasis which support the teachings of Jesus through the disciples, as fulfillment of Christ's plan for the Gentile world.

ACTS reassures believers that their faith in Christ rests on facts. The book tells what happened following Christ's ascension. He began work on His new body, the Christian Church, with the help of the Holy Spirit, using the talents of His initial crew of 11 disciples, They were supplemented later by a replacement for Judas, and the Apostle Paul. The disciples did not testify about a dead Christ, but the living Christ they had seen with their own eyes. He lives and works through His Church!

The main themes to be perceived are: 1-Emphasis on the work of the Holy Spirit, 2-A concern for outcasts and sinners, 3-An emphasis on women in the church, and 4-The piety of Jesus and His followers. The disciple Peter is the dominant character ministering to the Jews in the 1st 9 chapters; thereafter most activity revolves around the Apostle Paul.

Chapters 1-7 focus on the early church in Jerusalem, and the persecution by Jewish leaders that forced many new converts to leave for safer places. The hostility of the persecutors actually facilitated the spread of the gospel throughout Judea and Samaria, as related in Chapters 8-9. With Paul's conversion in Chapter 9, the gospel moved on to Gentile nations, beginning with major population centers of the Roman Empire, as related in Chapters 10-15. World outreach evangelism is described in Chapters 16-19, through Paul with the help of a few disciples, until his imprisonment in Chapters 20-28.

The spirituality and vision of the Christians in Antioch shaped the ministry described in chapters 12-19. Their sensitivity to God's Spirit prompted the three missionary journeys of Paul and the spread of the gospel throughout Asia Minor and later to Europe and Rome. Paul's arrival in Rome set the advent of Christ's message at the center of Gentile civilization; it also was the symbolic completion of Paul's mission which began in Acts 1:8.

In term's of God's agenda for evangelizing the world, the book of ACTS can be roughly divided into 4 parts, as follows:

1. God's preparations for the mission of Jesus to continue (Ch. 1-7)
2. He overcomes human barriers to continue Jesus' mission (Ch. 8-13)
3. He expands Jesus' mission beyond geographical boundaries (Ch. 14-20)
4. He prevents human limits from hindering Jesus' mission (Ch. 21-28)

CHAPTER 1:   Confirming his authorship, Luke tells his friend Theophilus in verses 1-2, just as he did in Ch. 1:1-3, of the Gospel of Luke, that he wrote that book to <u>tell what Jesus set out to do during His time on earth.</u> Now, in verses 3-9, he reviews what Jesus did during 40 days from His resurrection to His ascension to heaven.

Jesus commanded the 11 disciples to remain in Jerusalem to wait <u>for the baptism of the Holy Spirit,</u> (unison in the body of Jesus Christ) before commencing in great spiritual power their evangelistic mission to the Jews and the Gentiles. They wanted to know if He would then restore Israel as an independent kingdom, but He told them this was God's business, while their business was to <u>be witnesses of His teachings and to carry them to all the world.</u>

Verses 9-11, tell of Christ's ascension at Mount Olivet into the clouds, while 2 angels standing with the disciples, asked why they were looking up (thinking Jesus was gone forever), and assured them <u>He would return in the same manner as He left.</u>

Returning to Jerusalem in 12-14, a Sabbath day's distance of about ½ mile, the disciples assembled in an upper room abode they had used before <u>to spend time in prayer.</u> Those named included Peter, James, John, Andrew, Philip, Thomas, Bartholomew, Matthew, another James, Simon, and Jude (son of James), 11 in all. They were joined by women of Galilee who had followed Jesus, <u>along with Christ's mother Mary,</u> and His 4 brothers, James, Joses, Simon, and Judas (see Matt. 13:55).

About 120 other believers in Jesus had joined them during this waiting period, in verses 15 -26, when Peter in a leadership role, <u>proposed that a new disciple be chosen</u> to replace the betrayer Judas, citing prophetic words of David from Ps. 41:9 as justification. He described the death of Judas who fell from a tree, when the hanging rope broke, to be disemboweled; then he was buried in a field purchased with his betrayal money. Peter referred to Ps. 69:25 & Ps. 108:8 as God's word that a replacement should be chosen.

Peter specified that a dedicated long-standing follower of Christ up to the time of His ascension <u>should be selected as a reliable witness</u> of His resurrection. Two were proposed: a man named Joseph, or Barsabas, and another named Matthias. After prayer to God that the right one be identified, they drew lots to select <u>Matthias, who completed the original 12.</u>

CHAPTER 2:   This chapter is exclusively about the Day of Pentecost, or Feast of First Fruits, when <u>Christ's church was activated by the Holy Spirit,</u> said to have occurred 10 days after His ascension, and 50 days after His resurrection. In 1-13, while the 120 or so followers were gathered in what may have been a temple, a loud sound like a wind storm (hurricane) filled the place. Then fingers of fire seemed to emanate from each person, as each was enveloped and filled with the Holy Spirit, and given the <u>ability of speaking in other languages</u> not their own.

There is no indication in this narrative that such a gift was permanent, or was to be concurrent <u>with the infilling of the Holy Spirit in the future of the church.</u>

Many religious Jews from other parts were nearby, and on hearing the noise coming from the excited followers, they drew near to observe what was happening. Many of them may have understood and expected to hear Greek or Aramaic, but they were <u>amazed to hear their own locale language.</u> The text says that all the followers began to speak in other languages;

perhaps there were primary speakers, such as the chosen disciples of Christ, otherwise the din of many voices could made understanding. difficult to the hearers.

People from about 15 separate language locales are named in verses 9-11, that heard their language spoken, but verse 13 mentions others who did not understand any strange language, and thought the followers spoke gibberish because they were drunk from to much wine.

Verses 14-36 give an account of a sermon that Peter delivered to the crowd, presumably in his own language, Aramaic, or Greek. He pointed out that no one was drunk because it was early in the day, about 9 a.m. He proceeded to quote the prophet Joel in 17-21 (from Joel 2:28-32) where the gift of the Holy Spirit was promised 'in the last days' (prior to Christ's 2nd coming), to enable young and old people to prophesy, young men to have visions, and old men to have dreams.

Afterwards, there will be atmospheric and earthly disturbances that will bring fire and vapor (volcanic?), causing personal injury, blotting out the sun and turning the moon red. Yet, those who call on the name of God will be saved. Peter urged his listeners to hear his words about the miraculous and supernatural ministry of the Jesus they had crucified, who was now raised up according to God's plan.

Peter then quoted paraphrased words from David's Ps. 16:8-11, as added proof to what the disciples had witnessed, that the resurrected Jesus Christ is the Messiah who provides eternal life and joy to His own. Peter spoke of the life and death of David, who had received God's promise that He would raise up the Messiah to sit on a throne, after His resurrection from death, as they had witnessed.

In 37-47, the effect of Peter's words on the unsaved crowd is described as being a knife to their hearts, as a sharp conviction of their need. They asked what they should do, and Peter told them to repent of their sins, be baptized, and receive the anointing of the Holy Spirit This promise of God's salvation was available to them, their families, and all others.

Those who accepted his admonition, about 3000 of them, were baptized that day, and as a growing family, they continued learning from the disciples, eating and praying with them. They were in awe of the miracles and wondrous revelations rendered by them. At this point, the key followers of Jesus, the anointed 12 disciples, having been endowed with the spiritual gift of leadership to the church and the training of others for ministry, earned the title 'Apostle.'

Members of this embryo church merged into one big family, by pooling their possessions for all to share, enjoying meals together, and worshipping God. They were well liked and respected by others, many of whom were saved each day to join the church. A quality of spiritual fellowship was demonstrated that many churches of this age lack and need.

CHAPTER 3: At 3 p.m., Peter and John went to the local temple for a time of prayer, in verses 1-10. There they encountered a beggar man lame from birth who was carried to the temple gate daily. When he asked alms of them, Peter said, 'Look at us,' but gave no gift.

Then Peter said that he had no silver or gold to give, but he would give what he did have, and commanded, 'In the name of Jesus Christ of Nazareth, rise up and walk.' With a helping hand from Peter, the man readily got up and vigorously walked into the temple with them, where he leapt about and praised God. People who knew the man were amazed and filled with awe, because <u>they knew it was a genuine healing.</u>

More people gathered around them, giving Peter inspiration to do some preaching as related in verses 11-26. Peter immediately made it clear that Jesus, whom they had sent to the cross, <u>was still the source of healing,</u> because He had been glorified through resurrection by their God of Abraham, Isaac and Jacob. Faith in His power to heal enabled the man to walk for the 1st time, even though <u>he was about 40 years old</u> (see Ch. 4:22).

Peter acknowledged that the Jews had rejected Christ out of ignorance, which was also fulfillment of prophecy. He challenged them to repent of their sin of unbelief, and to accept Jesus as their Messiah, so they would <u>enjoy a time of spiritual refreshment</u> in His presence. For all Christians, that special time will be when Christ returns to gather His own for His millennial reign.

Peter paraphrased scripture from Deut. 18:17-19, that Moses (the favorite prophet of the Jews) spoke to the Israelites in the wilderness, concerning a prophetic being (Christ) that <u>God would give them to heed and obey,</u> or risk destruction if they refused to do so. He reminded them that other prophets from the time of Samuel had foretold such a happening. The Jews were God's chosen people to be given the first opportunity to accept Christ, and be <u>forgiven of their iniquities.</u>

CHAPTER 4:   In verses 1-4, persecution by the temple officials and Sadducees began from this time onward; they were disturbed that the preaching of Peter and John on the resurrection of Jesus had swelled the <u>number of believers to about 5000</u>. They took the two men into custody for an interrogation the following day.

The interrogation, described in verses 5-22, was conducted by the high priest group in a Jerusalem location. The 1st question asked of Peter and John was, 'In whose power or name did you heal the man?' How sad it was that they showed no compassion and joy for the lame man being healed.

With the Holy Spirit giving strength and boldness, Peter responded that he and John should not be tried for the good done to the lame man, because Jesus, whom God had raised from a death they had caused, <u>was the Great Healer in this case,</u> and this proved Him to be the Messiah. He quoted Ps. 118:22 to characterize Jesus as 'the stone which was rejected by you (Jews), the builders, but which became the chief corner stone,' the foundation of the new covenant church, as the door to salvation.

Knowing that the 2 apostles were relatively uneducated, the priestly jurors were amazed, and began to see them as Christ's spokesmen. They recessed the hearing for a bit to privately discuss what course of action they should take. They decided to threaten them with harm if they did not <u>cease preaching in the name of Jesus</u>. This testified of their hypocrisy, wickedness, and tyranny, as spiritual leaders blinded to the truth. (A modern day condition in some religious circles)

When told of this warning, the 2 apostles asked how could they comply with such a demand, and rightfully stop their service to the Lord, which He had commanded them to do. They said, 'You judge if it is more right in God's sight to obey you, or to obey Him.' The 2 men were released after hearing more threats to their safety, because <u>the people at large</u> <u>approved the healing of the 40 year old lame man</u> and praised God for it. Sadly, the temple leaders vainly attempted to serve two masters, God and the world, thus serving neither in an honest manner.

In 23-31, when the 2 apostles returned to their growing church of believers with a full report on their trial, all joined together with a mighty prayer to God in the words of David from Ps. 4:26, for boldness and courage in the face of danger. God gave evidence of His support by shaking the place, as <u>He renewed them again with His Holy Spirit</u>, and enabled them to testify of His word with greater boldness.

This experience served to transform the believers even more in verses 32-37 to be of one accord spiritually as well as materially. The apostles were more powerful in preaching and the people were more united in a common cause, as they <u>pooled their possessions for</u> <u>the common good of all.</u> By selling their property and giving the proceeds to the apostles to administer and distribute, all their needs where filled equally. One Levite man named Joses (or Barnabas, meaning Son of Encouragement) served as a good example in this action, by selling his land to give more money.

<u>VIEWPOINTS:</u>   Selfishness took a back seat in the early church, as a spirit of bonding compelled the members to share their material goods and property. This was a voluntary act of 'common-ism,' based on the love of God producing a mutual love amongst them. It did compare to state mandated communism. Contrariwise, it was meaningful evidence of the grace of God in them, with the <u>realization that all they owned had been given by Him</u>. This did not terminate the right to have privately owned property later in the life of the church. It was a unifying phenomenon for the moment, providing strength in numbers.

CHAPTER 5:   Verses 1-11 is about Ananais and Sapphira, a married couple, who sold their property and tried to give part of the proceeds to the believer fund as if it were the total amount received. When Ananais gave it, Peter <u>sensed through the Holy Spirit that he was</u> <u>dishonest</u>, and asked, 'Why have you yielded to Satan and lied to the Holy Spirit and to God in doing this.'

Hearing this charge, Ananias was convicted of his sin, and fell dead; young men took him out, and completed the task of his burial. Wife Sappira arrived 3 hours later and to Peter's question if the contribution was the total price received, she said it was. When Peter asked her <u>why she had agreed with her husband to deceive the Holy Spirit</u>, she too fell dead and was buried next to her husband. All believers who learned of this incident were filled with fear.

This act of deception by the couple revealed their covetous nature and shallow spiritual condition, which contributed to their hypocrisy. They could have honestly retained a portion of the price they had received, but their deliberate lie for the sake of self-glorification provoked God's anger and brought His judgment on them. Trying to cheat God can put a <u>fatal blight</u> <u>upon one's righteousness and being.</u>

The great number of signs and miracles at the hands of the apostles spurred the growth and unity of the new church as they witnessed at Solomon's Porch by the temple. <u>Believing</u> <u>in the power of God</u>, so many sick and disabled persons were brought for healing that they were put on cots in the street; some looked for Peter's shadow to fall on them for healing as he passed by. Verse 16 says this happened.

Imprisonment and trial followed on the heals of such supernatural works, in verses 17-42, as the high priests became enraged. They imprisoned all of the apostles, but that night an angel from God unlocked the doors, freed them, and told them to return to the temple in the morning to speak God's message boldly.

The priests sent escorts to the prison to bring the apostles before them, and were puzzled when the men returned to report the apostles were not in prison, even though the doors were secure and guards were on duty. When someone informed them the apostles were teaching back at the temple, they sent policemen to carefully retrieve the apostles, lest the people become violent.

The high priest chided the apostles for disobeying his previous order for them to stop teaching in Christ's name, thereby bringing blame on the priestly body for Christ's death. Peter and his brothers responded as before, that they had to obey God rather than the priests, because God had Jesus resurrected from the death they had brought on Him. In the power of the Holy Spirit, the apostles felt compelled to witness to all Israel, in the hope the people would repent and receive forgiveness.

This infuriated the priests and they began plotting how to kill the apostles. From their group, a Pharisee doctor of law named Gamaliel, asked for the apostles to be put outside; then he lectured the others to be careful of their actions, because judgmental errors of the past had caused major revolts with the loss of many lives.

Gamaliel recommend that no action be taken against the apostles, because if their work was of men, it would fail, but on the other hand, if it was of God, then it could not be stopped. The priestly body agreed with Gamaliel but yet they beat the apostles before releasing them, with another warning to stop preaching in Christ's name. Although hurting, the apostles rejoiced that they were counted worthy to suffer for God's glory, and they kept on witnessing in Christ's name.

CHAPTER 6: A church administrative problem arose in verses 1-7, which required consideration of priorities and preferential treatment. The church had grown considerably to the point where the daily distribution of food and other needs resulted in some inequities. This came to light when Hellenistic Jews, those from other areas where Greek was spoken, complained that their widows were being neglected.

The 12 apostles decided that special service coordinators should be selected to be responsible for fair distribution to everyone, because their own ministry duties demanded most of their time. To them, preaching the word of God was enough to take up their thoughts, cares, and time.

They called on the entire church to select 7 highly respected men, with Holy Spirit wisdom to be the special administrators. The members chose Stephen, Philip, Prochorus, Nicanor, Timon, Parmenas, and Nicolas, all spirit filled Grecian Jews. The apostles ordained them by prayer with the laying on of hands, thus imparting responsibility under divine grace. Many new converts became members of the church after the apostles were able to devote all of their time sharing the word of God.

In verses 8-15, Stephen became a thorn in the flesh of a separate Jewish synagogue for former slaves, whose members were in disagreement with some of his forward looking views, but they could not logically override the wisdom he imparted in the spirit. So they resorted to undermining his standing by <u>falsely accusing him of speaking blasphemous words against Moses and God.</u>

Stephen's accusers stirred up others in the membership to call him to task before their governing council. They brought false witnesses against him who claimed he spoke badly of their temple, the laws of Moses, and that Jesus would <u>bring destruction to change their Mosaic customs.</u> They were taken aback when his face took on an angelic look, maybe even aglow with compassion he felt for them.

<u>VIEWPOINTS:</u>   It is tragic that many Spirit filled Christians dedicated to serving the Lord in the ministry of saving grace, <u>must suffer persecution like a common criminal,</u> even become martyrs, because of hateful persons without conscience giving others no credit for doing good. Lack of understanding by the villains is not the problem, as much as their decadent heart, which is <u>deceitful above all things and desperately wicked</u>. They are a product of Satan's manipulation!

CHAPTER 7:   The presiding high priest asked Stephen if the false charges were true. Stephen delivers a lengthy but profound response in verses 2-53, in which he recounts the ancient history of the Jewish people back to Abraham <u>under the umbrella of God's care</u>. In summary, Stephen said the following, after his opening remark, 'Listen to me, brothers and fathers:'

- God told Abraham to leave his country to go to a land God would show him.
- After Abraham got there, God told him family ownership would come later.
- Abraham's descendants would become as slaves in Egypt for 400 years.
- Then they would possess a new land that God would give them.
- God's covenant assurance with Abraham was entwined in a circumcision rite.
- Abraham has a son, Isaac, the father of Jacob, the father of 12 sons.
- The 11 sons sold their younger brother Joseph as a slave into Egypt.
- After much difficulty, Joseph became prime minister of Egypt.
- When a famine struck, Jacob sent his 11 sons to Egypt twice for food.
- Joseph revealed his identity, and had Jacob's family, 75 in all, move toEgypt.
- The Israelites increased in number, continuing as slaves under a new pharaoh.
- Moses, born to an Israelite mother, was adopted by pharaoh's daughter.
- At age 40, Moses killed an Egyptian who mistreated an Israelite worker.
- Moses fled to Midian when he realized his crime would become known.
- He heard God speaking from a burning bush, that he should return toEgypt.
- Moses returned to Egypt, and after much difficulty, he led his people out.
- God told the Jews He would send a prophet (Jesus) that they would kill.
- The Israelites became rebellious, and asked Aaron to give them a new god.
- He made them a golden calf, which they worshipped with pagan sacrifices.
- God turned away from them, and allowed their enslavement in Babylon.
- A tabernacle created in the wilderness remained as a model in David's time.

- Solomon eventually built a more suitable temple replacement for worship.
- God clarified that He did not live in man-made structures, but in heaven.

Stephen concluded, calling the temple judges stiff-necked, with uncircumcised hearts and ears, just like their forefathers, resisting the Holy Spirit, and persecuting and killing God's messengers to them. In the end, they <u>killed Jesus, the Righteous One, as their ultimate disobedience of God's divine edict.</u>

The temple council ground their teeth in fury at hearing this indictment. Stephen looked heavenward and shared this observation, 'I see the door of heaven open, with Jesus standing at His right hand.' For a moment they covered their ears, and then with loud angry shouts, they drug Stephen to the city outskirts and began stoning him. Most interesting is the added comment, that the false witnesses left their outer garments <u>with a young man</u> named Saul, as <u>they stoned Stephen.</u>

In his final agony, Stephen asked Jesus to 'receive his spirit,' and on his knees, asked God 'to not hold this sin against them.' Saul voiced his approval of Stephen's death (8:1), although it appears he was not involved in the stoning. While religious leaders of Israel were at their worst, <u>Stephen was at his righteous best!</u> In ways, his grit, courage, and his death without rancor matched that of Jesus Christ.

God's new covenant gospel was offered to the Jews, as a better way than the laws of Moses, to have a right relationship with God through the infilling of the Holy Spirit. Yet they did not embrace it, for they <u>stubbornly resolved not to accept God's terms,</u> legally or spiritually. Guilt stung them to the heart, but instead of being sorrowful and asking for mercy, they sought to murder the one who cared for them.

CHAPTER 8: After Stephen's death, verses 1-3 state that persecution of the Jerusalem church, mainly the Hellenistic Jews, intensified to the point that many of the members fled to Judea and Samaria; however, the 12 apostles remained in Jerusalem. <u>Saul became a zealous persecutor of the church folks,</u> breaking into their homes and dragging them off to prison.

Verses 4-8 tell of an effective ministry in Samaria by Philip, one of the 7 deacons, where he drove out protesting demons and healed many cripples. The Samaritans rejoiced over this transformation in their beliefs, and how <u>God's word overcame their racial bias.</u> This was the 1st evangelistic movement away from the Jews towards the Gentile world. Persecution became God's instrument to spread the gospel of Jesus to new places.

As related in 9-13, there was a Samaritan magician named Simon, who took great pride in his art, and the people's praise of him as a 'Great Power of God.' When he observed how so many people believed in Philip's message, and were baptized, he too <u>professed belief and was baptized.</u> He was totally amazed at the miracles taking place under Philip's ministry.

Back in Jerusalem, in 14-17, when the apostles heard of the Samaritan conversions, they sent Peter and John to confirm this development and <u>to bring about a subsequent infilling (baptism) of the Holy Spirit</u> to all the converts who may have had an earlier water baptism. This was done through prayer and laying on of hands.

The magician Simon, coveted this power also, in 18-25, and <u>offered the apostles money</u>

to obtain it, but Peter rebuked him for his hypocrisy and wicked ambition. He advised Simon to repent of his sin and ask for God's forgiveness. But, Simon told them to do the praying for him so he would not be punished. He was ambitious to be like an apostle, for his own pride, not for the good of others. Neither could he humble himself to obtain God's mercy. Peter and John turned back to Jerusalem, preaching along the way in Samaritan villages.

Verses 26-40, God's angel instructed Philip to leave Samaria, to go south towards Gaza, where he encountered an Ethiopian eunuch, from the court of Candace, queen of Ethiopia. This man was returning from a visit to Jerusalem where he evidently worshipped with the new church. Philip found him seated in his chariot, reading from the book of Isaiah.

Under the prompting of the Spirit, Philip drew near to hear the eunuch reading aloud, and asked him if he understood the reading. The eunuch, admitting he needed help, invited Philip to sit with him, to explain what Isaiah 53:7-8 was all about. Philip clarified that the scripture spoke of Jesus and His crucifixion, adding much more about Jesus and the gift of salvation that He provided all mankind. The eunuch believed and asked to be baptized.

Coming to a small body of water, Philip said, 'If you believe with all your heart, you may.' After the eunuch confessed, 'I believe that Jesus Christ is the Son of God.' Stopping the chariot, the two went into the water and the baptism took place. As they came up out of the water, Philip was divinely whisked away to a place called Azotus, north of Gaza; from there he preached in towns on the way north to Caesarea on the Mediterranean coast. The eunuch went his way rejoicing, never to see Philip again.

VIEWPOINTS: God withheld the Holy Spirit at the time of baptism in Samaria, because of long held hostility between Jews and Samaritans. Conveying the Spirit through the Jewish apostles established the unity of the Samaritan believers with Jewish believers into Christ's church. Peter and Philip brought the full power of Pentecost to non-Jew converts.

The 1st instance of the Holy Spirit's delayed coming upon confirmed believers occurred at Pentecost (Ch. 2), to the 120 followers of Christ. Two other incidents of a delayed imparting of the Holy Spirit after conversion are described in Chapters 10 and 19. Later on, when Peter ministered to the Gentiles, the new believers received the Holy Spirit at the moment they repented of their sins and accepted forgiveness through Christ's atoning grace.

There is now no basis for a separate later baptism of the Holy Spirit after a true conversion experience has taken place. In this age, every believer receives the indwelling of the Holy Spirit at the instant of genuine belief (Eph. 1:13) in Christ's gift of salvation, with forgiveness of sins. Separate spiritual infusions of the Spirit may occur (called 'infilling'), as God's way of blessing the believer with new understanding of His sovereign grace, energizing one for special service, or to receive fresh new perception of scriptures.

CHAPTER 9:   This is a return to Saul, the persecutor of new believers, who stood by in approval of Stephen's death by stoning. Still breathing thunder and lighting against disciples of the Lord in verses 1-9, he obtained letters of authority to scout out new Christian (the Way) converts in the synagogues in Damascus, to bring them back to Jerusalem as prisoners.

As he came near to Damascus, an intense blinding light focused on him, and he fell to the ground. He heard a powerful voice saying, 'Saul, Saul, why do you persecute Me?' When he respectfully asked, 'Who are you, Sir (Lord)?' Jesus identified Himself as the speaker, and told him to stop resisting and go into Damascus where he would receive more instructions. Paul arose, as did the other men with him, all speechless, when Paul realized he had lost his vision. His comrades led him into the city to spend the next 3 days fasting in darkness, as he pondered what had happened to him.

In verses 10-19, Paul's sight is restored by an ordinary disciple named Ananias, after he was instructed to do so by the Lord Jesus in a vision. Ananias was told that Paul expected him, having seen him in a vision coming to restore his vision. Ananais was not keen about this mission because he had heard of Saul's unwavering zeal to persecute new believers. To allay his fears, Jesus told him that Saul was to become a witness in His name to the Jews, as well as kings and most of all Gentiles; he would also learn about suffering for His sake.

Ananias complied, went to Saul, laid hands on him, and informed him that through the filling of the Holy Spirit, Saul would recover his sight. Like scales falling off his eyes, it happened immediately and Saul was baptized into his new faith. Partaking of food, his strength returned over 3 days of rest with fellow believers.

It is amazing how God's grace changes and renews the greatest sinners! With scales of ignorance and pride removed by the Holy Spirit from his spiritual vision, Saul became a new creature, and with an attitudinal reversal he is ready to recommend his newly discovered Savior, the Son of God, to his former companions, and all others who will hear him. He is identified by his 3 days of blindness and days of rest. with Jesus' 3 days in the tomb.

In verses 20-25, Saul began preaching in the synagogues that Jesus really is the Son of God, with the same zeal he had when against Him. People were amazed at the strength of his conviction and power of his message delivery. As usual, dissenting Jews decided to get rid of him, but Saul got word of their plot, and with the help of other believers he escaped in a basket lowered through a hole in the city wall.

After his escape, Saul returns to Jerusalem in verses 26-31, where the church folks resisted his attempts at fellowship with them, for fear that he might betray them as before. The apostle Barnabas broke the ice for him, so he could relate to them how Jesus had confronted him on the road to Damascus, to give him new spiritual insight, and how he had preached there in the name of Jesus. Thereafter, he preached in Jerusalem, mainly to the Hellenist Jews, who also tried to kill him. His newfound believer fellowship came to his aid by safeguarding his departure to the City of Carsarea, where he sailed for his home town of Tarsus.

Jesus said Saul would learn of suffering in His name, but He also provided safety and a way of escape, to preserve him for protracted ministry. It was God's plan for Saul to be a major factor in reaching out to the Gentiles. With his departure, a time of peace prevailed in Judea, Galilee, and Samaria, with many converted to walk in obedience to the Lord and to rest in the comfort of the Holy Spirit.

The focus shifts to the ministry of Peter in verses 32-43, who traveled about 20 miles northwest of Jerusalem, to visit believers in Lydda. He was taken to a man named Aeneas, who had been paralyzed and bedridden for 8 years. When Peter told him that Jesus was healing him, the man arose immediately to become a witness that brought many to the Lord.

A short distance away, at Joppa, about 30 miles northwest of Lydda, a beloved woman named Tabitha became ill and died. When local disciples heard of Peter in Lydda, they sent word for him to quickly come to Joppa. When he <u>arrived, he found many widows in</u> <u>mourning</u>; he had them removed from the upper room where Tabitha's body lay, and knelt down to pray over her. Then as he said, 'Tabitha, rise,' she opened her eyes and sat up. With his help, she walked out to the believers and widows, who witnessed this so that <u>many believed in the</u> <u>Lord's healing power.</u>

CHAPTER 10:   The Gospel moves out of Jewish territory into the Gentile regions. In verses 1-8, God fingers a Roman army regimental officer named Cornelius to be an initial stepping stone for Gentiles to be reconciled to the Jews <u>as equals in Christ's church</u>. He and his family were devout God fearing people, always prayerful, and generous to the poor. They lived in Caesarea, about 40 miles north of Joppa, where Peter was located.

Cornelius was startled one day, when he saw an angel of God in a vision, calling him by name. The angel told him that his prayers and alms giving had found favor with God, and now he was to send for Peter in Joppa, who would give him further instructions. Promptly, he dispatched 2 reliable servants with a devout soldier aide to Joppa. Without dispute or delay <u>Cornelius was obedient to the heavenly vision</u>, an example for any believer to emulate.

The next day, in verses 9-24, as the 3 emissaries neared Joppa, Peter had a vision also while praying on the housetop where he was staying. Out of heaven, what appeared to be a <u>large 4 cornered sheet came down to earth.</u> It contained all kinds of animals, creeping things, and birds. God told him, 'Peter, get moving, kill some of these and eat them.

Peter decline to do so, saying, 'Lord, I never eat anything unclean and unfit to eat,' in keeping with Levitical Mosaic law (see Lev. Ch. 11 & Deut. 14:3-21). For a 2nd and 3rd time, this dialogue took place, and each time God told Peter, 'What I have cleansed should no longer be considered unclean.' Then the sheet returned to heaven.

This revelation in effect said that the law of Moses was to be replaced with a new standard for Gentiles, not to be considered unclean, but <u>equally acceptable to God and the Jews.</u> Only Jews, Samaritans, and those converts who had been circumcised, were welcome in the new Christian church, but now the Gentiles were to partake of all the privileges of God's people, without first becoming Jews in that manner. God was <u>diluting Peter's own prejudices against</u> <u>Gentiles.</u>

As Peter deeply pondered the meaning of this vision, the men from Cornelius arrived asking for him. The Holy Spirit aroused him with word of the 3 men sent by God, and <u>instructed him to go with them.</u> After being told how they happened to come to him, Peter invited them to stay the night.

The next morning Peter and six of his own fellow believers left with the 3 emissaries. The group arrived late the next day to find <u>Cornelius waiting with family and relatives.</u> Kneeling before Peter, Cornelius began to worship him, but Peter told him, 'Stand up, I'm only a human.' Then he told all those in the house that Jewish tradition forbade fraternization with non-Jews, viewed as unclean, but in this case God had informed him that <u>this was no longer applicable</u> <u>amongst God's people.</u>

To Peter's query as to why he was asked to come, Cornelius told Peter about the vision he had 4 days earlier, in which God said <u>Peter had some heavenly wisdom</u> to share with him. Peter admitted that he now understood God's vision of the sheet to mean that all people are <u>equal in God's sight without partiality.</u> God is pleased with all who worship Him, a message God gave the Israelites when He sent Jesus as a messenger of peace.

Peter reviewed how the ministry of Jesus flourished from the time of John the Baptist to His crucifixion, and how He commanded the disciples to <u>preach the new gospel of salvation to all the world,</u> that all who believe in Jesus will receive remission of sins.

As the people heard Peter's words, the Holy Spirit came down upon the Gentile folks, and the Jews with Peter were astonished as they heard them <u>speaking unknown languages to praise and magnify God.</u> This was a similar experience to what the Jews had at Pentecost. Since they were undeniably baptized with the Holy Ghost, Peter concluded they should <u>receive water baptism in the name of Jesus,</u> and the ordinance was administered. This confirmed that all were now united, the Jews and the Gentiles, into Christ's church, <u>with the gift of the Holy Spirit</u>. This was a startling eye-opener to the Jews!

<u>VIEWPOINTS:</u>   The manifestation of Holy Spirit endowment to speak in a strange language had a special purpose in the early church, and in the case of Cornelius and his household, to show the Jews the <u>reality of Gentile inclusion in Christ's church.</u> Peter's Jewish comrades may have doubted the authenticity of the conversion and baptism of the Holy Spirit upon Cornelius and his household, had this not been included.

There is no valid biblical reason to assume that 'speaking in tongues' is a necessary <u>evidence of salvation in Christian circles today.</u> Neither should Christians deem it necessary for this to occur during a separate moment called the baptism of the Holy Spirit, after one has become a believer. This Holy Spirit gift was meant to edify the church before New Testament Scriptures were in existence. Even then, Jesus did not speak in tongues or ever advocate it for new believers!

CHAPTER 11:   When Peter returned to Jerusalem, he was confronted by opposition from Jewish leaders who held to Mosaic tradition that a Gentile must become a circumcised Jew to be a true believer. In verses 1-18, Peter recounts all that had occurred in Chapter 10, about the visions from God that he and Cornelius experienced, how he was led to Caesarea to minister there, and <u>how the Gentile family of Cornelius was converted and filled with the</u> <u>Holy Spirit.</u>

He emphatically declared that they had received the same gift as the Jews during the Pentecost revival. Peter begged for understanding that he was compelled to visit Cornelius, for <u>whatever else could he do but obey God's command.</u> The Jews were convinced, they stopped arguing and praised God for this divine manifestation.

In this case, the imperfections of human nature were very apparent, as the Jewish believers showed their displeasure that the word of God has been received without conformance to their own doctrinal views. Sadly, churches in this modern era are often prone to consider true believers to be outside the parameters of the Christian Church, because of differing beliefs and interpretations on trivial issues.

Verses 19-30 focus on new developments at the Gentile Christian church in Antioch, about 300 miles north of Jerusalem, which was the capital of the Roman province of Syria. After

Stephen's death, many Jewish believers fled Jerusalem to Phaoenicia, Cyprus, and Antioch, where they witnessed to other traditional Jews, <u>converting many to the new</u> <u>Christian faith.</u>

Apostles at the Jerusalem church heard of this and sent Barnabas to Antioch to verify what God was doing to change lives. He was full of the grace of faith, and the fruits of the faith that grows from brotherly love. His delight was so great over the movement, that he <u>encouraged</u> <u>the new believers to continue with the Lord</u>. Then he decided to travel to Tarsus to find Saul to bring him back to Antioch, where they ministered together for a year. It was there that new believers were called Christians.

When a prophet named Agabus came from Jerusalem, he informed the church at Antioch that a great famine was to occur; it did happen during the reign of Claudius Caesar, about 46 AD. The members <u>collected a contribution to send to the believers</u> living in Judea. This was delivered by Barnabas and Saul.

This was evidence that true Christians will give aid to their afflicted brethren, thus producing the <u>fruit of praise and glory to God.</u> Would that all mankind were true Christians, to cheerfully help one another! This earth would be like one happy family, with every person striving to be generous and kind. But Satan is waging war on Christians through terrorism, brutality, and terrible evil deeds by some against others.

CHAPTER 12:   At that time, Herod Agrippa I, the grandson of Herod the Great who ruled when Jesus was born, was in Jerusalem, harassing the new church. For some untold reason, he had the Apostle James killed by a sword, probably beheaded. He was the brother of John, the beloved of Christ, who told both of them in Matt. 20:20-23, they would have to drink the same cup of suffering that He had to drink of, for their faith in Him. <u>James was the first of</u> <u>the apostles to be martyred</u>! One must wonder why God allowed this faithful servant to be taken out so early.

Since this pleased some of the traditional Jews, Herod had Peter seized (his 3rd arrest) and <u>jailed during the Feast of Unleavened Bread</u>, which delayed Peter's execution. The Christian Jews prayed fervently for Peter, and on the eve before he was to be killed, while he was sleeping in the jail, surrounded by many guards and chained to 2 of them, an angel appeared as a bright light and woke him.

The angel said, 'Arise, put on your garments and shoes and follow me.' The chains holding him to the guards fell off, and Peter followed the angel <u>thinking he was seeing a</u> <u>vision</u>. After they had passed all the guards and walked through the exterior locked iron gate (which opened automatically) into the street, the angel disappeared. Peter knew then it was no vision, but God's miracle that released him to disappoint Herod and the Jews.

The <u>prayers of the saints were answered</u> in God's will. This deliverance of Peter typifies a person's redemption by Christ, bringing peace and joy to the believer, in the knowledge they have been freed from the prison of sin. Often, new believers delivered out of unspiritual bondage, do not at first understand what God has done in them. They have the truth of grace, but they want evidence of it. Fellowship with a church and bible study will provide the evidence!

Peter then proceeded to the home of Mary, the mother of John Mark, the author of the

Gospel of Mark, and when he knocked at the street door, a maid named Rhoda went to the gate to ask his identity. Recognizing his voice, she was so excited that <u>she ran inside to</u> <u>tell the</u> <u>others, without letting Peter in</u>. Those who were gathered for prayer told her she was crazy, that it might have been his guardian angel.

Peter's persistent knocking brought others to the door. They were astonished when they saw him, but <u>remained silent when Peter signaled them to be quiet</u>. He told them all that had happened and instructed them to pass a warning word to James, the brother of Jesus, with the church brethren. He left them for a more secure place.

In the morning, the prison guards were dismayed over Peter's escape. When they had no answers or excuse to satisfy Herod, <u>he had them put to death.</u> Then Herod left Jerusalem to go to Caesarea.

While there, people of Tyre and Sidon came to see Herod about some kind of disagreement which angered him. His aide Blastus set up an appointment with Herod, who sat on his throne regally dressed, as he spoke eloquently to them. The people were impressed, and <u>perhaps in</u> <u>an attempt at appeasement</u>, they shouted, 'His is the voice of a god, not a man.'

When Herod accepted this accolade, no doubt with enjoyment, an angel from God <u>struck</u> <u>him down with a deadly malady</u>, appearing to be an infestation of intestinal roundworms that caused his death. Anyone with knowledge of God, who is puffed up with pride and vanity, is ripe for His swift vengeance. God is jealous for His own honor, and will preserve it on the backs of those who dishonor Him.

God's message kept on spreading, when Saul and Barnabas returned from Jerusalem, bringing with them John Mark as a witness and an aide.

CHAPTER 13:   The believers in the church at Antioch, being ministered to by Barnabas and Saul and other prophets and teachers, were inspired by the Holy Spirit in verses 1-3, to <u>send Barnabas and Saul out as missionaries to other lands</u>. After fasting and prayer, with the laying on of hands, they sent them on their way.

In 4-12, they went south a short distance to the seaport of Seleucia, to sail to Cyprus, where they preached the gospel to the Jews. John Mark accompanied them to help. At the west end of the island, they <u>encountered a Jew named Bar-Jesus,</u> known to be a sorcerer and false prophet, who was in the company of the Roman (Gentile) governor, Sergius Paulus.

Being an intelligent man, Paulus wanted to hear about the Christian message and sent for Barnabas and Saul, but Bar-Jesus tried to <u>prevent a dialogue between them.</u> Enemies to the doctrine of Jesus, are generally enemies to all that is right; and try to keep those with open minds from learning it.

In the power of the Holy Spirit, Paul (Roman name adopted here) denounced Bar-Jesus, calling him a son of the devil, a liar, a crook, and <u>an enemy of what was right.</u> After asking him when he would stop speaking against the Lord, Paul told him that God was making him blind for a time. Instantly, this happened and he asked others to lead him by the hand. This act plus some teaching about the Lord <u>made the governor another believer.</u>

Paul and his assistants then sailed north in verses 13-41 to the mainland port of Perga, where <u>John Mark left to return to Jerusalem.</u> The main party continued north to another city of Antioch in Pisidia, to attend services on the Sabbath at a Jewish synagogue. After reading the Old Testament scripture on Mosaic Law and Prophets, the synagogue leaders invited Paul and his party to say what they wanted that would be of spiritual help to those in attendance.

In his new role as the missionary leader, Paul stood up and with a gesture that all were included, Jews and Gentiles who worshipped one God, he delivered an historic account of the Jewish people similar to that which Stephen gave to the Jewish Council in chapter 7, to basically include the following details:

- God chose the Israelites, gave them greatness in Egypt, for about 400 years.
- He sustained them for another 40 years wandering in the wilderness, and
- Another 10 years to subjugate Canaan, for a total of 450 years.
- He allowed judges to rule over them, until Saul became their 1st king.
- He made David Saul's successor, because David was in His will.
- As a descendent of David, God brought Jesus to the Jews, as their Savior.
- Before Jesus began His ministry, John the Baptist proclaimed His coming.
- The message that Jesus brought was rejected by leaders in Jerusalem.
- They persecuted Him, and brought about His death on the cross.
- He was laid in a tomb, from which God raised Him to life again.
- He appeared many days to His followers, witnesses of His resurrection.
- Now we, the apostles, preach to all the good news that He is alive.

Paul quoted 3 passages of scripture that prophesied of Christ's resurrection as part of God's plan: Ps 2:7, Ps 16:10, and Is 55:3. Paul concluded his presentation with words of assurance that Jesus would forgive all who had faith in Him, and make them free of past sins, which the Law of Moses could not do. Christ was to serve all generations. Most importantly, he warned them not to become victims of disbelief as described in Hubakuk 1:5.

After the service, some Jews and Gentile believers asked for more teaching the following Sabbath, and received more counseling from Paul and Barnabas. The next Sabbath, almost all the people in the community attended, including many Gentiles, This made Jewish leaders envious, who then became hostile, and opposed the apostles preaching, by contradicting and blasphemed Christ and His message.

Boldly, Paul and Barnabas spoke out to say that it was necessary for them to bring the message first to the Jews, but since they had rejected it, the message would now be taken to the Gentiles, as the Lord commanded in Is. 49:6. This gladdened the hearts of the Gentiles, who enthusiastically embraced God's word.

The message of Jesus spread rapidly throughout the region, bringing joy to many, but Jews were intolerant of this and stirred up trouble with the support of prominent men and women of the city, so that Paul and Barnabas went to Iconium.

CHAPTER 14:   Iconium was located in the Roman province of Galatia in Paul's day; it is now the Turkish provincial capital Konya. At Iconium, the two apostles boldly preached the word in the Jewish synagogue, in verses 1-7, to convert many Jews and Greek Gentiles.

Division existed between the Gentiles and Jews, and those who were unbelievers united against Christians. They rose up against the apostles with the intent of stoning them. Learning of this, the <u>two apostles fled south to preach at Lystra.</u> When persecuted, believers have good reason to move on to another place to continue their Master's work.

In verses 8-20, while at Lystra, a lame man unable to walk listened intently to Paul's preaching. When Paul saw a receptive mind in the man, he loudly said, 'Stand upon your feet,' to which <u>the man vigorously responded.</u> The local Lyconian people said in awe, 'The gods have come down to us as humans.' Then they called Barnabas, 'Zeus,' and Paul, 'Hermes,' the one who did the talking. The local Zeus priest <u>brought oxen and flowers to the</u> <u>city gates</u> for a sacrifice to them. (Greek gods were Zeus and Hermes, the same as the Roman gods Jupiter and Mercury)

The two apostles reacted in horror at this idea, tore their clothes and pleaded with the people not to do this. They pointed out that <u>they too were humans,</u> just trying to tell others about a living God, the Creator of all, who in times past had provided the people's needs, even though they had not worshipped Him. Paul and Barnabas were rightfully more concerned about glory and honor to God than to themselves.

These words were hardly enough to restrain the people and their priest from making a sacrificial offering to the apostles, but <u>along came some hostile Jewish leaders</u> from Antioch and Iconium to turn the unbelievers against them. They stoned Paul and dumped his body outside the city <u>thinking he was dead.</u> Thankfully, when some true believers went to him, Paul recovered and went back into the city with them. The next day, he and Barnabas <u>departed</u> <u>south to the nearby city of Derbe.</u>

Without any trouble, they preached there to win many converts, before retracing their way to Lystra, Iconium, and Antioch. Along the way, they exhorted new believers <u>to remain</u> <u>steadfast in their faith,</u> in spite of tribulations that would come. They also appointed and anointed church elders to the Lord's service. At Antioch, the two apostles gave a full report of their missionary journey, how God had provided for them, and <u>how many Gentiles became</u> <u>believers.</u> They stayed with the first church for a time to rest, and receive new direction from the Holy Spirit.

CHAPTER 15: A doctrinal dispute arose in this chapter <u>between adherents to traditional</u> <u>Mosaic Law and new believers</u> in Christ's doctrine. In verses 1-5, men from Judea, probably Pharisees, came to Antioch to inform the new Gentile believers that they must be circumcised like a Jew to really be saved. This was to impose the yoke of Mosaic Law that <u>would limit</u> <u>Christian's freedom from the law.</u> Paul and Barnabas disagreed, and after much debate, the church elders decided that the two should return to Jerusalem to seek guidance from the Church leaders there.

They passed through Phoenicia and Samaria, taking every opportunity to spread Christ's message of joy through salvation in Him. Their arrival and their activities report was welcomed by the Jerusalem church leaders, but as usual some newly converted Pharisees contended that Gentile converts should be circumcised to comply with Mosaic Law.

Extensive discussion and debate ensued between the apostles and church leaders on this issue, in 6-21. The apostle and inveterate spokesman Peter arose to bring sensible perspective on the issue, by reminding them of his experience with visions that caused him to bring

Cornelius (see Ch. 10) into a faith relationship with Christ, through the Holy Spirit, <u>without the need for Mosaic Law requirements</u>, which the Jews had not always obeyed. He flatly stated that salvation is by the grace of Jesus, a gift from God for Jews and Gentiles alike. (Peter is no longer mentioned)

Paul and Barnabas elaborated on how God had worked signs and miracles through them unto the Gentiles. They persuaded the church that God ordained the preaching of Christ's gospel to the Gentiles apart from the law of Moses; therefore to impose that law upon them could <u>undo faith brought about by the Holy Spirit</u>.

Then James, the brother of Jesus and now the leader of the Jerusalem church, spoke up to remind them of a favorable report from Simeon, a prophet from the Antioch church, concerning <u>God's agenda to convert Gentiles by faith in Christ.</u> In support of this objective, James quoted prophecy from Amos 9:11-12, that pictures a future time when Christ would reign over a kingdom in which both Jew and Gentile <u>would exist equally believing in the supremacy of Christ.</u>

He recommended placing no strange burdens on new Gentile believers, but simply <u>admonish them to refrain from obvious troublesome sins</u>; these included eating meat offered to idols, or meat not properly drained of blood, and a variety of sexual sins. This was to warn them to avoid major evils they customarily practiced, or would be tempted to, and to caution them to be sensible in their new Christian liberty. As they heard the Mosaic laws preached, they were to reconcile differences.

In verses 22-35, the council and all church members agreed with James, and composed <u>a letter setting forth what James recommended.</u> Together with Paul and Barnabas, they sent two church elders, Judas Barsabas and Silas, to deliver the letter to churches in Antioch, Syria, and Cilicia.

The letter was well received by the believers in Antioch, who then <u>enjoyed teaching from Judas and Silas</u>. When finished with their mission, Judas and others with him returned to Jerusalem, but Silas stayed on to work with Paul and Barnabas.

Paul was then motivated to suggest to Barnabas that they return to churches they had established on his 1st missionary journey. When Barnabas proposed taking John Mark along, Paul disagreed and <u>unable to reconcile their differences, they separated.</u> Barnabas took Mark with him to sail to Cyprus, and Paul took Silas along to travel through Syria and Cilicia, servicing churches along the way.

God brought good out of the split by sending out <u>2 missionary groups instead of just one.</u> Fortunately, in keeping with Christian principles, this rift was temporary, and Paul spoke highly of both Barnabas and Mark in his later writing of epistles.

CHAPTER 16:   Paul and Silas went to Derbe and Lystra in verses 1-5, where they met a young man named Timothy, the son of a devout Jewish mother (Eunice), and a Greek Gentile father. Timothy was <u>well schooled in Old Testament scriptures</u> and witnessed effectively for the Lord in that area. Paul liked the man and wanted to take him along as an aide, but since Timothy had not been circumcised in accordance with Jewish practice, he had this done so <u>Jewish Christians would not reject him</u>. This did not change Paul's basic view about circumcision for Gentile believers!

The 3 men, proceeded to each city in the region where they had been earlier, to deliver the Jerusalem Church decree that had been put in letter format. This brought <u>satisfaction to the Gentile believers,</u> and their numbers increased steadily.

In 6-10, the trio moved on northwest through Galatia (central Turkey) towards Mysia, being restrained by the Holy Spirit from doing any preaching. They planned to enter the northern most region of Bithynia, which the Holy Spirit also vetoed. This was the beginning of Paul's 2nd missionary journey. (See map at end of this book)

The men moved southward, passing by Mysia to a port city of Troas, on the Agean Sea, where Paul had a vision of a Macedonian (Greek) man pleading for spiritual help. Paul accepted this as <u>a call from God to carry the gospel to Macedonia.</u> Evidently Luke, the author of this book, joined Paul somewhere, as this is implied by the new use of 'we' to describe their movements.

The 4 men sailed from Troas in 11-15, across the Agean Sea to the port city of Neapolis, on the southeastern shore of Macedonia (now Greece). From there, they walked about 10 miles westerly to Philippi, then a Roman colony of military veterans.

On the Sabbath they went to a riverside park where small groups of Jewish people held <u>prayer services because they had no synagogue</u>. There was a successful business woman named Lydia who believed in the God of Israel. She eagerly listened to and accepted all that Paul shared with her family and her servants. All were baptized in the river, and then the apostles <u>accepted her invitation to be guests at her home</u>. This is another case of emancipation of womanhood under Christianity.

Later at the prayer park, in 16-24, Paul and Silas met a slave girl, possessed of an evil spirit, who earned her masters an income as a fortune-teller. She followed them on repeated park visits, and yelled, 'These men are servants of the Most High God, telling us how to be saved.' This annoyed Paul, and he commanded the spirit to leave her in the name of Jesus Christ. The spirit left her and when her masters <u>realized their source of income had</u> <u>dried up,</u> they angrily seized Paul and Silas and brought them before local magistrates.

They charged the 2 men with causing trouble by preaching Jewish religion which was contrary to local Roman law. This aroused the fury of the magistrates and other people, who <u>tore off their clothes and severely beat them</u>, before throwing them in jail, in isolation with their feet in stocks.

In 25-34, at midnight in the jail Paul and Silas prayed and sang praise songs to God. Without warning, a strong earthquake shook the jail so violently that all <u>doors were opened and prisoner holding chains came loose</u>. The jailer saw all the doors open when he awoke, and was about to kill himself, thinking all had escaped.

Paul shouted, 'Don't do it, no one has escaped.' The shaken jailer got a light to enter the jail where he kneeled at Paul's feet and then led them out of the jail to ask, 'What must I do to be saved?' He was told to <u>have faith and believe in Jesus Christ,</u> so he and his household would be saved. These words softened and humbled the man, that he felt compassion, and took them to have their cuts and bruises cleansed.

At the jailer's home, Paul and Silas so effectively counseled his family that all confessed belief in Christ, and were then <u>baptized with rejoicing in the nearby river</u>. All returned to his home for a good meal. Love and kindness prevailed!

The next morning, in 35-40, local officials sent police to the jail where Paul and Silas spent the night, with word that they should be released. When Paul heard this, he informed the police that he and Silas were Roman citizens, and because they had been beaten and jailed, the <u>officials would have to personally apologize to them.</u>

It was a violation of law if a prisoner was beaten before being tried. This message caused the officials to be fearful and they quickly came to apologize and release them with a request to leave quickly. They stopped by the home of Lydia to encourage all new believers, and then left town.

<u>CHAPTER 17:</u> Moving westerly about 100 miles through two towns, in verses 1-9, Paul and Silas arrived in Thessalonica (now Thessaloniki), a large cosmopolitan city where Jews maintained a synagogue. Paul attended for 3 consecutive Sabbaths to introduce the Jews to Old Testament prophecy <u>on the suffering, death and resurrection of Jesus,</u> and how Jesus fulfilled that scripture. Some Jews believed, but many more Greeks and a few leading women believed and became followers of the Apostles.

The opposing Jews became envious of this turn of allegiance and stirred up trouble, <u>using some vagrant men to stir up a riot mob,</u> with the intent to give Paul and Silas over to it. The Jewish leaders sent men to the home of Jason (their host), but did not find them there, so they took Jason and other Christians before city officials to charge them as well as Paul and Silas of disturbing the peace, by claiming that Jesus was their king. This was upsetting to the officials but <u>they released Jason and the others after they posted bail.</u>

Paul and Silas left that night for Berea, in 10-15, about 50 miles southwesterly, where they appeared in the morning at the local synagogue, to receive a much better reception than in Thessalonica. Many Jews, Greeks, and some prominent women <u>believed the word of God as preached by Paul.</u>

Unfortunately, some of the bad apples from Thessalonica heard about Paul's success in Berea, and <u>came there to stir up more trouble.</u> As a precaution for Paul's safety, some believers accompanied him to the nearest dock, from where they sailed to Athens. They returned home with Paul's request that Silas and Timothy join him as soon as possible.

It is strange that some religious factions begrudge the success of others over a good thing <u>they will not themselves accept.</u> Rulers and church leaders should rejoice over the increase of real Christians, and not let evil spirits use trouble makers to make religion the pretext for mischief and persecution. Often Christians must temporarily withdraw from such situations, so as to demonstrate a desire <u>to be respectful of local laws and customs.</u> This does not mean to relinquish the right to worship God according to our consciences.

In 16-21, while waiting for his comrades, Paul became greatly distressed over the worship of idols throughout Athens. He made this a main topic of discussion in the synagogue, among both Jewish and Gentile worshippers, and also daily in the market place. As usual, dissent appeared in the form of <u>Epicureans</u> (happiness was their main goal in life), and <u>Stoics</u> (practiced self-control as one's conscience dictated), the leading philosophers of that day.

They called Paul 'a babbler' for proclaiming a foreign god to them, namely <u>the resurrected Christ.</u> They then forced him to appear before a Roman council, the Areopagus, where he was asked to explain his 'new doctrine,' a subject of great interest to them. Paul's lengthy discourse and the outcome is related in verses 22-34.

He acknowledged their religiosity, by referring to an altar marked 'TO AN UNKNOWN GOD, <u>which they worshipped but did not know.</u> He told them that his God of creation was their unknown god, and as God's children they were not to consider Him an idol. Paul said that as he served God, they were <u>also to serve Him.</u> Their ignorance of Him should come to an end, and all of them should repent of their idolatry to avoid God's wrath.

Paul also assures them that God is not remote from mankind but is <u>as near as family</u> <u>for daily fellowship</u>. He tried to convey the understanding that all mankind as God's creatures should be responsible to Him. After all, God ruled how from one blood all nations would emerge and live within prescribed boundaries.

The more so, because His Son was resurrected from death so that mankind might expect the same treatment in the last days. The idea of resurrection turned these intellectuals off, and they <u>dismissed Paul for lack of interest.</u> A few of the Greeks spent more time with him, including a woman named Damaris.

CHAPTER 18: Having little success in Athens, Paul moves on to Corinth, about 50 miles to the west, where he <u>makes the acquaintance of a Jewish man named Aquila,</u> and his wife Priscilla, in verses 1-6. They had lived in Rome but left after Emperor Claudius ordered all Jews to leave about 49 AD. Since they were tent makers, which was Paul's only trade, he stayed and worked with them.

Corinth had a famous temple dedicated to Asclepius, the god of healing, and his daughter Hygieia. Other buildings around the temple were for the sick who came for healing.

They <u>left terra cotta replicas of their body parts,</u> that had been healed, at the temple,. Some of these replicas have been discovered by archeologists.

At that time, Corinth was known for its licentious life-style, centered around the cult of Aphrodite. The pagan temple of 'the goddess of love' was so wealthy that it <u>maintained</u> <u>over 1000 slave prostitutes,</u> who had been provided by the local populace. These 'love slaves' provided much income from the patronage of sailors who freely squandered their money there.

Paul continued his efforts to convert traditional Jews and Greek Gentiles at the synagogue. When Silas and Timothy joined him from Macedonia, he spent all his time with the Jews telling them about Jesus. Typically, they finally rejected his teaching and became hostile. This angered Paul so much that he told them they would <u>have to bear the</u> <u>consequences of their rejection,</u> that it would no longer concern him, because he was going to focus entirely on the Greek Gentiles.

The Jews would not themselves believe, so they did all they could to <u>keep others from believing</u>. Thereafter, the Jews could not complain, for they first received the word from Paul. He had no reason to waste time with them; turning to the Greeks was <u>part of God's plan.</u>

It is puzzling why Paul left Aquila and Priscilla in verses 7-17, to move into the home of a Christian named Justus, next door to a Jewish synagogue. The leader of the synagogue, Crispus, and his household, became converted Christians, with many other Corinthians who believed, and all were baptized into their new faith.

Paul must have had some fear that traditional Jews would again give him trouble, because the Lord gave him assurance in a dream that he would not be harmed, and he should keep on preaching to reach many people. He continued his ministry for about 18 months.

During that time, some Jewish leaders did come against him, to take him before the local governor Gallio, with the charge that Paul was trying to change their manner of worship. Gallio wasted no time with them, telling them that their charge was not criminal, but only pertained to their religious beliefs. Dismissing the case, he told them it was their concern, not his. Then for some senseless reason, a mob beat up a Jewish leader in front of the court.

While it is obvious that Gallio had no personal interest in religious matters, it is also easily surmised that God used him to relieve Paul from justifying his ministry, and to chide the protesters for their petty fault-finding. His judicious decision saved Paul from the anger of more Jewish bigotry. This also confirmed God's promise to Paul in his dream.

Before leaving Corinth, Paul had all the hair of his head shaved off at the eastern port of Cenchrea, to fulfill a Nazarite vow he had made earlier, that prohibited drinking of wine or cutting of hair for a prescribed time. Then he rejoined Aquila and Priscilla, in verse 18-23 to sail for Syria, but when the ship got to Ephesus in Galatia, they debarked there to spend time counseling the local Jews.

Paul decided to leave for Jerusalem to attend a Jewish feast and sailed across the Mediterranean Sea to the port city of Caesarea, about 50 miles northwest from Jerusalem. After giving the Jerusalem church a full report on his 2nd missionary journey, Paul departed by land to Antioch, about 300 miles to the north, where he rested for a while. After a time, he left to travel by land to Galatia and Phyrgia, to refresh Christian believers in that area. That was the beginning of his 3rd missionary effort.

In verses 24-28, the scene shifts back to Ephesus, where Aquila and Priscilla were helpful to a devout Jew named Apollo, who knew little about Jesus. They coached him on the finished work of Jesus Christ, His death and resurrection, and His return to Heaven, and what this meant to believers in God. This empowered Apollo to travel to Achaia, a province in southern Greece, where he vigorously refuted traditional Jewish views, with scriptural proof that Jesus was their long awaited Messiah.

The help Aquila and Priscilla gave to Apollo illustrated how important it is for the uninformed to take advantage of the greater knowledge of seasoned Christians. Even though the young in Christ believe through grace, they still need help. As long as Christians remain in this world, there is a constant need for them to perfect their own faith, so they can be helpful to those who need their faith perfected.

CHAPTER 19:   Paul passed through the upper central part of Galatia to arrive at Ephesus in verses 1-10. There he found 12 believers in Christian doctrine who knew nothing about the Holy Spirit, but they were expecting a Messiah some day. When Paul asked them under what power they were baptized, they identified John the Baptist. Paul called his a baptism of repentance, and told the 12 that they needed to know and believe that Jesus Christ had already come as the Messiah for them.

They quickly believed and were baptized in the name of Jesus, after which Paul laid hands on them to receive the Holy Spirit, with gifts of prophecy and speaking in other languages. This established a measure of unity between them and the Jerusalem church, where the Holy Spirit was manifested in the same manner, as it was for the earliest Gentiles.

For 3 months, Paul boldly preached in the synagogue on Way of the Kingdom of God, until some stubborn Jews objected and spoke evil of him. As before, he withdrew with his followers to continue teaching for 2 years in a school operated by a philosopher named Tyrannus. His teaching reached many in that part of the land.

In 11-20 the matter of miracles by Paul and other Jewish men is discussed. For Paul, God brought healing of diseases and freedom from evil spirits, by the laying on of his hands, or his handkerchiefs and work aprons. This may have been God's way to overshadow the works of wizards and magicians in Ephesus.

Some Jewish exorcists tried to cast out evil spirits in the name of Jesus according to Paul's teachings. The 7 sons of a local chief priest tried this also, until an evil spirit challenged their authority, and the possessed man attacked them. With clothes torn off and injuries caused by the man, the phony exorcists fled the scene.

This episode spread so much fear in the populace, among Jews and Greeks, that many became believers in Jesus Christ. Also, many magicians gathered their magic books, worth 20,000 drachmas in silver, to burn them in public.

As the believers became more knowledgeable about the word of God under Paul's teaching, they demonstrated a willingness to put aside pagan beliefs and practices which impinged on their spiritual development. In the world today, if the word of God was given proper consideration, many evil lewd infidel books, video's and movies would be burned by their owners. To be sincerely committed to the benefits of Christ's gift of salvation, every evil pursuit, vice, or erotic entertainment, should be put aside, so that hearts and minds remain attuned to God's direction.

Verses 21-32 relate how a riot began in Ephesus at the time when Paul began planning his next move to Macedonia and Achaia in southern Greece. He dispatched 2 of his disciples, Timothy and Erastus to Macedonia to prepare for that mission.

A silversmith named Demetrius, who crafted silver images of the cities main pagan goddess Artemis (Diana), was losing business because of Paul's conversions of so many people to the Way (Christianity). He rallied others in the same trade, to convince them that this could put Diana's temple in disrepute, causing her to be despised and destroyed.

The tradesmen became angry and stirred up the city with their cry, 'Great is Artemis (Diana) of the Ephesians. They collared 2 of Paul's Macedonian aides, Gaius and Aristarchus, and brought them into a large amphitheater for a hearing before the people. Paul wanted to go there to rescue his comrades but other followers and local officials warned him it would not be safe for him to appear there.

Because the people were confused in verses 33-41, as to why they were there, some Jewish leaders persuaded Alexander, one of their articulate members to <u>explain to the crowd</u> <u>what the furor was all about,</u> but they rejected him by shouting for 2 hours, the same chant, 'Great is Artemis, the goddess of the Ephesians!'

Finally, a town official quieted them down to explain that nothing had been done to harm the image of Artemis, no crime against her had been committed by the 2 men, and therefore Demetrius and his cohorts should <u>take their charge before a local court.</u> Otherwise, their charges may have been heard before the city council. In any case, he convinced them that a riot was not what should happen without ample reason, and told them to return to their homes.

At that time, Rome would not tolerate public disturbances in cities under Roman control. The city official probably <u>reminded the mob of the consequences if they rioted</u> and became violent in their treatment of Paul's comrades. The public usually behaves properly in well-governed nations, being fearful of punishment if they did not. Most people stand more in awe of men's judgments than of God's.

While at Ephesus, historians believe Paul wrote the epistle of I Corinthians.

CHAPTER 20:   After public agitation subsided, Paul bid his followers good-bye and left for Macedonia in verses 1-6. He gave encouraging words to believers along the way to Greece, where he stayed 3 months. Some historians believe that he wrote the epistle II Corinthians during that time. He then planned to sail for Syria but was diverted to a land journey back through Macedonia when he <u>learned of a Jewish plot to kill him at sea.</u>

A total of 7 named followers went ahead to make arrangements for a stay at Troas. As Paul passed through Philippi, Luke apparently joined him, based on the use <u>of the pronouns 'we' and 'us' again.</u> Five days later, after sailing from Philippi, Paul and Luke rendezvous with the advance party of 7, to minister in Troas for 7 days.

On their last Sunday at Troas, Paul and his followers came together, in verses 7-12, to observe the Lord's Supper, and Paul <u>spoke to them until midnight</u>. With the room stuffy and hot from many lamps, and body heat, a young man named Eutychus fell asleep and fell out of the window where he was seated.

Having fallen from 3 stories up, he appeared to be dead, but Paul knelt down to embrace him, and rose up to <u>advise others that he was alive</u>. Paul then returned to the upper room to consummate the Lord's Supper, and continued speaking till dawn before he left. Later that morning, the young man was escorted to his home very much alive and well.

This is the first clear reference to the choice of Sunday as our Christian day of worship. This correlates with the appearance of Jesus before his disciples, after His Sunday resurrection, on 2 successive Sundays as recorded in John 20:19 and 26. Paul also told the church of Corinth in I Cor. 16:2, to gift to the Lord on each Sunday. Sunday become <u>a day of rejoicing and worship in the early Christian Church.</u>

Verses 13-17 tell of Paul's journey southward to Miletus, with him on foot for about 20 miles to Assos, while the 8 followers sailed there, <u>where he joined them on board.</u> Over 3 days, they sailed past Mitylene, to make stops on the islands of Chios and Samos, before reaching Miletus. From there, Paul sent word to Ephesus, about 40 miles to the north, for the elders of that church to join him. He obviously chose not to go to Ephesus because it <u>would have delayed his arrival in Jerusalem.</u>

Paul's only lengthy discourse to Christian Church leaders is recounted by Luke first hand in verses 18-38, after the elders joined him. His <u>main purpose was to say farewell to beloved believers</u> that he expected not to see again. He first reminded them how he humbly served the Lord, preaching the truth equally to Jews and Gentiles, even though the Jews caused him much trouble.

He admitted to them that he was unsure of his fate, but he was <u>directed by the Holy Spirit to return to Jerusalem,</u> and he was not concerned about trouble there as long as he was able to finish the ministry that Jesus gave him.

He confessed that he did not expect them to see him again, so they would be on their own, without his help. He said they had been told all that God wanted them to know, so with the help of the Holy Spirit, they could <u>take good care of themselves and their fellow church members.</u>

He warned them of antagonists attacking them like wolves, and backsliding amongst them. He reminded them that he had spoken of trouble to come for 3 years, often with tears in his eyes He admonished them to help the weak with the same commitment that he had demonstrated in working hard to provide for his own needs, while ministering to them. Then he quoted Jesus saying, 'It is more blessed to give than to receive.' He closed by placing them in God's care and kindness, with blessings to follow.

When he knelt down to pray for them, they all wept and showed their love for him with kisses and hugs, expressing <u>regret that they would not see him again.</u> They gave him a loving send-off as they accompanied him to his ship at dockside. There was no doubt about their affection for him and regret over his departure.

CHAPTER 21:   Paul and Luke sailed to the southeast, in verses 1-14, passing the islands of Cos and Rhodes, to arrive at the port city of Patera, in Lycia. There they secured passage on a larger ship that would sail to the south of Cyprus <u>to reach Tyre in Phonecia,</u> where it docked to off load cargo. This gave them an opportunity to spend a week with Christian followers, who made a point to <u>warn Paul of danger ahead, per the Holy Spirit.</u>

As they departed, all followers with their families walked with them from town to the seashore, where they <u>knelt and prayed together,</u> before farewell niceties. From Tyre they sailed a short distance to Ptolemais to spend a day there with followers. The next day they sailed further south to Caesarea to spend several days with Philip, a preacher and one of 7 men chosen to supervise resource distribution in Chapter 6. He also had 4 unmarried virgin daughters with the gift of prophesy (see Ch. 2:17)

While there, a prophet from Judea named Agabus borrowed Paul's long garment belt to bind himself hand and foot. He then shared with Paul a message he had from the Holy Spirit that <u>the belt owner, Paul, would be bound by the Jerusalem Jews</u> and handed over to Roman Gentile authority.

This caused his friends to beg Paul not to go there. Paul's response was to say that their weeping was breaking his heart, but <u>he had no choice</u> but to be bound and even die in

Jerusalem for the cause of Jesus Christ. His followers admired his courage and committed him to God, saying, 'The will of the Lord be done.'

As his followers foresaw trouble for him, in love they tried to keep him free from it, but this seemed to strengthen his resolve to do what he thought the Lord wanted of him. Christians are warned repeatedly in scriptures of much tribulation before entering into the kingdom of God, which they must face up to in the strength of the Holy Spirit as Paul demonstrated. Young Christians should aspire to be faithful disciples of Jesus Christ, steadfast in the faith, as they pass through life to a ripe old age, thereby honoring the Lord.

In 15-25, Paul, Luke, and other believers from Caesarea sailed on to Jerusalem with Cyprus believer Mnason, who would provide lodging for them there. They were well received by Christian brothers in Jerusalem, including James and the church elders, after they received a report of Paul's missionary success with the Gentiles. But they advised Paul of a false notion held by some Jews that he preached non-compliance with Jewish tradition, namely circumcision, to the Gentiles.

James and the elders then asked Paul to pacify the believing Jews, by compliance with some ceremonial purification law, with 4 other men, and to pay for their expenses. This was to show that he was trustworthy in obeying Mosaic law, as they had prescribed for the Gentiles in a letter to them earlier (see Ch.15:19-20).

In actuality, what Paul preached tended not to destroy the law, but to fulfill it. He preached righteousness through Christ, with repentance and faith, in which believers would make proper use of the new covenant law of the kingdom of God.

In verses 26-36, Paul went through the ceremony with the 4 men, but during a 7 day purification period while in the temple, he was accosted by some traditional Jews who accused him of bringing Greek Gentiles into the temple, in violation of temple rules. They arrived at this false notion because they had seen an Ephesian with him in the city, and perhaps Luke also. Typical of their mob mentality, the people were aroused by this accusation, and drug Paul out to beat him to death.

Fortunately, the local Roman military commander heard of the disturbance and brought soldiers to investigate. This stopped the beating and Paul was then chained as the officer tried to find out what the furor was all about. This was a futile attempt because some of the crowd said one thing and others said another thing against Paul. So Paul was quickly taken into the military headquarters to escape the wrath of the crowd, who shouted to kill him.

Paul surprised the Roman commander when he spoke to him in Greek. Before that, the officer thought Paul was an Egyptian that had led a band of 4000 assassins in a rebellion against Roman law. Paul clarified that he was a Jewish citizen from Tarsus, an important city of Cilicia, and asked to speak to the crowd. With permission granted, he stood on the entrance steps, motioned for silence, and spoke to them in Aramaic.

VIEWPOINTS: Paul's return to Jerusalem completed his 3rd missionary journey on an ominous note, despite his great effectiveness in spreading the Christian gospel to the Gentile people. Just as Jesus had persisted in returning to Jerusalem when His time had come, so Paul was inspired by the Holy Spirit to do likewise, without fear of the outcome, as predicted by those who loved him. Just as Jesus was rejected by traditional Jews, so Paul was rejected, in spite of his efforts at reconciliation. Truly, Paul was a type of Jesus in many ways, suffering much while doing his best to fulfill the will of God to reach out to sinners of the world.

CHAPTER 22:   Hearing Paul speak in Aramaic, in verses 1-21, the crowd respectfully became quiet, as he too respectfully addressed them as, 'Friends and community leaders (Brethren and fathers), let me tell you all about me.' After identifying himself as a Jew, he compared his zeal for God as being similar to theirs, another attempt at rapport with them.

Paul told them of his early history as a persecutor of new believers in Jesus, including his approval of the stoning death of Stephen (Ch. 7:58, 8:1) and his trip to Damascus to persecute more of them. Then he tells of his encounter with the light of Jesus Christ on the road to Damascus resulting in blindness, with follow-up healing by Ananias and his conversion to the service of the Lord, as related in Ch. 9:1-18.

He told them of a message received from God while praying in the temple, that he should leave Jerusalem, where the people paid no heed to the word of Jesus, and go far away to preach to the Gentiles.

As the Jews heard his remark about ministering to distant Gentiles in verse 22, they reacted angrily because of their bias against non-Jewish believers in Jesus without becoming Jews. In 23-30 Paul faces a crowd showing their hostility to him, by calling for his death, tearing their clothes, and throwing dirt in the air.

The Roman commander had him taken into the military barracks for examination under the whip. As he was being tied up, Paul asked if it was legal to beat a Roman citizen without a court hearing. A junior officer reported this to the commander who asked how Paul became a Roman citizen. When Paul said he was born as one, the military backed off in fear that they had broken a law. The next day the commander brought Paul unchained before the Jewish Sanhedrin to find out why they were so hostile to him, and to determine if any legal charges were justified.

Paul defended his dedication to minister to the Gentile world because it was ordained of God; he also defended himself as a Roman citizen to avoid beatings and other rough treatment by Roman authorities. His courage in both cases exemplified his willingness to endure public condemnation, as well as his effort to prevent physical suffering by legal means. So it should be with Christians in this wicked world!

CHAPTER 23:   Before the Sanhedrin, in verses 1-10, Paul unflinchingly looked at them and said, 'My friends, to this day I have served God with a clear conscience.' At this, the high priest, Ananais (not the one in Ch. 9), ordered a nearby man to strike Paul in the mouth. Paul angrily said to Ananais, 'You white-washed wall! Wait till God strikes you for breaking the Mosaic Law by having me struck, when you should judge me under it." In effect, he called the high priest a complete hypocrite. Paul's response was both a rebuke and a prediction of God's punishment.

Other men chided Paul for insulting 'God's high priest.' Paul then admitted that he didn't recognize Ananais as high priest, of which no evil should be spoken. Maybe he truly did not recognize him as such, or he spoke with veiled sarcasm.

Seeing that the Sanhedrin was made up of Pharisees and Sadducees, Paul cleverly announced that he too was a Pharisee, and he felt that he was being tried solely because <u>he believed in the resurrection of the dead</u>. This set off a firestorm of disagreement between the two factions, because the Pharisees agreed with Paul, while the Sadducees did not. Amidst much shouting back and forth, some Pharisees scholars declared that <u>they saw nothing wrong with Paul</u>, as an angel may have spoken to him.

The dispute between the two factions became so fierce that the Roman commander decided it was prudent for soldiers to escort Paul back to the barracks. By diverting the Pharisees from further antagonism, <u>Paul was taken to safety.</u>

The following night in verses 11-22, Jesus stood by Paul in a vision to tell him to be brave and not worry, because He would take <u>Paul to Rome to minister there too.</u> This had to be gratifying to Paul, since his desire was to honor God everywhere.

The next morning, 40 Jewish men made a pact not to eat or drink anything until they had killed Paul; then they asked the Sanhedrin leaders to have Paul brought before them again for more questioning, so <u>they could kill him enroute.</u>

For the only time in scriptures, a <u>member of Paul's family is mentioned</u>, a nephew, who had heard about the plot and went to Paul's barracks to inform him of it. Paul had the nephew taken to the commander to give him this information. The commander dismissed him with a request not to tell others what he had been told.

That night, in verses 23-35, the commander mobilized a 470 man escort, 200 regular foot soldiers, 70 riding horses, and 200 spear armed foot soldiers, <u>to take Paul on horseback to Caeserea</u>, about 70 miles to the north. The commander wrote a letter to Felix the governor at Caeserea, telling him about Paul's problem with the Sanhedrin and the plot to kill him. When Paul arrived, Felix inquired what province he was from. When Paul told him Celicia, the governor said he was then authorized to conduct a hearing when the Jewish accusers brought charges.

Paul was held in Herod's mansion, where he languished with visitation rights, <u>for about 2 years (probably 58-60 AD)</u>, until his case was resolved. God often used the resources and moral virtues of heathens as instruments to protect His persecuted servants for unscheduled periods of time.

CHAPTER 24:   After the escort soldiers returned to Jerusalem, to inform Ananais of Paul's situation, it only <u>took him 5 days to file charges</u> against Paul in verses 1-9, with the help of church elders and a legal spokesman named Tertullus. After flattery in his opening remarks to Felix, Tertullus charged Paul with treasonous disturbances, religious heresy (as a ringleader of the Nazarene sect), and temple desecration. He accused Commander Lysias, who had rescued Paul, with interference in their own hearing on Paul. The hostile Jews with him concurred in what he said.

These charges were much like those leveled against Jesus, as well as prophets of old, for their <u>well meant efforts to reach sinners for the Lord</u>. Motivated by selfish and evil ambitions, unbelievers historically have mislead and prejudiced men in positions of authority against the truth declared by honest and sincere servants of God. There can be no question how the revilers and the reviled will be judged by Him.

Paul respectfully voices his own defense before Felix in verses 10-21, <u>point by point</u> <u>against the charges as made</u>: '1-It was impossible for me to stir up a riot in just 7 days out of 12 that I was there, 2-I spoke nowhere publicly on religious matters, and 3-There is no substantiation to these charges or that I desecrated the temple.'

He admitted that he worshipped God according to 'the Way' (Christian gospel), and that he <u>also believed in the Mosaic Law and Old Testament prophecy</u>. This included his admission that he believed in resurrection of the dead, both the righteous and the wicked, to eventually come, apart from his own judgment.

Paul added that his presence in the temple was to bring a collection of funds to the local church fellowship <u>from more prosperous believers</u> in other lands. That was when the Jews from Asia (not from Jerusalem) saw him and stirred up trouble, trying to get local Jews turned against him. Paul asserted that those Jews should have been present in the hearing before Felix. This was a very good point!

Since Felix had been in Judea and Samaria for 6 years, where he learned about the Christian movement, he was not convinced <u>that the charges were legitimate</u>, and terminated the hearing until he heard from Commander Lysias. Paul was put in centurion protective custody with visitation rights.

Days later, Felix and his Jewish wife Drusilla had a conversation with Paul about his Christian faith. When Paul <u>emphasized the need for proper conduct to avoid later judgment,</u> Felix felt guilty about his own life, which was exceedingly wicked, and dismissed Paul. He did have more conversations with Paul with an ulterior motive of obtaining ransom money from him. Two years passed until Felix was replaced (60 AD) by a new governor, Porcius Festus, who <u>kept Paul confined to placate the Jews.</u>

Luke may have written the Book of Acts during Paul's 2 year confinement.

CHAPTER 25:   Three days after Festus arrived in Caesarea, he traveled to Jerusalem to meet with Jewish leaders in verses 1-12, for diplomatic reasons. Jewish temple leaders immediately <u>petitioned him to bring Paul back to Jerusalem</u>, with intent to ambush his escort and kill him on the road. Festus denied their request, and told them to come to Caesarea when he returned <u>to present their case against Paul.</u>

After 10 days, Festus returned to Caesarea accompanied by a representation of Jews, for a hearing of their charges against Paul. Their case was weak, and Paul asserted that he had <u>committed no wrong against Jewish law, temple rules, or Caesar.</u>

Festus tried to wiggle out of a ruling by offering to let Paul return to Jerusalem to be tried there, but Paul resorted to his best defense, that he was a Roman citizen <u>who should be</u> <u>tried under Roman laws</u>. He was more willing to submit to the rules of justice for Roman citizens, whatever the outcome, than to face certain death under Jewish judgment. His appeal to Caesar was granted, because Festus <u>could not ignore his request.</u>

In verses 13-27, Festus informed the visiting territorial ruler, King Agrippa and his sister, Bernice, of Paul's <u>situation and problem with hostile Jews</u>. He also expressed his puzzlement over Paul's assertion that Jesus had been raised from death. He admitted his uncertainty over what was proper justice, and therefore <u>approved Paul's request to be tried</u> <u>under Roman law.</u>

Agrippa asked to hear what Paul had to say for himself. Festus agreed to this because he needed tangible evidence for his written request to Caesar of reasonable cause for trying Paul. He obviously <u>hoped that Agrippa would be helpful.</u>

CHAPTER 26:   In verses 1-8, when Agrippa invited Paul to speak up, he first expressed his pleasure over Agrippa's involvement and interest because he was <u>familiar with Jewish customs and religious beliefs.</u>

Paul then summarized the story of his life from childhood to adulthood when he became a devout Pharisee, to <u>be then charged with beliefs and hope given to them</u> by God in Old Testament days. He asked why he should be charged with something the 12 tribes of Israel longed for, a Messiah, who came but was crucified and then resurrected by God. He queried Agrippa and those present with him why it was so difficult for them to <u>understand</u> that God <u>could raise people from death.</u>

In verses 9-18, Paul gave Agrippa a review of his previous persecution of new believers. He told how he was confronted by Jesus on the road to Damascus over this practice, and how he was <u>converted to the cause of the Christian Church,</u> to carry the gospel of Jesus to the entire world. (as recounted in Ch. 9:1-19; 22:6-16). He told how he was promised protection by God, from both Jews and Gentiles.

Paul emphasized in verses 19-23 that he had to be obedient to God on this mission, which he first took to Damascus, Jerusalem, and Judea, <u>before going to Gentile people.</u> His message to all was that they should repent of their sins, turn to God, and then live and behave in a manner that honored God in all ways. For thus preaching what the prophets and Moses predicted, that the Messiah would come to be put to death and then be resurrected to life, <u>the hostile Jews tried to kill him.</u>

When Paul spoke of Christ's resurrection in verse 23, Fetus yelled, 'Paul, you are crazy!. Your great learning has caused you to lose your senses.' Paul's courteous denial of this in 24-32, was prefixed by 'Honorable Festus.' Then he <u>expressed confidence in Agrippa's knowledge of such prophecy,</u> since it was not a hidden fact. Flattered, Agrippa said he was almost persuaded to become a Christian.

Paul declared that no matter when it would happen, he sincerely wished that all <u>who heard his testimony would become Christians.</u> This concluded the hearing before Agrippa and his entourage, who then privately discussed the charges against Paul and concluded that he was not guilty of any wrong doing justifying death or imprisonment.

Agrippa shared this with Festus, saying Paul <u>could have been freed except for his</u> appeal to Caesar, which was formally made and thus binding on them.

<u>VIEWPOINTS:</u>   Although seen as innocent of a civil wrong, Paul was <u>not released because of his own appeal</u> to a higher authority. In this way, Paul would also realize his ambition to carry Christ's salvation message to the Gentiles in Rome. God was working this out in His own way, while also giving Paul protection.

Contrary to the frequent failure of a Christian culture to observe the rules of truth, justice, and charity, <u>in judging their brethren,</u> the Roman authorities were quite diligent in adhering to their laws. In spite of their judicial stance, the concerns of the old Roman empire will have no favorable consequence before God, unless they <u>accepted Paul's message of</u> <u>repentance, belief in a living Christ, and a righteous life.</u>

Royalty and their willingness to hear charges against the innocent is often <u>overshadowed by the conduct and veracity of the poor prisoner at the bar,</u> as was demonstrated by Paul's self-defense. Their regal appearance and consideration, cannot be compared or deemed equal to Paul's wisdom, courtesy, dignity, courage, and constancy in defending his faith in Christ, as the living Son of God. How wonderful if all Christians could live up to his superb example of a dedicated believer!

CHAPTER 27: Luke used the pronoun 'we' again to indicate that he too traveled to Rome with Paul, along with other prisoners, <u>under the control of a band of soldiers</u> commanded by a Roman centurion named Julius. The journey is believed to have begun in late summer or early fall.

In verses 1-8, the first stage of the journey at sea is described, from Caesarea where they boarded a ship, to the first stopping point about 75 miles to the north at Sidon, and from there to Myra of Lycia (south coast of modern Turkey). Paul was given <u>permission by Julius</u> to go <u>ashore at Sidon</u> to visit friends who filled some of his needs for the trip.

Their 460 mile voyage from Sidon to Myra was first to the north and then westerly because of adverse winds. They transferred to a larger ship at Myra, which sailed slowly westward about 130 miles to reach Cnidus, where adverse winds caused a change of course to the southwest to the island of Crete. There they docked at the southern port of Fair Havens, after another 300 miles of rough sailing.

Considerable time had been lost and sailing conditions were becoming more dangerous, so Paul spoke up in 9-12, to suggest that they go no further, for fear of disaster at sea. Unfortunately Julius opted for the proposal of the ship's owner and his helmsman that they <u>go further to winter at a larger port</u> 60 miles away on the west coast of Crete. They considered the fair Haven harbor unsuitable for a winter layover.

In 13-20, with a gentle breeze at their backs, the ship headed west close to shore, but not for long. Shortly, a violent northeasterly wind <u>forced them to lower the sails and</u> <u>drift</u> to the south to gain some protection near an uncharted island called Claudia. There they secured the lifeboat and placed rope cables around the ship's hull for added strength <u>in case they ran aground.</u> During the next two days, some cargo and equipment was tossed overboard to lighten the ship. They had <u>no sun or star navigation</u> for days at a time, and persistent storms began to give them doubts of survival.

They also lacked food or were too seasick to retain it. At this point, in verses 21-26, Paul chides the ship's crew for not heeding his earlier warning at Crete, but simultaneously <u>assures them that there would be no loss of life or ship.</u> He had a dream in which an angel informed him it was God's will that they all survive so Paul would come before Caesar. Against this good news, he added that they would be ship-wrecked on some small island.

On the 14th night, in 27-38, the sailors realized they were close to land and a depth reading confirmed that they were in shallow waters, so they dropped anchor to wait until daylight. Then some sailors began lowering the lifeboat with intentions of deserting the ship. Paul saw this and warned Captain Julius that lives would be lost without them, so the soldiers were ordered to cut the ropes to let the boat fall into the water.

Before dawn, Paul is concerned over the hunger of all on board, and urges the 276 men to eat for renewed strength. He took a piece of bread, thanked God for it, and ate of it. This encouraged others to eat, which energized them to throw their entire cargo of wheat into the sea to lighten the ship.

As daylight came, in verses 37-44, they saw a coast line with a cove and beach. They cut the anchors loose, freed up the rudder oars, raised some sail, and began moving towards the beach. Unfortunately, the bow of the ship plowed into a sandbar; the ship was stalled and high waves smashed into the stern.

Thinking that the prisoners on board would jump overboard and try to swim to shore, the soldiers decided to kill them, for they feared execution if they allowed prisoners to escape. Captain Julius had special concern for Paul's life, and forbade the killing of any prisoners. Instead, he authorized all who could swim to go for the beach, and those who could not swim to get there on wooden planks or other floating ship parts. Everyone reach shore safely! Up to this point the ship had sailed about 1015 miles, in a time frame far in excess of normal travel.

VIEWPOINTS: Just as sailors must make take advantage of supporting winds, likewise Christians must do so, in their passage over the seas of life. Conversely, we must move forward as best we can when winds blow against us, or find a safe haven in the Lord's domain. We are not always certain of achieving our purpose in life, or of finding a safe haven when needed, but we know we will be quite safe when we enter heaven.

Faithful servants of God find comfort when in difficulties, knowing that the Lord will provide and prolong their lives if He has work for them to do. Now if Paul had placed himself in bad company, he might justly not have survived the storm; but with God taking him into the journey, he is secured with the rest of them. How fortunate that Paul was on board, as he not only communicated with the Lord, but he was a fountain of encouragement to all under life-threatening conditions. He demonstrated God given leadership under dire stress!

With the shore in view, the ship still did not make it, proving how uncertain security in life can be when the way is not known. The way of the God's promised salvation is secure for all believers, for they will safely get to that heavenly shore, in spite of sandbars and rocks along the way. What a joyful landing that will be!

CHAPTER 28: Having just made it to the shore of an island not known to them, one must wonder how God would deal with all 460 men, without a clue of dangers ahead, or their ultimate destination. As so often is shown, in His marvelous grace, the outcome was spectacular and far better than one would expect.

In verses 1-10, they learned that they were on the island of Malta, about 60 miles south of Sicily, when friendly (but pagan) natives welcomed them with fires to warm them as their clothes dried. When Paul gathered some wood for the fires, a poisonous snake sank its fangs into his hand.

Being superstitious, the natives jumped to the conclusion that Paul was a criminal, who was saved from drowning for a god of justice to kill him. Paul shook the snake into the fire, and when his hand did not swell and he didn't drop dead as the natives expected, their view changed to, 'This man is a god.' He suddenly earned greater respect which would benefit all of them!

Things got better for Paul after the island's friendly Governor Publius had him as a guest in his home for 3 days. The governor's father was sick in bed with fever and stomach problems. Paul used his God given gift of prayer over the elderly man, to bring complete healing. This brought many others to Paul for healing, from a fever sometimes lasting for months, that some accounts claim was caused by Maltese goat's milk. The result of his service to them was a generous outpouring of supplies for the entire group for the winter until they sailed for Rome.

It is remarkable how God made Paul special among these people, and so opened the way for the receiving of the gospel. The Lord provides friends for his people wherever He leads them, and makes them a blessing to those who are afflicted.

After a 3 month layover, in 11-16, the group boarded an Egyptian ship, called 'The Twin Gods,'(old Greek sailing gods, Castor and Pollux) that had docked there for the winter. It sailed north about 100 miles to the port of Syracuse on the island of Sicily, where it docked for 3 days. From there it sailed another 100 miles to reach the port of Rhegium on the southern toe of Italy. Two days later, about 200 miles to the northwest, they reached the port city of Puteoli, where Paul and his escort disembarked, and he enjoyed a week there with some Christian brothers.

As Paul's party traveled on foot, or some other mode of land travel to Rome, about 150 miles to the northwest, some Christian brothers came south to meet them at two other coastal towns. This was most encouraging to Paul, for which he gave thanks to God. Upon arriving in Rome, Julius delivered Paul and the other prisoners to the captain of the Roman guard, but Paul was given private quarters with a single guard over him.

After 3 days of rest, in verses 17-31, Paul called some Jewish leaders together to explain his presence in Rome, because they had no information about him from Jerusalem. He told them of the hostility he had faced there and why he became a prisoner, to be tried before Caesar. They were interested in hearing his story, and his explanation of the Christian Wa y.

Paul testified earnestly to them about the kingdom of God, introduced by the arrival of Jesus as the Messiah, in accordance with Mosaic Law and biblical prophesy. As usual, some believed and some did not. Then he quoted from Is. 6:9-10, presenting it as a message from the Holy Spirit to their forefathers, about their stubborn resistance to God's word.

He concluded by telling them that the message of salvation through Jesus, which they rejected, was being sent to the Gentile world which would accept it. The Jews departed from him in dispute over what to believe.

Paul resided 2 more years in his own rental house, keeping an open door to all who wished to hear his message, without hindrance from Roman authority. Historical evidence is that he wrote several New Testament letters (epistles) during this time.

SUMMARY: The Book of Acts, as written by Luke, is an inspirational account of how the gospel of Jesus Christ, pertaining to the kingdom of God, spread to the Gentile world, after repeated rejections by God's chosen people, the Jews, for whom it was meant first and foremost. The 1st 12 chapters focus mostly on the conversion of Jews to the Messianic faith, beginning with the Jerusalem Church, spreading to the prominent churches at Caesarea, Antioch, and throughout Galatia.

Chapters 13-28 focus almost totally on the ministry of Saul/Paul, first to the Jews wherever he went, but mostly to the Gentiles when the Jews became hostile and rejected his message. God's hand was on Paul more and more to send him to the Gentile world. His own conviction and commitment to this mission grew with time.

Luke did not complete the story of Paul's experience with Roman law, to tell whether he was allowed to preach the gospel as a free man after his 2 years of house arrest. Nothing is said of his hearing before the Roman emperor, or his death.

The reader is invited to the article at the end of this book, entitled 'Peter, Paul, and Mary' for historical data that various publications provide, particularly on the end times of Paul, and his contribution of a major portion of the New Testament.

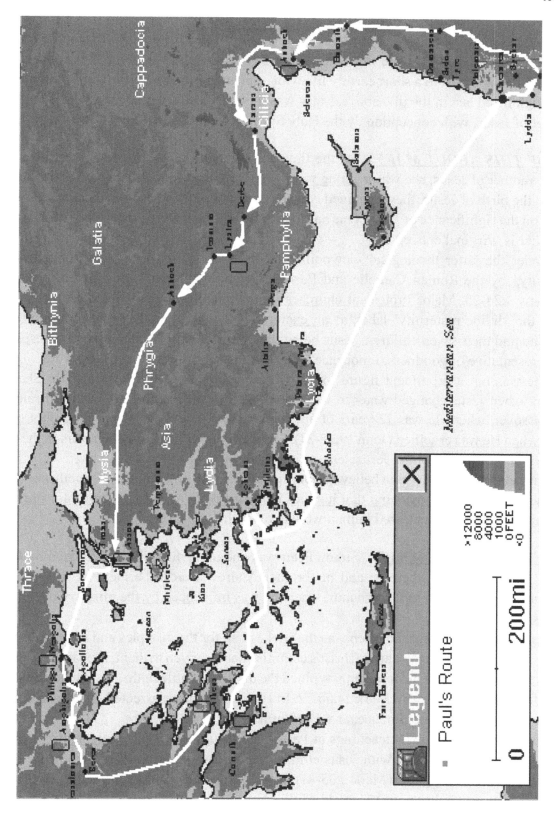

PAUL'S SECOND MISSIONARY JOURNEY

PETER, PAUL AND MARY

P eter, Paul and Mary were three important key figures used by God to introduced His son, Jesus Christ to a short earthly life with a spiritual mission for the souls of humanity. Although listed last in the title above, Mary was the first to be selected for a vital role, as the mother of Jesus, with conception by the Holy Spirit.

KNOW THIS ABOUT MARY: At the time she was notified by an angel that she would be the mother of Jesus, she was a young virgin engaged to Joseph. Although married to him before the birth of Jesus, they remained celibate until after His birth. Two theological beliefs focus on the significance of Mary. One has to do with what is referred to as 'divine maternity,' the other is 'virginal conception.'

Under the latter theological viewpoint, she has been raised to a status of 'perpetual virginity,' by the Roman Catholic and Eastern Orthodox churches, but this is refuted by Matthew 1:24-25. Major Protestant churches do not share this view. She more aptly lived up to the 'divine maternity' label, as an example of excellent motherhood, devoted to her husband and their seven children, Jesus being the first-born. In Christianity, she is respected as representative of goodness, innocence, and steadfast commitment to Godly ways.

She was not a prominent figure in the Gospel accounts of the early church. She was present when Jesus changed water to wine (John 2:1-11), she was with Him in Jerusalem at the Passover, when He was 12 years of age (Luke 2:41-51), and she stood at the foot of the cross when He was crucified (John 19:25-27). She was present with other believers in the early church, in the upper room at Jerusalem, as indicated in Acts 1:14.

It is befitting that Christian believers admire, respect, and honor her as the mother of Jesus, but there is no biblical teaching that justifies holding her up as a divine being for prayer or worship. She was just a blessed human woman of God.

PETER, THE ECCENTRIC: Simon Peter was one of the first disciples chosen by Jesus, at the Sea of Galilee, where he and his brother Andrew were fishermen. He was married and maintained a home in Capernaum, where he was influenced by the ministry of John the Baptist.

As a disciple for Jesus, he often was the spokesman for the disciples and raised questions they wanted to ask. Later on, after Christ's commission was given to them, he was the leader of the twelve disciples. Yet, he frequently typified the disciple of little faith, as he demonstrated in his infamous denial scene in Mark 14:66-72. In His mercy, the resurrected Jesus rehabilitated him to his position of prominence, as related in John 21:15-19.

Jesus often directed His teachings at Peter even though intended for the entire group of disciples. Peter was present with Jesus at many significant times, such as the raising of the synagogue ruler's daughter (Mark 5:35-41), at the Transfiguration (Mark 9:2-8), and at the arrest of Jesus in Gethsemene (Mark 14:43-50).

He played an influential role in establishing the Jerusalem church as related in the early chapters of Acts, from 2:14 to 5:16. Later, in 9:32 to 12:19, he was active in the early stages of the Gentile mission, before Paul became the "Apostle to the Gentiles." Peter may have forfeited the opportunity to be a continuing leader of either one of these ministries because of his commitment to doing his best to hold together the diverse strands of beginning Christianity.

It is believed that Peter died as a martyr in Rome during the reign of Emperor Nero, in the late 60s. His legacy lives on in his contribution to the New Testament in his books of I and II Peter, believed to have been written between 64-67 AD.

FROM SAUL TO PAUL: Most dramatic is how Saul, as a staunch believer in Old Testament Mosaic law, and an initial supporter of Pharisee bias against the teachings of Jesus, would be fingered by the resurrected Jesus to be the prime mover of the new covenant gospel of the kingdom to the Gentile world. His apostleship and writing of 13 Epistles (letters to churches) comprise an important part of the New Testament.

With the Jewish name of Saul, and an official Roman name of Paul (Paulos), he was born in the Roman city of Tarsus, possibly because his parents migrated from Galilee. At home he was well trained in Jewish scriptures and tradition, in both the ancient Hebrew language and Aramaic, and later learned to speak Greek.

In his teens, he went to Jerusalem to study under the famous rabbi, Gamaliel. one of the best Jewish teachers of that day, who instilled great zeal in him for the traditions of his people. This shaped his disagreement with the teachings of the apostle Stephen who placed Jesus superior to old Jewish law and temple worship. Paul then approved the stoning of Stephen as the first martyr of the new church.

Paul was converted about 32 AD, after his Damascus Road experience, as told in 3 passages of Acts: 9:3-19, 22:6-21, and 26:13-23. This radical change of his spiritual view initiated his motivation to preach throughout the Roman Gentile world, after he first preached in Damascus, and Jerusalem, and his home town of Tarsus for about 12 years.

Then, he completed 3 major missionary journeys in his remaining 23 years of service to the Lord. The 1st in 46-48 AD began in Antioch, under the leadership of Barnabas, who came to Tarsus to recruit Paul. They sailed to the island of Cyprus, then to Perga, Iconium, Lystra, Derbe, and from there they traced their way back to Antioch. He traveled about 14 50 miles, 730 at sea, and 720 on land, on foot, or possibly riding in an ox cart or on horses.

For his 2nd journey about 49-52, Paul with Silas as an associate, departed from Antioch, to go through Syria and Cilicia, back to Derbe and Lystra, and then to Troas, and Philippi in Macedonia, where they were jailed. From there they traveled to Thessalonica, Berea, Athens, Corinth, and back to Antioch in Syria. On this journey, he traveled about 1050 miles by sea, and 1150 by land, for a total of 2200 miles.

Much of Paul's time on his 3rd missionary venture in 52-57 AD was spent in the city of Ephesus from which he carried the gospel to 7 churches in surrounding cities. From there he went as far as Athens in the south of Greece and then retraced his path through Macedonia, northeastern Greece, Troas, Miletus, and back to Jerusalem. He traveled a total of about 2640 miles, 1340 by sea, and 1300 by land over a period of about 5 years.

Altogether, his total travels, from the beginning of his 1st missionary journey in 46 AD, through his sea journey to Rome for his first trial in 60 AD, covered a total of over 8420 miles, with 5150 by sea and 3270 miles on land. This does not include travel distance during his time of freedom between his 1st and 2nd imprisonment in Rome. He may easily have traveled over 10,000 miles. Only one mention is found that he rode a horse part way, in Acts 23:24.

Paul freely reminded the churches he visited that he possessed apostolic authority from the Lord, and was called by God to carry the gospel to the Gentiles, however he often preached first to the Jews in each region.

When Paul talked about a person accepting God's offer of reconciliation in Christ, he often referred to Old Testament persons of faith, using Abraham as a worthy example. He always advised a person of faith to fellowship with a church body. In his letters to the churches he established or encouraged, he emphasized that the basis of a righteous Christian lifestyle of love depended on the Holy Spirit.

During his 35 years of serving God as a fantastically dedicated evangelist to the Jews first and finally to the Gentile world, he spent many months and years in confinement. During such times, he wrote 13 epistles (letters) to the major churches, which became significant portions of the New Testament. Based on numerous published biblical textbooks, the following summary of these writings, as to location and time, is believed to be fairly accurate:

- Galations, in 48-49 AD, possibly at Antioch, after his 1st journey.
- I & II Thessalonians, in 52 AD, at Corinth, during his 2nd journey.
- I & II Corinthians, about 55-56 AD, at Ephesus, on his 3rd journey.
- Romans, about 56 AD, at Corinth, near end of his 3rd journey.
- Ephesians, Colossians, Philippians, and Philemon, about 61-62 AD, during his imprisonment in Rome.
- I Timothy, and Titus, about 62 AD, while in Macedonia, after 2 years imprisonment in Rome.
- II Timothy, about 67 AD, in Rome, during his second Roman time of imprisonment, shortly before his execution.

It is likely that Paul wrote the Book of Hebrews also, about 66-67 AD, during his 2nd imprisonment, although this is in dispute among historians.

He was arrested in Jerusalem, moved to Caesarea, and sailed for Rome, in 60 AD, for his first imprisonment, believed to have been for 2-3 years. Indications are that he was released, and taken captive again later, about 65 AD, before he was executed about 67 AD by Roman Emperor Nero, to end his 35 years of ministry.

Non-biblical records describe Paul as a small man, with crooked legs, a bald head, and converging eyebrows over a hooked nose. He suffered immensely, but God gave him supernatural power to cope and recover to preach another day.

His character was outstanding as a totally committed servant of the Lord. In his last days, he said in II Timothy 4:6-7, 'My life is being given as an offering to God. The time has come for me to leave this life. I have fought the good fight, I have finished the race, I have kept the faith.' This is a testimony for every believer!

ROMANS—BOOK SIX

What Romans is all about! This epistle was written by the Apostle Paul while in Corinth, in the south of Greece about 56 AD, to the believer group in Rome that he hoped to visit. He was nearing the end of his 3rd missionary journey, when he planned to visit Rome after a special trip to Jerusalem to deliver some contributions from Gentile believers in Greece and Asia Minor. This plan was tabled by his conflict with the Jerusalem traditional Jews who had him arrested by the Roman governing authority. He did not reach Rome until 3 years later, as a prisoner of Rome for a hearing before Caesar.

He wrote to introduce himself before his visit and to share some of his theology, with the hope that they would provide support for his intended journey on to Spain (15:24). He also beseeched the Roman believers to pray for him as he went to Jerusalem (15:30-31). Paul was concerned about the Jerusalem Church's reaction to the offering from Gentile churches and if it would tend to bring the Jewish and Gentile Christians closer together in their common faith.

The book is a great presentation of God's plan of salvation, both for the Jews and the Gentiles. Paul's ambition was to encourage the two factions to live harmoniously with each other. He stressed that there is only one God, for both groups. To this end, he focused on the core principles of the Christian faith: sin versus righteousness, faith with good works, and seeing God as a standard for a lifestyle pleasing to Him.

Paul added clarification on the righteousness of God's agenda, by setting things right through the life, death, and resurrection of Jesus. What Paul meant by righteousness is crucial for one's interpretation of Romans, which stimulates one's perception of justification so as to achieve high ethical standards. This encompasses both the new status of a believer before God and the new life that this status demands.

In this letter, Paul points out that a believer's union with Christ reveals the ugliness of sin. By obeying God as Jesus did, believers reject sin's dominion in life. Our salvation in Christ replaces the sting of death with a spiritual future with God. Christians have the resources of God to fight sin victoriously; but an intense lifetime struggle is unavoidable.

After his introduction, Paul clearly stated the theme of his letter—the righteousness of God, as revealed in the gospel. This is followed by an emphasis of God's provision of salvation through Jesus Christ on the basis of faith. This brings a realization of peace with God, with assurance of His love for us, and enables us to rejoice in the face of difficulties. Finally, he calls on Christians to practice obedience to God, by living transformed lives, and to demonstrate this in good stewardship of their spiritual gifts. Also, Christians should strive to edify one another in the fellowship of a good church.

CHAPTER 1:   As a chosen bond servant of God, Paul identified himself in verses 1-7, as an apostle to carry the salvation gospel of Jesus Christ, the good news, to everyone who would believe it. He identified Jesus with prophecy of His lineage from the house of David, to be the Son of God, as confirmed by His resurrection through the Holy Spirit. He acknowledged Christ's mercy to all who believe in Him, himself as well as all those in Rome, who are always in his prayers. As Saints of God, he wishes them grace and peace through His Son, Jesus Christ.

In 7-17, Paul expressed his thankfulness for the faith of the Roman believers which was drawing much attention in that part of the world, for which reason he praises them daily in prayer. He admits his desire for God to provide a way to visit them, so that he might bless them as they would also bless him, while sharing mutually in their faith. Because he owed God so much, he felt indebted and was proud to preach the gospel to Jew and Gentile alike, who in their wisdom and willingness to understanding and believe would then by faith live in righteousness.

Paul spoke of God's wrath against the sins of the world in verses 18-23, and deplored the wicked suppressing the true meaning of righteousness, even when they knew about God, His powers of creation, and divine nature. Foolishly, such persons are not thankful to Him, nor do they honor Him in any way. With no excuse, they turn to idolatry, worshipping pagan images of mankind, birds, animals, and serpents.

Paul stated that God would give up such wicked ones to the lusts of their hearts, in verses 24-32; This includes unnatural sexual passions wholly between women or between men, in place of a normal relationship between a man and a woman, for which they would suffer the consequences of disease and their sin.

With a debased mind devoid of spiritual concerns, such persons indulge in vile and unnatural passions with no thought of right or wrong. Thus, they become susceptible to other crimes of murder, strife, lying, slander, and other character aberrations, making them untrustworthy, unlovable in the normal sense, unforgiving, and unmerciful. Even though realizing that such a lifestyle leads to an early death, they justify their conduct as well as that of others doing the same thing. How tragic!

VIEWPOINTS: It seems odd that Paul would proceed into a condemnation of sin, with emphasis on sexual perversion, after his gracious opening remarks to a group of believers to which he had never ministered. Ordinarily, this could have alienated them rather than incline them to welcome Paul with open arms.

Paul may have heard about the rampant perversion and immorality that existed at that time in the culture of Rome. His remarks may have been intended to strengthen the resolve of the believers to resist such temptations and to be more righteous in their own conduct as worthy witnesses in their community. He warned them of the consequences of such sins under God's wrath judgment, in the hope that they would endure and stand fast in their faith, and be more obedient to God's moral code. This warning is greatly needed in this modern world!

CHAPTER 2:   In verses 1-16, Paul continued with his condemnation of sin and sinners. He declares that the unrighteous, who tend to judge others, have no excuse for their own sins, especially when they behave as those they fault. God's judgment will fall on the hypocrite as well if they don't repent and walk in His Ways.

God's rewards to the righteous, and punishment to the wicked, is equally imparted to the Jew and the Gentile; He shows no partiality. He has no favorites now, as He once had for the

Jews, His chosen people. God will 'render judgment to each person according to their deeds,' as stated in Ps. 62:12 and Prov. 24:12.

Under the Mosaic Law, the Jews considered themselves to be a holy people, entitled to their privileges by right, even while they were thankless and rebellious For their sins, they would be judged by God under that law. On the other hand, Gentiles not under the law, sometimes live in compliance with it, as their conscience dictates. Their conscience may sanction, acquit or condemn them as they either keep or break laws which they understand. In any case, God will judge all through Jesus Christ when that day comes, and in the meantime, bless or trouble them according to their deeds. Their secret and obvious sins will be revealed as a condition deserving wrath!

As for the Jews, Paul set them straight on their views in verses 17-29. They tended to take pride in their knowledge of the Mosaic Law and their relationship to God, and considered themselves to be a good example to the Gentiles. They failed to see that humility and thankfulness to God is the basis of a good faith religion. Spiritual pride is dangerous, and can be the inception of hypocrisy.

Paul pointed out that none can be an example, or lead others in the right way, without first learning what is right or wrong, and then live accordingly. To do otherwise is to dishonor God, and give non-believers cause to ridicule and blaspheme the proud but phony self-glorifying hearers of the word, but not doers of it. Every Christian should strive to be genuine outwardly, as well as inwardly, in their heart and spirit, anointed by the Holy Spirit to praise and honor God in every way.

The Jew is justified in his physical circumcision if he lives up to the Law, but disobedience to it nullifies the significance of the circumcision for salvation of the soul. On the other hand, those who are uncircumcised, the Gentiles, who live in obedience to God's word are more pleasing to Him than the circumcised Jew who does not.

A real Jew, whether circumcised or not, is one who obeys God's word, and is circumcised spiritually in the heart, that is, separated from the bondage of sin through faith in Jesus Christ, the great Savior. The uncircumcised Gentile is bound to the same formula for true righteousness and salvation in Christ.

CHAPTER 3:   To the questions, 'What value does a Jew have?' and 'What is the good of circumcision?' Paul said there was much, in verses 1-8. Most important is that the old Testament word of God was given to them for later sharing with the world. Because they did not live up to it, or believe completely in the messianic prophecies, God still used them for this purpose. It did give them an edge towards salvation through Jesus Christ, which many rejected, to prove that mankind needed a path to righteousness by faith, with justification for punishment of sin.

Some will say that evil deeds bring forth the truth of God's word; so why should evil be punished? This is a foolish notion, because if He did not judge and punish the wicked for their deeds, then His justice and awards to the righteous would be invalidated.

In 9-20, Paul makes it clear in the words of Ps. 14:1-3 & 53:1-4, that all mankind is sinful. This scripture says, 'There is none righteous, no not one,' for if none understand or seek God's ways, they have become empty of anything good, and they have replaced peace with violence because they have no fear of God.

The corrupt and depraved nature of all men, will prevail until God's grace restrains or changes them. Though the Law was provided for mankind to live by, it also points to their sins.

Paul turns to righteousness in verses 21-28, which is a characteristic independent of the Law, and totally dependent on faith in Jesus Christ. That is mankind's only hope, for all have fallen short of the glory of God and sinned. Our faith must be firmly on Christ as our Savior, to receive God's complete forgiveness of our sins. Christ's death fulfilled the justice requirements of God, in which He will not compromise His holiness. This applies to Jews and Gentiles equally. To receive His righteousness, faith and trust in Jesus is the only avenue for spiritual redemption.

In 27-31, Paul said that there is no basis for boasting, just by obeying a law, for mankind is acceptable to God solely on the basis of true faith. The way of justification by faith cancels out any reason for boasting. All believers, Jews and Gentiles, are not left lawless, because their faith and obedience reinforces the Law of Moses ordinances of the Old Testament, and confirms the Jesus ordained laws for Christian living.

CHAPTER 4:   Paul focused on 'justification' in one's relationship with God. A Webster's understanding of the word as it applies to religion is: an act whereby man is made or accounted just, or freed from the guilt or penalty of sin. In verses 1-5, Paul tried to correct a Jewish view by using their forefather Abraham as an example of accountability on God's terms.

It wasn't because of good deeds that he performed, or services for which he deserved payment, that Abraham was deemed justified before God. It was solely because of his firm belief in God, and trust in His promises, that Abraham was reckoned righteous, as a gift and not as compensation. (See Gen. 15:6)

However exalted in various respects, he had nothing to boast about in the presence of God, for he was saved by grace through faith, even as others are, both Jews and Gentiles. As such, Abraham was the spiritual forefather of all Christians, who are sanctified by the Holy Spirit for their genuine evidence of faith.

In 6-8, Paul quoted scripture written by David in Ps. 32:1, to make clear that God blesses the sinner who repents, is forgiven of sins, and has absolute faith in Him. Reverting back to Abraham in 9-14, Paul pointed out that Abraham was justified by his faith in God before he was circumcised, and therefore this rite had nothing to do with his righteousness before God. Thus, Abraham was the spiritual forefather of all believers, male or female, circumcision notwithstanding as it applies to males.

Circumcision was really a confirmation in Jewish eyes that Abraham had the gift of righteousness. It is not the key to salvation, but faith is! God's promise of a world empire from Abraham's heirs was not dependent on his obedience to the Mosaic Law, or his circumcision; it was and remains solely dependent on his true faith in Him. Abraham's faith added to his trust in God's promises.

Abraham's faith gave him strength to face up to the difficulties of becoming a father in his old age; he <u>did not waiver in facing this responsibility</u>. In this way, he gave glory to God for His miraculous powers with steady trust in His will.

Paul introduces Chapter 5 at this point by using Abraham's justification through faith as assurance that the <u>same formula applies to all believers in this age.</u> He made it clear, that our righteousness comes from our faith in Jesus Christ's atonement for our sins and His righteousness, which <u>makes us acceptable to God.</u>

CHAPTER 5:   The role of Jesus Christ in making us acceptable to God is the opener for this chapter. And what do we gain from Christ's intervention for us? Paul enumerated several advantages in verses 1-11. First of all, the believer has peace of mind and heart with more hope for life possibilities, <u>followed by joy as blessings flow</u> from the throne of God, and this adds endurance to handle the rough times much better. With guilt removed by justification, these gains justify the believer's faith, and sweeten the <u>awareness of the Holy Spirit's infusion of God's love</u> into our lives.

God's love for mankind is manifested by His Son Jesus Christ's death on the cross to atone for our sin, and with Him as our peace-maker and mediator before God, <u>we escape God's wrath for sins of the past.</u> We have reason to sing with thankful hearts, 'What a friend we have in Jesus,' for having reconciled us with His Father.

Paul again refers to the past in verses 12-19 when in the Garden of Eden, Adam's sin gave mankind a sin nature, with a sentence of spiritual death <u>unless reconciliation with God occurred.</u> Until God gave the Mosaic Law, a person's sin was not a matter of record with God, but during the interim, physical death was a punishment provoked by God's wrath over gross sinfulness with no fear of Him.

When Jesus Christ, the 2nd Adam, came on the scene, the consequences of sin took on a new dimension. Before Christ, the sin of one man, Adam, brought death to many; his disobedience led to misery. After Christ, mankind was <u>offered the free gift of salvation,</u> whereby forgiveness of many offenses resulted in justification, with the opportunity for righteous living under the guidance of the Holy Spirit. Christ died in our stead, with the provision that we accept His sacrifice and believe in His objective, to <u>gain forgiveness and acceptance with God.</u>

Under the Law, sin became magnified, but now God's <u>kindness overshadows sin</u>, as Jesus Christ gave us acceptance before God with eternal life. It is our choice to put on the garment of righteousness, or to pay the wages of sin!

<u>VIEWPOINTS:</u>   It is easy to wonder why Eve is not mentioned in connection with Adam's sin. After all, she was the first to sin and then <u>enticed Adam to do likewise</u>. Perhaps, Paul figuratively included her in his general reference to Adam, who was designated general manager of all that God created, with Eve <u>an aide to complement what Adam was to do</u>. It was Adam's choice to accept the forbidden fruit or to reject it. If he had rejected it, man's relationship with God may have survived without the consequent burden of sin. Eve could have been replaced, or punished separately. The final responsibility for guilt inheritance was Adam's.

CHAPTER 6:   Paul raised an important question in verse 1—should mankind sin more to receive <u>more of God's grace and forgiveness</u>? In 2-14, he refutes this foolish idea with a 'God forbid' expression. Just as Christ died on the cross to atone for our sin, we are to die to sin at the moment we <u>accept Him in faith as our Savior</u>. Just as He was resurrected to life, we too are resurrected to a new spiritual life in Him.

True believers should be dead to sin, apart from it, and <u>therefore not yield to it.</u> If that is not the case for a new professing believer, then the conversion can be suspect as insincere or unreal. Baptism by water is only a sign of our new status, but <u>baptism by the Holy Spirit</u> is <u>necessary</u> to give us freedom from the tentacles of sin

In a true conversion, our sins are hung on a cross to die just as Jesus did, and we are <u>then resurrected as He was to a new spiritual life</u>, to walk with God, sinless as the Holy Spirit enables us. In every true believer, our former corrupt nature, called the old man (woman), having been derived from the first Adam, is crucified with Christ. Then, by His grace that old nature is weakened into a dying state, even though it struggles to live to cause the new believer to backslide into sin.

As a believer is set free from the chains of sin, spiritual freedom unto God will flourish, as long as the believer is concerned and <u>strives for spiritual maturity.</u> With help of the Holy Spirit to resist sin, the believer achieves sanctification by grace and the <u>willpower</u> <u>to recognize and resist sin</u>, which brings compliance with Mosaic Law.

Yet, in verses 15-23, Paul explains that believers are not ruled by the Law, but are subject to God's mercy and kindness, having been forgiven of sin, and therefore <u>must strive</u> <u>to please God in every way.</u> We must become slaves in the righteousness of God, making every effort to conform to His word to achieve utmost holiness.

Sin does not bring the pleasure and nourishment of wholesome spiritual fruit, it <u>contributes to a wasted life with a second death</u> at the judgment seat of God. By becoming a sin resistant believer in Jesus Christ, the fruit of holiness and everlasting life (only one death) is given the believer. This is God's most cherished gift to us!

CHAPTER 7:   At first glance, the language in this chapter appears to be contradictory to some degree, and <u>convoluted to say the least.</u> Perusal of other publications to arrive at a common understanding added to my perplexity over the true basic meaning of Paul's dissertation. There seems to be a wide divergence in the interpretation of his language, which leaves this writer no choice but to say what Paul meant to say, as best <u>as common sense</u> <u>and divine guidance allows</u>.

In verses 1-6, the representation of lifetime marriage is used to illustrate that the Mosaic Law for the Jew, or some equivalent moral code for the non-Jew, is <u>binding for the life</u> <u>of each spouse</u>, not just the wife. God's original intention was for marriage to be a lifetime commitment, with infidelity as the only grounds for divorce (see Mark 10:2-12). Death of a spouse however frees the surviving spouse to remarry, thus the binding law of marriage <u>only applies when both spouses are alive.</u>

In like manner, a true believer becomes wedded spiritually to Christ, and <u>should become</u> <u>dead to sin</u>, as the power of sin is broken. Before becoming a believer, a person continues under the law while seeking justification for one's conduct, and continues to be a slave of sin in some form. On the other hand, the Holy Spirit received through Christ Jesus, can free any sinner from the bonds of sin and death. They are delivered from that power of the law, which condemns them for their sins, and provokes the sin that is inherent in them. When free from the law, the new believer can serve God in a productive manner, as never before. (For a better understanding of the Mosaic Law, and the word 'laws,' see VIEWPOINTS at end of this chapter)

Verses 7-12 say that the law itself is not sin, but it identifies sin. Speaking for himself, Paul says that he knew sin based on the law, which mainly prohibits actions that are displeasing to God. Knowing the law, he realized that his sins were more numerous than he had ever thought, and at one point, he died spiritually by committing a sin. This probably occurred before his experience on the road to Damascus. Afterward, He saw the law as holy and just, and realized that one's weakness to resist sin, would be the underlying cause for spiritual death, and separation from Christ.

Paul goes on to say in 13-14, that God's law cannot save a sinner from spiritual death, but through it the evil of sin becomes known, and the consequences are revealed. In his humanity, Paul did not understand why he was that way, wanting to do wrong things that he hated. He spoke of a conflict between good and evil which persists in the heart of man, since the sin of Adam, which God's law made apparent. Wanting to do good, but finding it offset by wrong-doing, gave him the feeling that it was the power of sin within him that caused the problem.

Yet, he acknowledged that the law gave him an understanding that some inner urge to do wrong battles with his conscience, to make him most miserable. Then he cries out to be rescued, and forthwith thanks God that Jesus Christ has done so. Now, in spite of his innate selfish unholy desires to sin, he testifies that he can serve God in good conscience, having won the victory over sin, with the Holy Spirit's help.

VIEWPOINTS: In the original Old Testament, the Hebrew word 'torah' (meaning law) could be found in about 200 places. It prescribed the way of life for faithful Israelites, as spelled out in the first five books of the Bible (the Pentateuch), known as books of the Law because they are based on commandments given to Moses by God. More specifically, the covenant agreement given by God to Moses at Mount Sinai provided the foundation for all of Israel's laws.

As found in the books of Exodus (Ch. 20-30), Deuteronomy, Numbers, and Leviticus, they are now commonly called the Mosaic Law or Mosaic Code. Before his death, as the Israelites were about to enter the land of Canaan, Moses reviewed God's laws as given earlier in most of the book of Deuteronomy.

In New Testament times 'torah' was understood to mean both the written Law of the Old Testament Scriptures and the oral law (unwritten law) of Israel, which religious leaders developed in adapting the written Law to new life situations.

Jesus inaugurated a new view in which the Law as understood by contemporary Jews would no longer be the guiding principle for the Kingdom of God He said that He did not come to destroy the Law, but to fulfill it in a spiritual sense.

Paul had difficulty with the Law, which he viewed as the Law of God of the Old Testament.

He also spoke of a kind of natural 'law of sin' which existed in human beings, troubling human conduct, and contrasted it to a "law of faith," that influenced <u>conduct as</u> <u>derived by faith in God.</u> (For more information, see Unger's Bible Dictionary, or the Holman Bible Dictionary)

CHAPTER 8:   Halley's Bible Handbook says that, 'This is one of the best loved chapters in the Bible.' Lets see what makes it so! Paul leaves the condemnation for sin matter behind and moves into a discussion of 'sanctification,' <u>the business of becoming righteous</u>, striving to become sinless by faith, in the likeness of Jesus Christ. God sent Jesus to earth in the likeness of man for this purpose, but He was <u>without man's sin nature</u>. With the spirit of life in Christ in our hearts, we can fulfill the requirements of God's laws. If we are obedient to what the Holy Spirit dictates, then our conduct will become pleasing to God <u>as our thoughts</u> <u>become more spiritual</u>. For most humans, this is a gradual process that becomes ingrained in us over time.

Seeking to please God, and concern over the welfare of the soul for an eternal future, are <u>productive influences of the Spirit</u>, which those with the Spirit do sense. A sanctified soul is alive in peace, being shielded from internal stress and struggle between our sin nature and compliance with God's Laws. With the Spirit of Christ as our mentor, our lifestyle and thoughts will become patterned <u>in the likeness of what Jesus Christ possessed and</u> <u>exemplified.</u>

If our minds focus on worldly interests and desires, we cannot have a good relationship with God, because we displease Him. Just as Jesus was resurrected from death, mankind must be spiritually resurrected (transformed) from the deadly effects of sin to live a new and <u>better life enriched under Holy Spirit control</u>. It is somewhat like a blood transfusion to revive health and vitality to regain strength to do our best.

Verses 12-17 speak of a father-son (daughter) relationship with God that evolves into spiritual maturity for the believer in Christ. Regeneration by the Holy Spirit plants a new divine nature in the soul of man, initially in a weakened state, that grows with time and effort. Like children, believers grow up <u>to become joint heirs with God and Christ,</u> <u>overcoming suffering so as to be glorified in eternity.</u>

In verses 18-30, Paul elucidates on the transition from suffering to glory, in which he labels suffering as insignificant when <u>compared to the glory a believer will receive.</u> He states that all of creation looks for a time when Christians will be delivered from the sin of a cursed world to live with Christ, as the first-fruits of becoming a believer portends. The first-fruits of the Spirit quickens our desire, hopes and expectations of a better time and circumstances apart from this world.

With the help of the Holy Spirit, believers overcome difficulties, even as He intercedes for them, according to the will of God, when they <u>know not how to pray</u> for help. Paul spoke these important words, 'We know that all things work for good to those who love God, to those who are called to His good purpose.'

In this context, our love for God is a response to the work of the Holy Spirit in us. Then the love of God, ruling in the hearts of those who once were His enemies, is proof that they have been <u>called according to His purpose</u>. Even though sinful mankind deserves destruction as enemies of God, He has provided a way of regeneration, so man can grow in conformity to the nature of Christ. That is love!

In verses 31-39, Paul asks, 'Well, what about it? With God on our side, who can be against us? He spoke in amazement and admiration as he pondered the scope of God's love for mankind, admitting that it <u>exceeded his understanding</u>. He marveled over the fact that believers have a best Friend at the right hand of God; with power to intercede for them.

Asking the question, 'Can anything separate us from the love of God.' Paul concluded convincingly that nothing can separate the soul that cleaves to Christ, from what God has promised the believer. When physical death comes to break earthly bonds, even the soul from the body, the <u>believer's soul is carried into an eternal union with the Lord Jesus,</u> for full enjoyment of Him for ever.

Yes, this is a most magnificent chapter of the Bible. It is filled with hope and promise of God's unfailing love and goodness <u>to those who love Him.</u> Hallelujah!

<u>VIEWPOINTS:</u>   The precise meaning of verse 29 has been a conundrum for biblical scholars. The word' foreknowledge' means to 'foreknow' or have prior knowledge of a thing or event before it happens. In a general sense, that God has this ability is indisputable, but it is difficult to understand that God would know who would choose to love Him and become a believer, <u>even before their birth.</u> There are two main schools of thought on this.

Either God has the ability to know this would happen to each person during their years of life on earth, or, He would know this <u>before a person was born, back over countless years of time.</u> In my own view, it means the former, that He knows us from the day of our birth, according to our childhood training, our nature as we mature, and our character as it develops. He is most <u>wise in discerning the direction a human life will take</u>. Of this, we can be certain! So be it!

CHAPTER 9:   Paul expressed his great concern with sadness and grief, in verses 1-5, for the <u>nation of Israel and his fellow Jews,</u> because of their unbelief in Christ's teachings, when they had been chosen and favored of God from day one. He admitted that he would accept God's judgment on himself to restore Israel spiritually. He is concerned for them also because they were the ancestors of Jesus Christ.

In 6-13, Paul stated that God did not fail all the people in Israel, because <u>some of them were not Israelites from the beginning,</u> as descendants of Abraham's son Ishmael, rather than from Isaac to whom God's promises were applicable. He added a reminder that God had also chosen Jacob for His love and favor, over Esau, the other twin son of Rebecca, who He hated. (Hated could more aptly mean 'rejected')

Asking if God was unfair in these matters, in 14-18, Paul denies this emphatically, because it is <u>always God's choice</u> on whom to show mercy and compassion. God does no wrong, however it might appear to men, who are <u>not enjoined as judges over God's affairs.</u>

In 19-29, Paul spoke of God's anger and mercy as it applied to those who would find fault with God. He used the analogy of an object formed by a potter out of clay, that found fault with the potter for the way it was shaped, to illustrate that it is <u>always God's choice that rules</u> over mankind, as it was the potter's choice on shape.

God could have shown anger and exerted His power against those who deserved destruction, both Jew and Gentile, but out of love <u>He chose to patiently give them time</u> to repent and become His children. To clarify this point, Paul quoted scripture from the book of Hosea and Isaiah to support the premise that many Gentiles not among His chosen people would become believers. Conversely, from His chosen people of Israel, relatively <u>few would escape His judgment against those who disbelieved.</u> Even among the vast number of 'professing' Christians in this modern world it is likely that only a remnant will be saved.

The Gentiles are not bound to the Law, therefore they normally <u>attain righteousness by faith,</u> without becoming involved in the Jewish religion and their ceremonial rites. Although the Jews spoke of justification and holiness, and were eager to be the favored of God, they expected justification by obedience to the law of Moses. They <u>excluded acceptance and faith in Christ,</u> with submission to the gospel.

<u>CHAPTER 10:</u> Paul bemoaned the spiritual plight of his Jewish brothers in verses 1-13, because they continued to hold to their traditional belief that <u>compliance with God's Law would lead to salvation of their souls.</u> They refused to accept and trust Jesus by faith as the fulfillment of the Law. While the Law is not null and void, the death of Christ for those who break the laws was because the people could not hope to keep the law without fail. Therefore Christ has fulfilled the whole law, for those who believe in Him are <u>by faith</u> <u>counted just and righteous before God.</u>

Even though Moses said that a person could become acceptable to God by obeying the Law, in God's new way, a person acceptable to God only by faith will not look for Christ to come down from heaven, or to come out of Hades <u>to prove His existence.</u> Justification by faith in Christ incorporates belief and trust in God's written Word that is to be preached everywhere, to every one, so <u>none will have an excuse for their unbelief.</u>

No Jew or Gentile will be disappointed for their faith in God's word and in His Son Jesus Christ. There is only one Lord; He welcomes everyone who turns to Him for salvation. No true believer will be shamed for their confident trust in the Lord Jesus. <u>Everyone has equal standing before God</u> who is generous in His mercy.

In verse 14, Paul asked these questions of the Jews: how could they expect to hear from a Messiah they rejected? —how could they believe in Him with hearing the truth? —as taught by a preacher—that was sent by God? Paul then <u>reproaches them for not obeying what</u> <u>they understood,</u> for not listening when the word was given to them, and for not knowing that all was done to inform them.

In essence, Paul then said in 15-21, that when the gospel is preached, it is for the <u>purpose of becoming informed,</u> believing by faith, <u>and for compliance.</u> The gospel is not just a bunch of ideas, it is rule book to be put into practice. The birth, growth, and strength of faith comes from hearing the word of God <u>to recognize how true it is.</u> God was disappointed that the people of Israel fell short of this mark because of disobedience, and refusal to yield their stubborn wills to His invitation to have faith.

Paul used several passages from the Old Testament to support his words, to show the Jews that God would turn to the Gentiles. They should have known it from Moses and Isaiah. Isaiah speaks plainly of the grace and favor of God being bestowed on the Gentiles, <u>which would arouse jealousy in the Jews.</u>

CHAPTER 11:   Paul gave assurance in this chapter that God had not forgotten His first chosen people, the Jews, and his promises to them for some future fulfillment. Reconciliation with their Jehovah God will come for them at the end of time.

In verses 1-10, Paul clarified that the Jews were not totally rejected by God, because He always retained a remnant of them no matter how disobedient they were. Paul presented himself as an example of this fact, and refers to the time when Elijah thought he was the only survivor of his people, in I Kings 19:14 & 18, and God informed him that He had, by grace only, saved 7000 who had not bowed to the pagan god Baal.

Paul added that God's policy of preservation was still in effect, and would always be that way because of His kindness and mercy. This was so, although it was through many Jews joining the Gentiles in a new faith in Christ's righteousness. The rest of the Jews were still too stubborn and blind to see the gospel truth.

In verses 11-24, the introduction of the gospel message to the Gentiles is related to the stubborn rejection of it by the Jews, who will be restored in God's grace someday, for the benefit of all believers. Paul addressed himself to the Gentiles, as an apostle to them, to make clear that he would zealously carry out his ministry in the hope that it would arouse jealousy in the Jews so they would also become believers.

The implication is that a future infusion of the Jews into the Christian church would be akin to a resurrection of the dead in sin to a life of righteousness. Until then, the nation of Israel will be as in a deep sleep, unaware or unconcerned over dangers ahead, with little sense of it's need of the Savior, or the danger of eternal ruin.

Then Paul gave 2 analogies to illustrate how the Gentiles would be grafted into the parent tree of God's chosen people, the Jews. First, he spoke of a piece of leavened dough (holy Gentile believers) being added to the main batch (the Jews), to convey life (holiness) to all. Second, he said that an entire tree would be holy if the roots were holy, meaning that Israel was really the root for salvation in Christ.

Going further on this allegory, Paul described Israel as a cultivated olive tree with branches broken or pruned off, with the Gentiles, as new branches from a wild olive tree, being grafted in to replace the discarded branches. The new branches then receive nourishment and life from the roots of the original tree, but they are no better than the other branches, which also receive life from the same roots.

True, Paul said, the discarded branches (disbelieving Jews) removed for lack of faith were replaced by Gentile branches of faith This means that the Gentile church must rely on God's grace, and be fruitful, or face the same pruning the Jews received.

Paul declared in verses 25-32 that the people of Israel would be fully restored to God after a time of hardening and separation until the fullness of the Gentiles has been completed. A mystery exists since the Old Testament did not explicitly predict this as part of God's plan, and the mystery continues concerning the length of time or spiritual conditions that will constitute fullness of the Gentiles. Presumably, this means that a time will come in God's view when further evangelization of the Gentiles is futile or non-productive of new converts.

In verses 26-27, where Paul said that the whole nation of Israel would be saved, as prophesied in Isaiah 59:20-21, he did not mean that every Israeli would be saved. The <u>nation itself would be preserved</u> to be part of God's endtimes program.

In the meantime, the Gentiles will be favored while Israel will be looked upon as an enemy of God, even though their restoration to believe in Christ is <u>assured as promised to their ancestors,</u> because God is merciful. His mercy is equally bestowed on both Jews and Gentiles, as all are sinners prone to disobedience.

With a form of doxology in 33-36, Paul marvels at the mystery of God's wisdom and knowledge, admitting his own limited understanding of it. Yes, a chasm of great proportions lies between God and mankind in this department. Therefore, it is <u>our humble duty to acknowledge His glory in all things</u> as the angels do in heaven.

<u>VIEWPOINTS:</u>   The word 'mystery or mysteries' appears many times in the New Testament, where the mystery may be explained, or is left for explanation later in the Word, or as God's endtimes agenda unfolds. (See the insert, entitled, Bible Mysteries, at the end of this book for more information.)

CHAPTER 12:   As part of the last 5 chapters on practical Christian service, Paul gave advice to believers in verses 1-8 on <u>faith-based relationships within the Christian community</u>. Self is to be subordinated in deference to God's will, by allowing Him to mold our thoughts and lifestyle to be more pleasing as a living sacrifice to Him. Above all, he admonishes us not to live as the world lives. We are to let our faith bring about a renewing of the mind, to <u>enhance the quality of our soul</u>.

Since God was so good to him, Paul tells believers not to think too highly of themselves, but to rate themselves <u>sensibly according to their faith in Him</u>. As individuals, Christians are to consider themselves a useful part of Christ's church body, using their God-given spiritual gifts to honor and glorify God, whether it be interpretation, service, teaching, encouragement, gifting, leadership, kindness or cheerful good-will. In summary, this <u>means to do all the good we can,</u> one to another, for the common benefit of the whole, with all done in humility from the heart.

In 9-21, Paul added more rules for Christian living, citing 'love' as number one. The love Christians have for each other should be sincere, without deceit, devoid of insincere compliments, or <u>considerate of their feelings for themselves</u>. It should encompass help to the poor and courteous hospitality to strangers according to their needs. True love will incline us to empathy in the sorrows and joys of others.

Being careful not to repay in kind those who do us harm, will often bring about an <u>improvement in the character of others</u>. Living in harmony and peace with others is a noble goal. Allow God to punish those who bring injury, rather <u>than seek personal revenge</u>. Showing kindness in the face of animosity or indifference is like heaping fiery coals on the head of the enemy.

It is not easily understood or practiced by the world, that in all strife and contention, those that seek revenge are losers, and <u>those that forgive are winners</u>. We are to stand above or apart from evil, rather than succumb to it. With God's help!

<u>VIEWPOINTS:</u>   The admonition not to seek revenge when someone harms or injures us

does not mean that the perpetrator should not be punished under civil or criminal laws that pertain to the offense committed. God's word reminds us that governments are for the purpose of protecting its citizens, and to administer punishment as deserved for law- breakers. This is discussed in the next chapter.

When the offense is personal and not really in violation of existing laws, then a Christian is to be charitable and not seek personal satisfaction by filing frivolous lawsuits, or doing anything similar to what was received. Christians may be no different than the offender if they react in a like manner to what offended them.

CHAPTER 13:   Paul advised in verses 1-7 that Christians should be obedient to governing authorities, because they are sanctioned by God for the good of the citizenry. Resistance against legitimate government is equivalent to resistance to God's laws. Good rulers look out for the interests of good people, and punish the evil doers. By cooperating with them, good will ensues with benefits to the respectful.

As God's servants, rulers have the responsibility to punish wrong doing, as if God's anger was shown, therefore all should obey their rulers, knowing that it is proper conduct to avoid God's anger. Taxes and fees levied by governing bodies should be paid with respect for the needs of government.

There can be times when a Christian is justified in speaking up against those who govern in violation of divine justice. There may be times when obedience should be to God's laws rather than the corrupt laws of wicked rulers. If conscience is offended by evil leadership, a Christian may have to fight against it with God's help.

Paul again spoke of 'love' in verses 8-10, as a component of obedience to existing laws pertaining to marriage, murder, theft, coveting, and kindness to others. It is like a debt that mankind owes to others, and is never overpaid. He cites the 10 commandments as the yardstick for loving a neighbor as one's self. This is the basis of the golden rule to, 'Do unto others as you would have them do unto you.'

In 11-14, Paul reminds believers to be aware of the wickedness of the world in which they live, and be ready and alert for the return of Christ when we will realize the fullness of salvation in Him. As each day passes in our lives, the darkness of Satan's world pollution is closer to the end, and the brightness of Christ's reign draws nearer. We must steadfastly avoid the darkness of sin, such as orgies and drunkenness, strife and envy, and let Christ's garment of righteousness envelop us. This will keep us from indulging in desires of our sin nature.

CHAPTER 14:   In this chapter, Paul seemed to be addressing the differences between Jewish and Gentile believers in the Roman fellowship, which could result in critical attitudes towards one another. In 1-13, he makes it clear that such differences should not be divisive, and the strong in faith should be understanding of the views of newer believers without judgmental disputes.

He used the example of different food tastes, or days of worship, and made it clear that they should not override one's commitment to please the Lord according to His Word. The Christian's business is to please God, not themselves or even others. During our lifetime, our different strengths, capacities, and practices should be <u>in keeping with the Lord's approval and pleasure</u>.

Paul cautioned against judging or despising others for their differences, as Christ will judge all believers some day, for all are accountable to Him in the end. Most important, believers should be careful not to say <u>or do things which may cause weaker ones to stumble or fall.</u>

The 'law of love' is again Paul's theme in verses 14-23. Interaction with other believers should always be tempered by loving kindness and the <u>goal of peace and joy</u>.

He suggested consideration of what is right and clean to eat, to be certain that the strong believer's preferences do not adversely affect the faith of the weaker believer. To avoid inconsiderate choices that may bring shame against God, Christians are to <u>please God by living in peace with fellow believers</u> to promote happiness for all.

Believers are to edify one another, mutually strengthen each other's faith, and avoid doing anything <u>that would weaken the faith of others</u>. Although all food not deemed unclean is fit to eat, there are times when they should be avoided, if eating them might offend a brother. This same principle is applicable when one's views or actions might be offensive to another believer with a difference outlook. Believers must deny themselves in many cases what they may lawfully do, when doing it <u>might hurt their standing before others and God.</u> Good fellowship does not depend on what one eats or drinks, it thrives when Christ's gift of salvation is shared.

CHAPTER 15:   Paul continued to expound on the topic of chapter 14, by emphasizing 3 points in this chapter: the faithful strong should <u>help the weak</u>, love and concern should <u>build unity in the church</u>, and believers should <u>accept one another as equals</u> before God.

In 1-6, Paul exhorts the more seasoned believers to be patient with the new believer, and to help them in the manner of Jesus Christ to <u>become happier in their Christian walk,</u> so that all will praise and honor God as one. Christ's life example as a self-denying, non self- pleasing person, is what a maturing Christian should emulate.

In 7-13, just as Christ reached out to the Jews to keep God's promises to their ancestors, He also was <u>kind and merciful to the Gentiles</u> so they would believe in God. The loving disposition of Jesus to all should be seen in the faithful strong by the weaker ones.

Our objective as believers in Christ is to glorify God in our relationship with other believers, <u>whether they be Jew or Gentile,</u> as brought out in scripture quotes by Paul. He added a short prayer for believer hope, happiness, and peace.

Paul reviewed his missionary service in verses 14-21, so the Roman believers would appreciate how good God had been to him. He cited his priestly role as a servant of Christ to the Gentiles, to give them help from the Holy Spirit to become holy. He expressed satisfaction over the help Jesus Christ gave in <u>bringing the Good News message to the Gentiles</u>. Through miracles and other signs made possible by the Holy Spirit, Paul preached effectively in many places far from Jerusalem, including Illyricum (modern day Albania). Now he wishes to minister to lands <u>where no one has preached.</u>

Paul expanded on his ambition in verses 22-33, to preach the gospel in new lands where it had not been taken. He mentions Spain as his objective after a time of fellowship with the Roman church. Before this journey though, he <u>planned to return to Jerusalem</u> with the contributions he had collected from Gentile churches during his 3rd journey to Macedonia and Achaia.

To this end, he asked for earnest prayer for a safe and successfully trip to Jerusalem, followed by his voyage to Rome for a happy time there in God's will.

CHAPTER 16:   Paul closed out this letter to believers in Rome in a loving and thoughtful manner, to express his appreciation for their faithfulness and to great them <u>in the name of the Lord</u>. In verses 1-16, he first asked that they give Phoebe, a leader in the church at Cenchreae, an eastern port city of Corinth, a warm welcome for her Christian leadership and help in his ministry.

Next, he extends a special greeting on behalf of all churches, to Priscilla and Aquila and their home fellowship group, for their service to him in Ephesus and Corinth, and for <u>risking their lives on his behalf</u>.

Greetings with kind words are extended to 25 more brothers and sisters now a <u>part of the Roman fellowship</u>, that he must have met during his previous journeys. Most names are of Roman origin and are listed in verses 5-16. They are not the kind of names that Gentile believers would select for their children. About 6 of them are thought to be female names, but there may be more.

Paul injected a warning in verses 17-20 for the Roman believers to be wary of pagan unbelievers who would try to <u>provoke dissension and division in the church.</u> He cautioned that their flattery and ridiculous ideas would fool the less informed. In addition, he said that he was pleased with their level of faith and encouraged them to continue to resist evil so that <u>Satan's evil intentions would be crushed by Christ.</u>

More greetings are extended in 21-24 by Timothy, Paul's beloved aide, and 3 of Paul's kinfolk. A surprising revelation is given by Tertius, who identifies himself as a believer who <u>wrote this letter as dictated by Paul</u>. Finally, 3 more believers, probably from churches in Ephesus and Corinth, included their greetings.

Paul ended the letter with a prayer of praise to God for making the Good News gospel available to all, both the Jews and the Gentiles, to be <u>united into one body through Jesus Christ.</u> This was revelation to prophecy mystery (11:25) in the Old Testament, about the Messiah's salvation message that the Jews could not understand.

SUMMARY: From this scripture, it is clear that Paul wrote the believers in Rome with about 5 main things in mind: 1-To ask for prayers for his impending trip to Jerusalem, 2- <u>To prepare them</u> for his planned visit, 3-<u>To share some of his understanding</u> of what God intended to accomplish through Christ, 4-<u>To strengthen them</u> in problem areas, and 5-To <u>enlist their aid</u> for his planned trip to Spain.

The theme of Romans is generally understood to be the "righteousness of God" whereby He sets things right through the life, death, and resurrection of Jesus, and <u>thereby</u> <u>acquits the sinner of their sins</u>. The new believer then rejects sin as a way of life, which initially results in a struggle with sin, until the Holy Spirit brings victory over evil. Salvation is thus God's gift of a righteous status before Him in Christ, and obedience through the Holy Spirit to live the new life

Paul also issued a summons to Christians to live transformed lives, make good use of spiritual gifts in Godly service, honor obligations to civil authority, have love and show kindness to other believers, and be helpful to those with little or no faith in Christ. All this should be done to honor and glorify God before the world.

The last chapter revealed that Paul had the services of Tertius as his writer of this letter. It will be of interest to learn if Tertius, or some other writer will assist him on the other 12 epistles for which authorship is credited to him.

The following article "Bible Mysteries' casts more light on the words, 'mystery or mysterious' that appear frequently in the remaining New Testament books. The reader is encouraged to seek understanding of those mysteries as explained, or for which the light of understanding will be given as God's endtimes plans unfold.

BIBLE MYSTERIES

After 6 years of intensive study and commentary writing on God's Holy Word, I have concluded that it is the most fascinating book ever written. First of all, ancient origin sets it apart as second to none. Second, the divine origin of it is obvious when one considers how early portions of it survived in parchment form in caves for thousands of years before all was brought together. Third, with so many authors involved, it is amazing how integrated and related the separate books are with respect to each other. And fourth, there is mystery galore contained in the early accounts of creation, the world-wide flood, the endtimes prophecy yet to be fulfilled, and the final creation of the new world.

I must confess that I have wondered often about the sum and substance of God Himself, in triune form with Jesus the Son and the Holy Spirit. In some respects, the Trinity, as they are called, resembles a business corporation in the way it serves the interests of stockholders. God is the Chairman of the Board, Jesus is the Executive Officer, the Holy Spirit is the Field Manager, and humanity represents the stockholders. Angel's are the Tech Reps, the headquarters assistants, and public relations experts.

One can speculate endlessly about the manner in which God carried out His spectacular and supernatural creation work. Some of the questions for which no detailed answers are given in the Genesis account could put one's imagination on a merry-go-round trip.

How did God create the land animals, the birds of the air, the creatures of the sea, and the insect population? Did He create them as fully grown ready for reproducing their own kind, or were they begun as genetic embryos that came together to produce each species in its infant form? Were they produced out of the dust and the earth as was Adam? Did God create only two of each specie, male and female, or did he create more of each kind? Also, how did God decide where to put different species of animal life, birds, and other land life throughout the earth?

The next area of wonderment pertains to the time of Noah, and the flood that Scripture says covered the world. Was the entire globe as we know it today covered completely by water, or did the flood waters only envelop the land mass known as the world at the time of Moses, who recorded this history?

Then wonderment can focus on how the wide diversity of mankind came about to give us Africans, Asians, Europeans, Indians, Orientals, and other ethnic groups. These peoples came from the family of Noah somehow, but his family members were presumably alike in appearance. Did genetic mutation play a part in bringing about the wide diversity of peoples we have in the world today? Did God bring about changes in features, habits, and intelligence levels as adaptations to environmental differences in locale? Did these changes happen when languages were multiplied after Babylon's Tower was destroyed, and people were dispersed?

Another mystery is how such a diversity of religions came into being over the history of mankind. These mystery religions featured sacred rites, called mysteries, in which the legend of the god or goddess worshipped in the cult was reenacted. Many of the deities in these mysteries were associated with fertility. The mystery religions impeded and disjoined the practice of Christianity when it was introduced in the Middle East. In the absence of Christianity, the nature of mankind obviously felt the need for an avenue of worship of a superior being.

That we have mystery in the Bible is unquestionable. The word mystery is found in many places in the old and new testament. A computer search of the entire book reveals that the words 'mystery or mysteries' is used about 35 times. It is found in 6 passages in the Old Testament book of Daniel, and about 29 times in the New Testament. Surprisingly, the mystery of creation is not spoken of in Genesis.

The 6 appearances of the word in the book of Daniel relates to interpretation of King Nebuchadnezzar's dreams by Daniel. There was mystery at that time, but Daniel's predictive interpretations have been fulfilled to end the mystery.

The number of times the 'mystery-mysteries' word appears in the New Testament depends on the translation version. It appears 25 times in the New Revised Standard Version from Romans 11:25 to Revelations 17:7, but it also appears in 3 gospel scriptures (Matt.

13:11, Mark 4:11, & Luke 8:10) in the King James and American Standard versions, where it refers to the secrets of the kingdom of God, as revealed to Christians, but made a mystery to non-believers. It also appears in I Corinthians 2:7, speaking of God's wisdom. The Book of Revelation is a supreme mystery in itself, yet to be unfolded.

The term has different meanings which will be clarified as much as possible where the word appears. The New Testament usage definitely differs from that of mystery religions, in that mysteries of the New Testament are related to the historical activity of the person of Christ. These mysteries are spiritually manifested in the proclamation of the gospel with disclosure that Gentiles share in the blessings of the gospel. Where a meaning can not be discerned, Christians have a promise of understanding when heaven is their home. Scriptures where mysteries are mentioned are listed below:

MYSTERY SCRIPTURES

Matthew 13:11	Ephesians 3:9
Mark 4:11	Ephesians 5:32
Luke 8:10	Ephesians 6:19
Romans 11:25	Colossians 1:26
Romans 16:25	Colossians 1:27
I Corinthians 2:1	Colossians 2:2
I Corinthians 2:7	Colossians 4:3
I Corinthians 4:1	II Thessalonians 2:7
I Corinthians 13:2	I Timothy 3:9
I Corinthians 14:2	I Timothy 3:16
I Corinthians 15:51	Revelations 1:20
Ephesians 1:9	Revelations 10:7
Ephesians 3:3	Revelations 17:5
Ephesians 3:4	Revelations 17:7
Ephesians 3:5	

I CORINTHIANS—BOOK SEVEN

The church at Corinth was a contentious fellowship of mostly Gentiles, with division over moral issues, marriage and divorce, pagan worship festivals, and resurrection of the dead in Christ. Paul's letter to them was written after he received several letters reporting these problems.

During his 2nd missionary journey about 53 AD, Paul left the church under the leadership of Prisilla and Aquila, who subsequently returned to Rome. In their immaturity and pride, the young church failed to protect itself from local cultural decadence, and they strayed from Christian ways.

Paul is named twice as the author of the book, in 1:1-2 & 16:21. It is believed that he wrote it at Ephesus during his 3rd missionary journey, between 54-57 AD. Paul expressed his concern over the spiritual welfare of this wayward fellowship, as he attempted to change their conduct to one more compatible with the gospel of Christ. His remarks include rebuke, advice on legal matters, clarification on matters of doctrine and spiritual gifts, and giving them understanding of bodily resurrection after death.

CHAPTER 1: Paul greeted the church in verses 1-7 with words to remind them of their status as saints in the name of Jesus. Then he expressed thanks for God's grace that gave them the added ability to communicate and understand the teachings of Jesus Christ, so they might serve Him well with their spiritual gifts, and be acceptable in His Day, when He returns to claim His own.

Without hesitation, in verses 8-17, Paul delved into the issue of divisions in the church. He pleaded with them to avoid taking sides, to try to get along better, and to stop arguing over differences on leadership from spiritual mentors. For this reason, he thanked God that he had not baptized any of them, other than Crispus, the synagogue high priest, Gaius, a former host, and the household of Stephanas. He reminded them that his role was to preach the gospel, not to baptize.

In verses 18-25, Paul sermonizes on Christ's message of salvation, which is foolishness to the unsaved, but a special power to the believer. He questioned the effectiveness of the intellectual members of society to solve problems of the day according to the scriptures, adding that their wisdom was foolishness, that God would not allow them to use in learning of Him.

God's choice was to use only those who believed in Christ's message, which most Jews would not accept, and many Gentiles thought was foolishness. If there is any foolishness in God, He is still wiser and stronger than everyone else.

Paul asked the Corinthians, in verses 26-30 to remember what they were when they became believers, and to consider what they had become since then. While the world thought they were foolish and unimportant, God chose them to put the wise and the powerful to shame with respect to spiritual knowledge. As God's children, God sent Jesus Christ to give them wisdom, acceptability, and righteousness. For this reason, Paul told them to brag about God and Jesus, if they wanted to brag, rather than brag about human attributes.

CHAPTER 2:   Paul explains his low key presentation of the gospel in verses 1-5, during his previous visit to Corinth. He wanted his hearers to gain faith in Jesus Christ through the Holy Spirit, rather than from eloquent oratory. When a crucified Christ is plainly preached, success comes with the Holy Spirit giving understanding, so hearers become believers and gain salvation of their souls.

From verses 6-16, an explanation of spiritual wisdom is gleaned. Paul admits that more complicated language is used with the more intellectual listeners, which includes mysterious wisdom from God that was revealed by Christ's first coming and His teachings. It is made known by the Holy Spirit to true believers as they mature and grow in spiritual understanding, so they will know and appreciate God's blessings.

It is only by Holy Spirit empowerment that clarification of bible mysteries are clarified for the Christian. The intelligence of intellectuals, apart from God, will not reveal the deeper meanings of scripture, because what they read and hear is foolishness to them. The mature Christian, on the other hand, can examine, judge the truth of what is read or heard, and arrive at logical conclusions that strengthen faith. They are given the reasoning power of Christ which produces good spiritual fruit.

CHAPTER 3:   Paul castigated the Corinthian church brethren in verses 1-4 for their shallow faith and limited spiritual understanding. So he spoke to them in elementary terms, which they still could not totally grasp, because of their divisive nature. As an example, Paul pointed out that some argue they should follow Paul and others say they prefer Apollos. Spiritual maturity generates Christian unity.

In 5-10, Paul clarified that both he and Apollos were merely servants of God, and therefore they counted as nothing before God, because He provides the growth of believers to become His church. Paul only admitted to laying the foundation for faith in Jesus Christ, on which others should build.

Paul added in 11-17, that any believer building on such a foundation, as if with durable gold, silver, or gems, or destructible wood, hay, or straw, will be judged according to the quality and durability of results, when Christ returns to judge and gather His children. Those who achieve durable results will be rewarded, whereas those whose results are perishable will not be rewarded, but they will be saved.

Using an analogy, Paul told the believers that they are the holy temple of God in which the Holy Spirit resides, and if anyone (believer or otherwise) defiles the temple, they will reap a physical death by God. Christians who receive the Holy Spirit through faith in Christ, are deemed holy by God, and therefore should always be concerned that they contribute to the peace, purity, and unity of the church.

In closing, Paul admonished the church that if any member acquires worldly wisdom in place of spiritual wisdom, they would have to become foolish to the worldly ideas to be restored spiritually. The best ambition is to humbly yield to God for spiritual wisdom to see and believe the simple truths of His Word.

Believers should know that God's blessings are theirs, if they are Christ's child. in true faith. We are subjects of His kingdom, both now and when He returns. He is Lord over us, we receive His gifts, and we should cheerfully submit to his command. God in Christ is the sum and substance of the gospel. There is no better way to spend time, than to study God's Holy Bible!

CHAPTER 4:   Paul asked the Corinthians in verses 1-5, to consider him and his associates (Apollo) as servants of Christ with the responsibility of <u>explaining the mysteries of God</u>. Believers should put their service to God above their concern for what others think of them. While Paul had a natural concern for his own reputation, he knew that proving himself a faithful servant of Christ <u>took precedence over pleasing mankind.</u> He had a clear conscience on this. Yet, he admitted that in the end Christ would judge him, just as He will judge all mankind, and reward those who deserved commendation. What a comfort it is that men are not to be our final judges!

At the Day of the Lord (Christ's 2nd coming) men's secret sins will be exposed to the light of day. Then faithful believers will be justified, approved and rewarded according to their record. Unbelievers will not be so benefited; they will suffer God's wrath judgment.

In 6-13, Paul admitted that he and Apollos were typical examples, who also had to learn the rules as others, and therefore <u>no one should think too highly of themselves</u>. Believers have no reason to be proud, for all they have, are, or do, that is good, comes to them by the generous grace of God.

With some perceived sarcasm, Paul likens the attitude of the Corinthians to those who think highly of themselves <u>for the wealth and power they have gained</u>. He expressed the wish that they really had such a status that he too could have. Then he pointed out that he and other Christians are not so disposed, since they <u>must often suffer greater hardships than others.</u> They are looked upon as fools by the high and mighty, they must endure malnutrition, have inadequate clothing, live in substandard abodes, work harder to survive, and be subject to scornful abusive language.

Those who strive to be faithful in Christ Jesus, must expect poverty and contempt at times. Whenever they suffer such treatment from men, they should follow the example of Christ, being <u>patient and kind in their reaction</u>. Even though treated as a vile castaway by the world, believers are precious to God, and someday will be gathered to Him for royal treatment as compared to their earthly experience.

In 14-21, Paul tempered his criticism with assurance that he did not wish to shame the Corinthians, rather, his purpose was to <u>help them with tough love,</u> as if he were their father, even if they had 10,000 others teaching them about Christ. He considered himself as their spiritual father because they were his converts, and he presented himself as a proper example along with his beloved aide (son) Timothy, who was to visit them.

He cautions them not to become egotistic about their influence over others, because he would soon visit them if God permitted, and would <u>then know who thought too highly of themselves.</u> He told them that God's kingdom with mankind was more dependent on Godly ability to lead, than in cheap and misleading language.

He said the choice was theirs, whether he came in the spirit of love and kindness, or as a parent with a stick to punish them.

CHAPTER 5:   Paul castigates the church in verses 1-8, for blindly tolerating immorality, as bad as in Gentile circles, <u>in their fellowship body</u>. Specifically, he cites the case of a man cohabiting with his stepmother, <u>which the church should condemn.</u> Paul said that he had judged this man as if he were before them, so they should feel his presence when they assembled to deal with the problem, probably a <u>termination of church membership and</u> shunning. They seemed to feel that a Christian's freedom was unlimited, because God's grace is limitless. Not so, my friend!

Paul compared the sin of incest to a piece of leavened bread which when added to an unleavened (sinless) batch (the church) <u>would contaminate the whole</u> with leaven, to make all sinful. He urged the church leaders to throw away the sin portion so the <u>purity of the church would be retained</u>. He reminded them that this was in keeping with Passover tradition, where unleavened bread is eaten.

In 9-13, Paul reminded the believers that his letter was to advise them to avoid company with any believer who was <u>sexually immoral, covetous, had anything to do with idols, reviled others, and was a drunkard or an extortioner</u>. He then corrected his message to exclude unbelievers, because this would mean that they could not do business in the pagan culture, or witness to unbelievers about Christ.

He admitted that it was not his place to judge those in the world, because <u>that was God's business</u>. But they were to be wise and wary of those in the world, so as not to be seduced by them into sinful ways.

CHAPTER 6:   In this chapter Paul emphatically condemned the filing of lawsuits by Christians against fellow believers. In verses 1-6, he raised several questions about this issue: did they take cases before a court of sinners, or before fellow believers?—were they aware that they would one day judge the world, and even the angels of Lucifer?—<u>aren't you wise enough to judge fellow believers</u> rather than let unbelievers do so, especially to settle everyday small matters?

Christians will not be given sole judicial license to judge humanity, or fallen angels, but in our association with Christ as He gathers the saints into His future kingdom, <u>we will share in His judgment process</u>. When it comes to great damage to ourselves, our property, or family members, from unbelievers, it is <u>permissible to resort to civil or criminal courts</u> under our judicial system. There are times when it is better to be wronged or cheated than to seek redress before unbeliever judges.

We must remember that the unrighteous will be punished by <u>not inheriting the kingdom of God.</u> The people who have committed the following acts, for which they have not repented and been forgiven by God, <u>will suffer eternal damnation</u>: sins of fornication, adultery, homosexuality, sodomy— idolatry, thievery, covetousness,—and being a drunkard, reviler, or extortioner. Those who have repented by faith in Christ, and been forgiven, are described as '<u>washed, sanctified, and justified</u>.' All who are made righteous in the sight of God, are made holy by the grace of God.

In 12-20, Paul told the Corinthians, as well as all Christians of the past and present, that they should <u>honor God with their bodies,</u> by obeying Him at all times. There are actions which are lawful, but not necessarily good for the body and soul.

He then said, contrary to Corinthian views, indulging in sexual immorality to satisfy sensual craving or lust, is <u>not justified on the basis of eating food</u> to sate pangs of hunger. If a Christian is a part of God's spiritual body, sexual immorality certainly does not glorify God, rather, it grossly dishonors Him. Our hope of a resurrection to glory with Christ, <u>should</u> <u>keep us from dishonoring our bodies</u> by fleshly lusts.

<u>PERSONAL VIEWS</u>: Filing lawsuits in the hope of receiving huge financial benefits is an <u>epidemic cultural flaw in our American society</u>. Trial lawyers become wealthy by taking unreasonably large portions of such settlements, which are usually <u>out of proportion</u> to the <u>wrong inflicted</u> on the victim. This trend has resulted in clogged court calendars, higher costs for healthcare, higher prices for medications, and a warped system of justice. Legislation to correct this problem has been slow in coming, probably due to the <u>added tax</u> <u>revenue that is generated</u> from huge awards.

To what extent Christians are involved in this undesirable aberration of justice is unknown, but it is safe to assume that a <u>growing number do resort to this remedy</u>. The Christian should staunchly oppose this kind of justice and demand that <u>corrective steps be</u> <u>taken by our elected legislators</u> to correct this practice for the good of our nation. Certainly, God would look with favor on such action and change for the better, in keeping with His desires.

CHAPTER 7: Marriage in the Christian life is the topic of this chapter, in response to questions Paul had received. In verses 1-9, Paul discusses the question of celibacy in marriage. He found no fault with staying single, in a celibate state, but recommended <u>marriage when sexual passions require satisfaction.</u> In such cases, husband and wife should be fair over their participation in the sex act, not withholding unless by mutual agreement. This approach keeps Satanic temptations at bay. Paul admitted that he knew of nothing said by Jesus on the subject; he saw nothing wrong if others were <u>single as he was, perhaps by choice,</u> or as a widower choosing celibacy.

In 10-16, Paul urged those who were married to faithfully honor their vows. There should be <u>no separations without cause,</u> each spouse should strive for reconciliation when separation occurs. If this does not take place and they are divorced, then both should remain unmarried, because <u>remarriage constitutes adultery.</u> Marriage is a divine institution and an engagement for life, by God's design.

If marriage becomes difficult because one spouse is a believer and the other is not, then the believer should remain faithful and make <u>every effort to win the unsaved spouse to</u> <u>Christ.</u> This outcome is always most favorable for children! But if the unbeliever insists on divorce, let it be so peacefully and in harmony with each other. The believer spouse may then consider <u>remarriage as permissible by God.</u>

An important understanding was given in verses 17-24, that every person should readily accept what God brings to them in life Christians should be content with their lot, and to <u>conduct themselves in obedience to God's commands.</u> Whether a male is circumcised or not, whether bonded to some responsibility or free to choose, it is best to abide in God's will. Let Him decide what changes to make, or show how changes should come about.

Verses 25-40 are words of advice to single folks, beginning with a state of virginity. Paul admits he lacks divine guidance on this matter but trusts in the Lord for good advice to be given. In a time of distress, he suggests staying single, with responsibility solely for one's self. Notwithstanding, he did not condemn marriage, because it may be the best way to avoid the snares of a sinful world.

Paul suggested that with the Lord's second coming, it won't matter whether one is married or not. It won't matter what a person has or enjoys doing because a new way of life will come about. The main thing is to have less worry! A single person may be concerned more over their spiritual condition with God than the married person, who has a family to care for. Paul expressed his desire for all to live right in God's love above all else.

In conclusion, he agreed that anyone desiring to marry should do so regardless of other circumstances, if this is their greatest wish. In a Christian marriage, if a spouse dies, then the surviving spouse is free to remarriage, however only to another Christian. But, in Paul's judgment, the survivor would be happier staying single.

CHAPTER 8: The Corinthians had asked Paul about eating meat that had been offered as temple sacrifice to idols. In verses 1-6, he attempts to answer this question by relating the act to their knowledge that idol worship had nothing to do with the purity of the meat, and therefore eating it was not a sin. He cautioned that a person can become vain over such knowledge and be a bad example to others who consider it a sin to eat such meat. Love and concern for the feelings of others is evidence of love for God. We should look to Him and to Jesus Christ for guidance rather than think we know it all, because human knowledge is worthless without spiritual love.

In verses 7-13, Paul made the point that eating one kind of food, and abstaining from another, has nothing to do with one's relationship to God. The harm that can come from eating idol sacrifice meat is that it may induce those with less understanding to eat it, and in their conscience feel guilty as if they had sinned. Paul called this putting a stumbling- block in the way of the weak. This can be considered a sin against Christ. With the Spirit of Christ in us, we will love those whom Christ loves, and be careful not to offend them with questionable choices. By offending other believers, we may offend Christ, and damage our own peace of mind.

CHAPTER 9: In this chapter, Paul used interesting and contemporary style language to explain his views on serving the Lord's churches with little or no pay. In verses 1-18, he spoke of his personal rights to choose to do whatever he wished to do, while acknowledging that it is customary to provide support to ministers of God.

With many questions, he asserted his status as an apostle to the church of Corinth, even though he took no pay from them. Some of the rights which he claimed as justification for not doing so included: eating or drinking what he preferred, the apostles taking wife and family with them, or he and Barnabas working for self-support. On the other hand, he supported the principle of fair pay for one's work, by citing a military man at war, a vineyard grower consuming some of his grown fruit, or a sheep herder enjoying milk from the ewes in his flock.

He refers to the law of Moses, which prohibits muzzling an ox to keep it from eating grain that it helps to harvest. From the New Testament, he includes the comment that, 'the one who plows should do so with hope for a good crop,' and 'a thresher of grain should partake of his harvest.' From this, his reasoning is that he has a right to glean satisfaction from the spiritual knowledge he had sown in their lives, rather than receive material things.

Without excuse, Paul agreed that he and his group had not asserted their rights for compensation for services rendered to the church, even though Jesus instructed his disciples to live on the gospel they preached, meaning to be sustained by those who received them in their homes with faith in their message. The principle was that those who provided soul food, should have body food and housing provided for them. Recipients of God's word should supply the needs of their full-time ministers!

Paul as much as stated that God, as his boss, had given him a stewardship to preach the gospel for blessings to be accrued from the fruit of his efforts. By denying himself the usual means of compensation, to serve Christ and save souls, he would enjoy God's blessings for his zeal and love for the spiritual crop he had sown. Voluntary self-sacrifice to serve God can bring unanticipated spiritual blessings!

In 19-27, Paul sums up his objectives for service to the Jews and the Gentiles, to be a servant to all of them, without being obligated to any, because his obligation was to the Lord. He conformed his ways to their ways, to make believers of as many as he could, without neglecting compliance to God's laws.

His objective was to win the contest for their souls, just as a marathon runner strives to win the race, or as a boxer strives to win by a knockout. For this purpose, he had prepared himself, conditioned himself, and applied himself. With constant self-discipline, he did this so he would not lose out on God's rewards for his success. All Christians, as well as ministers of the gospel, should persevere with all their strength to achieve what God has assigned to them, according to their God-given talents.

VIEWPOINTS: The race that all Christians should prepare themselves for is the calling of God, for the service that He has equipped them to accomplish. By diligent application to their calling, believers are assured of spiritual rewards, and often mundane rewards will also ensue. The objective should always be to please and honor God with our efforts, apart from any potential rewards. As with an athlete, we must condition ourselves with help from the Holy Spirit, to endure, to strive for the crown of victory, and to win the race or the match. All this for fulfillment of our calling from God, according to our God- given talents.

CHAPTER 10:   In this chapter, Paul recounts the exodus of the ancestral Jews from Egypt, in verses 1-14, as an example of people who lacked appreciation for blessings of God and persisted in sins of various kinds, for which they paid an awful price.

He describes their exodus through the sea as under a cloud, to symbolize redemption and baptism into Moses, as a representative of Christ. They ate manna, spiritual food from God, and drank from springs from the spiritual rock of Jesus. Yet, they displeased God so much that He <u>caused most of them to die before reaching the land of Canaan.</u> (only Joshua and Caleb made it there)

Their fate was to be a warning to the Corinthians, as it is to humanity in this age. Their sins of idolatry and immorality brought <u>God's judgment upon them.</u> Some died of snake bites, others grumbled over their lot and were killed by angels, and on one day, 23,000 died of a plague. (References for above: Ex. 13:21-22—14:15-29—16:4,15,35—17:2-7—32:6— Num. 25:1-9)

The punishment God brought on the early Israelites for their sins is an example for mankind to consider and expect to a greater extent at the end of earth time <u>when God's wrath judgment falls on the wicked.</u> The remedy is to resist temptation, with the help of the Holy Spirit. With the fear of God in our hearts, we cannot fail.

In verses 15-22, Paul pointed out that in the eating of the bread and drinking the wine of communion, with sins forgiven, we are <u>welded into the body of Christ,</u> and we share in the benefits of salvation that He brought to us. For this reason, there is no room for idolatry of any kind in the life of a Christian. Love of money, power, sensual pleasures, and other diversions from righteousness can be a form of idolatry, because demon influences often pervade them. Serving God and Satan according to our whims is a no-no.

Paul admitted in 23-33, that even though things may be lawful, not all things are helpful or edifying, <u>some may not contribute good to the well-being of others.</u> As an example, with a clear conscience, meat from a market may be eaten, without knowing if it was offered to idols. But if one learns it was so offered, then it should not be consumed. Whatever a Christian eats or drinks should be with thanks to God, and of <u>no offense to others,</u> whether they be Jew, Gentiles, or members of one's church. A holy, peaceable, and benevolent spirit, will foster unity within the church.

<u>VIEWPOINTS:</u>   The Israelites lived in Egypt for over 400 years, under increasing bondage and control as slaves, <u>before their liberation by God</u> under the leadership of Moses. The scripture says nothing of their conduct during that time, whether it was pleasing to God or if they were sinful and degenerate. No doubt they were too exhausted from hard labor or had little <u>time to indulge in deviant interests.</u>

With this background, one must wonder why they became so sinful during their 40 years in the wilderness. <u>The Holy Spirit was not in control of their liberated lives.</u> With God's presence manifested in so many ways to protect and preserve them, how could they ignore His benevolence and behave so shamefully? The answer may be found in one word, 'FREEDOM.'

They had a new found freedom which gave them more time to yield to their sin nature and act accordingly. Freedom can be a dangerous condition, as is evident in today's world. The word 'democracy' implies <u>freedom from unreasonable restraints,</u> without fear of the consequences. This actually goes contrary to the sin nature of man. What we need is the 1000 year theocratic reign of Christ, when He will rule with a rod of iron.

CHAPTER 11:   In this chapter Paul discussed 2 kinds of misconduct in the church fellowship, that of <u>proper head covering and excessive eating</u> with the Lord's Supper. He told the Corinthians to follow his example in verses 1-2, because it was example from the Lord, and then said he was proud of them for doing so. He spoke of the difference between men and women in a worship service, in verses 3-16.

Paul set out a pecking order as God intended for mankind, in that as He is the head over Christ, Christ is the head over man, and man is the head of woman. Under Jewish custom, this meant that man should be bare headed in the church, but the woman was to have her head covered (and wear a veil). A bareheaded woman was as shameful as a woman with her head shaved, which was punishment for prostitutes. The point was that in dress and habits, we should strive to always honor Christ.

Woman was made subject to man, for his help and comfort, and therefore, she should do nothing in Christian assemblies, which appeared to make her equal to man. Yes, man and woman were made for each other, to enjoy mutual comforts and blessings, without domination or total submission. For this reason, in the manner of angels submitting to God, a woman should wear something on her head to show that she is under her man's authority. Paul added that it was unnatural and disgraceful for a man to have long hair like a woman, but for her it is a part of her beauty.

In 17-34, Paul advised on the proper way to participate in the Lords' Supper. Apparently, the Corinthians combined the ceremony with gluttony, by overeating at a meal during or after the ritual part. They made light of the ritual, by making their important part a dinner party. He said the ceremony did them more harm than good, because it was corrupted by arguments and disputes. What should have been bonding in mutual love and affection, was more an affair of discord and disunion.

At the meal part, the wealthy despised the poor, consuming what they brought, while the poor went hungry. For this, Paul had no praise for them, saying this was no way to celebrate the Lord's Supper.

Paul gave them a review of the proper way to observe the Lord's Supper, as set forth in Matt. 26:26-29, Mark 14:22-25, and Luke 22:11-20. He reminded them that any deviation from the prescribed ritual was a sin against Christ's body and blood, which could bring divine punishment. In essence, he pointed out the danger of participating in it with an impious attitude, or impaired sense of propriety. This may have resulted in conscience guilt, which contributed to their many illnesses, and even death. His final word on this was to enjoy the dinner part together, or eat at home.

VIEWPOINTS: In these days, women rarely wear a hat or cover their heads with a scarf while attending church services. Outside of the church environment, many men now have long hair in an effeminate style. This appears more in some ethnic groups, such as the American Indian. This does not seem to be disgraceful in the eyes of most people, either from a religious or secular viewpoint. Is this way of the world displeasing to God, or is there biblical license to be this way? Who is to say!

CHAPTER 12: The Corinthians asked for enlightenment about spiritual gifts. Paul elucidated at length in this chapter on the gifts of the Holy Spirit that a Christian may receive at the time of conversion to the faith. They are not natural gifts as much as they are God endowed. Paul wanted them to be wiser about this matter because they formerly had been led astray by idol worship. They also made public displays of the gifts for self glorification, lacking a spirit of piety and respect for non-participants.

In 1-11, Paul mentioned 9 different gifts, all emanating from a single source, the Holy Spirit, that were to be for the benefit of all church members. They included: spiritual wisdom, divine knowledge, extraordinary faith, a healing ministry, working of miracles, special revelation prophecy, discerning of spirits, speaking in other languages, and interpretations of such languages. These gifts are given to believers singly, or in number, completely as God wills through the Holy Spirit. Believers should not become proud over gifts bestowed on them, or despise those without them.

In verses 12-26, Paul told how diverse gifts amongst the members of a church body should benefit all with unity in the Spirit, whether they be Jews, Gentiles, slaves, or from other walks of life. Each member is like a separate part of the physical body, an ear or an eye, the head or the feet, in which each part is dependent on the other parts, to be an effective whole. Each part, each member, has an assigned value!

In 27-31, Paul emphasized that all the members of a fellowship represent the body of Christ. As in the human body, members are to be closely united by the strong bonds of love; concerned about the good of the whole. Christians are typically dependent one upon another, giving and receiving help from the whole. A spirit of unity is essential, for the whole to prosper in the Spirit.

Everyone may have a gift, but none will possess all of them. We are to desire the best gift, which is usually the one the Spirit gives us. Paul ended with the wish that the Corinthians would seek the best gift, which he would make known to them.

CHAPTER 13: All 13 verses are about the greatest gift of the Spirit which Paul extols for the believer. Paul puts all 9 gifts of the previous chapter below the single most important one, which is 'LOVE'—the essence of God's nature. He declared that even though he possessed the gifts of speaking other languages, prophecy, knowledge, and faith, none of them would be significant unless he had love for others. His definition of love included kindness, patience, humility, courtesy, tolerance, generosity, and a gentle nature. Charity, or unselfish love, does not desire or seek its own praise, honor, profit, or pleasure. It is to be a quality inherent in all other gifts!

Paul stated unequivocally that knowledge would eventually become unimportant, and prophesies and speaking in unknown languages would cease at some future time, most likely as the New Testament was combined with the Old Testament to create God's Holy Bible, and believers are fully exposed to the knowledge of Christ.

The immaturity of the early Christian has been transformed into maturity for the modern church, with the help of God's Word, and even though we don't have all the answers we will know all when Christ's returns. For now, and until then, Paul said that faith, hope, and love should prevail, with love being the dominant one of all so that we may imitate the nature of Christ.

VIEWPOINTS: As with the church of Corinth, some charismatic branches of the Christian church in our time, put much emphasis on the gift of 'speaking in tongues.' They call it the language of angels or the Holy Spirit; it is an unknown, not another language. Often, the view of these believers is that one is not truly a Christian <u>unless they speak in</u> <u>tongues,</u> and they do look down on anyone not so gifted. Some say that this gift, as well as others, is received after conversion to faith in Christ, by a <u>separate baptism of the Holy</u> <u>Spirit.</u>

From Paul's words about this gift, 'tongues' can <u>include languages spoken by other</u> <u>people,</u> from other lands, apart from the church where they are spoken. If not another language, an 'unknown tongue' could be akin to an old pagan belief that it was divinely <u>inspired and</u> <u>understood by some divine power.</u> The interpretation of such utterances, as admonished by Paul, could <u>also have no God given quality.</u>

In short, Paul's statement that this gift was only temporary and it would pass away, when a <u>better source of spirituality would come,</u> (the Holy Bible) is reason enough to relegate this gift to the past. It can cause more division in a church body than it can unify! After all, Christ never spoke in tongues or <u>advocated it for believers.</u>

<u>CHAPTER 14:</u>   This chapter is about the proper use of two main spiritual gifts, that of <u>prophecy and speaking in tongues.</u> In verses 1-5, Paul opens by urging the Corinthians to strive for love while desiring other spiritual gifts, of which he <u>recommends the gift of</u> <u>prophecy.</u> Webster's definition of prophecy is, 'A foretelling or declaration of something to come, especially inspired by God.'

In Paul's day, the New Testament containing the teachings of Christ and prophecy of future events was <u>not yet in existence.</u> Holy Spirit inspiration was being given to devout scholars of the Old Testament prophecies, <u>of things to come</u> for the growing Christian church. Paul considered such forward looking revelations to be of <u>much greater value than</u> the tongues gift, which served no good purpose in the increase of understanding. Prophecy was edifying, exhorting, and comforting.

In the context of this chapter, 'tongues' seems to be the utterance of unintelligible sounds with <u>no meaning to any listener,</u> except one possessing the gift of interpretation. This is opposite of the speaking in other languages at Pentecost, as understood from Acts 2:4-11, where the languages were understood by people from other lands. Speaking in an unknown tongue can give the speaker spiritual satisfaction, but without interpretation, it <u>does nothing</u> <u>for the listener</u> except to perhaps cause them to view the speaker as divinely endowed.

In verses 6-18, Paul explained why tongues must be interpreted to be of any value, <u>in</u> <u>serving the spirituality of the church.</u> He said that utterances without meaning to others, is <u>like speaking into the air,</u> even though the speaker may think or feel that they are speaking to God. Other existing languages make sense to those who know the language, but 'unknown tongues' make no sense to the hearer. Everyday language that is easy to be understood, <u>is the</u> <u>best for worship,</u> and other religious purposes.

If one does speak in an unknown tongue, and no interpreter is present, Paul said they should pray for inspiration to explain their utterance. However, he clarified that when praying in tongues, spiritually the mind is useless, so the solution is to <u>pray in the spirit with</u> <u>the mind</u> <u>engaged.</u> This means to pray in an intelligible language.

Admitting that he spoke many languages (probably Hebrew, Aramaic, Greek, Latin, and others learned while ministering in present day Turkey), Paul said he would rather speak 5 words that made sense, than to speak 10,000 meaningless words

In verses 20-25, Paul chided the Corinthians to grow up, from childishness to maturity in their thinking. He quoted Isaiah 28:11-12 to point out that people still would not listen to God, even when He had prophets and others speaking to them in strange languages. While conceding that speaking in tongues could be viewed by unbelievers as a demonstration of divine power, they may also think it is a nutty act. Furthermore, it does not profit the believers.

On the other hand, Paul said that prophecy as a sign is of benefit to both believers and unbelievers, the latter possibly being persuaded to become believers, and associate with Christians. When scripture truth is revealed intelligibly, it has great power to quicken the conscience and move the heart to seek righteousness with God.

Orderly worship is the theme of verses 25-40. It should be orderly, sensible, peaceful and even handed, all for the purpose of edifying the entire fellowship. Whether prophesying or speaking in tongues, it should be done one at a time. Women also should remain silent, rather than disrupt a service with nonsensical questions.

CHAPTER 15: Some of the Corinthian church leaders were denying the resurrection of Christ and the dead in Christ. Paul addressed this issue in a classical manner at he closed out this letter, probably because it was most important. He virtually shouted that with no after life, the entire Christian message would be a lie. The Greek mind had difficulty accepting this concept.

In verses 1-11, Paul established the resurrection of Jesus as a historic fact by recalling his previous message to the Corinthians on the subject. He told them that this was part of the message of salvation they had to believe, otherwise their faith would be worthless.

He recounted Christ's death, burial, resurrection 3 days later, and then His many appearances. First, it was to the apostles Peter and to His brother James, then all the disciples, 500 other followers, and last to Paul on the road to Damascus. Since this happened about 26 years earlier, most of the witnesses were still living to confirm that Christ rose alive from death.

Paul lessened the importance of his own witness, because he was spiritually reborn after Christ's resurrection, and he had persecuted the church. God's grace meant so much to him that he worked much harder to be deserving of His goodness. Paul ascribed to God's grace all that was valuable in him, humility, diligence, and great faith, no doubt as he recalled how he had grieved God before conversion.

Challenging disbelief in the resurrection concept in verses 12-19, Paul cited the consequence of such disbelief, mainly that faith in and preaching of the Good News is without merit if Christ were not alive. Much worse, we would be saying that all the witnesses lied because they attested to His resurrection. Without it, there would be no hope for eternal life in Christ, and Christians would suffer for nothing of value during their earthly life. The faithful who died would then have perished in their sins, without hope of redemption and salvation.

In 20-28, Paul's comments turned to the positive side. Christ's resurrection insures that all the faithful dead will be resurrected and united with Him. As the first, Christ is called the first fruits, meaning <u>a good harvest of souls will follow</u>. Adam's sin brought the penalty of death, but Christ's resurrection and His 2nd coming will bring restoration to life for all believers resting in death, to be with Him for eternity. The <u>unsaved dead will be</u> <u>resurrected later</u> after Christ's millennial reign. For the believer, death as an enemy will be destroyed.

Shortly after Christ's 2nd coming, the living wicked on earth, plus Satan and his legions of fallen angels, will <u>suffer God's wrath judgment</u> of death, destruction, and/or confinement to a 'lake of fire.' There will come a time when everything is under God's control, presumably after Christ's millennial reign, <u>and Satan will be gone.</u>

Evidently the Corinthians had baptisms of the living for someone who had died, as indicated by verses 29-34. Paul asked them what good purpose this served if there would be no resurrections. Without the hope of resurrection, why risk one's life, as Paul implied he did at Ephesus (the beast may have been evil men). If no resurrection, then <u>why not 'eat, drink and be merry, for tomorrow we die</u>?' Paul then cautioned the Corinthians to be wary of evil men bent on their spiritual downfall.

Verses 35-49 relate Paul's description of the believer's resurrection body, and how it is raised up. He prefixed his words with the comment, 'Don't be foolish,' perhaps to get their full attention. He then <u>compared death to the planting of a seed</u> which decomposes in the ground before it germinates into a living sprout, with an appearance much different from the seed. This is part of God's creation and design program. From the beginning, man, animals, birds and fish are living creations different from each other. Heavenly bodies also have their own distinctive properties.

In like manner, when the dead in Christ are raised to life, infirmities, ugliness, weakness, and other flaws, will be <u>replaced by perfect health, strength, beauty</u>, and total body perfection. Actually, our physical bodies at death will be raised as spiritual bodies to live forever. This will also be true for those who are alive at Christ's 2nd coming!

Whereas, life was given to the 1st man Adam from the dust of the earth, the <u>life- giving essence of Christ originated in heaven.</u> All mankind has a body of limited duration like Adam's, but the righteous will receive a heavenly body like that of Jesus.

In 50-58, Paul clarifies the mystery of human body transformation into spiritual beings, to include <u>those living when the 'rapture' occurs</u>. Quicker than the eye can blink, as Christ comes again, at the sound of the last trumpet, the dead in Christ will be raised and changed into their spiritual body. That is when the sting of death will be neutralized. Living Christians will likewise be instantly changed into spiritual beings. Paul concluded by advising all believers to be steadfast in their faith, giving good service to the Lord, in the knowledge that they would be rewarded.

<u>VIEWPOINTS:</u>   The term 'at the last trumpet' in verse 51 is a bone of contention. Some believe that it refers to I Thess. 4:16-18, but others relate it to Rev. 11:15. While the 'last trumpet' could be the 7th trumpet sound spoken of in Revelations, the activity described there is clearly <u>not that of the Thessalonian event</u>, the 'rapture' of the dead and the living in Christ. The Revelation trumpet sounds appear to be <u>related to God's Great Wrath judgment</u>, following the rapture.

However, since the rapture is described as an event to be quickly carried out, and then immediately followed by God's wrath judgment, the 'last trump' and the 7th trumpet could be one and the same. If this is so, then the timing of the rapture will definitely be shortly before the end of the 7 year tribulation time (70th week of Daniel).

One may surmise that these 2 trumpet sounds are unrelated, and Paul's 'last trumpet' relates to the Thessalonian trumpet sound to signal the end of life on earth as we know it, namely the last days for Christians. If this is so, there still is no justification here, to conclude that the rapture will take place before the 7 year (70th week of Daniel) tribulation time begins, as some church doctrines claim. At this point, without exception, scripture seems to point to a rapture taking place near the end of the tribulation time, when Christ returns to claim His own, as Paul implied in 15:23. No scripture states that Christ's return will be in 2 steps, 6 or more years apart.

CHAPTER 16:   In this closing chapter, it is interesting in verses 1-4, that Paul asked the Corinthian church as well as those in Galatia to contribute funds for the less prosperous church in Jerusalem. This is a viable concern for a Christian minister towards needy followers who respond well to his labors.

Paul reviewed his travel plans in 5-12, that included a visit with the Corinthian church, possibly for an entire winter. He indicated that he planned to stay in Ephesus until Pentecost to complete some vital ministry. He asked them to give Timothy a good reception during his visit, and a blessed departure as he continued on to Ephesus. He added that he had tried to induce Apollos to visit them, but this was not agreeable to him at the time.

In verses 13-23, Paul both exhorts the Corinthians and acknowledges the work of others. He encouraged the church to hold fast to their faith, without fear of criticism from others, and to fellowship in love of one another. He recognized Stephanus and his household for their devoted ministry to the believers in Corinth, and asked the church to honor them for their service.

In closing. Paul sends greetings from churches in Asia, and Aquila and Priscilla with their home fellowship. He asked the Corinthian believers to greet one another with a holy kiss, a customary sign of brotherly affection and unity. He admitted that he wrote the ending words himself, which indicates that all other writing was done by his aide, Sosthenes, (see 1:1), per his dictation.

While extending his own love together with wishes for grace in the Lord Jesus, he oddly voices a denunciation on anyone without love for Jesus Christ.

SUMMARY: Prior to Paul's evangelization of the people of Corinth, they were deeply immersed in pagan worship of several gods. They had a temple dedicated to a god and goddess of healing, Asclepius and his daughter Hygieia. Another cult was that of Aphrodite, which they worshipped in a temple so wealthy that it owned more than 1000 temple sex slaves, which they primarily rented out to visiting sailors. Corinth was known for its licentious life- style in an age of great sexual immorality.

Because of these earlier influences, the church of Corinth had difficulty overcoming these pagan activities with spiritual values. Backsliding was prevalent and Paul was disturbed over reports of questionable practices in the church. Divisions over moral and spiritual issues was prevalent in the believer fellowship. For this reason, he wrote extensively in this letter about the gospel of Christ and how to live up to all it's precepts.

Perhaps the most troublesome subjects addressed in this letter apropos to the Corinthian church, as well as churches of today, was the matter of marriage and divorce, a proper and balanced use of spiritual gifts, and the <u>impact of Christ's death and resurrection</u> <u>on the spiritual future of mankind.</u> Paul's advice and admonitions were pertinent then, but even more so today, as contemporary Christians churches compromise spiritual values and principles, become more tolerant of immoral deviations, and question the Good News Gospel of Jesus Christ. Apostasy in it's ugly camouflage attire is a growing problem today in too many Christian churches in the world!

II CORINTHIANS—BOOK EIGHT

Paul's 2nd letter to the church in Corinth was to serve 2 purposes: 1st, that he still planned to visit Corinth as he had promised in his previous letter, and 2nd, that he wanted to reestablish his claim to be the primary apostle to their church. He bared his soul over his feelings of affinity with the Corinthian church, and defended his authority to preach Christ's message of love and unity.

While his 1st letter to the church had produced good results, there still were dissenters who questioned his right and authority to minister to them. Paul expressed his joy over the generally favorable response his 1st letter received, as he sought to justify his involvement in the creation and guidance of the church. Chapters 1-7 have a joyful and happy tone, but 10-

13 have a more somber and reserved tone, to reassert that his ministry to them as an apostle of Christ was for real. Chapters 8-9 are mainly an appeal to the church for financial aid to other churches.

It is believed that he wrote most of this letter, with some help from Timothy, less than a year after his 1st one, in late 56 AD, while in the city of Philippi in Macedonia, before keeping his promise of a visit.

CHAPTER 1: In the 7 opening verses of salutation, Paul identified himself and Timothy as the authors greeting the 'church of God at Corinth' and surrounding area. He wished them grace and peace from 'God our Father' (Father is a new term) and the Lord Jesus Christ, and voiced thanks to this divine twosome for the comfort given in earlier tribulations at Ephesus (perhaps the riot of Acts. 19).

Paul spoke of afflictions suffered in the manner of Christ and comfort received from God, as the conditioning they received to be better equipped to give comfort and consolation to the church brethren at Corinth. He extended this hope to them also.

In 8-11, Paul shared some of their experiences with trouble while in Asia, mainly Macedonia, some of them being life threatening, from which God delivered them. He thanks the church for many prayers that contributed to their safety.

In 12-14, Paul gave assurances of their good conduct and intentions, not as the world does, but as God's grace dictated. This was an effort to win confidence, so the church could testify of his integrity at the end of time as he would do for them.

Verses 15-24 is Paul's explanation why he failed to visit the church as planned earlier. He asked if they thought his planning was frivolous and insincere, causing them to think he meant 'yes' one day and 'no' on another day, just to please them. He assured them that this was not the case, because his plans at the time were based on his faith in Christ's direction for him. Just as God is trustworthy, Paul claims the same quality for himself, in that his promise to visit them was always a 'yes.'

In like manner, Jesus Christ's promises were always certain, just as God's promises to Him were certain; hence Christ can say 'Amen' for our glory in God. This gives all believers a common bond for unity with Christ, by which the Holy Spirit gives us assurance that we belong to God. This is a triune blessing!

Claiming God as his witness, Paul emphatically stated that he deferred his first plan to visit <u>to avoid harming them</u>, and whether they believed him or not, he wanted to give them joy and strength in their faith.

CHAPTER 2:   Continuing his fence mending dialogue, Paul explained in 1-11, that he refrained from visiting the Corinthian church for fear of causing sadness, which would make it <u>hard for them to give him happiness</u>. He spoke of his grief and anguished heart as he wrote a previous letter that he hoped would convey his love for them. That letter is thought to be one written between I and II Corinthians, that may have been lost, or may actually be chapters 10-13 of this letter.

Then he spoke of someone who had grieved them for some wrong-doing, perhaps against him personally, <u>for which he held no grievance</u>. Paul suggests that they should welcome the man back into their fellowship, for he was repentant and remorseful over his guilt. Perhaps Paul felt that too much discipline could cause the man to take his own life, or be <u>used by Satan to do something harmful to the church.</u>

In verses 12-17, Paul spoke of his God given ministry to the church at Troas which he suspended when his aide Titus did not arrive <u>with news from the Corinthians.</u>

He sailed across the Aegean Sea to Macedonia, perhaps the port city of Philippi, where he found Titus, who gave him good news from Corinth (see 7:5-7).

Paul gave thanks to God here, (see his comments in chapter 7), for diffusing the fragrance of His divine providence through Jesus Christ <u>to save some from spiritual death</u> when they <u>repented of their sins.</u> A believer triumphs over death through Christ, with joyful hearts over the success of His Gospel. Unfortunately, the <u>fragrance of death comes to those who reject Christ</u> and His Good News message.

To Paul's question, 'Who is sufficient for these things?' The answer is God—<u>no one else!</u> He stated that he was not peddling the word of God for personal profit, but was <u>doing it sincerely and devoutly in the power of God</u> through Jesus Christ.

CHAPTER 3:   Paul's words effectively describe the 'glory of ministry' in this chapter. In verses 1-3, he clarified that he did not need a letter of reference or accreditation from his home church in Jerusalem, according to the custom of those days, when <u>a believer or a minister moved from one church to another.</u>

He claimed the church of Corinth as his letter of reference because the members, as his converts, could <u>attest to his proficiency in preaching the gospel</u> of Christ. Their witness was heartwarming to him, as it came from the Holy Spirit through their hearts, <u>not from tablets of stone</u>. With the gospel of Christ written in their hearts, the love of Christ was shown to all. The effect of the Law on stone was external, while the force of the Spirit is internal.

In verses 4-6, Paul expressed trust in Christ for confidence given by God that enabled him <u>to do what God willed for him.</u> God was his 'sufficiency,' qualifying him to preach the new covenant gospel message with Holy Spirit endowment, rather than from Mosaic Law. The Law made men conscious of their sins without a Spirit passport to forgiveness. Thus, <u>the Spirit brings eternal life,</u> whereas the Law was condemnation for sins without a provision for life.

In verses 7-18, Paul extolled the glory of the new covenant, the New Testament, as being <u>superior to the Old Testament Mosiac Law,</u> having a fading glory.

The Old Testament dispensation identified sin subject to the wrath and curse of God. It put God above and against mankind, as opposed to the New Testament gospel <u>which makes known the grace of God in and with us.</u> This reveals the righteousness of God, by faith in a believer's heart, and enables us to attain righteousness by the grace and mercy of God through Jesus Christ, with forgiveness of sins and eternal life.

The glory of the new covenant so outshines the old covenant of the Law, that it <u>replaces the old which no longer shines</u> forth as it once did. The Law left a veil of ignorance or misunderstanding on the minds of the Israelites; this veil is removed when Christ's New Testament doctrine <u>permeates the heart of a new convert to God.</u> This brings joy to all who believe in the gospel, who aspire to live up to God's desires for His children, and who relish the new spiritual liberty for life as a Christian. Christ is revealed in the New Testament to new believers, as a bright image in a new mirror, which is also <u>reflected from the shining face of committed Christians.</u>

CHAPTER 4: Paul spoke of dedication and suffering entailed to <u>realize the glory of his ministry,</u> in verses 1-7. Entrusted with this mission, he and his aides did not give up, do shameful things, or try to fool anyone with a convoluted message. Speaking the truth simply, they tried to <u>make their message understood.</u> Unfortunately, it was often as if hidden to those under Satan's control, whose design was to keep men in opposition or ignorance of the light of Christ's gospel. **A growing problem today!**

The sun in the firmament is pleasant to behold. Much more pleasant and profitable it is for <u>Christ's gospel to shine in the heart of man,</u> as created by the Holy Spirit. God could have sent angels to preach the gospel, or selected the most prominent of men, but He <u>chose humbler, weaker vessels,</u> in which His divine power would be more glorified as He enabled them to serve effectively. The treasure of gospel light and God's grace are stored in fragile earthen vessels akin to a clay jar.

As a clay jar is sometimes roughly handled, so are the servants of God, but as Paul said in verses 8-15, <u>they were never broken or crushed.</u> Their suffering mirrored that of Jesus Christ, but yet the light of His grace could be seen in them. Paul himself was almost stoned to death (Acts 14:19-20), but he survived by God's grace so he could preach His Word. While death threatened him often, his ministry brought life to those who believed.

Having the spirit of faith in Jesus Christ, Paul and his helpers endured suffering for the <u>advantage of all those who became Christians</u> through their ministry. They knew God would reward them with eternal life with Jesus for their service was to glorify both Him and God. They would rendezvous with fellow believers in heaven! That is a future all Christians should aspire too.

Paul concluded that none should lose heart even though affliction and time brought on aging, because spiritually the <u>inward man was being renewed daily.</u> Our earthly vision should not be focused on what we see or experience in life, what is temporary, but we should <u>keep our eyes on the eternal rewards of heaven.</u>

CHAPTER 5:   As a tentmaker, it is natural that Paul compared man's earthly body to that of a tent in verses 1-10. Like a tent, the human body, although a marvel of creation, <u>is a temporary abode for the soul.</u> It is a burden to maintain physically, and in a spiritual sense, it is just a down payment (earnest) on a heavenly home. It is comparable to a motel or hotel on the journey of life to reach a preferred destination.

When our earthly body expires, we have a mansion in heaven to occupy rent free as our reward for faith in Jesus Christ, and the <u>good or bad that we do on earth.</u> We want the eternal shelter of that home just as we wear clothes for warmth on earth, which we should readily want <u>to exchange for what God will provide.</u> His Holy Spirit assures believing souls they will wear garments of praise, and robes of righteousness as they <u>enjoy the comfort of</u> an eternal home.

There is no doubt that the Lord pleads for the soul of the believer to be closely <u>united with Himself.</u> The Christian should strive for this unity while on earth and thus be amply <u>rewarded for the achievements that please the Lord</u>.

In verses 11-21 Paul spoke of the importance of bringing the unsaved to a living relationship with God. With scriptural knowledge of the frightful judgment God will bring upon the evil unbeliever, <u>Christians should do all they can</u> to bring others to a saving grace in the Lord Jesus. As His disciples, our zeal and diligence in this regard is for His glory and the healthy growth of our earthly church. It isn't for us to brag about, although it is a matter of pride in the circle of believers.

Paul spoke of motivation in serving God's purposes, as it applied to himself and his aides. He felt that their ministry was in obedience to God, even when others might think they were 'nutty,' because in their 'right' mind they were bringing good. It was the <u>love of Christ</u> that <u>compelled them to make converts out of the Corinthians.</u>

Paul said that believers should not judge others by outward appearances or visible characteristics, as Christ was once judged. A believer is a new person, who should <u>do everything possible to have peace with others</u>, and see them reconciled with each other and with God. As Christ's ambassadors, Christians are to persistently represent God in this rebellious world, with dignity, conviction, and purpose, so that the unsaved will receive and believe in the <u>priceless gift of salvation from Jesus Christ.</u>

CHAPTER 6:   More vindication is sought by Paul over his own ministry in the face of much trouble, suffering, and <u>disaffection from the Corinthian church</u>. In verses 1-10, Paul spoke on behalf of himself and his coworkers, as working together with God, when they asked the Corinthians to <u>benefit from God's goodness to them.</u>

He quoted Is. 49:8, 'At the acceptable time, I listened to you, and on the day of salvation, I helped you,' to tell them that now was the time to keep the faith. This is true for all mankind, because we know not where or what tomorrow will be; we must be careful <u>not</u> <u>to turn our back on a day of grace</u> in God's pleasure.

Paul said they tried hard, as God's servants, to be correct in all things, so no one would find fault with them. In spite of much trouble and hardship, including beatings, jail time, riots, deprivation of rest and food, they patiently endured with understanding, kindness, love, and purity of heart <u>to do what was right in God's sight.</u>

No matter what others said negatively of them, they were always truthful, as the Corinthians should have known. In the face of death, and cruelties, they survived to be happy; in the face of poverty, they had given others spiritual wealth, and reaped the satisfaction of spiritual wealth in serving the Lord.

In verses 11-18, Paul openly expressed love for the Corinthians and asked them to reciprocate with love in return. He evidently felt that they were being adversely influenced by pagan interests that bridled their affections. For this reason, he admonished them not to be 'unequally yoked' with them; this would be as incompatible as yoking an ox with a donkey (Deut. 22:10). Such a pairing is as unproductive as trying to mix righteousness with sinfulness. Just as light and darkness are opposites, Christ and Satan (Belial used here, only once in the N.T.) are completely irreconcilable.

Believers and unbelievers are spiritually unsuited to each other, for believers are spiritually a temple of God (see I Cor. 6:19), in which idolatry has no place. Paul quoted Lev. 26:11-12, Ezek. 37:27, Is. 52:11, and Ezek. 20:34, in support of his advice that the Corinthians separate themselves from pagan influences.

When believers are unequally yoked with unbelievers, they must expect trouble. Although it is normal to be with unbelievers at work, in public at sporting events, and other activities, we should not choose them for close friends. If a friendship ensues, the believer should strive to acquaint the unbeliever with the Good News of salvation through Christ. If this is a fruitless effort, then it is best to draw apart from the unbeliever, less we become defiled spiritually.

CHAPTER 7: Paul opened this chapter with a plea to the Corinthians to put aside all evil that would corrupt their physical bodies and their spiritual lives, so they would reap the blessings promised by God. Then in verses 2-12, he resumed his appeal for their love and respect for the ministry he had brought to them, because he trusted them, was proud of their spiritual progress, and was encouraged and happy over it.

He referred back to his time of trouble in Macedonia when Titus came from Corinth with good news about the church's response to a critical letter he had written, with some regret for having written it (a letter apart from I & II Cor.). The report from Titus gave him much satisfaction and joy because they had repented of their earlier errors as God willed for them. This lifted the regret that burdened Paul's heart.

He praised the Corinthians for their recovery from the sorrow they felt over their own actions, and how they accepted the will of God, to walk in newness of life. This included some kind of disciplinary action against someone in the church who had done wrong and involved the church somehow.

Paul concludes with words of appreciation for the courteous manner in which the church received Titus, which gave him much joy and increased his love for them. This added to Paul's joy and confidence in them. As their apostle, Paul typified the relationship between a pastor and his church, whereby the latter must lighten the burdens of pastoring, and the former should show his concern and love for his congregation with words of pleasure, caring, and comfort.

CHAPTER 8:   As an example of generous giving, Paul commended the churches in Macedonia, in verses 1-7, for giving gladly and generously, even during hard times, because they wanted <u>to help God's people</u>. It was their desire as children of God, to honor Him in their giving to the needy.

Titus evidently first induced the Corinthians to give, and now Paul asked them to <u>complete their giving program with him;</u> Paul commended them also for excelling in what they set out to do, with great faith, using their spiritual gifts, and <u>showing their love for him</u> and his <u>coworkers,</u> and suggested they do as well in their giving.

In 8-15, Paul mentioned Jesus Christ as most generous in giving up material riches <u>so He could make men spiritually wealthy</u>. He literally gave everything for the purpose of redeeming souls from eternal damnation. What better example is there for the Christian than the generous love of Christ?

Paul repeated his suggestion that the Corinthians complete their giving, not as an order from him, but <u>according to their ability and desire to give</u>. He pointed out that their relative prosperity was a good reason for generous giving. In life, when some have little to share, while others have more than they need, it is God's will that the <u>prosperous share of their abundance with the poor</u>. There should be a measure of equality! Some day the table may be turned, and the poor of today will help their benefactors of yesterday.

In verses 16-24, Paul informed the Corinthians that he was sending Titus back to receive their contribution, with 2 other trustworthy companions, to insure that their <u>gifts would be safeguarded and delivered</u> to the saints of Jerusalem. He qualified Titus as his personal aide and the others as followers of Christ representing several churches. His final request here is that these men be accorded a loving and courteous reception in Corinth.

CHAPTER 9:   Paul continued informing the Corinthians in verses 1-5 about the gathering and administration of their gifts, by the 3 men commissioned to do so, so the church would <u>complete their collection effort in advance</u>. He admitted having bragged about them to the churches in Macedonian, and therefore gave them advance notice so he and they would not be embarrassed by a failure to fulfill their giving plan.

Paul demonstrated a wise practice, by dealing prudently and considerately with contributors, to give them <u>the time needed to organize their effort</u>. Selling the justification for giving is important, because self-interest can work strongly against the will of God. Paul did say that their giving should be willing, not as if under pressure, which in a sense he applied, but <u>in the context of reminding them of their pledge</u>.

In 6-15, Paul expounded on the measure of a 'cheerful giver,' in terms of one who sows seed, which if done sparingly produces a small harvest, as opposed to one who sows <u>abundantly to reap a bountiful harvest</u>. By giving cheerfully and willingly, we please God, and He in turn may compensate us in greater measure than otherwise.

This attitude is somewhat in agreement with Ps. 112:9. At times, we should waste less on ourselves so we can <u>give more to those with less;</u> this would surely please God and bring an increase of both spiritual and temporal good things. We are blessed if we emulate the example of Christ, in doing good under the adage, 'it is more blessed to give than to receive.'

Verses 10-15 are in the form of prayer that Paul voiced for the Corinthian church, that they be blessed for their generosity by added prayers from the Christians in Jerusalem, who would want <u>fellowship with them if possible</u>. In closing, Paul gave thanks to God for His indescribable gift, the Lord Jesus Christ. There is no way that mankind can out give God— He is the Master Giver, second to none!

CHAPTER 10:   In saying, 'Now, I, Paul, myself' to open this chapter, it appears that Paul wrote this chapter through 13 <u>without Timothy's help</u>. This portion may be the missing letter in which Paul addressed some serious problems in the Corinthian church. It is commonly believed that some Jewish church leaders were challenging Paul's authority to be the primary apostle to the church.

In verses 1-6, Paul asked the main body of believers to deal with their problems so his visit with them <u>would be on friendlier terms</u>. He did not want to come before them in as stern a manner as he would have to show towards those who opposed him. He did not choose to contend with opponents using weapons of war, but he would <u>rely on God's powers</u> of <u>persuasion</u> to overcome their arguments and blind pride, so they would listen and obey Christ.

More than ever, the ministry for Christ involves spiritual warfare with spiritual enemies, and <u>for spiritual purposes</u>. Physical force is not the best choice, strong persuasions rendered in truth, humility, and wisdom, is a better way. Feeble this may appear to some, the might of God through the preaching of the cross, by men of faith and prayer, will normally decimate idolatry, impiety, and wickedness.

In verses 7 -11, Paul suggested common sense in judging who was a Christian, that it should <u>not be based on outward appearances,</u> which in his case was not truly impressive. He felt that his letters to them confirmed his authority from Christ to help them, not to harm or frighten them, as some would say. On this basis, he would say the same in person as in his letters.

Paul declined to compare his performance with that of his opponents, in verses 12-18, who because of their ego, <u>considered themselves greater than anyone</u> else. Rather than indulge in such foolish egotism, Paul gave credit to God for help in ministering to the Corinthians, for which he would rightfully boast in moderation. He said, 'After all, we are the ones who brought the message of Christ to you.'

Paul chose a good rule for his conduct; namely, not to boast of things without the measure, or yardstick, <u>that God had given to him</u>. He elected not to praise his own achievements, which were for God's approval—to promote His glory, and then to receive honor from Him.

Strengthening the faith of the Corinthian church was Paul's goal, so they would <u>increase the Christian population</u> in Corinth, and make it possible for he and his coworkers to move on to other lands with the gospel message. He told them to boast about the Lord in their lives, because only His approval had any value.

CHAPTER 11:   In verses 1-6, Paul asked the Corinthians to accept some foolishness from him, while <u>matching his concern</u> (jealousy) for them to God's. He called them a virgin bride that he had chosen for Christ, but now feared they were being deceived as Eve was tricked by the serpent in the garden of Eden. He feared that they were being corrupted by teachings from some false apostles, causing them to lose their faithfulness in the only true son of God, Jesus Christ; he thought they were being drawn away into a belief different from what they had learned from him. He believed that his conduct and knowledge was as good or better than the false apostles, even though they were able to orate better than he.

Paul asked if he had demeaned himself in verses 7-15, by preaching the gospel before them without compensation. By accepting support from other churches, to bring the gospel to Corinth, it could be said that he robbed the other churches. He told them, 'When I needed help, I received help from followers in Macedonia, and refrained from being a burden on you,' all because he loved them.

He stated his intentions to keep on ministering to them in this manner, so his dishonest opponents would have no basis for comparing themselves to him, even though they were dishonest apostle pretenders. In his eyes, they were as deceptive as Satan in what they were doing, and would get what they deserved in God's time.

In verses 16-33, Paul enumerated all the suffering and tribulation he had suffered, after chiding them for thinking he was a fool, which gave him reason to be foolish and boast of what he had endured for their benefit. He also reminded them of how foolish they had been when others enslaved them, cheated and stole from them.

First he does some comparing by stating that he was as they were, a Hebrew Jew, and from the family of Abraham. But, as a servant of Christ, he felt that he was better than they were because he worked harder at it, been jailed, whipped, and near death more often they had experienced.

He listed the following persecutions and hardships: 5 times of 39 whip lashes by the Jews, 3 beatings by Romans, a stoning, 3 shipwrecks with a day in the sea, life threatening dangers from rivers, robbers, Jews, foreigners, in cities, deserts, at sea, and from false followers. In addition, he endured many sleepless nights after hard times, hunger and thirst, cold for lack of garments, and finally, burdensome worry over his churches. In his weakest moments, God saved him, as he did in Damascus when his followers lowered him in a basket through a city wall window to escape capture.

Paul gave this account of his labors and sufferings; not for self-glorification, **but to honor God,** for enabling him to do and suffer so much for the cause of Christ. In this way, he greatly eclipsed the false apostles, who tried to diminish his character and accomplishments.

CHAPTER 12: Paul said he would do some boasting even though it would not personally gain him a thing. He may have done it to offset some boasting about a special spiritual experience that a false apostle in the church of Corinth boasted about. In verses 1-10, Paul revealed that he, as a 'follower of Christ.' had a God given visual revelation about 14 years earlier, about 42 AD, while on his 1st missionary trip.

He admitted that he could not say whether he was alive or not, as he was caught up in God's 3rd heaven (Paradise), only God knew this. There he heard things that were not lawful to share with others, or perhaps too marvelous for others to believe. If he could tell of the wonderful things he saw or heard, it would be the truth, but he felt it would be foolish to say too much, else it would <u>improperly magnify himself</u> in the eyes of the Corinthians.

NOTE: This experience could have occurred at Lystra when a mob <u>stoned him</u> <u>and left</u> <u>him for dead,</u> as related in Acts 14:19-20. His spirit could have left his body for a rendezvous with God, and then been returned to bodily presence, so that he could continue to <u>carry out</u> <u>his assigned mission</u> for God's glory. The alternative, is that this vision was given to him while in an unconscious state, as if a dream.

Paul also revealed that he was given a painful physical affliction about that time, by one of Satan's fallen angels, which <u>constrained pride in his accomplishments</u> so that God would receive more credit. For healing or relief, he prayed 3 times for God's mercy, but was told 'All you need is my kindness, for my power is strongest through your weakness.' (Popular belief is that Paul suffered from some kind of eye infection, which made him look grotesque, and required him to enlarge his writings)

Even though God permitted his affliction as a factor for good, it is logical to assume that Paul prayed thereafter more than 3 times for comfort. There is <u>no limit on the praying one</u> <u>may do to receive aid</u> from our heavenly Doctor. As with Paul, a Christian with impairments can be a spiritual tower of strength. In our weakness, we can be strong in the grace of our Lord; He is the source of spiritual and physical strength, and the <u>Supplier of the blessings we</u> <u>receive in His power</u>.

In verses 11-21, after speaking as a fool, Paul said it was quite necessary, to make the Corinthians see that he was every bit as good as any false apostle in their midst. He reminded them of the miracles, sign, and wonders of his ministry to them, for which <u>they only missed</u> <u>the blessing of giving him support</u>. For this 'wrong' he asked for their forgiveness! (For 'this right' he deserved praise and thanks.)

He spoke of his intentions to visit a 3rd time, without being a burden to them, so he could enjoy them, <u>as a father enjoys his children.</u> Paul's loving nature and kind intentions are obvious in his words, which <u>typify a faithful minister of God.</u> He explained that parents ought to leave inheritance for their children, and not vice versa. Just as this does not always buy love from the children, Paul stated his desire to do his best out of love, for the spirituality of the Corinthians, <u>without receiving love in return.</u>

Emphasizing his honest intentions, Paul asked them if he had cheated them personally, or through his ambassador Titus. As Christ's apostle, <u>everything done for them was intended</u> <u>for</u> <u>their good.</u> Therefore, he desired that they settle their petty differences and be on their good behavior during his visit, else he would be ashamed and sad over their sinful ways, including things immoral, indecent, and shameful.

CHAPTER 13:   Saying that he would be visiting them for the 3rd time, Paul made it clear in verses 1-10, that it would be for disciplinary purposes if necessary, to punish those who persisted in sin, when 2 or 3 witnesses attested to their wrong-doing. This had been promised to them during his 2nd visit. Now as he spoke for Christ, he warns them that <u>he would act</u> <u>under</u> <u>His power to do what was necessary.</u>

He challenged them to take a measure of their faith in Christ, with hope and prayers that they <u>would not come up short in their spiritual relationship</u> with Him. He stated that the truth must rule the day, and not be denied. With prayers that the Corinthians would do well, better than before, Paul stated that he hoped that he would not need to <u>exact his God given</u> authority <u>too stringently</u> during his visit.

Verses 11-12, are words of adieu, goodwill, and blessings to the church. Again, Paul asked them <u>to take heed to his words, act on them,</u> and restore peace and unity in the church so they could greet each other with a holy kiss. His benediction is that they may partake of all the benefits of grace in Christ, and the love of God in union with the Holy spirit, for such <u>major blessings are freely given to the faithful.</u>

SUMMARY: Most noticeable about Paul's ministry is how he firmly reminded the churches he established that his apostolic authority came from the Lord, and that he preached the true <u>gospel of Christ as divinely revealed to him.</u> He acknowledged that he was called by God to carry the Good News Message to the Gentiles, as an apostle of Christ Jesus. Yet, he did not depart from his love and concern for fellow Jews.

He did not command or dictate to his churches, but used persuasion as demonstrated in his letters to the church at Corinth, in an effort to <u>induce them to properly deal with specific problems,</u> as well as toward himself. He used the power of the gospel to admonish them, as any dedicated minister should do.

Paul's writings to the church of Corinth constitute a major part of Christian theology, because of the volume and his intensely theological writing style. He presented <u>Christ as God's reconciling gift to humankind,</u> which he graphically portrayed in the death, burial, and resurrection of Jesus. This was the focal point of all that he preached and wrote. He credited Christ as the mediator to <u>reestablish broken relationships between God and humankind,</u> as stated in II Cor. 5:19, 'God was in Christ reconciling the world unto himself.'

Reconciliation with God happens best in a congregation of believers known as a church. Paul began his missionary activities out of the mother church in Jerusalem, and thereafter advised persons of faith to <u>affiliate with a fellowship of consecrated believers,</u> who considered Christ to be the Head of the church.

Paul's ministry portrayed him as a person of great humility, but with <u>equally great courage and persistence</u> in fulfilling his God given mission to the Gentiles. Second only to Jesus in the New Testament, he was an <u>example of dedication that all Christians should emulate.</u> More of that can be seen in his epistle of Galations.

TITHES AND STEWARDSHIP

Tithing is first mentioned in Genesis 14:18-20, where Abraham gifted a tenth part of war booty to King Melchizedek, and again in Gen. 28:22, where Jacob pledged a tenth of his possessions to God for safety from Esau, while away from his parents. Tithing was required of the Israelites for the support of the Levite priests, orphans, widows, and visitors from other lands, most often in the form of animals and harvested grain.

In Malachi 3:8, failure to tithe is equated with robbing God. Jesus said that tithing should be with sincere concern and compassion for the needs of the less fortunate, with mercy, justice and fairness, rather than as an obligation under law. (See Matt. 23:23; Luke 11:42).

Stewardship is the management of assets or resources possessed or assigned to another by the owner. The word 'steward' as found in Genesis 43:19,24, and 44:1,4, is applicable to the servant who managed food supplies that Jacob's sons received from Joseph in Egypt. In John 2:8-9, it identifies the man in charge of the wine supply, when Jesus changed water into wine. In Titus 1:7, it refers to a responsible pastor managing the property of the church. Often, stewardship is thought of solely in terms of finances, but the Bible teaches that God approved stewardship includes sharing with others in the manner of Jesus giving His life for mankind's benefit.

The most comprehensive discussion of giving is Paul's dissertation in II Corinthians, chapters 8 and 9, where he told the Corinthians why and how they should give. Some people think only the wealthy should give, but Paul said that all believers should give according to their means, no matter how poor they might be.

He next emphasized that giving should be done willingly and cheerfully, without a feeling of compulsion. The amount to be given is not specified as a 10% tithe in the New Testament, but is measured according to what the heart of the giver dictates, preferably on the generous side, even to the point of personal sacrifice. Jesus was more pleased with the sacrificial giving of a widow, than in the tithe or substantial offering from the wealthy, who took pride in their giving.

The good attitude of church members to what they possess, should be that all of it came from the loving heart of God, given to them for good stewardship. The New Testament concept of stewardship correlates to our commitment to Jesus Christ, the Steward of our time, talents, finances, and ambitions. We are not our own, but we are His, bought with a price, and giving of our resources is our thanks to Him.

Giving is not a one way street, there are many dividends to be enjoyed. Giving is important for the giver, for whom it is a test of sincerity and love for God and His children. In Matt. 6:19-21, how we manage our earthly wealth is a barometer of our spiritual health. The bonus often comes in greater wealth as a reward from heaven, and always as spiritual blessing for reflecting God's love.

Contributions to the church or other Christian causes should always be handled with integrity by a person of accountability, having a good reputation for honesty and management ability. Periodic reports on contributions received, and an accounting of disbursements, should be provided to the church body, so that contributors can be assured of responsible stewardship by the pastor and others.

GALATIANS—BOOK NINE

At the time, Paul wrote this letter, Galatia was a large Roman province stretching in a north-south direction across central Turkey from the Baltic Sea nearly to the Mediterranean. There is some question among scholars of history, whether Paul wrote to churches in the northern part or southern part of Galatia. This also brings into speculation the most precise time this letter was written.

Paul and Barnabas evangelized the southern region during his 1st missionary journey, which would place the writing date at about 48 AD. If the letter was written to the northern churches established by Paul on his 2nd missionary journey, then the date may have been about 52-55 AD.

There is good reason to favor the 1st scenario, because the problem of Judaizer adulteration of Paul's 'salvation through faith in Jesus Christ' gospel was the main reason for his letter to the Galatian churches. The Judaizer's were certain Jewish Christians who held to traditional Jewish customs, and followed in Paul's footsteps to preach that true Christianity for non-Jewish believers required observing Jewish customs, including the rite of circumcision.

The Jerusalem Council dealt with this problem in 49 AD, and issued a letter to clarify that non-Jews did not have to comply with Jewish custom, as set forth in Chapter 15 of Acts. If Paul's Galatian letter had been addressed to the northern churches, it is logical that he would have referred to the council letter as justification for writing this epistle.

Therefore, it is most likely that he wrote this letter o/a 48 AD to the southern churches. It is doubtful that the Judaizers would have dogged the northern churches with their views, after the Jerusalem council issued its exemption letter for non-Jews.

To defend his position, Paul wrote this letter to challenge the false views of the Judaizers, and to clarify that salvation was solely dependent on faith in Christ's Good News gospel, without incorporating Jewish Mosaic Law requirements. His message of justification by faith and freedom in the Spirit is a basic tenet of Christianity.

CHAPTER 1: Declaring himself to be an apostle chosen only by Jesus Christ with God's approval in verses 1-11, Paul quickly passed by words of greeting to express his surprise (and perhaps shock) that the Galatians were defecting from the gospel of Christ as he had first preached to them. He added that anyone, even angels, who preached another line should be severely punished, and he hoped God would do it.

To his question, 'Do I preach to please men,' he declared that it was to please God, otherwise he would not be a true servant of Jesus Christ. He added that his message to them was not originated by men, but it was solely Christ's revelation.

In 12-17, Paul gave them a summary of his beginning as an apostle of Christ, as given in Acts 9:1-25. First, he emphasized that his message came straight from Christ, after his confrontation with Him on the road to Damascus (Acts 9:1-19). Then he was converted from his strictly Jewish hostile attitude towards Christians, to become a servant of the Lord. Paul objected to any change in the doctrine of Christ, and held to the vital principle for all

Christians, that the true meaning of God's word should be <u>perceived and accepted without any modification</u> for personal reasons.

Paul accepted God's purpose for him as divinely ordained from his birth, that he was <u>to be an apostle to the Gentiles</u>. He did not seek the advice of other apostles, or church leaders in Jerusalem, to confirm this inspiration.

Without an explanation of his reason, he related how he went away for a time to Arabia before returning to Damascus. He ministered there before visiting Jerusalem about 3 years after his conversion (perhaps about 36 AD), to spend 15 days with the apostle Peter, and to meet James, the brother of Jesus. After that visit, he moved to the regions of Syria and Cilicia, probably to <u>spend time in his home town of Tarsus</u>.

He stated that he had visited none of the Judean churches, but their members were thankful and praised God that he no longer persecuted them as before.

CHAPTER 2:   Paul defends his presentation of the gospel message in verses 1-10. Presumably from the date of his 1st visit, Paul returned about 14 years later (12 years plus small fractions of the 1st and last year) to Jerusalem with his Gentile converts Barnabas and Titus, in obedience to God's direction to do so. This may have been the visit also recorded in Acts 15:3-21 in about 48 AD. He met privately with the important leaders of the Jerusalem church, (presumably Peter, James, and John), to <u>inform them of his central</u> theme in preaching the gospel.

Paul explained his reason for the visit was to refute what false apostles (Judaizers) were preaching, that non-Jews must be circumcised and conform to other Mosaic Laws to be truly Christian. They were attempting to impose legalism in place of spiritual freedom in Christ. He pointed out that Titus, as a Greek, was not circumcised, yet he was recognized to be a devout Christian.

He discounted the importance of the Jerusalem church leaders in presenting the true gospel to the Gentiles, because James, Peter, and John knew that he was God's choice in this service. Though he conferred with the Jerusalem apostles, he received no additions to his knowledge or authority from them. Perceiving that he was spiritually endowed, they gave unto him and Barnabas the right hand of fellowship, <u>acknowledging that he was divinely</u> anointed to be an apostle as much as they were. They agreed with Paul that he should help the poor of Judea in his ministry.

Paul related in verses 11-14, how he chastised Peter in Antioch for his hypocrisy, when he <u>stopped eating with the Gentiles</u> for fear of some Jews, that James had sent, who objected because the Gentiles were not circumcised. He saw this as a violation of the principle that Christ's death removed the <u>partition wall between Jewish and Gentile believers</u>. Other Jews joined Peter, and Barnabas became biased.

A double standard was implied in Paul's words to Peter, 'You are a Jew, but you live like a Gentile, so how can you force Gentiles to live like Jews?' Peter knew this was true, and <u>accepted this rebuke without retort.</u>

In verses 15-21, no matter whether people are born as Jews or Gentiles, God accepts only those who become believers with faith in Jesus Christ. All sinners <u>must adhere to this</u>

requirement, regardless of their ethnicity. Simply obeying Mosaic Law is not enough under the new covenant gospel of salvation through Christ.

Declaring that he too was nailed to the cross with Christ, Paul voiced his intent to live by faith in Christ, and therefore <u>would not reject God's kindness and mercy.</u> Otherwise, Christ's death was useless, and sinner's would endure death under the Law.

<u>VIEWPOINTS:</u>   In his own being, Paul operated under the spiritual or hidden life of a believer. Although, being freed from the negatives of the Law, through the blessings of God's grace, <u>that grace make him dependent on Christ.</u> God's grace is incompatible with man's nature to achieve all independently of grace. But, grace is not grace unless it is freely given and received by faith at all times.

The more completely a believer relies on Christ for every thing, the more devotedly he <u>dwells before Him in obedience</u> to His ordinances and commandments. With Christ as part and parcel of the believer's life, the more he lives here on earth by faith in the Son of God, neither abusing the grace of God, nor making it useless.

CHAPTER 3:   Most bluntly, Paul calls the Galatians stupid in verses 1-5, for allowing false beliefs to <u>corrupt their original true faith in Christ.</u> He asks a series of questions of them: How did they receive Christ's spirit in the 1ˢᵗ place, was it by trying to obey all the laws of Moses, or by hearing the Good News gospel from him?; are you stupid enough to think that you can complete what the Holy Spirit has started in you?; and have you come this far in knowing the truth for nothing?

He asked this crucial question, 'When the Holy Spirit works miraculously in you, does this happen because you try to live by the Law of Moses, or because you have learned enough about Christ to have faith in Him?'

To more fully make his point understood, Paul goes back to the days of Abraham in verses 6-9, to point out that Abraham received righteousness by God's grace because <u>he had</u> <u>faith in God.</u> His faith in the promises of God brought blessings, and it works the same way for all other believers, whether Jew or Gentile, as confirmed by Gen. 12:3, 'I will bless all people in other nations who believe in me as Abraham did!'

In verses 10-14, Paul said that those who try to please God by obeying the Law will be cursed, Because there are so many laws, it is impossible to be in obedience to all of them at all times, so <u>one will sin regularly by failing to obey</u> one or more of them. He cited Rom. 1:17, which says, 'The righteous man shall live by faith.' This can mean to live on this earth to please God, and to live eternally with Him, <u>through faith in Christ.</u> Trying to exclusively live by the Law, would leave no room or freedom for faith, because <u>one would</u> <u>become a slave to the Law</u>.

Being a slave to the Law adds up to a curse under which there is <u>no justification (righteousness) before God</u>. Freedom from this bondage is the only way to find favor with God, and Christ provided this way as he became a curse for us on the cross (See Deut. 21:23). His death on the cross was <u>ransom paid for our delivery from bondage</u> under the Law, to <u>freely live by faith in Him.</u>

In verses 15-25, Paul described God's promises to mankind as descendants of Abraham, in the <u>context of a Last Will and Testament,</u> which when signed before a Notary becomes legally binding. While the promises were made to all mankind, Christ was the Notary to bring them into fruition. God's promises to Abraham, made 430 years before the Law was given to Moses, could not be overridden or annulled by the Law. The provisions of the law were presented directly to every Israelite, but the promises of the Good News gospel were first given to Christ, for an inheritance to those who by faith become engrafted into Him.

Paul stated that the purpose of the Law was to make man conscious of his sin, until the fulfillment of God's promise of Christ as the fulfillment of the Law. While angels transmitted the Law to Moses, God Himself gave His promise directly to Abraham, thus making His promises superior to the Law. Even though the Law is not in opposition to God's promises, it still shows the need for a better way through faith. The Law merely served as a teacher constraining people from gross sin until Christ came with the honor system of faith in Him, to take precedence over the Law.

Paul assures the believers of Galatia in 26-29, that they still remained children of God by faith in Jesus Christ, whether they were Jew or Gentile, and thus they were recipients of God's promises through Abraham. Since Christ makes believers to be heirs, He will also provide spiritual nourishment and strength for their faith in Him.

CHAPTER 4:   Paul continued speaking of the Christian's status as heirs of God, as mentioned in verses 26-29 of the preceding chapter. In verses 1-8, he illustrates the point by stating that minors are much like slaves, under the care and supervision of parents, or guardians, until of legal age, when they become heirs for inheritances. The Israelites under Mosiac Law were like that, as children living under strict rules, which they often violated.

Their status changed when God in His own time had His Son Jesus born of the virgin Mary to come in human form, for the purpose of bringing the children of Israel to spiritual maturity apart from the bondage of the Law. Now, Israelites and Gentiles of the world become children of God as they become believers in Jesus Christ. With Holy Spirit discernment, God's children know Him as their Heavenly Father, to inherit His blessings after being freed from the bondage of sin.

Although Christians retain the old sin nature deserving God's wrath, as His children they are changed to have a nature of love resembling the love of God. In our day, the eldest son does not normally inherit all of a parent's estate, but estate values are usually divided equally when there are 2 or more heirs. With God, all believers will receive an inheritance of grace, as if they were the oldest son in former days.

Paul changed subjects in verses 8-20, to express his concerns over the apostasy creeping into the Galatian church, by way of former pagan deities. He asked them how could they abandon the one true God they had learned of and become slaves of their former gods again.

He begged them to come back to his own spiritual beliefs, so his time with them would not be a total waste. He credited them for being kind to him during his first visit, caring for him through some illness, as if he were an angel, or even Jesus Christ. He wondered where that old relationship had gone, and if they were now hostile because he had opened their eyes to the truth.

He warned the Galatians that the designing Judaizers were being attentive to them purely for the purpose of destroying their initial faith in Christ's salvation message. Like a mother in labor as her child is born, he was feeling pain again as when his ministry to them gave birth to their faith in Christ.

In verses 21-31, Paul reverts again to the difference between living under the Law and the new life of faith in Christ. He described the difference in terms of the 2 sons born to Abraham (see Genesis 16), the 1st by natural physical union with a servant named Hagar, and the 2nd by God's promised conception of wife Sarah.

The birth of Ishmael to Hagar is representative of bondage under Mosiac Law, (as given to Moses at Mount Sinai), but the birth of Isaac to Sarah, a free woman, is representative of freedom promised under the Abrahamic covenant, to believe in Christ with Holy Spirit conviction. One problem would arise, the descendants of Ishmael would be trouble makers for the descendants of Isaac; this has been true over the centuries and continues today, inasmuch as Muslims of the Islamic faith wage warfare with non-Muslims, particularly Christians of the gentile world.

Concluding his remarks, Paul told the Galations to rid themselves of the Mosaic Law and those who were part of it, who were not God's children or heirs of His grace. He declares that he and other believers in Christ are the children of Abraham's wife, and they are no longer slaves to the Law. Nor should they allow themselves to become enslaved by the descendants of Ishmael, whether they be Muslims or some other pagan people.

NOTE: A better understanding of the spiritual ramifications and differences between The Mosiac Law and the Abrahamic covenant, now known as the covenant of grace through Jesus Christ, can be gained from the special article at the end of this epistle, entitled, "Law versus Grace.'

CHAPTER 5:   Paul made it clear up to this point that as Christian believers, we are children of God, no longer under the spiritual legalism of the slave line of Ishmael, but we are in the freedom line of Isaac. We are to hold unto the freedom that Christ gave us. This is what he conveyed to the Galatians in verses 1-6, adding that if they submit to circumcision under the Law, they will gain nothing from Christ's gift.

As a believer in Christ's atonement, it matters not whether one is circumcised or not. Meddling with requirements of the Law will just lead to a falling away from God's grace. And then, as Jesus said in John 15:5, 'Apart from me you can do nothing.' What matters most is having a true working faith that produces God's love for others. Without faith working by love, there is little else of real value.

In verses 7-15, Paul clarified that love fulfills the Law, but he first questioned how the Galatians could fall away from their initial good beginning in faith? By accepting some false teachings from apostates, the fundamentals of their faith changed, just as the addition of yeast changes a batch of dough. He believed that the purveyors of pollution would be punished, because the Galatians were God's property, and He is a jealous God.

Paul acknowledged if he still preached that circumcision was necessary, there would be no problem, he would not be provoked, and no one would be offended. But the Judaizers were offended, because Christ was preached as the only way of salvation for sinners. Since the opposition to Paul's gospel still existed, it was proof that he adhered to the true gospel of salvation through Christ, <u>without works of the Law as a requirement.</u> He was so angered by the opposition that he wished they would castrate themselves.

Paul then pointed out that the freedom from legalism a Christian enjoys is not a license to do as one pleases, including sin, but it is meant as an <u>opportunity to serve one another</u> <u>in love</u> as Jesus would want done. In reality, the Law is fulfilled by obeying Christ's command to love others as much as self.

The desirability of walking (living) as the Holy Spirit leads is Paul's theme in verses 16-26. First of all, in so doing, the lusts of the flesh to sin will be neutralized, and the Mosaic Law becomes secondary to a believer's life of faith in Christ. Being led by the Holy Spirit <u>frees the</u> <u>believer from the curse of the Law.</u> With a distaste for sin replaced by desires after holiness, believers show their true faith in God's gospel.

Paul listed the sins of that day which are most <u>prevalent in today's world too</u>: sexual immorality, drunkenness and debauchery, idolatry and witchcraft, hatred and strife, jealousy, envy and anger, selfishness and greed, brutality and murder, and other evil things. Those who persist in these sins <u>will never enter the kingdom of God.</u>

In contrast to these sins, Paul enumerated 'fruits' of the Spirit as: love and joy, peace and patience, kindness and goodness, faithfulness, gentleness and self-control. When one is a true believer in Christ, the Holy Spirit helps us to overcome selfish desires and lusts, and <u>keeps us</u> <u>from thinking too highly of ourselves</u> as righteous ones. The Holy Spirit gives the believer a good life; it is best to yield to the Spirit.

CHAPTER 6:   Paul concluded this epistle with some good advice to the church. In 1-6, he advised believers to be gentle and careful when giving assistance to another believer <u>who has</u> <u>fallen from grace into some sin.</u> When others are burdened somehow, a believer should share their burden as much as possible, in love and understanding, as God would do. One should be modest about their own achievements, to see them for what they are, so that what others do is not looked down upon, and <u>better help is thus given to those under infirmities and afflictions.</u>

Paul advised generosity and good deeds in verses 6-10, especially to <u>teachers and preachers</u> <u>of the word.</u> Whatever we do as a believer, we should not try to fool God, because <u>He is not</u> <u>deceived by the nature of our motives.</u> If we do wrong, He will punish; if we do good, He will bless us with heavenly rewards and most of all, eternal life. Whenever possible, without fail, help fellow believers above all others.

In 11-18, Paul pointed out that he was replacing his secretary by writing with large script to close out the letter, probably because of his own eyesight problem. Oddly, he again addressed the matter of circumcision, which was being promoted by the Judaizers for self- glorification and their boasting over <u>converting Galatians to their viewpoints.</u> Even though they did this, they failed to obey Mosaic Law any better than anyone else.

Paul declared that he would only boast about the price that Christ paid on the cross, that separated him (as if crucified also) from worldly ways. Circumcision contributes nothing towards this objective, only a truly repentant heart counts.

His benediction invokes peace, harmony, and grace on those who share in his beliefs,

Gentiles as well as Jews. He asked for no more trouble to his scarred body <u>and his heart</u> <u>which suffered in the cause of Jesus.</u>

<u>SUMMARY:</u>   There is little doubt that Paul was unhappy over the apostasy creeping into the Galatian church body, because Judaizers <u>promoted the doctrine of living under the Mosaic Law</u>. He convincingly argued that believers are no longer slaves to the Law, but are free to life a godly life as led by the Holy Spirit. Does his view, that pleasing God by faith living in Christ clearly <u>nullifies Mosaic Law supremacy</u>? YES, it does!

LAW VS. GRACE

The first 5 books of the Bible are commonly known as the Pentateuch. The first 4 books, Exodus, Deuteronomy, Numbers, and Leviticus, include laws based on the 10 commandments which God gave to Moses on Mount Sinai as part of a <u>covenant agreement between God and His people</u>. They provided the foundation for all of Israel's laws, as found in the 'Torah,' the Hebrew word for the law portion of the Old Testament.

These laws were prescribed as a way of life, covering all areas of community living. They constitute one of the most important concepts in the Bible for committed Israelites striving to please God. For a wording of the 10 Commandments, see Exodus 20:2-17 and Deuteronomy 5:6-21.

Laws in the Old Testament are of two kinds. First, the broad categorical laws, such as the 10 Commandments which set forth general principles, without rules for enforcement or penalties for violations of them. <u>Second are the case laws,</u> often beginning with an "if" or a "when," that usually deal with specific situations. Many times they prescribe solutions for problems, or they prescribe a punishment for violations (see Exodus, chapters 21, 22, and 23)

While the 10 Commandments were first given to the Hebrew people, they were <u>intended for all people down through the ages</u>. They have universal validity for all persons who are committed to God, who is behind them. What makes them unique is the character of the God who gave them. Without Him, the Commandments lose their distinctiveness.

The enemies of Jesus frequently accused Him of violating the Law; He was both a critic and a supporter of it. Keeping the letter of the Law had become more important to some of the Jews than the purpose behind it. Jesus declared that He came to fulfill the Law, not to destroy it. Forthwith, He inaugurated a new covenant in which the Law as understood by the Jews of old <u>would no longer be the guiding principle</u> for Kingdom of God believers. (see Luke 16:15-16)

Jesus taught His followers that inherent spiritual motivation and commitment to the spirit of the Law was <u>more important than outward obedience</u> as observed by others. He advocated a deeper level of meaning, with observance of the Law in ways that God intended from the beginning. (see Matthew, chapters 5-7)

In Matthew 22:36-40, Jesus was asked which commandment was the greatest. He said, 'Love the Lord your God with all your heart, soul, and mind.' Then He added a 2nd commandment related to the 1st, 'Love others as much as you love yourself.' He concluded with these words, 'All the Laws of Moses as well as the Books of the Prophets are tied in with these basic commandments.' This matching up of the Law and the teaching of the prophets, with these love commandments, <u>implied that the principles of love for God and</u> others were <u>inherent in the Law</u> from the day one.

Paul had a personal battle with the term "law," which to him was <u>analogous with the Laws of God</u> in the Old Testament. His attitude toward the Mosaic Law was that it had been given for a good purpose, and it was holy, just and good (Rom. 7:12-14). He did not view the demands of the Law as evil, but felt it was primarily for the purpose of pointing out the sin of human beings. But, because of man's sinfulness, the Law <u>became a curse instead</u> of a blessing (Gal.

3:10-13). Even so, he believed the Law was given for a good purpose, but it <u>could not save souls</u> (Gal. 3:11; Rom. 3:20).

A central theme of Paul's epistles is that the death and resurrection of Christ freed us from the requirements of the Law (Rom. 8:3-4). That meant that Christ fulfilled the Law for Christians (Rom. 10:4), and it is faith that saves by God's 'grace,' apart from the Law.

Paul, as did Jesus, saw the Law fulfilled in the command to love (Rom. 13:8; Gal. 5:13). <u>With the help of the Holy Spirit,</u> believers can have love to meet the requirement of fulfilling the Law (Gal. 5:16; Rom. 8). Believers should realize that the Law is relevant, because it is the revelation of God, <u>meant to help Christians</u> understand the nature of living under the 'gospel of grace' with faith in and through Christ (Rom. 8:3; 13:8-10; Gal. 3:24).

Webster's theological definition of grace is 'the inherited renewing and moral strengthening of man; a state of reconciliation with God.' The apostle Paul deserves much credit for the Christian understanding of grace as used in the New Testament. In his epistles, <u>he used the word and related forms twice as often</u> as all the other authors of New Testament writings. For example, he urged his readers to make their speech "gracious" or "attractive" (Col. 4:6; Eph. 4:29), and referred to his visit to Corinth as a "grace" which would bring them pleasure Paul preached that grace is God's way of salvation, totally unearned (Rom. 3:24; 4:4; 11:6; Eph. 2:8). He believed that grace is <u>appropriated by faith in what God has done in Christ</u> (Rom. 4:16), and. it is through Christ's crucifixion atonement that God's grace gives mankind optimum freedom from the bondage of sin (Rom. 3:24-31). Paul strongly preached that grace brings salvation (Eph. 2:5, 8), and eternal life (Rom. 5:21; Titus 3:7).

Paul also emphasized that grace does not give one freedom to sin. His own experience showed him the power of divine grace working in his ministry to <u>overcome his own weaknesses</u> (II Cor. 12:9). He brought out that all who experience God's grace have special gifts for ministry and service (Rom. 12:6; Eph. 4:7).

Yet, God's grace can be and is often spurned (Heb. 10:29; 12:14-15), or <u>misapplied to pervert the gospel</u> to suggest that freedom from the law gives man freedom to sin without judgment (Jude 4). As a positive, grace is a badge of the Christian faith, when used in pastoral benedictions.

(Paraphrased excerpts from Holman's Bible Dictionary were used for the above)

EPHESIANS—BOOK TEN

Ephesians and 3 other epistles, Phillippians, Colossians, and Philemon, commonly referred to as the Prison Epistles, were all written by Paul during his imprisonment in Rome between 61-62 AD. This epistle was written primarily to the church of Ephesus, but it was also <u>circulated to other churches in Asia Minor.</u>

Paul spent more than 3 years in Ephesus, on his 3rd missionary journey, before he returned to Jerusalem to be <u>arrested by the Jews and given over to the Romans.</u> After 2 years of imprisonment in Caesarea (Acts 21:27-36), he was transferred to Rome for another 2 years in prison (Acts 27:1-2, 28:16 & 30).

Paul emphasized that all believers, Jews and Gentiles, are united in the church body of Christ, and he <u>exhorted church fellowships to live out this truth.</u> Each member must do his part in order for the entire body to function properly, especially <u>against the forces of evil.</u> Believers should apply the qualities of Christ's character in the use of their God given gifts to <u>make the entire church a testimony to Him.</u>

As in all his epistles, these words were part of his greeting: 'Grace be to you, and peace, from God our Father, and from the Lord Jesus Christ.' In that order, 'grace and peace'—grace from God gave salvation from sin, and peace is the believer's heart condition after grace has done its work. Paul's message is that there can be no peace in the heart until grace has done its work.

Paul was convinced that the message he preached was the <u>only way of redemption from sin</u> to become children of God. He presented the precept that redemption is gifted at the moment of conversion, as the triune work of the God the Father, God the Son, and the Holy Spirit. He was thankful for the blessings of redemption through the blood of Christ, and the <u>unity of believers through Him.</u>

To avoid Satan's temptations, Paul urged his followers to put on the armor of God, which enhances ones prayer life, and <u>concern for fellow believers.</u> To this end, he wrote this epistle to give basic doctrine in the first part and a summary of duties in the last half.

CHAPTER 1:   After his typical greeting to the 'saints' with grace and peace, in verses 1-2, Paul addressed the <u>blessings of redemption through Christ</u> in verses 3-14.

With a word of praise to God for the spiritual blessings received through Christ, Paul stated that God's plan of salvation was <u>established even before the world was created,</u> and He choose Christ to introduce the plan and promulgate it to the world. It is God's desire that man become His children, by separation from sin through belief in Christ as His Son, and <u>to grow spiritually by sanctification in the Holy Spirit</u>

Through God's wisdom and understanding, Christ carried out His mission on earth, to provide forgiveness of sins and an eternal home in God's domain, provided that man <u>accepted and believed in Him as the provider of redemption.</u> This was done first for the Jews, but was then extended to the Gentiles of the world, and in God's time and for His glory, Christ will reap the harvest of souls, from the grave, and from the living. <u>Those who are by faith secured</u>

in Christ by the Holy Spirit will receive the gift of redemption for eternity, as their promised inheritance.

Verses 15-23 are an expression of gratefulness by Paul for the faithfulness of the Ephesian church. He told them of his prayers for greater wisdom and the light of understanding for them, so they would know and be grateful for the glorious spiritual inheritance that God has provided for all mankind. He wants them to know more about God's power, such as He used for Christ's resurrection, and Christ's equal power over things of the world and heaven. Christ is the Head over the church, meaning every true believer comprising the fellowship of saints, through which He reaches out to the unsaved of the world.

Paul's apostolic prayer for his converts is a fitting example for every pastor and believer to emulate. The best Christians need to be prayed for, and even the unsaved are deserving of our prayers. Our nation's leaders definitely need our prayers for greater wisdom and integrity in fulfilling their responsibilities.

CHAPTER 2:   Paul explained how man can be transformed from spiritual death to spiritual life in Christ in verses 1-10. Sin rings the death knell of the soul and deadens human desire for spiritual qualities in life. This comes about when a person follows the ways of this world and submits to the power of Satan. People who are predisposed to sensual or spiritual wickedness, are by their Adamic nature disobedient and disrespectful of God's yardstick for righteousness.

Converted sinners are delivered from sin and wrath by God's grace through faith in Christ Jesus God's grace is a free gift, flavored by His undeserved kindness and mercy. This salvation comes to the sinner, not by the works of the law, but strictly by grace, because of the price Jesus paid on the cross. Our faith, our conversion, and our eternal salvation, are totally the free gift of God, enhanced by the quickening of the Holy Spirit in the believer's heart.

In verses 11-22, Paul spoke of the need for unity of Christ's body, to overcome racial, religious, cultural and social barriers. He reminded the Ephesians that once they were known as 'uncircumcised' Gentiles in the eyes of the Jews, who were proud they were circumcised. That was before they came to know Christ, and the promises that God made through Him. Because they had no part in Christ, they were without hope.

Paul said that Christ became the peacemaker between Jews and Gentiles, to break down the wall of hatred that separated them over the centuries. This truce is still in the process of enactment, since much anti-Semitism still prevails in this world. The peace option came through Christ's crucifixion, which fulfilled the Law of Moses, and made way for unification of all peoples in one spiritual realm, for the ultimate objective of peace with God for all mankind. Because of Christ, all mankind can now come to God through the Holy Spirit, apart from the Law.

As encouragement to the Ephesians, as well as all Gentiles of the world, Paul proclaimed Gentiles as no longer strangers or foreigners in the family of God, because they can now become citizens of one body of believers, through faith in Christ. He also compared the church to a building, founded on the doctrine of Christ; as prophesied by the prophets of the Old Testament, and constructed by the apostles of the New. God dwells in all believers now; so they become the temple of God through the working of the blessed Spirit. No matter what ethnic group a believer is from, each one is like a stone used in the construction of a building, carefully fitted together to give strength and durability, <u>Christ being the binding cornerstone</u> that provides unity. This then becomes God's house, as believer's become His temple, through the working of the blessed Spirit.

It behooves every Christian to desire and submit to His gracious presence, and His influences upon our hearts. Then we can <u>more effectively use our spiritual gifts</u> to discharge the duties allotted to us, all for the glory of God.

CHAPTER 3:   In verses 1-6, Paul as a prisoner in Rome, claimed to be a prisoner of Jesus Christ, Who provided care and safety by way of suffering with him, so he could bring Christ's message to the Gentiles. He stated that his epistle to the Ephesians was to reveal to them how God had shared a mystery with him; which he would now clarify as <u>His plan of salvation for Gentiles to share equally with the Jews</u> in all of His promises. Both could now become coequals in the body of Christ.

Paul spoke of his God given role to enlighten believers on the divine mystery in verses 7-12 as revealed by the coming of Jesus, that <u>unfathomable riches (blessings) awaited all believers in a united body.</u> As part of His salvation package, Jesus now provides courage and confidence for believers to approach the throne of God by faith. If we are not enriched in this way it is our own fault!

In 13-21, Paul told the church members in Ephesus not to be troubled over his suffering because it was <u>part of bringing honor to them,</u> for which he prayed to God. For their benefit, he asked God to give them inner spiritual strength, a firm foundation of faith and love, and to be enriched with <u>greater understanding of the magnitude of His love</u> in providing a great plan for heavenly happiness and glory. He prayed that the church as the body of Jesus Christ would forever praise God for the power He gives to <u>serve Him beyond our wildest dreams.</u>

CHAPTER 4:   Paul again mentioned his status as a prisoner as he advised the church on unity with Christ, in verses 1-6, with a plea that they <u>live up to a high standard worthy of God's chosen ones.</u> He cited these desirable attributes: humility with gentleness, patience with love for one another, and peaceful relationships, all under the influence of the Holy Spirit.

Paul stated that all Christians are one in the Holy Spirit, as part of the one body in Christ, the source of all hope, <u>and therefore of one heart in faith.</u> With a common belief in the indisputable truths of Christ's Good News gospel, all believers (both Jew or Gentile) become <u>members of one church by spiritual (and/or water) baptism,</u> in the name of the Father, the Son, and the Holy Ghost.

In verses 7-16, God the Father dwells in the believer, as His holy temple, to whom He gives special gifts by his Spirit, as deemed best by Christ, and <u>especially the gift of the Holy Ghost.</u> Quoting Ps. 68:18, Paul spoke of Christ's death, resurrection, and ascension, as the reason for spiritual gifts to mankind, in a way <u>to glorify His victory over Satan and the bondage of sin.</u>

Some of the more important gifts are apostles and prophets for that day, until the Word of God came into being, and <u>thereafter evangelists, pastors and teachers.</u> These gifts are to keep

God's children growing, as long as they are in this world, until they reach a <u>mature spiritual level with unity of faith</u> manifested by wisdom and love.

The spiritual maturity Paul spoke of incorporates doctrinal and spiritual understanding and stability, responsibility and determination, and the strength of faith in God's Word to <u>stand against false doctrine from deceitful teachings</u>. By lending strength to others weak in the faith, the spiritually gifted can weld believers together to become a fortress for the Lord.

Paul set forth standards in verses 17-24, for the believer as taught by Christ, not to live foolishly as the world does, so as not to become greedy and decadent. Believers are to <u>let the Holy Spirit remold them into a new person</u> with spiritual characteristics pleasing to God.

Verses 25-32 give Paul's views for proper conduct as a believer in the body of Christ. He listed the following as undesirable traits; lying, anger, stealing, foul language, bitterness, unseemly rudeness when speaking to others, and anything else that would grieve the Holy Spirit. These bad traits should be replaced with: honesty, forgiveness, honest work, clean language, gratitude, courtesy, kindness and compassion, in the likeness of Christ.

<u>CHAPTER 5:</u> Paul admonishes the Ephesian church members in verses 1-5, to imitate God with the love of Christ in their hearts, as if they were children loving their own father. As His children, they were not to displease God with sins of immorality, greed, foul or crude language, idolatry, or succumbing to deception by others. These actions <u>can bring God's wrath as punishment</u> upon those who disobey His commands.

In verses 6-20, Paul said that they (all believers) should live as if in the light of day, <u>as fruit of the Holy Spirit</u>, to show goodness, godliness, integrity, and separation from the darkness of evil, such that is shameful to describe. Let the light of the Holy Spirit reveal all that is bad to be avoided. The works of darkness are unfruitful for they bring <u>destruction to the remorseless sinner</u>. Joining others in their sin is reason enough to expect punishment with them. Not censuring sin is equivalent to association with those that sin.

In these evil days, we are to use common sense in all that we do, so as to please God, which excludes getting drunk. With Holy Spirit inspiration, join in the singing of spiritual songs, with <u>heartfelt feelings of praise for God's goodness,</u> in the name of Jesus Christ, to honor others as we honor Him.

The proper relationship between husband and wife in Paul's view, is given in verses 21-33. A wife should be responsive to her husband as if responding to God. The wife should <u>hold her husband in high esteem</u> just as the church holds Christ in high esteem. He should be the man in her life, to be honored, respected and obeyed out of her deep felt love for him.

The husband should be responsible to his wife as head of the home, just as Christ is responsible as the head of His church. The husband's love for his wife should be <u>sacrificially unsurpassed as Christ's love</u> is for the church, to make their marriage as perfect as possible. Make it a sterling Christian example of unity!

A husband should love his wife as much as he loves himself, better yet, more than he loves himself, <u>as shown by how he provides for her</u>. The goal is to have a perfect union as if twins, or of one flesh, just as Eve was of Adam's flesh and bones. The union should be perfected <u>as Christ is perfected by His union with His church.</u>

CHAPTER 6: Paul admonishes children in verses 1-4, to honor their parents with obedience during their dependency years, and with respect as they step out into life. This can best be shown with inward reverence, as well as outward signs; God promises a long and happy life for this kind of relationship. To make this relationship more fruitful, parents should not be overly strict or unkind towards their children.

Verses 5-9 relate to a master/slave relationship, but it could also apply to a boss/ employee relationship. Again, Paul stressed obedience on the part of the worker, with respect and a desire to please at all times, just as a Christian should strive to please God with all their heart. Bosses should reciprocate with kindness and love.

A firm believer commitment to serve the Lord Jesus Christ promotes faithful and sincere effort in every situation, without ill will or anger, but in true love. Thus, service is easier to provide, and more pleasing and acceptable, to our boss, the Lord Jesus Christ. When bosses avoid harshness, they are rewarded with better service!

In verses 10-20, Paul encouraged the Ephesian believers, as well as all others, to find spiritual strength and courage by wearing the armor of God, so as to stand against temptations and evil. The armor of God includes accepting the truth of God's word, living righteously with peace and assurance of God's salvation through grace, and being guided by the Holy Spirit through God's Word, and His response to prayers. A Christian's armor is to be donned at the moment of conversion, for onward protection, and not delayed until a time when buffeted by Satan's wiles.

In so doing, the Christian is ready, as if buckled with the belt of truth and God's justice around the waist and shoulders, the good news gospel as shoes, the shield of faith out front to stop Satan's barbs, covered with salvation like a helmet, and armed with the naked sword of the Holy Bible to battle against ways of the world.

To this spiritual armor, the power of diligent prayer should be added on behalf of God's people, the effectiveness of pastors, and courage to speak up in faith to share the Word of God with the weak and unsaved. Paul asked for prayers that he be better equipped to preach the gospel of Christ.

He closed with a most gracious farewell greeting, through his servant Tychicus, who was to go to Ephesus. He wished them peace, love with faith, from God and Jesus, and grace to all for loving the Lord Jesus Christ.

SUMMARY: In this epistle, Paul hammered away at one point repeatedly—unity of the church for all believers, particularly the Jews and Gentiles. He wanted to see an end of prejudice between the two factions. He seemed to feel that a common bond of unity in the one Christ, the one faith, and the one baptism by the Holy Spirit, should enable all believers, regardless of their ancestry, to live and worship together in harmony and peace, without doctrinal disagreements.

The first believers in Jerusalem demonstrated the principle of unity as they shared their possessions and were of one heart and soul (Acts 2:1,43; 4:32). Yet, the sins of covetousness (Ananias and Sapphira, in Acts 5:1-11), prejudice against Greek-speaking widows, and the obsession of the Jews over circumcision,—all threatened the unity of the early church. Even though one in the body of Christ, they were biased.

Today, in this modern era, we have disunity, as manifested in the wide variety of denomination factions in the Protestant church body, each having separate and distinct viewpoints, interpretations, and formats for worship. We have some ecumenical movements trying to promote unity within the Christian church body, but they also try to create some kind of unity between Christians and non-Christian faiths. We also have a wide breach between the Protestant churches and the Catholic faith.

Some denominations appear to be more apostate than others, so lacking in spiritual discernment of the Word, that they hardly seem Christian in a true sense. It appears that Satan is doing his best to corrupt some branches of the Christian community to prevent any kind of God approved unity from happening. There does not seem to be any possibility for the kind of unity that Paul preached, until Christ returns to gather His own for His millennial reign.

When local faith-based Christian churches do cooperate with each other on social issues, vacation bible school training for children, and Christian holiday events, the benefits are obvious as members are blessed by fellowship as Christians apart from their own church membership. This is a good thing, as it demonstrates to non-believers in the community that a common faith in Christ is a beneficial unifying factor. Maybe this was what Paul was advocating.

PHILIPPIANS—BOOK ELEVEN

The church of Philippi was founded about 50-51 AD by Paul, on his 2nd missionary journey as related in Acts 16:12-40. The city was located about 10 miles inland from the northern tip of the Aegean Sea. This was Paul's 1st European church founding, at that time within a Roman colony. The city may have been the main home of Luke, who ministered to the church for about 6 years.

Paul's 1st 3 converts to start the church included Lydia, a seller of purple royal robes (Acts 16:14-15), a middle-class jailer (Acts 16:22-34), and a young girl from which he exorcised a demon (Acts 16:16-18). It grew primarily as a Gentile congregation, but also had a number of Jewish members, who had typical differences of opinion on how to be a Christian.

Paul wrote this epistle while in a Roman prison in 61-62 AD. His purpose in writing it was to thank the Philippi church for their generous support and gifts, the latest of which was brought to him by Epaphroditus. The letter is the most upbeat of all Paul's writings, with less admonition and more praise; it contains exhortations to rejoice and to remain faithful. Epaphroditus took it back to Philippi after he recovered from a serious illness in Rome.

CHAPTER 1: Paul included Timothy as he greeted the church of Philippi with his customary grace and peace from God and Jesus Christ opening, in verses 1-2. His expressions of thanks and prayers for them are given in verses 3-11; he wrote the epistle from his imprisonment in Rome. He thanked God for his memories of them and told them of his prayers for their faithfulness as believers in the gospel of Jesus Christ. This gave him great joy because the church had a special place in his heart.

Paul expressed his longing to visit the church again, because he loved them as Christ loved them. He also hoped that their love for Christ would continue to grow, so their choices would always be for good things and good deeds until the day of Christ, when He returns. The goal of every believer is to stand before the Lord as faultless as possible when He comes to gather His own.

In verses 12-30, Paul shared details of his imprisonment and how it affected his spiritual views. He felt that it enhanced his ability to preach the Good News, to his jailers and to his believer followers, who became braver as witnesses to their faith. While others are preaching for spiteful reasons, being jealous of Paul's success, his true followers were preaching with much love in their hearts for what Paul taught them; what mattered most to Paul was that all preached about Christ and His gospel.

Paul expressed his joy for the prayers of the Philippians which would keep him safe through the help of the Holy Spirit, to keep him from wrong doing, and courageous in life and death. He saw his life as being for Christ, whether he lived or died. He trusted in Christ for whatever way he could be serviceable to His glory, in preaching or in suffering, by zeal or fortitude, and by living to honor Him whether working or suffering death for Him. Continuing on or dying to be with the Lord was a difficult choice since he looked forward to joining Christ for eternity. But, he concluded that he should remain because his followers still needed his leadership, to grow in their faith, so they would be joyful for it when he next visited them.

Paul then encouraged them to live honorably in accordance with Christ's gospel, so their reputation for steadfastness in faith and obedience would be good news to him on his next visit. He wanted them to be united in their efforts to convert others to the Good News. He urged them to be fearless against opponents of their beliefs, as God would preserve them in their sufferings for their faith, just as He had done for Paul many times. Such suffering brings eternal rewards, but it also serves to mature us as Christians so we may glorify Christ and God until our days are ended.

CHAPTER 2:   In verses 1-5, Paul exhorted the church to give him great joy by emulating the example of Jesus Christ for encouragement, compassion, unity in fellowship, Christian love for one another, without selfish desires, and humility in all ways. Kindly caring for others, without being intrusive in personal matters, will lead to inward and outward peace. There appeared to have been some conflicts in the church that gave Paul reason to render this advice.

In verses 5-11, Paul cited Christ as the epitome of humility, which contributed to His exaltation in heaven. His words may have been from a hymn or worship creed. Christ as God came to earth in complete humility as a man, giving up his divine equality with God, to obey God's will for Him, even to die on the cross.

With His 2 natures, divine and human, Christ became like us in all things except sin. While His whole life was one of poverty and suffering, this is not expected of mankind in a material sense, but more so in the realm of enduring hardship for one's faith in Christ, if this becomes necessary. Mankind must pattern after Christ's life on earth, for the benefit of His death to be realized.

Having been exalted by God for His sacrificial love for mankind, Christ now deserves honor from all mankind, but especially from all who believe in Him as the Lord of Salvation. By doing so, glory is given also to God the Father.

Paul reminded the Philippians in verses 12-18, of their obligations to live as Christ lived, and to preserve their salvation in Him in obedience, fear and trembling. He admonished them to do their duty without complaints, argument, flaws and sin, so as to be God's children above reproach, beacons of light in the darkness of this world. They were to be different from the perverse people of the world, especially in keeping themselves blameless and harmless as consistent believers.

Paul wanted them to share the salvation message with the unsaved so that his work would not be a waste, for which he would rejoice, and they too would rejoice, especially in the last days. It is God's will that believers rejoice in their own service, and also to be happy over good people who minister to them.

Paul expressed his hope, in verses 19-24, to send Timothy to Philippi in the near future, to get more news about them, before he would be able to visit them. He lauded Timothy for his faith, his caring spirit, and his great service in spreading the gospel. Immediately though, he was sending Epaproditus, a brother and coworker in Christ, who wished to return to them so their anxiety over his near fatal illness would be put aside. He asked that they receive him with open arms as a survivor by God's grace, because of his work for the Lord, and the help he gave to Paul. What is given in answer to prayer, should be <u>received with</u> <u>great thankfulness and joy</u>. Even in prison, Paul demonstrated his concern over others, their health, and their spirituality.

CHAPTER 3:   Referring to some advice he had given previously, Paul again cautions the Philippians in verses 1-11, to beware of the 'dogs,' those evil workers (Judaizers) who insisted that Gentile believers must become Jews through circumcision and obedience to the Mosaic Law. They opposed faith in Christ as a primary goal. Paul considered true circumcision to mean worship of God in the Spirit, with rejoicing in Christ, and <u>no human</u> <u>accomplishment</u> <u>as a gateway to heaven.</u>

If this was not true, then Paul had more reason to believe as they did, since he was circumcised at 8 day's age, as a Hebrew of the Israeli tribe of Benjamin, educated as a Pharisee, and under the Mosaic Law <u>persecuted the first Christian church.</u>

But, he learned an important lesson, what he thought was important was nothing but <u>rubbish</u> <u>in the eyes of God,</u> compared with knowing Christ as his Savior, and having righteousness simply by faith in Him. This knowledge gives a believer a new outlook on life, that riches in Christ are more valuable than all worldly riches.

In 12-16, Paul admitted that he still had not achieved his goal of perfection in Christ, but with His help, he was determined to forget his past mistakes and struggle on <u>to win the</u> <u>prize of</u> <u>a heavenly home,</u> made available by God because of Christ's atonement for mankind. He was willing to do or to suffer any thing, to gain the glorious resurrection of saints, not through his own merit and righteousness, but <u>through the divinity of Jesus Christ.</u> This is a commitment and goal for all believers to embrace until life on earth is over!

Offering himself as an example in 17-21, along with other true believers, Paul tearfully <u>encouraged all to hold to their Christian faith,</u> so that the unsaved in their life would not contaminate them with their wayward passions and appetites for evil. Rather than suffer eternal damnation with the unsaved, Paul pointed out that the <u>believer's citizenship is in</u> <u>heaven,</u> to be with the Lord, Whose power will transform our physical bodies to conform to His own. What a change that will be, to have a body without disease, sin, nonperishable, and deathless, in a new spiritual world!

CHAPTER 4:   Paul clearly spoke from his heart in verse 1 as he addressed the church of Philippi with love and longing, crediting them as the source of his joy and pride for them. In the same breath, he <u>encouraged them to stand fast in the Lord,</u> in their faith, and in His strength and grace.

He implored the church to strive for unity and joy in the Lord in verses 2-7, with a specific appeal to 2 women, Euodia and Syntyche to <u>put aside their differences,</u> and for a 3rd person to assist the women in doing so.

He urged all members to rejoice (be glad) at all times under all circumstances, because their <u>joy was founded in their relationship with God,</u> through Jesus Christ. Joy in the Christian life should be constant, and a counter balance to sorrow and tribulation. It should overcome harshness towards others, anxiety over problems, and bring the believer to <u>lean</u> <u>on the Lord</u>

through faith and prayer, for victory over negatives. With thanksgiving to God, peace like a river will flow to set things right.

Paul urged them to focus on the right things that build good character, such as honesty, purity, that which is beautiful in a virtuous way, and that which is proper. Strive for what is really worthwhile and worthy of praise, as measured by God's rules. Thus, in doing so, the God of peace will bless the believer with joy and comfort.

In verses 10-20, Paul gave thanks for the generosity of the Philippians, shown to him out of their genuine concern for his welfare. He expressed his contentment with what had been provided, through abundance and destitution, when well fed or without sufficient food. He was able to do this because Christ strengthened him!

He commended them for giving help after he left the churches in Macedonia and while he ministered in Thessalonica. This was help that he did not request of them; for that reason he wished blessings upon them. Their gift to him was equivalent to a gift to God. Having the grace to do good through Christ, brings His rewards, for which we should do our best to do more in His honor and for His glory.

Paul closed this epistle in 21-22, with his usual words of greetings to the saints, from himself and his aides, even converts from Caesar's staff, that the grace of Christ Jesus be upon them, as purchased for them by His own merits.

SUMMARY: The most striking quality in this epistle is Paul's 18 expressions of joy and thankfulness, in spite of severe testing he had endured. It appears that no hardship could rob him of this joy, even confinement in a Roman prison. He allowed God to work through him to share the gospel and to encourage others, even when under duress. He shared God's scriptural wisdom and encouragement for mankind, and held up Jesus as a model for all believers, with urging that they stand united in Him with love and kindness to one another. Great advice for today's Christians!

COLOSSIANS—BOOK TWELVE

Colossians was written by Paul from his prison in Rome around 61 AD, to the church at Colosse which was located about 100 miles east of the port city of Ephesus. It is believed that the membership of the church was typical of that region, <u>a mixture of Greeks, Roman, and Jews.</u>

No evidence exists that Paul founded the church by personal visits, rather, it may have become an offshoot branch during his 3 years of ministry to the Ephesus church. A Christian man from Colosse, named Epaphras, <u>may have been the initial inspiration for the church,</u> through his contact with Paul at Ephesus. He later became a companion prisoner with Paul in Rome. Another convert of Paul's during his work in Ephesus, a man named Philemon from Colosse, may also have been <u>instrumental in founding the Colossian church.</u>

Epaphras brought word to Paul about some kind of heresy, in the nature of a philosophical combination of Jewish and pagan beliefs, considered to be a more enlightened form of Christianity, <u>also known as 'gnosticism.'</u> Simply stated, it was a cult which combined Jewish legalism, Greek speculations, and Oriental mysticism. Paul viewed it to be a <u>subversion of true and complete faith in Christ.</u> Such deviations from a genuine Christian faith are still prevalent in this world.

Paul's letter was intended to restore the supremacy of Christ as the central and <u>only true Deity worthy of recognition and worship.</u> He emphasized the significance of Christ as the divine Creator, for which there could be no viable substitute, or reason for false doctrines.

The epistle has 2 main themes. The 1st is argument against false teachings, as found in chapters 1-2. The 2nd is <u>exhortations for proper Christian living,</u> as given in chapters 3-4. Chapter 1 also recounts Paul's prayers for the church and his thankfulness for their basic Christian beliefs.

CHAPTER 1:   Paul's usual grace and peace greeting opens the epistle, as coming <u>from him and faithful follower Timothy.</u> This is followed by his prayer of thanks in verses 3-8, for their faith in Christ, love for one another, and hope for heavenly rewards. He pointed out that these 3 qualities are in accord with the true gospel they first heard, and <u>as taught by their</u> own believer Epaphras.

In verses 9-14, Paul told them of his continuing prayers that they be filled with <u>divine wisdom and understanding of God's will</u> for their lives. Specifically, his prayer was that they live in a way that honors and pleases God, that their service be spiritually fruitful, and that their <u>understanding of Him would continue to grow.</u>

He prayed that they be strengthened by God's glorious power, to acquire patience, durability, and happiness, and thereby <u>be thankful for their heavenly Christ given inheritance</u> of deliverance from Satan's dark domain of sin. All Christians should consider it a great blessing and gift, to be translated from Satan's control to that of Christ, which brings an end to many trials and best of all, will <u>enable them to survive the worst of end times tribulation.</u> Their faith in Christ gives them joy over this redemption, and gratitude that He purchased it with His atoning blood.

Paul exalts Christ in verses 15-20 as the image of God before creation took place, and as creation occurred. The created world exists because He is Lord over all, the Head of the Church, and the 1st to be resurrected from death with an immortal glorious body like God's. He is important to God, and pleased Him with His sacrificial peace offering on the cross, because this opened the door for mankind to be reconciled with God. Christ as a human, was the incarnation of our invisible God, and all that see Christ spiritually by faith will have also seen the Father.

Paul took note of the former state of the Colossians as sinful unbelievers in verses 21-23, before they were converted to stand before God as faultless without sin by Christ's redeeming grace. This relationship would continue as they kept their faith in Christ's Good News gospel, which was preached everywhere with Paul's help.

In verses 24-29, Paul spoke of his own pleasure in serving Christ and His church, in spite of much suffering. The sufferings of Christ and of those in His church are somewhat commensurate, but yet different, in that He suffered for the redemption of the church, while believers suffer for other more mundane reasons.

Paul said that his task was to preach a message kept unknown for ages past, which God now wanted made known to all the world, that Christ is man's only hope for glory. With an infusion of God's strength and spiritual power, Paul vows to keep on bringing this message to all, but especially for the benefit of believers who gave him added inspiration. Church members should be an inspiration to their pastors!

CHAPTER 2:   Paul admitted in verses 1-7, how difficult it was for him to be spiritually concerned for the Colossians, no doubt because of his own dire straits as a prisoner. Yet he wished to encourage them to stand fast in their faith and love for each other, so they would come to know Christ as the key figure in God's mystery, and the source of spiritual wisdom and knowledge. This was so they would not be deceived by phony philosophy, for which Paul would derive great joy. To be strengthened or enlarged in Christ, believers must be firmly rooted in Him, and remain so grounded, with a desire to keep on improving as a child of God.

In verses 8-18, Paul sounded a warning again for the church to beware of false doctrine which promoted worldly Satanic ideas that diminished Christ as a central divinity of the Godhead. Being united with Him by faith, believers are spiritually circumcised from sin and the curse of legalism, and thus have a new life in Christ, as if resurrected as He was. We are victorious through His victory over death, which diminished the Mosaic Law as a Jewish yoke and a dividing wall to the Gentiles.

Paul admonished the church to not allow anyone to dictate what food or drink they should consume, what special days to celebrate, that angels should be worshipped, or that visions are essential. Those who advocate these self-serving desires are not true believers in Christ, for they lack spiritual strength and unity in His body. Their views are just plain nonsense!

He said that they had died to worldly ways through their faith in Christ, and asked why should they submit to ridiculous suggestions which on the surface may seem intelligent but are actually worthless concepts. By worshipping angels, Christ is put aside as the only Mediator between God and man. Christ, as Head of the Christian church, is insulted when mankind replaces Him with some minor thing.

CHAPTER 3:   Paul continued his dissertation on the preeminence of Christ in the Christian life in verses 1-11, by pointing out that <u>a new life in Christ should condition the heart</u> to cherish eternal life in God's heavenly home. Christ gave real meaning to life on earth, along with the bonus of a heavenly mansion for retirement.

We are to always focus on God's provision for the hereafter, more than on the temporary and mundane. To much affection for our earthly domain lessens our affection for our heavenly rewards as Christ calls us home. One way or another, by resurrection or a living rapture, <u>we will have a glorious role when Christ returns</u> to make us part of His millennial reign.

Until then, as Paul said to the Colossians, we are to live worthy of our salvation, by <u>squelching all sins of the flesh,</u> such as immorality, indecency. pornography, greed, forms of idolatry, malicious anger, hate, dishonesty, and vicious or insulting talk to others. We should rid ourselves of such ways as if <u>eradicating weeds or vermin which spread and destroy good things</u>. As a new person in Christ, whether a Jew, Gentile, circumcised or not, a free man or a slave, <u>Christ must be the dominant influence in life</u> for us to be holy and happy.

In verses 12-17, Paul gave his recipe for developing a Christian character, as God desires of us, with the ingredients of <u>gentleness, kindness, humility, meekness, forgiveness, patience, and binding love</u> above all else. As a member of Christ's church, we are to live in peace with one another with thanksgiving to God, when we can <u>help others in their Christian walk</u>. Let the gospel of Christ prosper and grow in our soul as we regularly partake of God's Word in the name of Jesus.

Paul ends the chapter with some personal rules for Christian home life in verses 18-25, much <u>as also stated in Eph. 5:21-6:9.</u> Wives are to be submissive to husbands, husbands are to love wives without bitterness, children are to obey parents, fathers are to deal fairly with their children, and servants are to be diligent in service to their boss. In every relationship, the Christian should try to behave as if serving Christ, apart from one's personal nature, knowing that <u>to do otherwise may earn His chastisement.</u>

CHAPTER 4:   The 1st verse is the conclusion to chapter 3, in which Paul advised slave owners to be fair and honest with their slaves, keeping in mind <u>their Master in heaven.</u> Paul urged the Colossians in verses 2-6 to be ever diligent in prayer, especially <u>for the spreading of the gospel,</u> and to take every opportunity to share it with unbelievers. He asked that they pray for his ability to make God's Word as clear as possible, just as they should do when sharing the gospel. God's Word should be discussed with grace and clarity!

Verses 7-15 are words of final greetings with mention of numerous fellow workers. Paul said he was sending his beloved brother in the Lord, Tychicus, to give <u>them this epistle,</u> and to <u>get information about them.</u> A slave, Onesimus, would be with him to return to his own master, Philemon (see Phil. 10).

Paul extended greeting for others: Aristarchus, a fellow prisoner; Mark, the cousin of Barnabas; a fellow worker named Jesus (Justus); Epaphras, an ardent supporter of the Colosse church; a man named Demas; and last, Luke the beloved physician. These <u>greetings</u> <u>were to be shared</u> with the believers in Laodicea and Nymphas. Paul asked that this epistle be read at Colosse and also Laodicea.

Paul signed the letter, which may have been dictated to Timothy, with a reminder that he was in prison, and his <u>prayers were for God's blessing on them.</u>

<u>SUMMARY:</u>   There is much value in this epistle for Christians of today. Paul's warning against false doctrine is germane to the present apostate trend in the world, with the introduction of cultist concepts which <u>serve selfish interest more than they serve God.</u> His sketch of Jesus Christ as the central spiritual force of the Godhead on behalf of mankind is <u>vital to a healthy growth of Christianity</u> in the world.

His repetitive advice for commendable personal relationships in the family, the home, and for better employee/employer relationships is vital to a good life, especially when problems and tribulations grow as God's endtimes scenario unfolds.

Paul's plea for prayers to help him preach the gospel as clearly as possible speaks of his concern that hearers of the message have good understanding so they will <u>believe, accept, and live by God's Word without procrastination.</u> The writing of this commentary was motivated with this same objective in mind, to make scriptures more meaning ful for lay persons, those who are hard at work making a living, with little time, or inclination to spend much <u>time in exhaustive study of the Bible</u>.

I THESSALONIANS—BOOK THIRTEEN

Paul founded the church of Thessalonica, the capital of Macedonia, on his 2nd missionary journey about 51 AD, as related in Acts 17. Paul may have spent less than a month preaching in a local synagogue before the Jews forced him out; then he may have ministered to non- Jews in private homes for a short time, before leaving the city and a church membership that was mostly Gentile.

He may have been assisted by Timothy and Silas, who were coworkers during that time; Timothy returned to the church with this letter to encourage them in their new faith. The church grew rapidly and as time went on, the gospel spread from there to other parts of Macedonia and Greece.

This epistle was one of Paul's earliest, believed to have been written in Corinth, after he had preached in Berea and in Athens (Acts 17:13-15). After a visit to the church by Timothy, based on the report he brought back, Paul was motivated to write to commend them for their spiritual strength to resist evil persuasions. Since they had questions about the 2nd coming of Christ and the gathering of saints by Him, Paul wrote to clarify what he had preached initially.

For Christians of today, Paul's letters to the Thessalonians are of great value in understanding the general pattern of events encompassing God's endtimes scenario, including Christ's 2nd coming to rapture His believers, and the Day of the Lord.

CHAPTER 1: Greetings from Paul, Silas, and Timothy were extended to the church in verse 1-3, with Paul's usual grace and peace wording, and his prayers for God's blessings because of their faith and good works.

Their faith is cited as an excellent example in verses 4-10, with assurances that God loved them for conforming to Christ's gospel of faith, love and hope, which they accepted with Holy Spirit inspiration. They had abandoned idol worship to become great examples of true believers to surrounding regions, in spite of threats and persecution from opposing Jews. They were steadfast in their expectation of Christ's 2nd coming to receive His own before God's wrath fell upon the wicked.

Clearly, the response of these Gentiles was most encouraging to Paul.

CHAPTER 2: Paul began with a review of his brief ministry in Thessalonica in verses 1-9, which he considered to be worthwhile—not in vain. He gave God credit for renewed courage to minister to them, even after his mistreatment at Philippi (Acts 16:22-24. He brought the message to them in all honesty, for which God was pleased; he had no up-the- sleeve personal motives.

He reminded them that he flattered no one, nor did he seek their praise, but he served as Christ desired of him, without demanding compensation. He asserted his affection for them was so great, that he would have given his life to share God's word. He spoke of his self-support, as a tent-maker, so as not to be a burden on them.

In verses 10-12, Paul portrayed himself as a father to them, working hard making a living to support his children, while sharing God's message with them. In complete honesty of purpose, he and his coworkers gave the new converts what any loving parent would do, by encouraging them to live rightly to honor God for accepting them as His own children.

Christians should live up to their calling, to honor, serve, and please God, and seek to be worthy of him. The mature believer serves well, who like a father gives direction to the new believer, to grow in faith.

Paul thanked God in verses 13-15, for their positive response to the gospel which God gave him to share, which was now bearing fruit in their lives. Just as churches in Judea had done, the Thessalonians withstood mistreatment by Judaizers, some of which brought death to Christ and prophets in the past, and forced Paul and his workers to flee for their lives. Neither God nor his servants cared for this because it interfered with the saving of lost souls. God's angry punishment would fall on the Jews for their extreme opposition to His purposes.

In 17-20, Paul expressed the longing of his team to visit them, as if they had been 'orphaned' away from their children, thwarted by Satan from realizing their hopes and dreams. He said they would ever keep the Thessalonians in mind for the glorious crown of hope and joy the church gave them.

CHAPTER 3: Paul continued with his expressions of longing and love for the church at Thessalonica in verses 1-5, apparently a reason for sending Timothy to them to give spiritual encouragement and strength to overcome afflictions. Suffering difficulties is a common experience in the life of a Christian, as Paul reminded them, and as he acknowledged in his own service to the Lord. A caring attitude, as he had, is also a commendable trait, in keeping with Christ's character.

The good news Timothy brought back of their faith and love, and fond memories of Paul's ministry was most comforting to him, and like a breath of fresh air. He said in effect that he didn't have enough words to thank them for their faithfulness. All he could do was to pray for their continued spiritual growth.

The prayer of Paul and his coworkers was that they be allowed to visit the church again, but until then, they prayed for love in the church and for continued growth, so that all would have a sterling record for Christ to share at His 2nd coming, with God the Father. When Christ comes in glory with all His saints (angels?), excellence of character with godliness will be important to receive rewards rather than punishment. Paul said believers are to have hearts that are pure and righteous, no doubt meaning— purged of sins that have been forgiven by repentance before Christ.

VIEWPOINTS: The phrase at the end of verse 13, pertaining to the return of Jesus Christ with all His 'saints, or holy ones, or those who belong to Him, or angels' is a point of difference from one Bible translation to another. Some scholars say that 'holy ones' or angels is the correct understanding, but the Greek word is 'hagios, meaning 'saints.' One school of thought is that 'saints' is correct, because it refers to the spirits of those believers who died in ages past, that will be implanted in a new resurrection body. Some say both angels and saints could come with Christ.

If 'angels' is the correct word, then Christ's return in this context, would seem to be in a preliminary status, for His initial action to gather (rapture) His own from the 4 corners of the earth, in which angels would assist (see Matt. 24:31, Mark 13:27). On the other hand, Matt. 25:31-34 speaks of Christ's return with His angels to separate the sheep (the righteous) from the goats (the unsaved), which seems to be a later judgment action to save those who become believers after the rapture.

It seems most logical that Christ would return with both angels and the spirits of deceased believers. The angels would first assist in the 'rapture' of the dead and the living as spiritually recreated beings, and then help to select those who will be citizens of His millennial kingdom, after and apart from God's Wrath Judgment.

CHAPTER 4:   Paul began this chapter in verses 1-12, with exhortations to the church to live a life that pleases God, as he had taught them. Even though on track already, he urged them to do even better, by avoiding immorality, domestic strife, being creatures of questionable habits, dishonesty, and obedient to all of God's rules. With respect to transformation of one's soul unto holiness, self-discipline must be imposed on the appetites of the body, including the thoughts and inclinations of one's desires, to avoid the wrong uses of them to earn God's displeasure.

Love of each other was also an important trait Paul advised, along with a peaceful life, not meddling in other people's affairs, and working diligently, so as to earn respect from others without owing them anything.

In 13-15, Paul spoke of several aspects related to Christ's 2nd coming, one of which related to the death of some fellow believers. With respect to the dead in Christ, Paul expressed his belief that they would be restored with new bodies in like fashion to Christ's resurrection, to be with the Lord forever. For that reason, excessive grieving over their death was not justified. As for the living when He comes, they too would be given new bodies as they are taken up to be with Him.

His coming, in verses 16-18, will be introduced by His own loud joyful command, a following word from an archangel (possibly Michael), and the traditional Jewish trumpet sound, to get the attention of the dead and the living in Christ. Both will be taken up in one massive movement (raptured) as if in a cloud to join Christ somewhere above the earth. With this assurance for the believers, Paul exhorted them to comfort one another accordingly.

VIEWPOINTS: From the language used by Paul, he evidently thought Christ would return during his lifetime. From his description, the return of Christ will have sound effects to announce His arrival in the stratosphere, but no indication about who will hear them; undoubtedly all believers would be alerted by them, but the unsaved may not be aware of the event until believers are gone and missed. Will they rethink their spiritual views to turn from their wicked way to become believers?

Paul's prediction gave no clue about the timing of the rapture within God's endtimes scenario. From this scripture, no legitimate claim can be made for the rapture to occur at the beginning of Daniel's 70th week, the 7 year tribulation time, as some contemporary doctrines contend. Again, it appears most logical that the rapture will take place immediately preceding God's Wrath Judgment (The Day of the Lord), in conjunction with Christ's master plan to establish His earthly kingdom, near the end of the tribulation period.

CHAPTER 5:   Paul makes it clear in verses 1-1, that the timing of Christ's return will not be determined by any earthly measures or formulas. It will come unexpectedly like a thief breaking into a house during the night, <u>when people think they are secure.</u> Paul's claim that destruction will strike suddenly like birth pains when a baby is due, indicates that something devastating and painful will take place, such as the Day of the Lord judgment of the nations <u>near the end of the tribulation period.</u>

He stated that the Thessalonian church, just as for all believers, should not be unprepared for such an event, complacent about it, or <u>ignore the reality of world developments</u> that relate to biblical prophecies, else they will be as if drunk or asleep. We should be prepared as good soldiers for the inevitable, whenever it happens, wearing the breastplate of faith and love, and a helmet of salvation assurance. We know that God has <u>foreordained that</u> <u>His children will not suffer His end of tribulation wrath</u> judgment, since Christ will have gathered them beforehand. Let this be an encouragement to us!

With final instructions in 12-28, Paul also closed the letter with his usual greetings in the name of the Lord. He asked them to be considerate of their hard working leaders, giving them respect and love, and by being cooperative with them. He told them to <u>help the spiritually weak,</u> by warning them of improper life styles. They were to be patient with the unsaved persons, and show kindness and love to all.

Happiness through prayer and thanksgiving to God, heeding the Holy Spirit, and keeping prophesies in mind, should be a <u>source of strength, holiness, and trust.</u> Paul asked for prayers for him and his coworkers, as he would pray for God's blessing on them.

<u>VIEWPOINTS:</u>   There is no hint in this chapter that Christ's church, true believers in His salvation gospel, <u>will be raptured anytime before or at the beginning of the tribulation years.</u> As a matter of fact, who will be able to say when Daniel's 70th week period will begin? Tribulation will creep up on the world, as <u>it already appears to be happening.</u>

If a pre-tribulation rapture should occur, the unsaved with some knowledge of scripture would know that the Day of the Lord and Christ's 2nd coming would be 7 years ahead, which <u>would motivate them to become believers.</u> That would be a good thing, and it will probably happen, <u>no matter</u> when the rapture occurs. Again, the rapture of the saints fits into the pre-wrath escape teachings of Paul. Scripture up to this point confirms that supposition!

SUMMARY: Readers of scripture might well wonder how Paul came by his revelations on Christ's 2nd coming. Inspiration from the Holy Spirit is relevant, but his understanding of Christ's teachings must also have <u>influenced his thinking.</u> Christ's predictions in Matt. 24, about wars, famines and earthquakes as just the beginning of much trouble on earth, appears to be a warning to all believers to remain strong and courageous in their Christian faith, so as to <u>endure until the time is shortened for them,</u> by the rapture event.

The separation of mankind into 2 groups, sheep and goats, as related in Matt. 25:31-46, seems to describe the final sifting of the good and the bad, immediately before Christ's millennial reign begins. This could be to <u>publicly identify those who may become saved</u> after the rapture, as they realize that prophecy was being fulfilled.

II THESSALONIANS—BOOK FOURTEEN

This epistle, also written from Corinth, about 51 AD shortly after the preceding one, contains further instruction about the Day of the Lord. The church members at Thessolonica somehow became concerned over a false notion that the <u>event had already began to unfold.</u> Persecution had increased and many had stopped working and sponged off of others, thinking that they would <u>shortly be taken to be with Christ.</u>

Paul clarified that a time of lawlessness and apostasy would precede Christ's return, as he asserted that the <u>Day of the Lord had not yet come.</u> For this reason, they were to stand firm in their faith and wait patiently for Christ's return.

CHAPTER 1: Paul again included Silas and Timothy, in his grace with peace in God and Jesus greeting to the church in verses 1-2. Words of commendation and encouragement follow in verses 3-12. He praised them for growing stronger in their faith and love for one another as persecution came against them. He spoke of them as an example for all of God's churches at that time, and perhaps for churches of today.

Paul asserted that their suffering was God's way of preparing them for <u>a role in His kingdom,</u> when Christ and His powerful angels would come to punish their persecutors, as if by fire. Their enemies would be doomed to eternal destruction. This would happen <u>when a glorified Christ returns</u> to receive praise and honor from his own, of which they would be a part. This comforting expectation is for all believers!

Because God had chosen them, Paul and his coworkers prayed for them to be empowered to accomplish all that their faith prompted them to do. In so doing, they would be honoring God and Jesus, for which honor would come to them.

CHAPTER 2: Paul urged the church, in verses 1-12, not to believe false claims that Christ had already come, and not to be upset by the <u>thought that they had been left behind.</u> They were not to be fooled by allegations that the Holy Spirit or letters from Paul had given this idea.

Christ had not yet returned and He would not until a <u>time of rebellion against God (apostasy) would take place,</u> bringing conditions in which a demon inspired world leader (man of sin, son of perdition, lawless one, or antichrist) would appear, take a seat in a temple of God (presumably in Jerusalem), <u>and proclaim himself to be the God mankind</u> <u>should worship.</u> His main objective will be to attract Jews.

Reminding them that he had previously told them all this, Paul said they should also <u>know who or what was delaying the appearance of the 'lawless one.'</u> A bit of mystery is injected here since Paul did not identify the 'restrainer.' One popular view is that the Holy Spirit working through Christ's church will be the roadblock to the antichrist, possibly until that time <u>when the gospel has been proclaimed to all the world.</u> Another view is that the archangel Michael will be the one, based on Dan. 10:13 & 21, and 12:1, which portrays Michael as a 'chief prince' protector of saints.

The antichrist will be Satan's tool to deceive the unsaved with all kinds of signs, miracles, and wonders in defiance of God. Disillusionment will be allowed by God, primarily as punishment of hard-hearted Jews for rejection of Christ. They could be saved but most will reject the truth, so God will let them go their chosen way.

After Christ returns to gather His own, He will join God to destroy the antichrist during the Day of the Lord judgment, preceding Christ's millennial reign.

Paul added words of encouragement to the church in verses 13-17, with thanks to God for work of the Holy Spirit in them to see the truth of Christ's glory. He assured them of God's love evidenced by His promise of eternal hope and comfort. Prayers for their good conduct and wisdom of expression were added.

VIEWPOINTS: Verse 1 conforms to what is said in Matthew 24:29-31, Mark 13:23-27, and Luke 21:25-27, where Jesus describes His own return as occurring after much tribulation (near the end of it), with His initial action to gather (rapture) His saints.

Another pre-condition to His coming, and the Day of the Lord, as given in verses 3-4, will be a time of pronounced rebellion against anything related to God, Christ, and the Bible. This apostasy development will lead to the appearance of Satan's antichrist, who will try to replace God as a divine authority over mankind.

Clearly no inference is given that Christians will escape the tribulation by an early rapture 6-7 years before the Day of the Lord wrath judgment. With Christ's divination of endtimes developments, plus Paul's amplifications, it becomes increasingly difficult to envision a pre-tribulation rapture of God's glorified saints.

The book of Revelations has more to say on this matter!

CHAPTER 3:   Paul opened with a request for prayers for his team in verses 1-2, for success in quickly spreading the gospel without harm from evil and unscrupulous unbelievers, or the Judaizers of Corinth. He expressed confidence in 3-5, that God would also shield the church from evil, so they will also accomplish what they should in obedience and love for God and Christ.

Paul issues a command in Christ's name, in verses 6-15, about working for self- support rather than be a charity case. He asked the church to stand apart from those who elected to remain idle in the expectation that others would provide their needs. Paul cited his team as an example of those who worked hard to support themselves, to avoid being a burden on others. He clearly denounced laziness!

He cited the principle of 'those who do not work, shall not eat.' He admonished all of this ilk to get to work in an orderly fashion so they could eat their own bread. However, he encouraged charity when necessary, but if an able-bodied person refused to work, the church should help to energize them, but not support them. All should be done as to a Christian brother, not as to an enemy.

Paul's benediction is one of peace and grace to the church from the Lord Jesus, with his own signature to validate his letter, probably written by Timothy.

SUMMARY: Paul's letters often spoke of deception and disillusionment in the endtimes as part of a 'falling away' from <u>Godly truths and lifestyle</u>. In this letter, he admits that this was already happening as Satan prepares the way <u>for the antichrist's appearance.</u> Apostasy has penetrated extensively into the <u>Christian foundation of America,</u> as established by our pilgrim forefathers. It has already permeated deeply into the spiritual character of Europe and other lands and cultures. Tribulation of all kinds is plaguing the world; clearly God's endtimes scenario is unfolding.

I TIMOTHY—BOOK FIFTEEN

Paul wrote this letter to his trusted friend and coworker Timothy as pastoral instruction, sometime after release from his 1st imprisonment in Rome, during his 5 years of freedom before his 2nd imprisonment, between 62-67 AD. It may have been written while Paul revisited Macedonia, and Timothy was a pastor at Ephesus.

Popular opinion is that Timothy, a Greek, became a convert of Paul's during his 1st missionary journey, when he visited Timothy's home in Lystra. Later, when Paul visited Lystra on his 2nd missionary trip, Timothy is mentioned as a faithful follower in Acts 16:1-3. He then became a coworker with Paul and Silas, after Paul had him circumcised to make him more acceptable to new Jewish converts.

He became like a son to Paul, and a very valuable coworker, as evidenced by liaison trips to the churches of Thesssalonica, Corinth and Philippi, to represent Paul's teachings, and his subsequent time as a pastor to the church of Ephesus. His name is mentioned as a coworker in the beginning of 6 Pauline letters: II Corinthians, Philippians, Colossians, I & II Thessalonians, and Philemon.

As Paul faced death during his 2nd imprisonment in Rome, he wrote another letter to encourage Timothy to stand fast in his calling to preach the gospel of Jesus, and to be a comfort to Paul during his last days.

CHAPTER 1:   Paul opened this letter with gracious words to Timothy as a true son in the faith, wishing for him grace, mercy, and peace from God and Jesus Christ. He followed with warnings in verses 3-11, for Timothy to guard against false teachers of the Mosiac Law, who propagated mythology and genealogies which drew believers away from the gospel of Christ.

Timothy was urged to adhere to and preach the importance of genuine love, with a conscience clear of wrong ideas, because of steadfast faith in the gospel. Faith in the truths and promises of God is essential to godliness of heart and life. Timothy's objective was to neutralize influence of the false teachers, who did not understand the error of their views or know what was most important.

With respect to the law, Paul acknowledged that it served well to reveal the sins of the ungodly, those who committed all kinds of wicked things that went against the Good News gospel of God. It serves as a restraint against evil in those who have any kind of concern for right and wrong. Those who are righteous according to God's word, are not bound by the law, for their faith sustains them.

Paul added a bit of his own views in verses 12-17, about God's grace for him when he was such a scoundrel as a persecutor of the Jerusalem church. He was thankful and amazed that Christ had chosen him to preach the gospel to the unsaved. God's mercy and grace was imparted to him, because of his ignorance of the truth, and he became a believer through the patience of Jesus Christ during his waywardness. For this reason, Paul prayed that honor and glory be given to the only true God, who is eternal, immortal, a fountain of wisdom, and yet invisible.

In verses 18-20, Paul commits his 'son' Timothy to live up to his reputation with others, to be a brave soldier, faithful with a clear conscience, and not be like 2 men, given over to Satan, Hymenaeus and Alexander, who opposed God's gospel.

CHAPTER 2:   Paul exhorts Timothy in verses 1-7 to pray much for all mankind, both believers and unbelievers, both men and women, royalty and commoners, using 4 modes of prayer: general prayers, supplications for specific help, intercessions for forgiveness, and prayers of thanksgiving. A general objective is to attain a peaceful life with regular worship of God.

It is pleasing to God for mankind to be saved and to know spiritual truth; this He desires of all mankind, that they believe in Him and His Son, Christ Jesus. We are to know that there is only one mediator between us and God, and that is Jesus Christ, Who came in human form to make this truth known to man.

These facts are why God chose Paul to become an apostle to convey spiritual truth to the Gentile world with all of his integrity and ability. This goal is also for all pastors who answer the call to serve as messengers of the gospel. All believers in Christ should be praying people, no matter what their status in life might be, in keeping with a primary duty to be godly and honest in their faith. All believers should grow in the knowledge of the truth, God's way to save sinners, so as to be ruled by it.

In verses 8-15, Paul expressed his personal opinion and preferences for the conduct and role of men and women in the church. Briefly, he wanted to see men praying fervently, with uplifted hands, without anger or doubt over God's Word. This was also true for women, but they were to be modestly dressed, without overdoing hair styles, makeup and jewelry. Women should be motivated to be ambassadors of goodwill to fellow believers in sorrow or in need of daily resources.

Paul felt that women should not be teachers of men, that they should be silent in the company of men, because Eve first sinned and then caused Adam to do likewise. He thought woman's primary God-given role was to bear children as faithful, loving, righteous, and modest mothers, and thus be spared other concerns of life.

VIEWPOINTS: Paul's ideas on the proper role of Christian women in the life of a church seem to be his personal views apart from teachings from Christ, as also expressed in I Cor. 11:5-15 & 14:35 Although women do attire and adorn themselves discreetly and modestly for the most part, when attending religious service, they are not always silent or without leadership responsibility over men. Some churches of today ordain women to be ministers, and teachers in general, and in many cases, they do an admirable job. Whether this is displeasing to God is difficult to say, or conclude. It does not appear to be a sin!

CHAPTER 3:   In verses 1-12, Paul instructs Timothy on the proper role of male church officials, if they are to be effective. His 1st requirement is that they have a good reputation and if married, it must be a first and only marriage. Then he listed 15 other qualities: having self-control, being sensible, well-behaved, and friendly to others; good teachers, not heavy drinkers or troublemakers, kindly, and not greedy over money; manage their families well, have well-behaved children, be honest, be seasoned believers, be well-respected in their community, and demonstrate a strong faith and commitment to God's word. These pre- requisites for leadership in the church apply to elders, deacons, trustees, and other church officials.

As for women, they should be serious minded, non-gossips, not heavy drinkers, and be faithful in what they stand for, especially as wives of church officials.

In verses 14-16, Paul spoke of his hope to visit Timothy in Ephesus, but until then, these instructions were given to help Timothy better perform his pastoral duties. Then he quoted what may be words of an old song, about the mystery of God, as manifested in Christ's resurrection, the work of the Holy Spirit as witnessed by angels, now preached to Gentiles, believed by many, and Christ's ascension to heaven.

CHAPTER 4: As part of the endtimes apostasy, Paul spoke of spiritual revelation that many believers will be deceived by demonic teachings from hypocritical liars, who will forbid marriage and the eating of certain foods. They will forbid as evil what God has permitted; giving the Christian reason for great caution to not be lured away. If not strictly forbidden by God's Word, through the teachings of Christ and His apostles, everything should be accepted as good with thanksgiving to God.

Paul got personal with Timothy in verses 6-16, about his role as a teacher and pastor of the church, saying he would be a great minister by holding to his faith and correct doctrine. He was to reject stupid untrue concepts and doctrine; and work hard to be truly righteous (religious) at all times. He was to preach that the hope and strength of all Christians is founded in a living God, who provides an enduring salvation to mankind. Timothy was to teach and commend this faith to all!

Paul told him not to be concerned about his youth, because his good example would earn proper respect from his fellow believers. Until he came for a visit, Paul exhorted Timothy to regularly read and teach from scriptures that were available then, including his own letters. He was to mediate on spiritual matters and hold fast in obedience to God's instructions for believers. Thus, they would listen to him!

Paul's advice to Timothy is most apropos for all ministers, pastors, deacons, and other church officials. These officials must diligently strive for spiritual wisdom and knowledge, to better endow spiritual profit and gain to their church fellowship. Their teaching, preaching, and advice to the church must be scriptural, understandable, evangelical, and given in practical terms, in accord with biblical doctrine. When well taught and informed, all believers are then better equipped to witness to others how the power of the Holy Spirit bears good fruit in their lives.

CHAPTER 5: Paul said not to find fault unkindly with an older man in verses 1-2, respect must be shown for the dignity of years. He said to treat younger men like a brother, older women as one's own mother, and younger women as a sister.

He gave instructions on honoring widows in verses 3-16, helping them as needed. If a widow has children, and no other relatives, it is her children's duty to care for her as she once cared for them, inasmuch as a woman of faith she would pray often to God for help. Widowhood is a desolate state; widows must trust in the Lord, and continue in prayer.

If believers neglect their poor relatives, they belittle their faith, and if a widow kicks up her heels in heedless pleasure, she likely is signing her death warrant early.

For church support, a widow should be at least 60 years of age or older and married only once. She must also have lived a good life, as a mother and as a good Samaritan, helping others in need, and be helpful in many ways. Younger widows should work to support themselves, since their youthful sensual desires may cause them to displease God, or they may remarry and not need help. If they receive help when they are able to fend for themselves, they will become lazy busybodies, gossiping improperly about others, and wasting good time.

In 17-25, Paul gave instructions for the respectful treatment of church elders, who work hard at teaching and preaching, even paying them double the normal wage. He quoted Deut. 25:4 and Luke 10:7 as justification for adequate compensation.

Accusations against elders should not be considered unless 2-3 witnesses can provide factual detail on alleged misconduct, but if they have sinned, make that known before the church body, as a warning to all.

Paul charged Timothy under the authority of God, Jesus Christ, and chief angels to carry out his duties without prejudice or partiality. He urged other things: not to be hasty in restoring a failed elder, or getting involved in their sin; and also to drink small amounts of wine only for stomach comfort or infirmities, but otherwise drink water.

Timothy was to keep in mind that some sinners are exposed before they do great harm, but other's keep their sins hidden; this was true also of good deeds. In all cases, God will bring to light the hidden things, and make known the good and the bad, for reward or punishment.

CHAPTER 6: The relationship between slaves and their master, when both are believers, was clarified in verses 1-2. The spiritual bond should give slaves a desire to give even better service than otherwise, but if the master is not a believer, the slave should still honor and obey him. This then reflects favorable on the slave's spiritual status!

Paul said more about dealing with false teachers in verses 3-5. He categorizes them as conceited and wicked in their ignorance of truth and fact, when they advocate a doctrine that clashes with that which Jesus Christ gave the world. Such sick and deviant doctrine usually results in much dispute, harsh language, and evil suspicions. Promotion of false doctrine is also done to gain monetary wealth, but in the process of gaining such riches, spiritual wealth can be destroyed.

Paul discussed the matter of earthly riches versus spiritual gains in verses 6-10. Uppermost to consider, is that Christian faith makes us rich through contentment with what God gives us. Having come into this world with nothing, we will leave it with nothing of material value, but hopefully with the spiritual value of eternal life. Satisfaction in having the necessities of life is a Christian attribute.

Those who covet material wealth often succumb to temptations and traps of lust which lead to depravity and destruction of character and soul. A love of money (covetousness) is the true evil; money itself is not evil. One can have wealth but not love it; if such is the case, one is more likely to use it for good purposes in the Lord's domain and to help the needy.

Unfortunately, some men of the cloth preach a prosperity gospel, often for selfish gain, by telling their congregations to give more seed, to reap a bigger harvest. This tends to promote covetousness in the hearts of the preacher and his followers.

In 11-16, Paul pleaded with Timothy to avoid such temptations, and strive for righteousness, godliness, faith, love, patience, and gentleness. He urged him to fight hard against the powers of darkness, to justify his faith in Christ to earn a reward of eternal life. He asked Timothy to vow to hold fast to God's Word, and to confess it completely, just as Jesus did before Pontius Pilate before His crucifixion.

In so doing, Timothy and his believers, as well as all believers down through the ages, will be rewarded when Christ returns, as approved by our glorious immortal God, the bright light of divine glory that mortal eye cannot envision.

Timothy was told in verses 17-19, to command the rich not to have vain pride or trust in their wealth, but to trust God who offers His own wealth for our needs and enjoyment. They were to give generously of their material wealth to lay up spiritual treasure for themselves and to realize what the good life is all about.

On closing, Paul urged Timothy in verses 20-21, to guard what God had put in his care, and to shun godless talk and ideas passed off as great knowledge, that could cause loss of faith in the true gospel of Christ. He added: Grace be with you!

SUMMARY: Much as a loving parent, Paul counseled his 'adopted son' Timothy on the basics of serving God nobly as a young man, according to the reputation that he had already earned as a coworker with Paul. Much of his own experience is encompassed in the wisdom he imparted to his beloved brother in Christ. What he shared with Timothy is advice of the best kind that every young person with potential and the heart to serve God should receive as they step into their chosen endeavor.

Paul's admonition on relationships between lay people and church leaders is much needed in today's world, where disputes and disharmony contribute to division and church splits that have a weakening effect on church growth and strength. Unity of each body of believers is essential for fruitful witnessing to the unsaved.

Finally, his warning against false teachers and doctrine is most applicable as our world slides into apostasy, with the dilution of the wholesome and biblically based faith of believers in Christ's Good News Gospel. It is the duty of every believer to stand fast in their faith and to give those of weaker faith as much help as possible to growth in their spiritual walk, by shunning all Satanic deviations from God's Word

II TIMOTHY—BOOK SIXTEEN

Realizing that his death was imminent, Paul wrote this 2nd letter to his 'beloved son' Timothy to 'pass the torch' of his ministry to his 'best soldier of Jesus Christ.' Imprisoned to, be martyred under Nero's reign of terror possibly under a charge of having burned Rome (to cover Nero's own crime), <u>Paul was lonely and cold in his dungeon.</u> Yet, he wrote this letter in 67 AD, to outline the course of action for a faithful servant of Jesus Christ <u>for a time of doctrinal and spiritual decline.</u> Paul urged Timothy to use all of his divine talent and courage as a faithful pastor to fight evil.

Paul was trying to instill great determination in Timothy to convey truths of Christ's gospel based on God's Word as written up to that time and to come, <u>apart from regional or denominational doctrine.</u> All that preachers of scripture, or witnessing believers do or say, should be completely founded on God's Word, or their <u>efforts will be little more than wishful thinking</u>, possibly erroneous or of no value.

These last words of Paul's, of wisdom and guidance, are just as applicable in this age for our Christian church, as they were when written to Timothy. Our lives would be enriched <u>if we adopted and applied the values and principles of this letter.</u>

<u>CHAPTER 1:</u> Identifying himself as an Apostle of Jesus Christ, as God willed, Paul greeted Timothy in verses 1-2 in his usual gracious way, with God-given grace, mercy and peace extended, <u>according to Christ' promise of eternal life.</u>

He wrote words of thanks and appreciation in verses 3-10, for Timothy's faith and commitment, for which he prayed as faithfully <u>as he had served God unceasingly.</u> Remembering a moment when Timothy shed tears of sorrow, Paul wished that he could visit with him again to rejoice over his Christian commitment that was <u>inherited from his grandmother Lois and mother Eunice.</u>

He urged Timothy to zealously use his spiritual gifts with the courage that God provides, <u>but with strength and love, in a sensible manner.</u> Timothy was not to be ashamed of Christ's gospel, or of Paul imprisonment, but he was to <u>let God's power work in him</u> to share the gospel, even if it brought suffering.

He was to remember that God's calling for him, as it was for Paul, had nothing to do with their personal preferences, but it <u>served the divine purposes and will of God.</u> This was demonstrated by Christ's suffering to bring an enduring light of truth and immortality to believers through His gospel.

In 11-18, Paul spoke again of his own commissioning as an apostle, preacher, and teacher, a task that brought him much suffering, for which <u>he had no shame or regrets.</u> He knew in whom he trusted, and was convinced that the Lord would preserve all the good that he had accomplished <u>to bring the gospel to the Gentiles.</u> He asked Timothy to let Christ's example be his teacher advocate to assist in sound sharing of the gospel <u>as inspired by the Holy Spirit,</u> and as given by Paul to him.

Paul spoke of two persons who had turned their back on him, probably for <u>fear of being imprisoned</u> as he was. He also asked God's mercy for Onesiphorus, and his family; this man had often uplifted Paul before and again when he came to Rome to spend time with him. He had been a big help with the church of Ephesus.

CHAPTER 2:   Paul compared a Christian to a soldier, an athlete, and a farmer in verses 1-7. In all these roles, endurance is a necessity, whether it be suffering and pain, winning or losing a contest, or extremely hard work to survive. In each capacity, one must be faithful to something, just as a Christian must be faithful to Jesus Christ to win the battle against temptation and sin, so as to reap the rewards.

As the soldier must be loyal and obedient to his commander, the athlete must abide by the rules for his sport and for physical fitness, and the farmer must conform to nature in the planting of good seed, cultivation for good growth, and harvesting at the proper time. Self-discipline is necessary in all cases! Also, doing the will of God, with patience, will contribute greatly to winning the prize for which we aspire.

In verses 8-13, Paul said that keeping his mind always on the resurrected eternal Jesus Christ, and the suffering He endured, made it possible for him to endure his imprisonment. He was willing to put up with his lot, as long as he could get Christ's message of salvation out to others. He used the words of a song to say we must suffer in Christ's death, endure in all things, not deny Him, and be faithful to obtain His favor and grace if we are to live and reign with Him.

In verses 14-26, Paul gave his views on what makes a servant of the Lord pleasing to God, or otherwise. Futile arguments over small matters should be avoided, but teaching the true message is most important. Discussion over worthless concepts are detrimental to a Christian's relationship with God. Everything should be on solid ground, the foundation of God's Word, if evil is to be avoided.

Paul used imagery of a large house containing gold and silver utensils, and some made of wood or clay, to represent believers faithful and useful in Christ's service, or those of little value which dishonor the Lord in their service. Removing or reforming the worthless servants adds to the fulfillment of the valuable effective servants. Christians are to be holy vessels in God's church, devoted in His service.

A strong Christian avoids the temptations of youth, by doing right in a loyal, loving, and leisurely way. Worship is best with people whose hearts are pure, whose views are sensible, who are good teachers in a kind and patient manner. We are to correct others who oppose us, in a humble and considerate way, hopefully so God will also help them escape evil as they see and understand what Christianity is all about.

CHAPTER 3:   Once again, in verses 1-9, Paul spoke of 'last days' as perilous, with evil men causing much trouble. For him, last days included the time elapsing from the writing of this letter to the 2nd coming of Christ, which he felt was imminent then, as it is now according to the views of many. The state of believer's preparedness is an individual's measure of time until Christ returns.

Conditions will become progressively worse, as mankind loves themselves and money more and more. Having difficult attitude and character traits, such as with vain pride, snobbishness, rudeness, and disrespect for parents, the younger generations will <u>become</u> <u>ungrateful, godless,</u> <u>heartless, and hateful</u> in their ways.

With no love for what is good, they will be sneaky, reckless, and <u>full of self- indulgence.</u> They will love pleasure more than God, even when professing religious beliefs. Men will seduce women lacking will-power to resist sin. All apostates will be like 2 Egyptian magicians, Jannes and Jambres, in their foolish opposition to truth. But the character and false doctrine of wicked deceivers <u>will be exposed in the end.</u>

In verses 10-15, Paul became personal with Timothy, as he spoke of his teaching to Timothy, his beliefs, his patience and love for him, and the trouble and suffering he had endured at Antioch, Iconium, and Lystra. Just as he had been rescued by God from trouble, anyone who is a follower of Christ Jesus will have trouble and will need divine protection.

Good men grow better in God's grace, and bad men in Satan's hands will grow worse. Sin is a down-hill slide, from bad to worse, <u>until the sinner turns to Christ.</u> It is never too late to do this, even on one's death bed.

Security for the Christian can be found in faithful adherence to the gospel, just as Timothy had learned from his grandmother, mother, and from Paul. All scripture is the product of the Holy Spirit, by the inspiration of the writer with divine truth, which <u>trains</u> <u>and leads God's</u> <u>servants to be masters of good deeds.</u>

Paul gave this classic scripture in verses 16-17: 'All scripture is given by inspiration of God, and is profitable for doctrine, for reproof, for correction, for instruction in righteousness, that the man of God may be complete, thoroughly (adequately) equipped for every good work.'

CHAPTER 4: In this final chapter to Timothy, Paul clearly wants him to carry on in the ministry as stated in verses 1-5. With God and Jesus Christ as his witnesses, he <u>commands</u> <u>Timothy to preach the word willingly,</u> and to help people see their sins and repent of them. He is to do this more so as people turn their back on God's message to listen to more <u>exciting</u> <u>and titillating religious concepts.</u> This will happen in the latter days of God's time table for humanity. Hard work in a calm manner, and through suffering, is the way to do the job well.

In 6-8, Paul spoke of his own short time, in which his life would be taken as if <u>poured</u> <u>out as a sacrificial offering to the Lord.</u> With great satisfaction, he said, 'I have fought a good fight, I have finished the race, and I have kept the faith.' How wonderful it would be for every person to feel this way about their service to God. He was looking forward to that crown of righteousness which Christ, as a righteous Judge, would award him on reunion day, after the <u>resurrection of the dead in Christ.</u> Every believer can earn rich rewards for faithful service to God!

As Paul once again expressed a desire to see Timothy in verses 9-15, he <u>commented on</u> <u>those who had left him</u> for one reason or another, Demas for one had returned to Thessalonica to indulge in worldly pleasures. Only Luke remained in Rome to be a trusted comforting friend. Paul sent coworker Tychicus back to Ephesus, hoping that Timothy would then come to him, with Mark, and bring a warm <u>garment and some books and manuscript he had left</u> there.

Paul commented on the harm that a man named Alexander had caused him, at some previous time in Ephesus, as indicated in I Timothy 1:20 and Acts 19:33. He may also have testified against Paul before the Roman court. Paul considered him to be very detrimental to the spread of the gospel.

In verses 16-22, Paul spoke of Christ's support of him at his trial, just as during his time of ministry, to deliver him from evil and danger, and praised Him for doing so. He closed with greetings to fellow believers, and a prayer for God's spirit and grace to be with Timothy. He also pleaded for him to come to Rome before winter.

SUMMARY: It is somewhat significant that near the end of his life, Paul had a dim view of the future spiritual condition of this world. He spoke of growing tribulation, immorality, and false Satan inspired religious doctrines which will oppose God's Word. His message to Timothy and all believers down through the ages was to resist in the strength of the Holy Spirit, and in the truth of God's Holy Word, the Bible.

His admonition and words of encouragement to Timothy were somewhat like a last will and testament bequeathing a rich inheritance to the chief beneficiary. His dying wish was that Timothy carry the banner of Christ as faithfully as he had. Oddly, scripture does not reveal what Timothy accomplished after Paul's death.

In his waning hours, Paul craved the company of his dearly beloved son, Timothy, but there is no evidence that he returned to Rome. As learned as he was, Paul also wanted his scripture texts and manuscripts, no doubt to receive inspiration from them. This is a need for all Christians, to help them stay focused on their walk with the Lord, and to resist the ways of the world, especially reptile apostasy.

Finally, Paul conveyed the message that if we do our best to stand holy before God, that He will stand by us, strengthening us in difficulties and dangers, and being present always to more than supply all our needs.

TITUS—BOOK SEVENTEEN

Titus was a convert and faithful young Gentile coworker of Paul's for about 15 years, assisting him much the same as Timothy. He was sent to Corinth twice where he effectively dealt with some church problems. At the time of this letter, he was assigned by Paul to further evangelize the people on the island of Crete, south of Greece.

It is believed that Paul wrote this letter to Titus personally, before his 2nd imprisonment in Rome, some time after writing I Timothy, about 64-65 AD. The letter was intended as guidance and instruction to help Titus deal with the Cretans, a rough sea-going mixture of 'liars, crude beasts, and lazy gluttons,' as characterized by one of their own people.

Some Cretan Jews had been present in Jerusalem, when Peter spoke on the Day of Pentecost, as related in Acts 2:11, and they may have planted a primitive gospel faith at Crete. Paul may have visited the island several years after his 1st imprisonment release. However it happened, the gospel was planted on 'rough ground.'

The main themes in this letter are: good works, purity, kindness and service to others, and proper witnessing of the gospel to the unsaved.

CHAPTER 1: Paul's greeting verses 1-4, to Titus, his 'true son in their common faith,' was given as a servant and apostle of Jesus Christ, in the knowledge of divine truth leading to righteousness, for the sake of His believers. He said that his service was based on his certainty of eternal life for believers, as God had promised from the time of creation, and as he had also preached. He extended his wish that grace, mercy, and peace from God and Jesus Christ be upon Titus.

In verses 5-9, Paul clarified that he had left Titus at Crete to select and appoint responsible and qualified leaders (bishops, elders, deacons), to better organize churches. Qualifications that he cited were: outstanding character, marriage to only one wife, thoughtful of others and slow to anger, self-restrained with wine, faithful to the gospel message, having obedient children faithful to the gospel, and an able teacher of the word. This yardstick is equally suitable for pastors in today's churches!

In 10-16, Titus is to silence or countermand the false views of the usual Jewish dissenters, called Judaizers elsewhere, who tried to dishonestly profit monetarily by upsetting the faith structure of the local churches. It is here that Paul referred to the Cretans as liars, greedy and lazy as wild animals. Paul instructed Titus to resist and put to shame these false witnesses, by preaching true doctrine from the gospel.

He pointed out that the pure of heart would recognize purity and live pure lives, while unbelievers with a corrupt viewpoint would not know purity, even though they claimed to know God. As hypocrites, they would deny and reject Him in their way of life. Such were disobedient, worthless, and unqualified to be church leaders!

CHAPTER 2: Verses 1-10 gives Paul's views on the desired qualities of a strong church. Pastors are to preach from sound doctrine, older men are to be level-headed, faithful, loving and patient, and older women should be the same, and not gossip or be addicted to wine, so they will be a good example for teaching of younger women.

Senior ladies should teach the younger women to be good faithful wives and mothers, good homemakers, and supporters of their husbands, so as to glorify God. Young men are also to be serious-minded, in all ways being a good example to their peers, demonstrating honesty, respect for elders, godly character, and proper language, so that the less wholesome have no reason to find fault, and may reform themselves.

Titus was to exhort slaves to be carefully obedient to their masters, courteous and honest, so as to honor God's word in all ways. If the master is an unbeliever, he could be influenced to become a believer and be more charitable to his servants.

In verses 11-15, Paul explained how God's grace can improve quality of life for believers, as they turn from evil and worldly temptations, to live godly lives. In so doing, we are filled with justified hope (trust) that we will be acceptable to Christ as one of His elect when He returns. He paid the price on the cross in the desire that we be saved from sin and then strive to live righteously for Him.

Titus was to teach these precepts diligently, rebuking those who would stand against his doctrine, and thus earn the respect of his church.

CHAPTER 3:   Paul gave instruction to Titus in verses 1-11 on how to have a good relationship with those elected or appointed to positions of governing, all other people, and false teachers. He is to tell the Cretans to get along with rulers and others in authority over them, and do their best to cooperate in kindness and understanding.

They should also be kind and helpful to people in their community, friends and neighbors, even though they may not be believers, prone to sinning. In this regard, all believers should remember their own past faults of stupidity, disobedience, jealousy and hatred, and other sins of lust and desire. This helps us to be patient with unbelievers over their sins, and to be more understanding with fellow believers who need help to restore their spiritual standards.

Our conduct and willingness to do good is to be based on the goodness and mercy that Jesus Christ demonstrated while on earth, and the influence of the Holy Spirit, to give us a fresh start in life. Christ did more for us than we deserve, by making us acceptable to God, for eternal life with Him.

These truthful teachings are helpful to everyone. Paul wanted the Cretans to abide by them to overcome their inconsiderate ways with good deeds for others. He told Titus to avoid stupid arguments with the Jewish people (Judaizers) who put great stock in their genealogies, and adherence to the Mosaic Law. Conflicts over such issues were a waste of time and senseless. Troublemakers were to be warned several times and if they did not desist in their ways, then Titus was to shun them, because their minds would be warped by evil.

Paul stated that he planned to send Artemas or Tychicus, so Titus could come to Paul at Nicopolis, his winter abode. He asked Titus to help 2 men, Zenas and Apollos, prepare for their return—they probably delivered this letter to Titus. Paul felt that believers should always do useful and worthwhile things.

He closed with greetings, including his coworkers, to all believer friends in Crete, with a prayer for <u>God's kindness to all of them.</u> In brotherly love, Paul showed affection for these believers, and his desire for good to come to them, with God's grace to be the essence of what is good, for <u>fruitfulness in their faith walk in Christ.</u>

<u>SUMMARY:</u> It is clear Paul wanted Titus to do his best to temper the crude and somewhat rebellious nature of the Cretans They were not to be quarrelsome, but they were to show meekness and consideration on all occasions, not only toward friends, but to all men, and <u>with wisdom in every way performing good deeds</u>.

No credible evidence exists to confirm any visit by Titus with Paul after receiving this letter. It may be that Paul's arrest for his 2nd imprisonment prevented it. But in II Timothy 4:10, Paul stated that Titus had gone to Dalmatia (north of Greece, in modern day Yugoslavia and Albania), <u>presumably after putting things in order</u> at Crete. It is possible that Titus visited Paul in prison on his way there.

PHILEMON—BOOK EIGHTEEN

Philemon was a wealthy member of a church in Colosse, who may have been converted to Christianity during Paul's ministry in Ephesus. Paul considered Philemon to be a 'beloved fellow laborer in Christ.'

He owned a slave, named Onesimus, who had robbed him of money and fled to Rome, where he somehow met Paul, who was then imprisoned his first time in 60-61 AD. Onesimus became a believer under Paul's persuasion, and evidently endeared himself to Paul, who convinced him that he should return to Philemon and make amends for his crime, no matter what the consequences might be, even death.

Paul wrote this courteous, tactful letter to plead for mercy, asking Philemon to receive and forgive Onesimus, as he would have welcomed Paul himself. He offered to pay any damages caused by Onesimus. There is no biblical clue as to how Philemon treated Onesimus, when he returned in the custody of Tychicus who delivered this letter, as indicated in Col. 4:7-9.

Paul opened the letter, in verses 1-7, as coming from himself, a prisoner of Christ Jesus, and his coworker Timothy, with greetings to beloved Philemon, Apphia (his wife?), and Archippus (son or church elder), and other believers, in the grace and peace of God and Jesus Christ.

He thanked God for Philemon's Christian character of love and faith, which was effective in serving Christ Jesus. He and Timothy received great joy and consolation from Philemon's ministry to the saints under him.

Verses 8-21 constitute Paul's appeal to Philemon on behalf of 'son' Onesimus, that he had adopted as a brother in Christ, who he wished could stay to comfort him in prison, with ministry help too. However without Philimon's consent, he could not do so, because it was the slave master's decision how to deal with a runaway slave, hopefully with kindness to Onesimus.

Paul suggested that Onesimus may have been induced to run away so he could return in the Lord's will, more as a brother of faith than a slave deserving punishment. Paul said, 'If I am your friend and partner, take him back as you would receive me, and whatever he owes you, I will pay.' (Even though Philemon owed Paul for his spiritual salvation) He validated this with his own writing.

He asked Philemon to give him refreshing joy in the Lord, with confidence in his response, and asked him to prepare a guest room for his visit, which Philemon's prayers could make possible.

His farewell words included Epapras, as a fellow prisoner, and 4 other coworkers including Luke, with a prayer for Christ's spirit of grace on Philemon.

SUMMARY: Paul's gracious letter avoided any pretense of a direct request to Philemon to give Onesimus his freedom, rather than suffer the possibility of death, or the branding of an 'R" on his forehead, that was customarily done to runaway slaves. Paul clearly appealed to his Christian principles out of faith and love for the Lord.

Paul appealed on the basis of his own love, rather than his authority, to give Onesimus credit for being useful to him in prison, even though he was of no help during his absence, to his master Philemon, but he could now be more useful.

Hebrews is a mystery book in itself, according to some scholars, who contend that the author, the recipient, and the time of writing cannot be clearly determined from biblical <u>or historical data</u>. They say consensus is not possible, as an examination of many biblical publications produced a wide divergence of opinion or speculation.

Many think Paul was the author, even though the style, vocabulary, theology, and other writing attributes <u>differ somewhat from his known writings</u>. The Greek version of the original book manuscript represents the Greek language <u>as used by highly educated and cultural Greeks of that day</u>, and the Hebrew version is described as polished, deliberate, and lacking in emotional expressions characteristic of Paul. In 2:3, the writer identifies himself as one who had not heard the gospel of salvation directly from Jesus, whereas Paul presented himself as <u>one who had received the word from Christ.</u>

Some think the author may have been Luke, Clement of Rome, Barnabas, Apollos, or Priscilla. Of these, Luke appears to be a logical candidate since he spent much time with Paul, and he may have <u>collaborated with Paul on the writing</u>. He was the only one with Paul during his 2nd <u>imprisonment in Rome in 67-69</u>; Luke also had the education and Greek background to put Paul's dictation into the language used in this book. He also admitted that he had to rely on the witness of others for the truth of Christ's message. The ending of the book in Chapter 13 is <u>typical of Paul's style,</u> including greetings from believers in Italy as stated in verses 24. There are 2 other clues in this chapter that identify Paul with some authorship of the book.

The book may have been written during the years 67-68 AD, the time most commonly <u>thought to be reasonable</u>. Speculation over the 1st recipient of this book includes a church in Rome, with another receiving it later. Most scholars believe it was written to Jewish Christians because of the book's frequent <u>referrals to Jewish topics</u> from the Old Testament. If it was written from Rome, then it would most logically have been written to a church somewhere else, perhaps in Corinth. From the language used, the recipients faced severe persecution that tested their faith to the point where they were <u>tempted to deny being a Christian to avoid suffering</u>.

Encouragement to the beneficiary church also stresses the superiority of Jesus over Judaism. Since Jesus had suffered as they may have, and was tempted as they were being tempted, He could best sympathize with their weakness and help them ably. The recipients were also <u>urged to remain faithful in the midst of their suffering</u>, by giving them examples of others who remained faithful through suffering. The book emphasizes the supremacy and sufficiency of Christ over all things!

For this commentary, authorship of the book will be credited to Paul, with the able assistance of Luke as the actual writer.

CHAPTER 1: Without any form of greeting in verses 1-4, Paul wrote of God's superiority and supreme revelation as spoken through prophets of old, but now <u>through His Son, Jesus Christ.</u> Having created the universe through Him, God has also made him an heir of all things in the last days. Jesus mirrors the brightness of God's glory and appearance, plus His power, wisdom, and mercy. Jesus, being superior to all the angels, <u>now sits at the right</u> <u>hand of God</u>, His inheritance for giving mankind a doorway to salvation.

The remainder of the chapter, verses 5-14, gives the reasons why Christ is greater than God's angels. Many Jews had a special respect for angels, because they had received the law and other guidance from them in Old Testament days. They credited them as mediators between God and man, and <u>some were inclined to show them a manner of religious homage</u> <u>or worship.</u>

Some quotations from the Old Testament were used to convince the reader that Jesus, as the Son of God, was <u>superior to any angel.</u> The sum total of these references —Psalm 2:7, 45:6-7, 89:27, 110:1, and 103:20—points out that God considered Jesus as His Son, for <u>angels</u> <u>as servants of God to worship,</u> for Jesus was instrumental in creating the earth and heavens, and He will reign as a divine King over His own kingdom—as the Anointed of God.

On the other hand, angels have not been invited to sit at God's right hand, because they are to <u>serve believers who will inherit eternal life</u> in Christ's kingdom. Even Michael, a most exalted angel, is a ministering spirit, a servant of Christ, to execute His commands. Angels will gather all the saints together for Christ's joy.

CHAPTER 2: To what may have been an immature spiritual audience, Paul warned of waywardness from the gospel they had heard. When truth directions from God through His angels, as heard in Old Testament times, were rejected and disregarded, God <u>brought</u> <u>punishment as deserved.</u> So now, if Christ's divine message of salvation is refused, how much more likely it is that punishment will come. This is an alarm bell to the consciences of sinners, that neglect in accepting divine direction–even though partial, <u>will bring a</u> <u>measure of rebuke</u> <u>and divine discipline</u> for the besmirching of the soul before it is brought to ruin.

Christ gave us the message of salvation, which has been carried to the unsaved by his evangelists and apostles, including those who first witnessed and heard Him, <u>with the help of</u> <u>the Holy Spirit,</u> and the miracles and wonders He performed. Luke admitted his own reliance on those who first heard the message.

In verses 5-9, Christ's relationship to mankind and the angels of heaven is more clearly defined by a quotation from Ps. 8:4-6, which refers to the original estate of Adam. Most important is this statement—that God <u>will not put the endtimes kingdom under the</u> <u>rule of</u> <u>angels</u>—Christ will be the sovereign king!

Christ in His human form, was made a little lower than angels during His earthly time, just as is true for all humanity. But God <u>rewarded Him with unlimited dominion over</u> <u>all things,</u> when He suffered humiliation and death on the cross for mankind. Christ is <u>now</u> <u>at a level far</u> <u>above that of angels,</u> in honor, glory, and power.

In his omnipotence, as stated in verses 10-13, God did a marvelous thing when He perfected His Son Jesus through suffering, so that mankind could become God's children through Jesus. This means that all believers, together with Christ, are <u>members of God's</u> <u>family;</u> therefore Christ can call them 'Brothers' or 'Sisters.'

Using Ps. 22:22 and Is. 8:17-18 as references, Paul said that Christ will present all believers to God, in complete trust that He and His children will be acceptable to God. Then Christ and believers <u>will be of one heavenly Father, our God.</u>

Verses 14-18 tells us that Jesus became one of us, a creature of flesh and blood, and <u>suffered a human death so He could defeat Satan</u> and give His saved children victory over death. His help was for mankind, not the angels, and therefore He <u>had to become a man in human form,</u> but with a sinless nature, to become our intercessor and atonement for our sins.

He paved the way to heaven for mankind!

CHAPTER 3: For the edification of Jewish believers, Christ is presented in verses 1-6, as a <u>superior personality in the eyes of God.</u> This was to offset the high regard the Jews had for the faithfulness of Moses, who in reality was just a type of Christ. Both were extremely faithful to God, but Jesus deserves more credit than Moses because He became Lord and Master over the Christian church, as God's Son, whereas Moses was <u>merely a faithful</u> <u>servant member.</u> In effect, Christ became the builder of the church, our spiritual residence as long as we trust our Landlord, while <u>Moses did nothing more than lay the foundation.</u>

Using Ps. 95:7-11, Paul exhorts his audience in verses 7-15, to hold fast to their faith in God and the salvation plan He provided through Jesus Christ. Jewish believers were <u>warned not to harden their hearts against His word</u> in the manner of the Hebrews in their 40 years of wilderness wanderings. Many exceeded God's patience and thus suffered His wrath unto death, without arriving in the promised land.

Vigilance is necessary to prevent disbelief which separates one from God, <u>all need support from fellow believers,</u> the weak more so than the strong in faith. This is a day by day need, lest sin creeps in to harden the heart. Saints of God have His Holy Spirit to fortify their spiritual stance in the grace, righteousness, and glory of Jesus Christ, and all that He has done, or will do for His church. <u>This position in Christ must be maintained until He returns</u> to claim His own. Christians are to endure!

In 16-19, the focus returns to the Hebrews in the wilderness after their rescue from slavery in Egypt under the leadership of Moses. To the question, 'Who were they?' (or Why did it happen?) the answer given is that they were the <u>people who angered God for 40 years,</u> who died in the desert for their sins, who were denied entry into the land God intended for them, all because they lacked enduring faith and obedience. Christian have the joy of being heirs of Christ's salvation rest, the fear of God's wrath without it, and <u>motivation to persevere in a life of obedient faith.</u>

CHAPTER 4: God's promised salvation rest, through Christ's obedience on the cross, is the theme of verses 1-10. The promise is for an indefinite time, until Christ <u>returns to gather His own,</u> those who have believed and kept the faith. Christians of today must heed and believe in God's word, and <u>not turn their back on it</u> as did the Hebrews of old, which closed the gate to heaven for them.

Just as God finished His '6 day's work of creation,' and rested from it on His 7th day, so may <u>believers enjoy their day of rest as Jesus Christ appears</u> in the clouds to redeem His own. Gen. 2:2, and Ps. 95:7-11, clarify that entry into God's rest is not automatic, for <u>unbelievers</u>

have no passport to it, since they lack the required belief and enduring faith in His promises, through Jesus Christ, to be admitted.

The 'day' of repentance, is the day that sinners receive God's <u>Passport to Heaven!</u> Although Joshua finally led the Hebrews in to their 'promised land,' it did not constitute a 'day of rest,' <u>as Christ will provide to all believers</u> of His church, on 'that day' when He comes in glory.

In 11-13, Paul urged diligence to be ready for 'that day,' for which all mankind can qualify, by <u>becoming a faithful and obedient believer</u> on this earth, before Christ returns.

On that day, mankind will be tested by God's living and powerful word, sharper than a double-edged sword, as it <u>penetrates to the depth of our souls.</u>

Christ is portrayed as our heavenly High Priest in verses 14-16, qualified to intercede for us <u>by virtue of His own experience in the form of a man,</u> being tempted as a human, but not having yielded to sin. This gives humanity a ready source of understanding help during times of need, to receive undeserved mercy and grace.

CHAPTER 5: Qualifications for a Jewish High Priest are briefly stated in verses 1-4. Since a high priest represents men before God, he must be a human selected by God, having the normal weaknesses of mankind so he also has compassion for those he serves. He must make sacrifices on his own behalf before doing so for the sins of others. He cannot elect to become a priest of his own will, he <u>must be anointed by God as Aaron was,</u> otherwise he may suffer death as related in Numbers 16.

Likewise, as stated in verses 5-11, Christ was selected by God to be our High Priest, as confirmed by Ps. 2:7 and 110:4, in the likeness of Melchizedek (king of righteousness) of Gen. 14:18-20. Having been born of the tribe of Judah, Christ <u>could not be compared to a</u> <u>Levite priest.</u>

At the end of His earthly time, Christ prayed passionately to God to spare Him the agony of the cross, and although God heard Him, it was <u>God's will for Christ to suffer death</u> as an act of obedience. By doing so, Christ's perfection was confirmed, and He became our High Priest <u>to save all who would obey and come to Him.</u>

In 11-14, Paul felt he could say more on this subject but it might be pointless to do so, as his audience was somewhat dense in their understanding. For the time they had been believers, they <u>should have been teachers by now</u> instead of in need of a refresher course. They were like a baby feeding on milk instead of solid foods suitable for a mature person, who knew right from wrong. Being slow of understanding makes one a poor listener, a shortcoming of even those of some faith.

The solid spiritual food of the gospel is what mature believers should have, to fully <u>challenge their discernment of right and wrong.</u> They are the ones to win victories in the service of the Lord.

CHAPTER 6: Paul contended in verses 1-3, that a truly mature believer must go beyond the basics of his faith, to grow spiritually and become more effective in his faith. We should <u>not need frequent reminders of sins to be avoided</u> that endanger our faith in God. This growth should not be associated solely with concerns over true repentance and baptisms, the laying on of hands, resurrection from death, or endtimes judgment. God desires for us to continually grow spiritually, by striving to comprehend and conform to all of His Holy Word.

In verses 4-6, Paul raised the matter of losing the gift of salvation by turning away, rejecting all that had been learned and understood about Christ, with heartfelt enmity towards Him and His believers. The statement is made that those of this category cannot be renewed again, to be eligible for salvation through Christ.

A Christian is compared to farm land on which sufficient rain falls to produce a good crop, but without enough rain, a crop of thorns and briars is grown. A Christian receiving good spiritual nourishment from God's Word, will be fruitful and blessed; the lack of spiritual food will bring nothing of value and God's displeasure.

Paul reassured his 'beloved' in verses 9-20 of better results ahead for them based on their Christian status, that God would remember their good works done in His name, from their ministry to other committed believers. He urged them to not be lazy in their spiritual walk, but to imitate those (Abraham) who inherited God's promises through genuine faith and patience.

As great as God is, He still made a promise to Abraham on the strength of His own name, just as mankind does when a vow is made or an argument is settled, by taking an oath based on a higher authority, such as God's Holy Bible. God's promises and vows are irrefutable because He does not tell a falsehood.

The believer's faith in Christ is secure like an anchor in a storm, giving us a sure hope and stability in our Christian walk, to gain the salvation He prepared for us. God's promises to faithful believers are in accord with His purposes as ordained by Him, His Son, and the Holy Spirit. We have a refuge to flee to for the mercy of God, with forgiveness of sins purchased by Christ's redemption. God's Word is also a firm anchor in the storms of life. Therefore we should set our affections on things above, and by waiting patiently for His appearance, we shall be with Him in glory.

VIEWPOINTS: The correct interpretation of verses 4-6 is debatable and in dispute. Some scholars insist that these verses speak of someone who is a professing Christian, appearing as such in the public view, who has learned much about God and Jesus Christ from scriptures, but has not experienced a Holy Spirit infusion of true faith and commitment to live a life pleasing to God. This may be someone who conforms to Christian living for the sake of appearances and public esteem, without truly yielding to the will of God and Holy Spirit guidance and direction.

On the other hand, the use of phrases such as, 'who were once enlightened,' 'tasted the heavenly gift,' 'became partakers of the Holy Spirit,' 'and have tasted the good word of God,' (6:4-5) seems to speak of a truly deeply committed believer. To say that it is impossible for these to be saved, if they fall away, puts the onus on the clear meaning of 'falling away.' Scriptures in the book of John (John 3:16, 18; 5:24; 6:37, 39, 40; & 10:27-29) give the impression that all who believe in Christ as their personal savior, who hear God's word and believe in it, who believe that God has given Christ ownership of true believers, and that nothing can take a believer away from Christ, is definitely and unequivocally saved for eternal life with Him. The assumption must be made that a believer in this category has not 'fallen away' from his beliefs completely, although <u>allowance must be made for stumbling</u> in the faith, or backsliding through weakness.

The Hebrew's criterion appears to encompass a total willful rejection of God, Christ, and the Holy Spirit, after a period of spiritual relationship akin to that of a believer, as an action <u>without any concern for the consequences</u>. It is a turning of the back, with anger, hatred, scorn, and other negative feelings, brought about by something drastic, and induced by Satan. It is total irrevocable apostasy towards anything pertaining to Christianity, with a hardening of the heart to stone against God.

In the final analysis, only God and Jesus Christ will know who is or is not a <u>true</u> <u>believer</u> <u>worthy of spiritual salvation</u>. When Christ returns to separate the sheep from the goats, mankind will also know the truth of one's spiritual nature. All who relish eternal life with Christ, should diligently <u>adhere to God's Word without fail!</u>

CHAPTER 7: As related in Gen. 14:17-20, Melchizedek, a high priest and king in the type of Jesus, is extolled in verses 1-10 (see 5:10-11, for a previous mention). No record is given of his birth or death, <u>making him a representation of Christ</u>, whose existence is forever. In the time of Abraham, as a priest greater than the Levites, he received tithes as the 'king of righteousness, or peace,' and blessed Abraham's victory.

In verses 11-19, Paul contended that a superior high priest like Melchizedek, rather than one from Aaron's Levitic priestly family, was <u>needed to bring a lasting reconciliation</u> between <u>mankind and God.</u> Our Lord and Savior Jesus Christ, from the tribe of Judah, is identified as that better High Priest (Ps. 110:4).

Christ holds His office by the power of endless life in Himself; giving spiritual and eternal perfection to all who rely upon His sacrifice and intercession, thus <u>replacing the</u> <u>limitations of the Mosaic Law</u>. This better covenant in Christ brings the church and every believer into clearer light, with more perfect freedom and privileges. It adds <u>safety and</u> <u>happiness in the life of the believer</u>, for this everlasting High Priest is able to save to the uttermost, in all times and situations.

God appointed Christ with a lasting promise in verses 20-28, when He appointed Christ as our High Priest, giving us assurance <u>that it was forever</u>. A better relationship with God is thus guaranteed when we come to Him through Christ. Jesus is the right kind of High Priest, since He is holy, innocent of sin, and faultless in His love for us. Unlike the Levitical priests, He does not need to make sacrifices to God for Himself or our sins, <u>because He gave</u> <u>Himself</u> <u>as our sacrifice on the cross.</u> He is always available to us, with ready forgiveness when we fall short of the mark. He is the strength we need to endure!

CHAPTER 8: This chapter presents the new Christ given covenant as far superior to <u>the</u> <u>inferior Mosaic Law covenant</u>. As stated in verses 1-6, Christ does not occupy an earthly man-made tabernacle (tent) but sits at the <u>right hand of God on a heavenly throne.</u> In the time of Moses, earthly priests were of the tribe of Levi, of which Christ was not, but they served as a copy of Christ, the supreme High Priest to come; they performed on earth in a manner <u>equivalent to what Christ would accomplish</u> from heaven.

The sacrifices and gifts offered by Levite priests have been replaced by Christ, who as a human gave Himself to God as a sacrifice to atone for the sins of man; now we are <u>acceptable to God only through His Son, Jesus Christ.</u> The blood sacrifices of old were replaced by Christ's own blood on the cross.

The Mosaic Law covenant proved to be flawed because mankind could not live up to it's intended purpose, it <u>made nothing perfect</u> because of man's sinfulness. Verses 7-13 describe the new covenant which God promised to give nearly 700 years before Christ, in Jer. 31:31-34, to the house of Israel and of Judah, a covenant far <u>different than the one they</u> <u>received when they were led out of Egypt.</u>

The new agreement was not written on stone, but it will be <u>inscribed on the hearts and minds of believers;</u> they will be transformed internally as they have an ongoing spiritual relationship with God, through Jesus Christ and the Holy Spirit. They will learn of Him, and get to know Him through the reading and preaching of the <u>gospel from His Holy Word, the Bible</u>.

Continual sacrifices of animals will not be required to atone for sins, because <u>Christ became the ultimate sacrifice</u> for all mankind, who will be forgiven their sins as they repent of them and turn away from them. Forgiven sins will be blotted out, as each sinner becomes a believer with a true knowledge of God.

All this, because the old covenant is outdated, on the shelf, to only be used as a reference to understand how much better the new covenant is for sinful man.

VIEWPOINTS: The new covenant promised in Jer. 31 was related to the people of Israel and Judah. One should not think it was thus <u>limited to God's chosen Jewish people.</u> In his epistles, Paul made it clear that the rejection of Christ by the Jews opened the door of <u>evangelization to the entire Gentile world,</u> and therefore the new covenant of Christ applies to everyone, whether Jew or Gentile.

CHAPTER 9:   The earthly place of worship and the protocol of atonement for sin, under the Mosaic Law, is summarized in verses 1-10. The house of God was a tent or tabernacle <u>erected and arranged according to God's blueprint,</u> with 2 main parts, separated by a veil. The outer room (holy place) was where regular priests perform daily rituals, and the inner room (the Most Holy Place) where only the High Priest (Aaron at time of Moses) would enter once a year to offer a blood sacrifice for himself and for all others, to <u>obtain forgiveness of known and unknown sins</u>. The tabernacle, as a movable temple, typified the undetermined state of churches on earth.

Access to God by an individual was non-existent, for the priests represented everyone, including themselves. The Israelites in general could go no further than the outward forms of worship, which <u>could not take away the defilement or dominion of sin.</u> Now, under the new covenant, all believers under divine teaching and inspiration of the Holy Spirit, can find easy access to God, for communion with him, and be <u>assured of admission into heaven</u> <u>through the Jesus Christ,</u> as the Redeemer, who atoned for their sins with His own blood.

The better way is the theme for verses 11-14, through Christ as our High Priest, who resides in an eternal holy place, where repeated blood offerings of animals is not necessary, because of His <u>one time sacrificial offering of His own sinless blood.</u> He fulfilled the once a year atonement for sin by the Levite High Priest through His year around presence in heaven (the Most Holy Place), which believers can <u>access through faith and prayer</u> for forgiveness of sin on a 24 hour daily basis.

Christ's once-for-all atonement provided an open path to eternal redemption, <u>not merely a temporary cover up of sins</u> once a year, as under the old covenant. We cannot begin to comprehend the depth and height of the mystery of Christ's sinless sacrifice, but by faith, we can know that guilt over sin can be cleared from our consciences through cleansing by the Holy Spirit, so <u>we can better serve God.</u>

In verses 15-22, Christ became the Mediator of the new covenant, on behalf of sinners before God, so that we may receive <u>an inheritance of eternal life with Him.</u> In the life of man, a Last Will and Testament is nothing more than a piece of paper, until the testator dies; it <u>becomes legal and binding after death.</u> In like manner, Christ had to die in order for mankind to become beneficiaries (heirs) of His estate, and for it to become <u>transferable</u> <u>under the new agreement.</u>

Under the old covenant, much animal blood was sprinkled in many ways to attest to the binding effects of the old law for the remission of sins, for a limited time. Under the new covenant, Christ's blood alone provides the <u>blessings of salvation with a blotting out</u> <u>of forgiven sins.</u> While we are all guilty of sin before God, He has mercifully provided forgiveness, when sinners come to Him with repentant hearts.

How great was Christ's sacrifice? Verses 23-28 shed light on that question. Most important, Christ's presence in the life of a believer is not founded in a temporary earthly abode, but it exists in an <u>eternal heavenly tabernacle offering ready access to Him, as</u> He intercedes before God to obtain forgiveness of our sins. His one-time earthly blood sacrifice was a complete year around substitute for all the old covenant repeated blood sacrifices. As the Sinless One, His death in human form was not for judgment, rather it earned Him the role of judge and redeemer at His 2ⁿᵈ coming, to <u>save all of His faithful believers that eagerly</u> <u>await him.</u>

CHAPTER 10: The writer pictured the Mosaic Law to be a shadow of the new and better covenant, in verses 1-18, with one great shortcoming—the <u>animal blood sacrifices did not remove sins</u> but merely reminded people of them on an annual basis.

In Ps. 40:6-8, David prophesied that Christ's perfect sacrifice would be <u>manifested by His 1ˢᵗ coming in human form.</u> It reads as if Christ spoke to God before His crucifixion, to say that He was a willing substitute, as God willed, <u>for animal sacrifices which were no longer pleasing to God.</u>

By offering Himself as a one-time sacrifice, in obedience to God's wishes, Christ <u>made our righteousness possible,</u> with a reward of eternal salvation in His kingdom. Christ's way is better than that of temple priests repeatedly offering sacrifices that did not remove sin. Reference is again made to Jer. 31:33-34 (see Ch. 8) to confirm that the Holy Spirit predicted this new covenant would be <u>enacted as an effective way to overcome sin.</u>

The scope of all that Christ has done for his people, in the sovereign will and grace of God, <u>is replete with eternal power</u> in the enduring salvation option His sacrifice purchased on Calvary. His one-time sacrifice has made spiritual pardon a gift <u>available to all nations, ages, and ethnic groups,</u> to escape God's wrath judgment on the wicked preceding Christ's millennial reign.

Verses 19-25 give encouragement to have an interest in Christ's salvation gift, to accept it by faith, and receive it as a seal on our souls by the sanctification of the Holy Spirit, so we may know that we are <u>justified by forgiveness of sins which God will erase from our</u> record. Then we are to live in a godly way with pure hearts, a conscience free from evil, and a public demeanor as if <u>freshly washed with pure water.</u>

Most important is that we regularly encourage one another with thoughtful and helpful deeds and words at worship services, and elsewhere. With the gospel being written in our hearts, we can know that we are justified, with sins forgiven, <u>unto that day when Christ returns to take us home.</u>

With language similar to Ch. 6:4-6, in verses 26-31, Paul warned of the unsaved status of those who choose to <u>keep on sinning after realizing the truth</u> of God's Word. This 'falling away' sin involves a total rejection of Christ, resistance to the call of the Holy Spirit, repudiation of the gospel and Christ's message of salvation, <u>in effect blaspheming God in every way,</u> all with determined will and resolve. Such will suffer God's wrath as enemies burned by fire, just as Numbers 15:30-31 ordained <u>judgment for the Hebrews who violated</u> Mosaic Law.

In verses 32-39, the writer encourages the believers to recall the suffering they endured after their spiritual conversion, as they were mistreated in public, and when their property was taken away. In all this, <u>they still had compassion on those in prison,</u> which may have included the writer according to some bible versions.

They were told to be brave and patient so as to receive God's pleasure and rewards. Scripture from Hab. 2:3-4, is paraphrased to assure the believers they <u>would be rewarded when Christ returns,</u> as long as they lived by faith, or died in the faith. Paul was confident that those believers would persevere in all ways, and that <u>Christ would return soon,</u> as he stated several times in his writings.

CHAPTER 11:   The entire chapter is about faith with examples of Old Testament men of faith who exemplified the meaning of the word. Faith is defined by Webster's Dictionary as:

'Confidence or trust in a person or thing; a belief not substantiated by proof; spiritual acceptance of truth or realities not certified by reason; and belief in God, and doctrines or teachings of a religion.'

In verses 1-3, what faith produces is a certainty, or conviction, of <u>the truth of something not visible or tangible.</u> Men of old pleased God with such faith. By faith all Christians believe in God's creation of earth and life in all forms, even though <u>we do not know how, or when, or from what it was made.</u>

In a spiritual sense, faith is an inner persuasion or expectation that God has done everything that has been, is now, and what will be; <u>based on promises in His word and as given through Christ Jesus.</u> Faith is a form of proof of the reality of what the human eye cannot see, and <u>acceptance of all that God provides or promises,</u> as being holy, just, and good.

Verses 4-11 identify 5 Old Testament people in whom faith was the key to their <u>godly holy obedience, remarkable achievements, and patient sufferings</u>. They are as follows:
- Abel: who pleased God with his 1ˢᵗ offerings as stated in Gen. 4:3-5
- Enoch: pleased God, and was translated directly to heaven in Gen. 5:22-24
- Noah: built an ark, saved his faithful family from a flood, Gen. 6:13-22
- Abraham: moved to a strange land to face hardship, Gen. 12: 1-10
- Sarah: conceived and gave birth to Isaac in her old age, Gen. 21:1-7

These saints of old died without losing confidence in God and His promises, as stated in verses 13-16, even though <u>they did not receive all of them</u> as they may have expected. The best promise of an eternal rest with God will be their ultimate reward for faithfulness, <u>which was their hope while still alive.</u>

More examples of great faithfulness are given in verses 17-31, beginning with Abraham's testing and obedience to God as he <u>proceeded to sacrifice Isaac, which God canceled.</u> Isaac blessed his sons Jacob and Esau, Jacob blessed Joseph's 2 sons, and Joseph provided food for his family and was later buried with his father in Canaan.

Moses, by faith chose to forego a life of ease and wealth as the adopted son of Pharaoh's daughter to <u>lead his own Hebrew people out of slavery from Egypt</u>. By faith, the Hebrews followed him through the Red Sea water corridor, which God closed to drown the Egyptian pursuing army.

The walls of Jericho fell after a faithful march of Joshua's army around the city for 7 days. The harlot Rahab was spared death when she helped Joshua's spies.

In verses 32-40, Paul asked, 'What more can I say? If I had time, I could tell of Gideon, Barak, Samson, Jephthah, David, Samuel, and the many prophets, all who through faith won battles, brought justice where needed, overcame lions, put out fires, and escaped battle wounds.' They <u>overcame weakness with divinely given strength</u>. Some women had the life of a loved one restored; some of the faithful were tortured, jeered, flogged, chained, and imprisoned. Others were stoned, cut in two, killed by the sword, suffered poverty without adequate clothing or food, and live in caves and holes in the ground in mountains or on deserts. The world treated them unkindly!

All these faithful ones pleased God, yet <u>none received what had been promised</u> before they died. This was because God had something better for mankind, and He did not want saints of old to reach the full reward of their faith apart from all mankind,.—the <u>coming of Christ with His salvation gift</u>, and His many earthly and heavenly blessings for believers.

May all believers constantly pray for an increase of their faith, that they may equal or surpass the historic examples cited above; and join them, perfected in holiness and happiness, to <u>shine like the sun in the kingdom of our Father for eternity.</u>

<u>CHAPTER 12:</u> Paul invited his audience church in verses 1-11, to jointly run the marathon race of life with a faith <u>equal to the heroic example and tenacity of the Old Testament saints</u> enumerated in the previous chapter. For the necessary endurance to win, the believers must be stripped of unnecessary baggage, sins which are an <u>anchor against steady progress and incentive,</u> or a weak faith which is out of focus with the objective of the race. Determination to gain a victory is supplied when we keep in mind the lesson given to us by our divine Savior Coach who endured the suffering of <u>death on the cross to win a big one for all mankind</u>—the salvation award. The church at that time had not yet suffered bloodshed for their sins.

As any good coach would do to help his aspiring runner, or a parent would do to set a child on course, God will <u>discipline to correct and perfect those that He loves,</u> when they are off their game or walk of life. As children of God, we are not to take such correction lightly, but we are to be <u>persistent in our efforts to respond positively.</u> God corrects us for our own good, just as a parent does, inflicting pain at times, always <u>for the purpose of obedience</u> <u>leading to a good outcome</u>. His correction is for our profit, out of love, since He <u>does not grieve or afflict us without a purpose</u>.

Exhortation and warning were combined in verses 12-17, to urge believers to shape up spiritually to renew their faith, to keep on track without injury, to win peace and holiness, and <u>to qualify for God's grace</u>. In this way, they would avoid bitter conflicts in their fellowship, and be <u>on guard against poor examples of faith</u> like Esau, who traded his birthright for just one meal. Later, his tears would not recover his loss.

In verses 18-24, the church was reminded that they had been spared the terrifying sight of Mount Sinai, aflame, or covered with dark clouds or heavy storms, from which God's awesome trumpet sound and commanding voice boomed out. This was <u>more than the</u> <u>Hebrews of the exodus could endure</u> as they received the Mosaic Law; they and Moses shook with fear at the sight and sound of it all.

In contrast, the Christian church addressed by Paul was now before Mount Zion, a heavenly Jerusalem, surrounded by angels and the spirits of God's redeemed children. They were also before God and Jesus, <u>to receive a new and better covenant,</u> far better than what Abel had between him and God.

In verses 25-29, the church is exhorted to obey divine authority under the new covenant, else <u>they would suffer punishment as those before God at Mount Sinai</u>. When He spoke then, it was to shake the earth for a short time, but His next anger with wrath judgment will shake both heaven and earth, to <u>remove the dross of wickedness</u>. Only the steadfast in Christ will endure to that coming event, and be <u>part of God's unshakable kingdom.</u>

Believers should be grateful for the grace they receive through the Good News gospel of Jesus Christ, so they are <u>able to serve God with reverence</u>. Yes, God will be a consuming fire, but Christ is our safe haven from His wrath.

CHAPTER 13:   Paul encouraged the church to excel in doing things that would please God in verses 1-9, as an <u>expression of their faith in Him</u>. Believers were to be concerned about each other, make strangers feel welcome in their homes (this could include angels), show kindness to God's own in jail, help the suffering, respect and honor marriage vows with fidelity and true love, and avoid greed for money or material things.

We are to be satisfied with what we have, and not fear what others may do to harm us, <u>for the Lord is our helper</u>. Spiritual leaders in authority should be respected, assisted, and obeyed. We must keep in mind that 'Jesus never changes.' He is forever the same, as in the past, today, and in the future, and we are not to be fooled by teachings that <u>deviate from our understanding of Him</u>, as given in God's Word.,

Our strength should come from our dependence on God's kindness more than from the kind of food we eat. Feeding on a diet of stability and God's grace is <u>far more nourishing</u> than <u>worldly food</u>, for our spiritual growth.

Under the new covenant, in verses 10-19, believers have a convenient altar for worship without the intervention of a priest other than Jesus Christ, who intercedes for us directly <u>as we beseech Him for mercy</u>. Just as the bodies of animal offerings were burned outside the Hebrew camp, Christ suffered death outside the city gate, and that is where Christians should worship, apart from ceremonial rites in the tabernacle of the old covenant. At His exclusive altar, we should praise God in the name of Jesus, as we willingly <u>separate ourselves from worldly distractions and wickedness</u>.

More admonition for believers includes helping others by sharing materially, as if <u>making a sacrificial offering to God</u>, and obeying and giving church leaders satisfaction as they show concern for a believer's soul, for their <u>happiness in service is part of their</u> motivation. Prayers are essential to keep servants right with the Lord! Paul again asks for prayer so he can soon visit his brothers in Christ, just as he <u>desired at the end of</u> <u>Philemon</u>, verse 22, and as he hoped in Phil 1:25-26.

Paul's comments and benediction is typical of language used in his other books, including the words 'grace' and 'peace.' Here he prays for God to equip the church to do everything to please God, through their faith in Jesus Christ, and <u>by heeding his words of</u> <u>exhortation.</u>

Then he mentions that Timothy had been released from prison, and if he came to see Paul (II Tim. 4:9 & 21), <u>they would visit the church together</u>. Greetings from those in Italy with him were extended to all of the recipient church.

SUMMARY: Paul's request for prayers so he could visit the church to which he wrote, (similar to comments in Philemon and Philippians), also as <u>tied in with the visit he hoped Timothy would make to him</u>, and the greetings from those in Italy, add more credence to my conclusion that Paul was the author behind this book, very likely with Luke doing the writing in his own style.

Admonitions to this church to adhere to their faith in Christ to better serve God, and his exhortations on <u>how to live as Christians pleasing to God</u>, is also very much like what he wrote to the other churches. His language is tailored as advice to Jewish Christians by his references to <u>Old Testament beliefs and covenant principles,</u> most likely to a church in Macdonia or Greece.

His encouragement to remain faithful through suffering was given by <u>examples of</u> <u>Old Testament saints</u> who were able to endure by means of their steadfast faith. History was used to teach a lesson in bravery by faith to a new generation. How marvelous it would be if our modern generation of believers and pastors would make more of an effort to do the same for our younger generations.

JAMES—BOOK TWENTY

James is believed by most authorities to have been written by James, the half brother of Jesus, to Christian Jews in general throughout the Roman empire. Some biblical references suggest that it was written early in his role as the chief apostle to the Jerusalem church, dating it as early as 48 AD. Others think it was written much later, perhaps shortly before he was martyred in 62 to 66 AD.

The theme of the book, in his practical expression of faith, is that Christianity must manifest itself in works superior to those of the world. He also promoted principles of conduct for pastoral leadership relating to ethical standards of early Christians. This included the best and proper response to temptations and trials, treatment of the poor and administration of wealth, controlling a wayward tongue, avoiding conflicts and peaceful attitudes between Christians.

Some of his views have provoked concern, such as his argument that "faith without works is dead" (2:17). This on the surface contradiction to the teaching of the apostle Paul has caused consternation, even with Martin Luther who referred to the book as "an epistle of straw" when compared to Paul's writings.

Nevertheless, the book of James has lasting value and consequence to the Christian confronted by an increasingly secular world. He preached that Christ ought to make a difference in one's life, as true today as ever in the past.

CHAPTER 1: Getting to the point quickly, unlike the Apostle Paul, James introduced himself in verses 1 as a servant of God and Jesus Christ, writing to Christians of all Jewish tribes scattered outside of Palestine.

In verses 2-8, he tells the brethren how to deal with trials of life. The first remedy is to have joy over the testing of their faith, which will produce patience with endurance to the end when blessings can be counted. That is when maturity arises, a type of spiritual perfection, which enables the Christian to ward off troubles to finish the race of endurance. Our prayers should be for wisdom to benefit the most from it.

Any request to God for help should be with complete faith, without doubts, that He will provide what is necessary to come through. If one is mentally whiplashed, requests to God will be nothing more than a wind driven wave washing out on shore.

Verses 9-11 contrast the poor with the wealthy in terms of spiritual attitude and reality. The poor brother is more likely to rejoice in spirituality as heirs of God's mercy, and be thankful for small benefits that add comfort to life, while the wealthy man might find joy when humbled by circumstances which reveal that God is more important than his wealth, and possibly lead to better use of wealth to help the poor.

How to deal with trials and temptations is the gist of verses 12-20. Out of His manifest love, God's eternal life reward comes to those who resist temptation with love in their hearts for Him. We must not blame God for temptations towards evil, because God has nothing to do with evil, and will never tempt us with it. He may allow us to be tempted by Satan, for the purpose of strengthening our faith, as occurred in the life of Job.

It is weakness of character, our personal desires of the flesh, and our inherited sin nature, that leads us into sin and misery, and deadens our spiritual wisdom in God.

James urged his friends to know that all good and perfect gifts originate with God, just as He provided the illumination that comes from the sun, the moon, and the stars, which are for a believer's benefit. It was the will of God that these Jews became Christians through the truth of Christ's gospel, in order that they could be more fruitful in spreading the faith to the unsaved. As the sun is to life, God brightens the life of man with His grace, mercy and blessings. His unmatchable gift of eternal life with all its holy, happy consequences, gives us reason to be first-fruits to others.

A word about hearing and obeying during trials and temptations is given in verses 19-27. Believers should be alert to what they hear, prudent in their speech, and slow to anger; letting tempers flare interferes with whatever good Gods wants to bring about. With the saving gospel implanted in our meek hearts, we can better separate ourselves from the wickedness of this world.

Believers are to obey His Word, not hear and ignore it! When we hear and ignore the word, we are like persons who look at their image in a mirror, and then forget what they look like. The person that looks at the word of God that can liberate from sin, and heeds it by comprehending and obeying, will receive divine blessing in all things.

All who profess to being a Christian, but let their tongue say unwise and harmful things, demean their faith. Everyone has faults which should be corrected by the word of God, which when given to humble and teachable minds, makes it possible for a level of perfection to be attained patiently and most thankfully.

Our religious faith will be pleasing to God, if we keep ourselves untainted by the evil of this world, and do good things, such as helping orphans and widows in their time of need and distress. Studying and heeding the scriptures turns our spiritual nature towards good deeds for the less fortunate, with genuine love and charity in our hearts. Having a faith that fosters love, purifies the heart, and subdues carnal lusts, brings eternal rewards from our Heavenly Father.

CHAPTER 2: James gave advise on the relationship of faith to impartiality and good works towards others in this chapter. In verses 1-13, he belittled the value of faith when partiality is shown on the basis of outward appearances, wealth, social status, influence, or other superfluous characteristics.

Just as God and Christ show no favoritism between persons, whether rich or poor, a Christian should do likewise by treating everyone as equals. The wealthy nicely dressed person who attends church should not be given open deference while a poorly dressed person is relegated to second-rate hospitality. Based on the inherent character of the two persons, partiality to one could be a gross judgmental error.

Partiality often goes contrary to God's inclination to give the poor an enriched spiritual life, because they tend to be dependent on divine providence more than the wealthy person, who looks to his wealth for the qualities of life. The wealthy all to often oppress the poor for selfish gain, and ridicule them for their religious faith.

To avoid the sin of partiality, believers must comply with God's most royal rule to, 'Love your neighbor as yourself!' <u>Failure to do so constitutes a sin,</u> and even though it may seem like a minor sin in our eyes, it equates to the violation of all God's laws, including adultery and murder. The believer should conduct themselves in accordance with God's rules, so as to <u>avoid His judgment for disobedience of them.</u>

The negative view James had of spiritual faith which is lacking in good works in verses 14-26, seems to go against Paul's teaching in Romans 2:28, and Galatians 2:16, that man is <u>justified in his faith apart from good works.</u> James implied that true faith in Christ will manifest itself in an open demonstration of love and caring for others who need help; but if such good works are missing, one's faith is not fruitful, <u>as good as dead.</u> Fruitless faith is not pleasing to God—workless faith is worthless faith!

Suppose 2 people believe there is only one God, and one says, 'Because I do good deeds, I have true faith in God,' but the other might say 'I can have true faith without doing good works.' This foolish one should remember Abraham of old who willingly <u>put Isaac on a sacrificial altar in obedience to God</u> (Gen. 22), as living proof of his faith. His faith was justified by his actions, to earn God's pleasure and blessings.

In like manner, Rahab, the harlot of Joshua 2:1-21, pleased God when she acted on faith to <u>save men of Israel from death</u> at the hands of the enemy. James concluded that as a dead body does not breath, so faith without action is dead. By faith, what we do good in obedience to God, is the <u>fruit of a well rooted and spiritually fed faith.</u> Where there is no fruit, the root may withhold nourishment and be as if dead! What every believer should covet and attain, is a faith that produces <u>good fruit through acts of love and kindness</u> as the Holy Spirit directs.

CHAPTER 3:   James gave a rather lengthy dissertation in verses 1-12, on the proper and controlled use of the tongue. He warned at the beginning that <u>not everyone should become a teacher,</u> because they are judged more critically than others for what they say. Only those who are mature in their self-control are qualified to teach.

Using 3 ordinary examples, James gave analogous ways to control the tongue. A small bridle bit in mouth of a large horse provides direction control, by using a small rudder a sail ship captain can override the direction of strong winds, and a very small flame can ignite a huge forest. Although a tongue is a small part of a large body, it too <u>can cause a wayward conduct, big waves, and hot fires.</u>

Out of control, the human tongue can throw the affairs of mankind into utter confusion, creating <u>havoc as if a fire from hell.</u> A tongue can be restless and evil, as if spreading deadly poison. No person can tame the tongue without Divine grace and assistance from the Holy Spirit. In this respect, humans are not like animals, birds, reptiles, and creatures of the sea that can be and have been tamed.

Our tongues can speak both good and bad things, from <u>praises to God to curses against His created images.</u> How is it possible that the tongue can be so diverse? In contrast, a spring does not gush forth both clean and dirty water, and a fig tree does not produce olives, nor does grapevine produce figs.

James' view that the tongue is uncontrollable should not be so construed. Yes, it can be difficult, but it is not impossible; a proper and <u>controlled use of the tongue is possible</u> where there is a sanctified heart, committed to Christian principles and respect for God's rules of conduct.

The key to tongue control is a healthy dose of wisdom from our heavenly Doctor Jesus, as implied in verses 13-18. We must be humble, free of bitter jealousy and selfishness, and honest in every way. Bragging or lying to conceal the truth is not a God given trait, but it comes from Satan, to often cause cruelty and trouble. Wisdom from above <u>leads a believer to be pure of heart and mind</u>, friendly and gentle, sensible and sincere, helpful and kind, and true blue in manner and personality. Such persons plant many seeds of peace, and reap a rich harvest of justice and joy.

May our lives confirm the gift of heavenly wisdom in all of our actions and the use of our tongue, with <u>diverse fruits of righteousness forthcoming to bless others.</u>

CHAPTER 4:   In essence, James asked if man should live as the world does or as God desires of all humanity. Citing the consequences of worldly living in verses 1-10, in terms of strife, selfish desires, covetousness, and prayers for selfish reasons, James admonishes <u>prayer and godly purpose of the right kind to overcome sinful conduct.</u>

Being a friend of the world makes one an enemy of God. God cares about the spirit He implanted in our human bodies, but He will oppose us when we do as the world does, and withhold blessings reserved for the humble in spirit before Him. James commanded his brethren to resist the devil, and to cause him to depart, <u>by submitting to God in a close</u> personal relationship with pure hearts and clean hands.

Submission to God in a contrite spirit can turn laughter into tears of remorse and sadness over sins of life, but <u>God does a wonderful job of restoration.</u> He does not withhold comfort when a sinner grieves, or blessings to the humble before Him.

In verses 11-17, James gave some 'do nots' for the believer. We should not speak evil of a brother, or judge him unfairly and unjustly, <u>because God alone is the authorized judge</u>. By this, James does not rule out a system of justice for the purpose of maintaining law and order in a governmental system. Neither does he rule out corporate discipline in a church body, as exercised in accordance with biblical truths.

Finally, he reproached those who brag about grandiose plans and schemes for personal gain in the future—for who knows what tomorrow will bring? All our plans should be conditioned by this concession to the Lord, 'If He lets us live, we hope to do such and such.' Anyone stupid enough to brag about hoped for achievements without the blessing of God, has too much vain pride, and in that vein can sin.

All that we plan, and all that we do, <u>should be with submissive dependence on God.</u> It is foolish and harmful to boast of worldly things and aspiring projects; the outcome can be much disappointment, and even dismal failure in the end.

CHAPTER 5:   James voiced a vicious indictment against the wealthy in verses 1-6. Historically, Jews have been looked upon as the unscrupulous rich of society, partly because of their exceptional talent to produce wealth, but also because of their all too often <u>inclination</u>

to take unfair advantage of employees or the less fortunate. Evidently, the churches James addressed had a number of these types.

In categorizing their riches as corrupt, their fine garments as moth-eaten, their jewelry as corroded, James was implying that their accumulated idolized wealth was worthless because the return of Christ was imminent.(as Paul also believed). For this reason also, judgment awaited them because they had short-changed wages of field worker's and other employees, while they enjoyed living it up without concerns for the poor. Just as the Jews brought about the death of innocent Jesus to justify their own vanity, James accused the rich of persecuting and murdering innocent people, probably by destroying their opportunities for improvement in their own quality of life.

Patience, perseverance and integrity were advised on verses 7-12. Believers are to be patient as they await the return of Jesus, just as a farmer awaits a good harvest, during months of expectation for adequate moisture. Grumbling against one another during times of trouble can earn punishment, or loss of rewards, in the endtimes judgment of man.

We have the example of the prophets who suffered persecution, just as Job endured, but who received God's compassionate mercy on earth and for eternity. In faith, we should serve God, to the best of our ability, as He helps us with our trials, believing that the end will bring us crowns of glory.

As for integrity, James advised his audience not to swear, which appears to refer to profanity, or attesting to truth of something by taking an oath based on a worldly or frivolous value, that may even be idolatrous. Profanity is a sin, because it usually shows contempt of God's name and authority. As for taking an oath to attest to a truthful testimony in court or to bind a legal matter, if it is sincerely and truthfully rendered in the name of God, it is hard to label it as sin. In taking an oath, we must not take His name in vain however, as that would be sinful.

Meeting specific needs through fervent prayer is prescribed in verses 13-18. Suffering physically or spiritually, for health reasons or committed sin, or when in trouble of any kind, prayer for the mercy of God in His will is an effective remedy. It is essential that faith be exercised when one is afflicted, to receive the balm of God's grace. When one is happy and cheerful for lack of troubles, praise the Lord as if singing.

When severely sick, James advised enlisting the intercessory prayers of the elders and saints of the church, with the anointing or application of oil in the healing name of Jesus. The prayer of faith is what really heals in this case, but the oil is symbolic of the Holy Spirit and therefore can do no harm. Along with such prayers, it is always wise to ask for forgiveness of sins, known and unknown. Our prayers should be as earnest and strong in faith as the prayers of Elijah for no rain and then for more rain. (I Kin. 17:1 & 18:1, 42)

In closing, James exhorts believers in verses 19-20, to do their best to restore backsliders or to save sinners, because this is like saving a life, and the pleasure it gives God is translated into blessing for the good Samaritan.

SUMMARY: With the exception of the somewhat arbitrary conditions that James placed on his views for perfection in the life of a Christian, his advice is suitable and applicable for

<u>Christians of this age</u>, as much as it was in his time. His advice was intended for hard-headed Jewish Christians who sometimes tended to revert back to Judaistic principles.

His unequivocal condemnation of faith without works in 2:14-16, words against swearing in 5:2, and instructions to apply olive oil when praying for the sick in 5:14, can be misconstrued as to meaning and application. Charitable works is not always possible for the new believer, or the poor believer, because their <u>faith is not sufficiently matured by the Holy Spirit </u>to be inclined to such actions.

Taking an oath on the Holy Bible, in the name of God, is a modern practice in Christian circles, and as such seems appropriate since the <u>oath is related to the highest supreme being in our Christian faith.</u> As for the application of oil (anointing), when praying for the sick, many denominations do this primarily as a demonstration of their faith in the healing power of Christ and God. If may also <u>enhance the faith of the sick person for whom prayers are rendered.</u> It is hard to see anything wrong with this practice!

I PETER—BOOK TWENTY ONE

Peter, an early disciple of Jesus Christ, and later an Apostle for the Christian church in Jerusalem and Judea, wrote this book much later to Christian Jews and Gentiles in Asia Minor, during a time of growing persecution under Nero's rule of the Roman Empire about 64-67 AD. There is speculation that he may have written it from Rome, shortly after Paul's execution in 66-67 AD, but this most logically applies only to II Peter.

The letter was written to strengthen the resolve of Christians to endure the persecution by non-believers in the hope that Christ, who suffered much, would soon return to rescue them. He admonished the brethren that suffering has a purpose, it must be expected and borne patiently, with rejoicing as much as possible for the Lord's intervention. He referred to Christ's return about 6 times, to give the believers more hope for survival.

Silas (Silvanus), who also assisted Paul on some of his writings, may have also assisted Peter in the writing of this part of his letter, which Silas then carried to the intended churches, possibly those in Galatia, Ephesus, Colosse, and Philippi.

Historical data gives credence to the martyrdom of Peter in Rome shortly after Paul's death. Tradition is that he was crucified upside down, because he did not see himself worthy of being crucified normally as Christ was hung on the cross.

CHAPTER 1: After his greetings in verses 1-2, to the 'Pilgrims of the Dispersion' (scattered believers), in 5 different locations, chosen by God—sanctified by the Holy Spirit— to serve Jesus Christ, Peter wishes them God's abundant grace and peace.

With praises to God and Jesus Christ, Peter spoke of the heavenly eternal inheritance believers can expect in verses 3-12. Through faith in God, more precious than gold, and with His gift of endurance, all believers will rejoice in their reward when Christ returns to claim His Own. Until then, we are 'strangers in the world.'

Even though these believers had not seen Jesus, and He would remain invisible to them, Peter commended them for their faith and love of Jesus. This gave them great joy in their well-grounded hope of salvation, also serving as a vital stimulus of obedience in their soul. In the unity of God's glory and our own godliness, this hope of salvation renders our soul free from the bondage of sin.

Jesus Christ was the primary concern of the prophets of old, as they studied and pondered the predicted sufferings of Christ and the salvation He would provide to mankind. As they strove to determine who the Messiah would be and when He would come, they realized that their efforts were to benefit future generations rather than themselves. It would lead to a gospel of salvation through the sacrificial death and resurrection of Christ.

In verses 13-25, Peter emphasized how these early believers were chosen by God to live a holy life in spite of suffering and tribulation, just as all believers down through the ages would experience. With a disciplined mind, purposefully alert to all spiritual hazards and enemies, and in total dependence on God, we are to maintain a strong and constant trust in God and Jesus Christ, remembering His adage, 'Be holy, because I am holy.' We are to remember that God will judge us fairly according to our works, nevertheless, we are to fearfully obey Him.

Early believers were rescued from the aimless and confusing way of life of their ancestors, not by perishable silver and gold, but <u>by the precious blood of Jesus Christ.</u> Even though He was ordained to come to earth, even before creation, He did not come until God willed for Him to bring salvation, with restoring hope in God, as He desires in faithful believers.

By obedience to the truth of the gospel, their souls became purified, and they were <u>filled with a new quality of love for one another</u> that would last as long as God's word endured in their hearts. Not as grass or flowers pass away, but durable as His Word, which is explained further in Chapter 2.

CHAPTER 2: To mature as a Christian worthy of God's mercy, Peter said in verses 1-3, that character flaws of evil intentions, deceit and hypocrisy, slanderous language, and envy, should be put aside, and <u>replaced with a spiritual thirst for the Word of God,</u> as a baby craves pure milk. God's nourishing Word provides spiritual growth and development!

In verses 4-10, people are to become believers in Jesus Christ, even though He was rejected by His chosen people. As God's precious Son, He became <u>highly honored as the Cornerstone of the Christian church,</u> into which believers are united as 'living stones' into the priesthood (servant and witness) of an everlasting temple. Though the framework of the world falls to pieces, the person who is part of this structure can bear <u>persecution without fear or disappointment</u> in the Christian life. True Christians are a chosen generation, members of God's family, distinctly <u>apart from the world in spirit</u>, <u>principle, and practice.</u> They are to be a 'light of redemption' to the unsaved.

To those who are not believers, the rejecters of the Cornerstone, and thus not part of this enduring structure, Jesus is <u>more like a stone over which they stumble and fall</u> in their disobedience. From their world of gross darkness, God wants them out of it, to come <u>into a state of joy, pleasure, and prosperity;</u> that they may be filled with praises of the Lord in their acknowledgment of His holiness and saving grace.

Peter reminded believers in verses 11-17, that they are more like foreigners visiting earth, until they arrive at their eternal home, and therefore they <u>should not succumb to</u> <u>the evils of the world</u> that endanger the soul. Christians must endeavor, at all times in all circumstances, to behave as God desires, and remember that they are servants of God. They are to be <u>worthy examples of righteous living,</u> to honor God and be acceptable to Jesus Christ when He returns.

Included in this good conduct is obedience to civil authority and appointed justices of earthly laws, and in so doing, give stupid and ignorant people no reason to complain. <u>Respect should be shown for everyone,</u> especially for fellow believers, and thus God is honored by our example.

Since a large portion of the Roman population, as much as one-half, were slaves, Peter exhorted the believers among them to be submissive to their masters in verses 18-25, whether masters were good or cruel. <u>Blessings would accrue to them,</u> just as Christ was honored and blessed for His obedience under God's plan. Just as He suffered, believers can expect to suffer, but our perseverance and <u>endurance earn God's pleasure and mercy.</u> Christ was brutalized and crucified as a sacrifice for our sins, and by His wounds and death our spiritual healing was made possible. God gave Him to us (lost sheep) as a watchful and caring Shepherd.

CHAPTER 3:   As a married man, Peter was well qualified to give advice to husbands and wives <u>on a proper marriage relationship,</u> as he did in verses 1-7. Wives are to give their husbands first consideration, so that if he is an unbeliever, her treatment may win him to the Lord. Her example of Christian living and her inner beauty can<u> influence her husband in a positive way.</u> The outward beauty of fine attire, jewelry, makeup, and fancy hairdos is not as important as the inner qualities of a gentle and calm spirit. Sarah is cited as an ideal wife, for she respectfully called Abraham 'lord' and was<u> totally submissive to him.</u>

Husbands are to be understanding of their wife's needs and emotions, respectful of her authority in the home, and <u>give her safety and trust.</u> A man should live with his wife as a partner in the blessings of life, obtaining peace through prayer together, to <u>maintain sweetness in their union.</u>

Peter had a word for believers in general in verses 8-17, that love with understanding, kindness and caring <u>be at the center of their relationship with one another.</u> As God's chosen ones, He will bless us with kindly virtues that <u>contribute to a happy life with love for others.</u> With God watching over us, who can harm us for our good deeds. We are to put aside fear and worry, and let the will of God deal with those who give us trouble.

Courteous responses to questions about your faith position will <u>cause others to be more respectful</u> about your conduct as a child of God. Suffering for doing right in God's view is preferable to suffering for doing wrong.

In verses 18-22, Peter reviewed Christ's suffering for sinful mankind, wherein He <u>gave His life to reconcile us to God.</u> His comment that Christ went to preach to spirits in prison is difficult to understand and explain. The most plausible meaning is that Christ's spirit communicated somehow to the unbelievers of Noah's day, during the 120 years of ark construction. These souls were spiritually imprisoned by their rejection of Noah's message, just <u>as the Jews were who rejected Christ's Good News gospel</u> when He lived on earth. Christ's offer of a 2nd chance was/is His great gift to mankind!

The 8 members of Noah's family were saved from drowning during the year they spent afloat on the ark, symbolically as <u>water baptism confirms our faith in a living Christ,</u> who was saved from death to now reign over angels, authorities and powers in heaven at God's right side. Their temporal salvation in the ark on top of the water typifies the eternal salvation of true believers through baptism of the Holy Spirit, to <u>float the believer above</u> the sins of the world.

CHAPTER 4:   Peter continued his dissertation about the suffering of Christ, and it's effect on the faith of believers, in verses 1-6. Just as Christ suffered, we too must suffer in our effort to avoid sin, with the <u>objective of living in God's will.</u> As sinners, we waste good time apart from God, when the sins of the flesh, immorality, boozing and partying, and even forms of idolatry <u>becoming a barrier to righteousness.</u>

After a conversion, unsaved friends may wonder what caused the sinner to become a believer, to forsake sins of the past, and <u>they may revile the new convert.</u> God will judge them for this wickedness and their rejection of the Good News gospel of salvation, as <u>preached to all who were spiritually dead.</u> The new convert wins!

In verses 7-19, Peter spoke of the suffering believers would have to endure until the return of Christ, which he portrayed <u>as an event to happen soon,</u> much as Paul did. To endure, Christians are to pray earnestly for strength, show love and support for one another, be a welcoming host to strangers, and <u>use God given gifts to serve Him better.</u> Whether it be speaking, charitable deeds, or whatever else that honors the majesty of God, it should be <u>done in the example of Jesus Christ.</u>

Peter again warned the believers to be prepared for trials and tribulation, which they would suffer through <u>until Christ's 2nd coming, to save His Church</u> from God's wrath on the wicked of the world. Such suffering is really a blessing because it identifies the believer as a chosen child of God, to His glory. It is better to suffer in this capacity than to suffer for the sins of murder, theft, other crimes, or being a general troublemaker.

Peter expressed the view in verse 17, that God's day of judgment was just around the corner, when the believer will be held accountable, and the wicked are doomed to eternal hell. He did not imply that the Christian Church body will be raptured at a separate and remote time from when the wicked will be judged—but the sheep and the goats will be subjected to His examination, <u>for acceptance or rejection, in close proximity to Christ's 2nd coming.</u> The faithful in Christ who suffer as God wills, should trust in Him as the Creator of all, <u>in the knowledge that He will judge them fairly.</u>

CHAPTER 5: Identifying himself as an elder who had witnessed the sufferings of Christ in verses 1-4, Peter encourages the church elders (deacons, pastors), to willingly <u>shepherd their flock of believers so as to please God,</u> and share in Christ's glorified 2nd coming to redeem His own. When they do this according to God's will, and not for personal gain, but as good examples to the believers, they will have also <u>earned everlasting crowns of glory.</u>

The young people are exhorted in verses 5-11, to obey church leaders in sincere humility before God, so they will be <u>honored also when Christ returns.</u> They are to give their worries over to God, be on guard to withstand the temptations of Satan, keep the faith through suffering that comes to them, and be <u>happy as God's kindness encircles them.</u> Christ is the source of perfection, confirmation, strengthening in the faith, and stability in life for all young people aspiring to be a beloved child of God.

Peter closed with word that his faithful brother in Christ, Silas (Silvanus), had assisted him in writing this portion of his epistles, which was conveyed with greetings from the church in Rome (also called Babylon), and his son in the faith, Mark. He asks his audience to <u>greet</u> one <u>another with a kiss of love, in the peace of Christ.</u>

SUMMARY: This letter is remarkable for the many times it refers to a believer's lot in life before <u>Christ returns to give them something better,</u> namely eternity with Him. There are 9 different remarks pertaining to suffering, trials and tribulations that Christians must endure for their faith. <u>In at least 6 locations, these are related to the 2nd coming of Christ</u> to end their time of endurance, and in no case is it implied that Christians will be spared much before God's endtimes scenario of judgment upon the wicked begins.

Clearly, this epistle was written at a time in history when Christians came under increasing persecution from atheist Roman leaders, Nero in particular, for the purpose of encouraging them to <u>keep their faith no matter how difficult life became</u>.

Today, the situation in the world is no different, Christians are maligned regularly in many lands, and severely persecuted in some, to a point where some might wonder where God's protection has gone. We must remember that God's Word warned this was coming!

It is incumbent upon pastors, priests, deacons, elders, and others in positions of leadership and spiritual guidance, to <u>encourage their fellowship of believers constantly</u> to stand firm in their faith against these mounting troubles of life.

Clearly, tribulation days are filling our calendars more and more, signaling that the time of Christ's return is definitely nearing. After all, about 1925 years have passed since Peter and Paul both considered His coming to be near.

II PETER—BOOK TWENTY TWO

The importance of a steadfast faith in the face of <u>increasing apostasy from false teachings</u> is the main theme of this short book of 3 chapters. In Peter's day, false teachers were peddling their own brand of religious beliefs, a practice that has reoccurred many times up to this age, and will continue until the end of time.

Peter was accepted somewhat belatedly by church councils as the likely author, perhaps with the help of Mark. There is general agreement that it also was <u>written from</u> <u>Rome about</u> <u>67 AD</u>, shortly before Paul died as a martyr, and was written <u>to a specific</u> <u>Gentile church</u> that Peter knew was afflicted by false teachings.

Scholars have speculated on the similarity between this letter and Jude's epistle. That in itself <u>does not invalidate the scriptural relevance of either letter</u>, as the two writers may have been together from time to time to reach agreement on pertinent subject matter.

<u>CHAPTER 1:</u> The faithful are greeted in verses 1-4, with Peter's identification as a servant and apostle of Jesus Christ. He equated with his audience as being one with them in their <u>righteous faith in God and Jesus Christ.</u> He wished them abundant grace and peace according to their knowledge of God and Jesus, which increased their faith, and <u>brought forth to them</u> <u>God's promised divine power</u> by which to escape corruption prevalent in the world.

In verses 5-16, Peter encouraged further diligent growth in their faith, with the addition of virtue, knowledge, self-control, perseverance, godliness, brotherly kindness, <u>and</u> to all these—love. This healthy package of spiritual nourishment can give the Christian clear <u>identity and</u> <u>productivity in service to God.</u> Lacking these qualities, a believer is shortsighted, virtually blind, and without appreciation that past sins were forgiven.

Peter adjured the brethren to diligently strive to do their best to walk persistently in <u>the</u> <u>path God has set before them</u>, which will eventually lead to a triumphal entrance into God's everlasting kingdom to be with our Lord and Savior Jesus Christ. This was an appeal to make their salvation a certainty!

Even though he recognized their knowledge of these truths, Peter declared that he would not neglect to remind them repeatedly, so <u>they would not forget</u> what he told them after his death. This he did as Jesus had told him to do.

Peter assured them in verses 16-21, that what he had preached to them about the power of Jesus for holy living and His later coming in glory, <u>was not the spinning of fictitious or</u> <u>fanciful tales.</u> He described his own eyewitness experience, including hearing God's words which <u>conveyed special honor and glory on Jesus,</u> 'This is my beloved Son, in whom I am well pleased,' This was a proclamation from heaven when on the mountain with Jesus (possibly Mount Hermon, see Matt. 17:1-5).

Peter emphasized that his personal witnessing, as well as that of others, <u>confirmed the truth</u> <u>of prophecy about Jesus,</u> which is a light in the darkness of ignorance, until the daybreak of some future day when Christ returns in full glory. Since no prophecy originates with man, it must be received as <u>divinely inspired by the Holy Spirit in chosen men of God.</u>

CHAPTER 2: This entire chapter (as in Jude 4-16) is about false teachers, their destructiveness, their depravity, their deceptions and their fate. In verses 1-3, Peter warned that false teachers <u>are found everywhere</u> (as Jesus warned in Matt. 24:4-5), bringing their distortion of biblical truths into the Christian church, sometimes for monetary gains. Peter urged the church to always guard against corruption from within. He feared that many weak believers would succumb to blasphemy, <u>and go down the primrose path of destruction</u> with the false teachers.

Peter cited several Old Testament accounts of wickedness being punished in verses 4-11. He spoke of the fallen angels (Gen. 6:1-6) who were consigned to chains in the pit of hell, the <u>doom of a sinful civilization except for Noah's family</u> in a world flood, the burning of Sodom and Gomorrah for gross immorality, and the related deliverance of Lot from a homosexual culture.

He contrasted this judgment record to God's ability to deliver the godly from temptations, while <u>keeping His foot of restraint on the wicked</u> until judgment day. Here Peter added special emphasis on the wickedness of homosexuals, who have a <u>fearless disregard for divine doctrine on sexual purity</u>. While angels, endowed with heavenly power and strength, do not revile these promoters of false virtues, these evil doers do not hesitate to revile divine precepts, or administrators of proper laws on sexual relationships.

The depravity of false teachers is decried in verses 12-17, where they are compared to carnivorous animals that should be destroyed, because such persons have no understanding of the evil they commit, <u>for which they will be destroyed.</u> Their erroneous concept of Christian liberty led them into the dissipation of drunken orgies, gluttony, adultery, immorality, and the <u>enticement of innocent but unprepared ones into such sins.</u>

All these wayward souls have figuratively stumbled and fallen unto the wrong path, as taken by Balaam of Numbers 22, who was rebuked for his transgressions by a donkey speaking as a man. False teachers are <u>compared here to dry springs and storm driven mists,</u> which lack the provision of needed refreshment.

In 18-22, Peter denounced the deceptions of false teachers who aroused the lust of the flesh with <u>phony enticement of personal liberties</u> apart from moral restraints found in spiritual reality. They were enslaved by their own moral corruption, even though they may have earlier been professors of the truth about God and Jesus Christ. In this condition, it might have been <u>better not to have known the way of righteousness,</u> because it could be said of them, that, 'A dog will return to it's own vomit' and 'A washed pig will again roll in mud.' This means that a fool will repeat his folly, and not learn from past mistakes (Prov. 26:11).

CHAPTER 3: Peter reminded the recipient church in verses 1-7, that he had written earlier to encourage them to give serious thought about Old Testament prophecy about God's endtimes plan, as also <u>confirmed by New Testament apostles</u> according to Christ's commissioning of them. They are to realize that many people, in their selfish lifestyle, <u>will not be concerned</u> about the end of time. They will ridicule the believers, and <u>scoff at Christ's promise of His 2nd coming,</u> because it had not happened since creation and during the many millenniums of ancestral deaths.

The endtimes scoffers will ignore the fact that God created the heavens and the earth, consisting of water and dry land, and later in the time of Noah, how He <u>used water to destroy</u>

most living creatures as His judgment against evil. Afterwards, He ordained that earth would continue in it's present form until His judgment day, when fire will renovate the earth and ungodly people will die.

In 8-13, Peter addressed the issue of timing, when Christ would return and when God would exact His endtimes judgment against the ungodly and earth in it's present form. To put God's timing in perspective, Peter quoted Ps. 90:4, that 'With the Lord a day is like 1000 years, and 1000 years is as 1 day.'

His equation is most significant but largely ignored by students of the Bible. It may have applied to the 6 days of creation, as it now applies to the time that may elapse until the endtimes unfolds. With man, there is a great difference between 1 day and 1000 years, but with God there is little difference. Past, present, and the future are part of His everlasting history, so a delay of 1000-2000-or more years is not a concern of His, as a delay of hours, days, or weeks, can be upsetting to man.

We should appreciate the likelihood that God will delay the last days for the purpose of giving more people time to become redeemed believers, since He does not want anyone to suffer eternal damnation with Satan. When Christ returns the 2nd time, it will surprise mankind like a thief breaking into a home when least expected. Peter told the church that the earth and it's atmospheric blanket will be subjected to an explosive cataclysmic fiery purification and renovation, not a total destruction.

Naturally, all of man's prized possessions will then be destroyed, which raises the question, 'what is the most important value that we should aspire to?' It is incumbent on everyone to become a believer in Christ, God, and all that the Holy Spirit reveals to us through God's Word, and then live to please God. Thus, we will have assurance that we will inherit His promise of eternal life in a remodeled and refined kingdom. That is the future which we should look forward to with joy!

In 14-18, Peter encouraged the 'beloved' to look forward to these events, and diligently live in peace without sin, in the knowledge that Christ paid the price in full for our salvation, just as Paul so wisely stated in his letters. Some of what Paul said is difficult to understand, which causes stupid and unwise people to distort facts.

Peter quoted this advance warning from Paul, exhorting believers to beware of false teachings, that can lead one astray, and to let the kindness and understanding that Jesus provides through the Holy Spirit keep them (us) on the growth path to Christian maturity. For this, praise Jesus forever (PTL).

SUMMARY: Many of Peter's comments can be tied in with Old Testament prophecy about the degeneration and timing of the last days on earth, before God does a complete house cleaning and refurbishment of earth as we know it. Here are a few to consider: Prov. 4:18-19, Ps. 34:15-19, Ps. 24:1-2, Ps. 136:6, Hab. 2:3, Ezek. 33:11, Ps. 102:25-26, Ps. 50:3, Mic. 1:3-4, Is. 65:17-66:22, and Zeph. 1:17-18 & 3:8.

Once again, Peter's description of the endtimes points towards Christ's 2nd coming closely preceding the beginning of God's wrath judgment on earth and all the wicked, to produce a totally refurbished earth for Christ' millennial reign.

I JOHN—BOOK TWENTY THREE

Written at a time when the Christian faith was over a half century old, this book was written by the last surviving apostle, John, the 'beloved son' of Christ, known early in his discipleship as a 'Son of Thunder.' It appears to have been written about 90 AD during his senior years in Ephesus, to a group of churches in Asia Minor in which heretical views were being promoted by false teachers, that endangered the true basics of Christianity.

The general theme of the book is 'Fellowship with God,' with advice on the standards of conduct for effective and productive service in the church. Christian fellowship with an abundance of love is a dominant view. John's views are quite similar to those of Paul and Peter, as expressed in their writings.

CHAPTER 1:   With words similar to those used to open his Gospel book, John spoke of the beginning of time, in verses 1-4, what was learned since then from history, and most of all, what he had witnessed personally as a disciple of Christ. His purpose was to joyfully share this with the church in the spirit of fellowship. The close communion John had with the Father and the Son, was to be shared with all believers, under the influences of the Holy Spirit, to bring them closer in every way.

In verses 5-7, he sets forth the true and best qualities of fellowship, as that of walking in the light of God's Word, for if that is not done, then we are in spiritual darkness. By living in God's spiritual light, we are a light to other believers, and everyone is benefited by purification from sin by Christ's sacrificial blood.

Verses 8-10 deal with the truthful confession of sin without self-deception, to have them forgiven and wiped away by Christ, the faithful and righteous Redeemer. We must know and confess our sin, else we might say we are sinless, meaning that His word is not ours, and this would make Christ a liar and much displeased.

By providing a sufficient, effectual sacrifice for sin, through Christ's death on the cross, God gave testimony to the sinfulness of the world from Adam's fall through all ages. The sinfulness of believers is evidenced by requiring them to continually confess their sins, and to submit by faith to Christ's blood cleansing.

CHAPTER 2:   John spoke of the help Christ gives to keep believers from sin, in verses 1-11. Addressing his church as 'little children,' John told them that his writing was to keep them from sinning, but if they did so, they had a defender, an intercessor before God, Jesus Christ, who would plead effectively for their forgiveness, since He perfected obedience to God's law by His own example.

Knowing God means keeping His commandments; not doing so makes one a liar. Conforming to His word is proof that the abiding love of God is a perfecting light in our lives, in the example of Jesus Christ, and as the Holy Spirit leads us.

John made clear that he was not speaking of a new commandment, but was referring to old commandments they were familiar with—but mainly to love one another! This commandment was <u>renewed by Christ's love for humanity,</u> as a new light in the darkness of a sinful world. Loving others puts us in God's light!

John claimed he was writing to his 'little children' (parents and young people), in verses 12-17, to remind them that God existed from the beginning of time, that their <u>sins were forgiven through Christ,</u> and thus they were defeating Satan. All were admonished not to love the evil of the world, because that would stand in opposition to true love of God. All of our <u>selfish desires are to be put aside,</u> because the time is coming when they will be destroyed with the world. By doing so, eternal life is ours!

In 18-29, John expressed the belief that the endtimes was near for the prophesied antichrist to appear, since <u>many false teachers had already appeared</u> in their community, but had felt uncomfortable and had gone elsewhere. This was an indication that Christ was shielding the church, by keeping them from false doctrine, <u>from those who denied Christ and God.</u>

He encouraged them to hold fast to the truth of all of God's Word, from the time they became a believer and thereafter, to <u>assure their gift of eternal life with God.</u> While warning them to avoid deceivers, John saw the Holy Spirit as their spiritual instructor on good and evil, and <u>their keeper in the faith.</u> With this faith quality, they would be able to recognize those who are righteous, and knowing also that Christ is righteous would <u>enable them to live without shame</u> until His return, a one time event near the end of the tribulation years.

<u>CHAPTER 3:</u> John described God's love for humanity in the same context <u>as a father loving his children,</u> in opening verses 1-3, whereby believers become His 'little children.' As strangers in this world, where God is not known, <u>believers must walk by faith,</u> and live by hope, until Christ returns. Then we will be identified as the 'beloved' of God, and be <u>transformed into His likeness.</u> With this hope, we maintain uprightness, independent of our inherited sin nature.

How sin affects our relationship with God is the theme of verses 4-10. The habitual commission of sin is breaking the law, as encompassed by the old Mosiac Laws, and Christ's specific emphasis on the most important rules for Christian living. As a sinless human, Christ became <u>the perfect agent to remove the onus of sin</u> in the life of mankind. As we conform to His example, we must put aside sin, but those who keep on sinning really don't know Christ, or <u>have Him as their redeemer.</u>

Those who have godly lives, possess the righteousness of God. In their regenerated spiritual condition, they <u>avoid sin as the Holy Spirit enables them.</u> In their new nature, they evidence their obvious love for their Christian brothers and sisters. In contrast, habitual sinners, and those who strive to be righteous but grievously sin in their weakness, <u>are associated with Satan,</u> a gross sinner since his fall from grace with God. Even for these unfortunate ones, Christ is God's provision for a new life with <u>forgiveness and separation</u> from sin, if they would turn to Him.

The regenerated person is predisposed not to sin as before, as others do who are not born again. With God given illumination of their mind, <u>the evil and malignancy of sin is revealed,</u> and growing bias in the heart generates a determination to avoid sins. True believers are like a fertile garden, with God's seed of righteousness planted in their hearts; they are then <u>endowed</u>

to produce fruits of righteousness, without contamination from the weeds of evil planted by Satan.

In verses 11-23, John spoke of the imperative outworking of love in the life of a Christian. It must not be like Cain who, lacking brotherly love, murdered his good brother. It must be like God's love, which if planted in our hearts, as a certain sign of our true faith and status as a believer, is manifested by genuine love for others. Yet, we must not be surprised if the world hates us, because it is mainly dead to love.

By hating others, one is as bad as a murderer, without eternal life, and lacking the love of Jesus who gave His life for us out of love. By His measure, we too must give of ourselves and our resources for the good of others, out of love for them. Our love must be demonstrated by deeds and not mere words, if we are to know and feel the truth of God's Word. The life of grace in the heart of a regenerate person, is the beginning and first principle of a life of glory.

If we realize that we do not measure up to God's standards for true love, God understands also, and will give us an infusion of love to restore our confidence in Him. Since the Holy Spirit deplores selfishness, which if not realized by anyone, will engender dissatisfaction, with doubts and fear of the future.

On the other hand, if we feel at ease about our love relationship with others, we will be encouraged to draw closer to Him, knowing that He will supply all our needs. With enduring faith in Christ, manifested by love for others as Jesus commanded, the Holy Spirit provides all the proof we need of our union with God. When we dwell in Christ, as our ark, refuge, and haven of rest, we receive God's grace to keep His commandments as His Holy Spirit leads us.

CHAPTER 4: John admonished his 'beloved' in verses 1-3, not to believe everyone who claims to speak what the Holy Spirit tells them, because many false spirits were promoting false ideas in the 1st century time. Believers were to test these devious ones, by discerning whether their views about Christ were in accord with God's Word, or in contradiction.

If they confessed the true doctrine that Jesus was both man and God, they were most likely a true prophet of God. In opposition to this view, they should be considered as under the influences of false demons in the spirit of the antichrist. John spoke with confidence of the true faith of his 'little children' as having overcome false teachings, by knowing the spirit of truth versus the spirit of error.

Reverting again to the essence of love (the 3rd time) in verses 7-19, John said that everyone who loved their fellow believers was of God, because love is His supreme quality, and our love came from Him. His love for us was confirmed by His gift of Christ as our Savior, with His New Covenant gospel of sin forgiveness leading to salvation of the soul. Having so loved us, we should love others as well.

Even though we have not seen God, if we love our fellow believers, his Love is imbedded in us by the Holy Spirit. John admitted that he was telling the world about Jesus, because he had seen Jesus in the flesh, and knew Him as the Son of God. Thus it appears that God dwelt in him with a new Spirit of understanding and love.

By living as Christ did, with love in our hearts, we can look forward to God's day of judgment without fear. We must abide by His commandments, 'Love God, and love one another.' If we say we love God, and have hatred for someone, we are liars! The longer we live with love, the greater is our confidence in His love for us!

CHAPTER 5: The victory of faith is John's topic in verses 1-5, where he again stresses that faith and trust in Jesus Christ is the foundation of a believer's faith in God, with love and obedience as evidence thereof. Love of fellow believers is also a dominant factor.

Jointly, these spiritual qualities enable the believer to stand against and overcome the evil of the world. There is victory in faith!

Verification of Christ's credentials is what John spoke of in verses 6-13. His major identification, as a super human born of God, was His baptism by water and later, the emission of blood and water as He died on the cross. In heaven, there are 3 divine sources of evidence to this truth: God the Father, His Holy Word, and the Holy Spirit. On earth, there are also 3 that bear witness of Christ's divinity: the Holy Spirit, the water, and the blood. The Holy Spirit is involved in both cases.

Receiving the testimony of human witnesses, such as John and Peter, and as preached by servants of God, is important, but not as significant as the testimony of God that Christ was His beloved Son in whom He was well pleased. God has also said that His gift of eternal life will come to us through Jesus Christ. We must believe in Christ as our Redeemer, to receive God's gift. John wanted his brethren to know this without a doubt, so they would continue in their faith.

With a solid faith in God through our acceptance of Christ as His Son, we can have assurance that God hears our prayers, as John stated in verses 14-17. Prayer for what we want or need should be in submission to His will. This will be most applicable when we pray for a believer that we know is sinning, because it is the will of God for sinners to repent and seek His face, when that sin is not unto death.

We should pray for others, as well as for ourselves, to ask the Lord to pardon and restore, and to retrieve the tempted and afflicted, and be thankful that no sin, of which any one truly repents, is unto death. Being born of God is our insurance plan for eternal life. In Jesus, we can be spiritually born of God, and reject all idols.

SUMMARY: John's advice on fellowship with love towards other believers is needed as much today as in his time. There is strength in numbers in the church when this quality is present. Walking in the light of Cod's Word and rules for godly living is essential to maintaining our faith at a level that will give greater resistance to evil influences, and encourage non-believers to turn from sin towards God and Christ.

Regular and searching study of God's word is vital to a vibrant Christian life pleasing to God. The character trait of love as demonstrated by God and Jesus Christ, and as described in His Word, should be a great witness of our faith, to the world and fellow believers. It sets us apart as born of God, and as recipients of eternal rest with Him.

II JOHN—BOOK TWENTY FOUR

False teachers became the plague of early churches after the ministry of Paul ended. The Apostle John wrote this letter shortly after I John, but to members of a particular church, (referred to as a lady and her children), about 90 AD. He opened with praise for adherence to truth, with an appeal to continue to grow in love.

He warned of the dangers of false teaching to the integrity of the church body. Those who claimed that Jesus Christ did not come in the flesh, were to be rejected by the church as deceivers in the spirit of the antichrist.

*****

Referring to himself as the 'elder,' John greets the 'lady and her children' with love, in verses 1-3, from himself and all others (unidentified) who were believers in truth. He extends wishes for grace, mercy, and peace to be with the addressee.

He expressed his joy, in verses 4-6, over learning that some of the members were diligent in their walk in the truth of God's Word, and begged for the church (lady) to join him in a fellowship of love, according to God's wishes.

In 7-11, John called the deceivers of that day antichrists, since they did not believe Jesus came in human form. Believers were to be wary of them, and not be lured away from their true faith in Christ, lest they lose their eternal reward.

The deceivers did not love God because they violated the doctrine of Christ's purpose, and therefore, they were to be shunned and not received with hospitality. Anyone who fraternized with them would be equally guilty of their evil. However, we must be fair with those who differ from us on minor points, as long as they hold firmly to the significant doctrines of Christ's person, atonement, and salvation gift.

John closed with an explanation that he had more to say and would rather visit them soon for the pleasure of a personal discussion. He extended greetings from a local church or another Christian woman.

SUMMARY: This epistle is doctrinally much like John's 1st epistle, giving encouragement to hold fast to one's faith with an element of love within a church body, and warnings to identify and avoid false teachings. This advice is needed in churches of today, as much as at any time in the past.

III JOHN—BOOK TWENTY FIVE

Gaius, a faithful leader of some church in Asia Minor, was the <u>intended recipient of this</u> letter written by the Apostle (Elder) John, probably shortly after writing his earlier 2 about 90 AD, from his home in Ephesus. This shortest book of the bible was intended to encourage Gaius to continue in love, truth and obedience to Christ's gospel message, as probably preached earlier by Paul.

It also warned of a selfish detractor in the church who was not cooperating.

*****

Identifying Gaius as a beloved brother in Christ, John added in 1-4, how happy he was that Gaius diligently lived according to God's dictates, and for that he <u>prayed for his good health and prosperity of body and soul.</u>

He applauded Gaius in verses 5-8, for his hospitality to visiting men of God, whether he knew them or not, and for the <u>good report these men gave about Gaius</u>. The traveling missionaries needed gratuitous help because they asked for no pay for their services, which they rendered in obedience to God.

In verses 9-12, John spoke of an earlier letter he had written to this church but an egotistical man named <u>Diotrephes disregarded John's advice,</u> and voiced negative gossip about John and his cohorts. This man also was lacking in hospitality to visiting believers and canceled the membership <u>of those who were kind to visitors.</u>

John tells Gaius not to mimic evil deeds of the godless, but follow the example of <u>God's good folks and their deeds.</u> As an example of a good person, he approved what a man named Demetrius said about Christ's message.

Closing greetings are given in 13-15, from his church to theirs, with a prayer for the blessing of peace, and an explanation that he had more to say but <u>hoped to visit them in person.</u>

<u>SUMMARY:</u> The Gaius of this letter may have been the new convert of Paul's mentioned in I Cor. 1:14. He is <u>commended for his love and godly hospitality</u> to God's servants, which Diotrephes refused to give out of jealousy and self-pride. John also contrasted Demetrius (possibly the courier for this letter) against the other man. John made it clear that he consider <u>those who did good out of love, were of God.</u>

The lesson here is that we should not practice something out of selfish pride to cause us to do something that dishonors God, even if we follow the example of a person of rank and power. Rather, <u>as followers of God we should walk in love and kindness,</u> after the example of our Lord Jesus.

JUDE—BOOK TWENTY SIX

Popular belief is that this short book of 25 verses was written by Jude, the half-brother of Jesus and brother of James, to an unknown church, sometime during a 20 year period, most commonly identified as 60-80 AD. It is a letter of exhortation, directly attacking some wicked opponents of Christ's true gospel, who had infiltrated a church and corrupted sound doctrine with false teachings.

The congregation may have been 2nd generation Jewish Christians, possibly located in Syria, where heresy as described was common. The trouble makers were an arrogant self-centered lot, who boasted of visions while reviling angelic beings. Their views contributed to division in the church and disruptions of orderly worship.

At the end of his writing, Jude committed the church congregation to the Lord's safekeeping in a most beautiful benediction, commonly used by theologians of today, to close worship services.

*****

After his greeting in verses 1-2, Jude gave his reason for writing the message in verses 3-4. After personal identification, he addressed his message to the chosen and loved of God, as preserved by Jesus Christ, with a prayer that they be blessed with kindness, peace, and love. Then he explained that he had intended writing about salvation working in their lives, but then was forced to encourage them to stand firm in their faith, because some godless people had invaded the church with false notions.

The primary evil of the godless ones was to contend that God's grace allowed them to be immoral and they denied Jesus as the Master and Lord over humanity. As examples of how God dealt with such gross apostates, Jude reminded the church in verses 5-11, of Old Testament cases where God's judgment was invoked. Among those cited were:

- the faithless out of all those liberated from slavery in Egypt.(Num. 14:1-45)
- rebellious angels who corrupted humanity on earth (Gen. 6:1-4, Pet. 2:4)
- the homosexual immorality of Sodom and Gomorrah (Gen. 19:1-25)
- the false and vile prophets (dreamers) who rejected authority (Deut.13:1-5)
- the angel Michael's dispute with Satan and his rebuke, to come from God.*
- foolish false teacher's with animal like knowledge and ways (Phil. 3:19)
- having false pride and self-righteousness as Cain had (Gen. 4:4-12)
- the greed and deceit of Balaam to reap a profit (Num. 22-24, 2 Pet. 2:15)
- rebellion against God's authority by Korah (Num. 16:1-3, 31-35)
- (*) taken from an apocryphal book, The Assumption of Moses.

More is said about the spiritual character of evil false prophets who corrupt the churches, in verses 12-16. They are like spoilers of good food, like dry clouds which bring no refreshing moisture, and like leafless, or dead and uprooted fruit trees.

Their shameful deeds are as dissipating foam on wild ocean waves, or like stars falling into darkness. They are like the evil people Enoch spoke of, which the Lord would judge and condemn to eternal damnation at the end of the tribulation, as taken from another apocryphal book, The Book of Enoch.

All such persons are unhappy complainer's who live selfishly, flattering others for self-gain, over which they bragged. God's punishment would be certain for every sin committed by these ungodly people.

Jude reminded the church in verses 17-23, to remember warnings given by apostles about the godless, apostate people who will ridicule God in the endtimes. He said they would turn the members against each other, by their unholy way of life.

He advised them to let the Holy Spirit help them to grow in their faith, to walk with Christ until He returns with the gift of eternal life. They were to be helpful to those of little faith, heroic in their efforts to save the unsaved or backsliders, be merciful where needed, but hate and shun those who persist in filthy deeds.

Jude then closed this book with the classical benediction we often hear at the end of Christian church services, as follows: (paraphrased from popular biblical versions)

'To God who is able to keep believers from falling, to keep them pure and acceptable to appear before Him, our great God and Savior, who is worthy of glory, majesty, power, and authority, through Jesus Christ our Lord, down through the ages, now and forevermore! Amen.'

SUMMARY: The Old Testament pictures Israel's history as one of turning from God to idolatry, from His law to injustice and lawlessness, from His anointed leaders to others, including kings, and from His divine word to false teachings. They forsook God without fearing Him, or the consequences of their faithlessness.

Since those days, apostasy, the falling away from God, has prevailed over the ages, as it will into the last days of God's agenda for mankind. Today, the Christian community is being plagued at an accelerated rate, by doctrinal deception, moral insensitivity, and ethical departures from God's truth.

It is more urgent than ever that Christians contend for the truth of God's gospel and our faith in it, in opposition to those who try to corrupt or deprave it. Those who infiltrate our churches, like invading cockroaches or reptiles, who then foster bold sinning, and who are hardened against the divinity of God's gospel grace, can expect God's most severe punishment according to His endtimes judgment.

Nothing but the renewal of our souls in the image of Christ, by the Holy Spirit, can preserve us from destruction to be vented on God's enemies. It behooves churches of today to heed Jude's exhortation to an unknown church of his day.

<u>FOREWORD TO REVELATION</u>

After 6 years of intermittent writing on Richard's Bible Commentary, including Part 1-Old Testament, which has now been published, the completion of Part 2-New Testament will be accomplished as soon as I work through the book of Revelation. The culmination of six years of hard work brings me to the most daunting task of all, to try to make the most complex and mysterious book of the Bible understandable to everyday non-theologian students of God's Holy Word. I recognize the challenge for what it is and with the help of the Holy Spirit I hope to give you the best understanding you have ever had on this revelation of what is yet to come.

As I have done throughout this work of love, my comments on this book will be as literal as possible, with every effort to clarify the tough hidden meaning behind Scripture language regardless of biblical versions or translations that I peruse, and most of all not dictated by any denominational doctrine that comes my way. My hope is that this book will be opened up to you in the way it has never been before.

John's vision of the future for mankind and the Christian Church represents God's confirmation of Old Testament and early New Testament prophecy about His endtimes plan. I am aware that many of my Christian friends have a different viewpoint from mine about a most important issue, the rapture timing for the Saints of God. Some of my dearest Christian brothers and sisters stand firm on the belief that the Christian Church will be raptured before Daniel's 70th week of tribulation begins, so that none of God's children will be subjected to the horrors and persecutions of the 7 year tribulation time. That is a debatable issue in the Church today!

I sincerely regret that my exhaustive study of God's word up to this point does not support this expectation. Without wishful thinking, reliance on John Darby's doctrinal dogma, and without credence given to a Scottish maiden's (Margaret MacDonald) personal vision, or any other interpretation of scripture, God's Word to this point tells me that the Christian Church will suffer through most of the tribulation time in a manner no different than the disciples of Jesus suffered as apostles in their day. Up to this point, based on numerous scripture references, the picture that unfolds is that the Church will be raptured shortly before God's wrath judgment on the forces of evil, generated by Satan through the antichrist, in the last days of the tribulation time.

So I ask you, regardless of your present viewpoints, to join me with an open mind as you study through the book of Revelation with the help of this commentary to see if it confirms or revises my/your understanding on this contentious point. May God bless you as you do so, with the help of the Holy Spirit. Please remember that truth is the essence of God's wisdom.

RICHARD C. HIRSCH

REVELATION—BOOK TWENTY SEVEN

Mystery unfolds in a mighty way in this book of Revelation, as God Word opens a window of illumination into what is ahead for this world and mankind. With symbolic language, that he had to use for lack of any conception of the technological age to come, <u>John shared his vision experience, received from Jesus Christ</u> on the island of Patmos, where he was in exile.

Common belief is that he had this experience and wrote this account of it, at a time that is difficult to ascertain, but is generally thought to be during the harsh and tyrannical reign of Domitian in 81-96 AD. Somewhere during this time, John was exiled to Patmos for perhaps 1-2 years before he was released and relocated to Ephesus, where it is thought he wrote his 3 epistles. Since his epistles are given a date of 90 AD., one may surmise that John may have written Revelation before that date, <u>perhaps during the time 81-89 AD.</u>

Let us consider what the words 'revelation' or 'apocalypse' connotes. They generally mean to reveal or disclose something not previously known or realized, an uncovering or <u>removal of a veil to disclose hidden facts</u>. The book of Revelation is God's manifestation of Himself through Jesus Christ, to make known a small bit about <u>His endtimes scenario for a glorious world to come</u>, where there will be no more death or persecution of mankind.

It is like a railroad crossing where gates and warning lights operate to give travelers safety by controlling their <u>crossing at the right time</u>. In like manner this book gives all the signals to guide mankind to a spiritual relationship with God through Jesus Christ, to <u>insure a timely and safe crossing through the gate to eternal life</u>, rather than ignore the signals and reap a disastrous and destructive aftermath.

John's language involves allusion to biblical prophecy and apocalyptic symbolism surrounding the <u>role of Jesus Christ in God's endtimes plan</u>. His account clearly predicts the return of Jesus Christ to wrap up world history as now lived by humanity, with the <u>destruction of all enemies of God</u>, the salvation of all believers from the worst days of tribulation, and the reworking of heaven and earth as a new creation wonder. Christ's appearance to do all this will not occur before Satan's antichrist organization of evil doers have <u>inflicted</u> <u>terrible persecution on all of God's children</u>, those who are faithful to the testimony and glory of Jesus Christ.

The book should be understood to serve these purposes: 1—to make known what is ahead, 2—to make known the blessings promised for all who read, hear, and obey what God's expects of a believer, and 3—it is a divine revelation given to John in a vision with Jesus Christ as the communicator. <u>Jesus Christ is the central figure all the way through the book.</u>

Basically, the sequence of events portrayed are as follows:

1. The Christian church faces increasing persecution as the tribulation continues, with all kinds of <u>disturbances, afflictions, and supernal events</u>.
2. The tribulation week of Daniel intensifies with the appearance of the antichrist, his reneging on peace deals, and his <u>attack on God's people</u>.
3. The rapture (resurrection and glorification) of God's people takes place with Jesus Christ as the judge and coordinator of raising the dead and taking up the living, to <u>preserve them from the wrath of God</u> which follows shortly afterward.

4. God's Wrath Judgment on the nations of the world, the wicked operating under Satan's rule, will <u>relegate them to eternal damnation.</u>

5. Christ brings the redeemed to assist in judging the remnant of humanity at the end of God's judgment, to separate the sheep from the goats, to make sure that those who repent and accept Jesus Christ as the Messiah, are also <u>given a reward of eternal life,</u> as a part of His millennial reign.

6. A total renovation of heaven, the earth structure and environment, occurs prior to Christ's millennial reign with <u>Jerusalem as the new spiritual world</u> <u>headquarters.</u>

7. After the millennium, a final judgment on Satan, his angels, and the lost souls he gathered to himself, will occur before God's kingdom goes on forever, with no more evil or sin <u>to contaminate His perfect future.</u>

There are 3 basic sections to the book: 1—<u>what John saw</u> in his vision, Ch. 1; 2—<u>letters</u> <u>to 7 churches,</u> Ch. 2-3, about the <u>things which are;</u> and 3—the things which shall take place in the future, the <u>history of tomorrow,</u> Ch. 4-22.

CHAPTER 1:   In verses 1-3, John spoke of Revelation as what God shared with Jesus Christ to tell His angels, and <u>what Christ had an angel share with John,</u> who then wrote it down to tell the world. John said that God would bless those who shared the book with others and will <u>bless those who hear and obey it</u> until the time came, in the near future (foreshortened, as Paul predicted-Romans 13:11).

John spoke a salutary prayer in verses 4-7 for the 7 churches in Asia Minor (western Turkey) that he would write to, as instructed by Jesus Christ through the spokesman angel. He ended with a benediction in verse 8, in which he quoted God, 'I am Alpha (the first-the beginning) and Omega (the last, the end), the one who is, was, and is coming again, God All-Powerful.'

In his prayer, the 7 spirits speak of the Holy Spirit as a complete spiritual entity. Christ was cited as the first to conquer death, to now prevail over all earthly kings. He <u>gave believers</u> <u>freedom from sin</u> so they could serve as spiritual leaders to His Church. He declared that every person will see Christ when He returns, including those who stuck a sword through Him, perhaps meaning <u>those who wounded Him with apostasy and blasphemy</u>. Many will weep over His return, most certainly the Jews who were reluctant to acknowledge Him as their Messiah.

John described his vision in verses 9-20, with the assertion that all believers will suffer as Jesus did, but He will give us strength and courage to endure, <u>presumably through</u> <u>the</u> <u>tribulation years until He returns</u>. He explained that this vision came to him on the island of Patmos on the Lord's day, Sunday, as the <u>Holy Spirit took control of him</u> with a loud voice like a trumpet call. He was told to record what he saw and heard for a special report to 7 churches in: Ephesus, Smyra, Pergamum, Thyatira, Sardis, Philadelphia, and Laodicea. (Ephesus was somewhat central to the other 6 churches)

When John turned to see where the voice came from, he saw 7 gold lamp stands surrounding the <u>image of the Son of God, Jesus Christ.</u> He was dressed in a long robe held shut by a wide gold waistband. With snow white hair, eyes like flames of fire, feet like polished bronze, with

7 stars in His right hand, a sharp double edged sword for a tongue, a face as bright as the sun, and a voice like the sound of rushing water, He was an awesome one-of-kind sight.

The 7 gold lamp stands represented the 7 selected churches to which John would write, symbolic of the status of churches in the last days before Christ returns. Christ's appearance can be said to represent His eternal wisdom, His righteousness and priesthood, His love and affection for His children, His all knowing insight as a divine judge to know the innermost secrets of all hearts, His ability and will to tread the wine press of God's wrath to pronounce sharp judgment according to God's will, and having the powerful voice of a mighty King to save, remove, or to destroy.

As would any human, John fell prostrate at the feet of Jesus as if dead, but the Lord assured him with the touch of His right hand that He was the everlasting living Christ, with the keys to the place of the dead (and also to the doors of heaven), and that John had nothing to fear. With these words of comfort, Christ instructed John to write down what he had seen, what he now knew about the representative churches, and what he had been shown of things to happen in the future.

As for the 7 stars, and 7 golden lamp stands, the stars were emblems of the ministering angels (pastors, priests?), of the seven churches (the lamp stands) to which the apostle was to write an individual letter, along with an account of what was to come in the end.

VIEWPOINTS: In this chapter, the number 7 comes to the forefront in the 7 stars, and lamp stands, representing ministering angels to the churches of that day and in the endtimes, plus the 7 letters to be written by John to these churches. This number will be manifested in many ways as we move further into this book.

Some may ask, 'Why 7?' for which an answer is deserved. Going back to creation, we are told that God's creation time table encompassed 7 days, (which may have been 7000 years because with Him 1 day of human time can be 1000 of His time). He rested on His 7th day to mark the completion of a vastly complex achievement.

In the Old Testament, the number 7 was significant in the fall of Jericho, when 7 priests with 7 trumpets, marched around the city walls for 7 days, and the walls collapsed on the 7th day (Joshua 6). The army Captain Naaman dipped in the Jordan 7 times for healing (II Kings 5:14).

The number 7 must be a favorite with God, for He put 7 colors in the rainbow, made music with 7 notes, and allowed Satan to make 7 a lucky number for dice. It is definitely a number signifying completeness, victory, and success. It will be a number repeated in the unfolding of God's endtimes scenario.

CHAPTER 2:   The angel of the Lord told John to write first to the church of Ephesus in verses 1-7, **a part good-part bad church.** Christ introduces Himself as the holder of the 7 stars (angels) in His right hand, and the one who walks among the 7 candlesticks (churches).

Acknowledging that the church worked hard to endure persecution, Christ commended it for discernment of evil and lies by false prophets. He also charged it with the sin of waning love for Him and encouraged them to regain a warm fervent love. If they did not, He warned He would take away (judge accordingly) their church.

Even so, the church had no love for the Nicolaitans, who indulged in idolatry and immorality, for which Christ complimented them. He gave a final warning to heed His message to all churches so believers would be certain of enjoying eternal life with the Lord in God's Paradise (Kingdom). Ephesus is no longer in existence.

In 8-11, John wrote the letter Christ (the everlasting living Lord) dictated to the good church in Smyrna. He sympathized with their suffering from poverty and persecution by Jews under Satan's control, for which they gained spiritual wealth, with special gifts and hope. Although they would suffer more at Satan's hand, for a short time, He promised them eternal life for faithfulness even if they were killed.

This church was also urged to heed what the Holy Spirit communicated to all churches, so they would overcome evil, and be assured of eternal life with God. A believer with an imbedded hope to be kept from the second death at God's Wrath Judgment to come, has strength to patiently endure whatever happens in this world.

The 3rd church addressed by Christ in verses 12-17, another part bad-part good, was the one at Pergamum. As the one with a sharp-edged tongue, Christ commended this church for standing strong in their faith in the midst of Satan's domain, where a faithful Antipas was martyred. However, Christ found fault with those who followed the teachings of Balaam who condoned the eating of food offered to idols. They also had some who were practitioners of the Nicolaitans.

Christ warned them to turn away from such sins, else He would punish them as if using His sword tongue. This church is also admonished to heed this message, so as to earn spiritual food and win the reward of a 'white stone' of victory over sin.

In verses 18-29, the 4th church, Thyatira, another part good-part bad, is addressed by Christ as the Son of God with blazing eyes, and glistening bronze feet. He acknowledged their good deeds, love and faith, service and perseverance, and their spiritual growth.

After this summary of good, He spoke strongly against their toleration of a woman named Jezebel, one who called herself a prophetess but who led believers astray into immorality and the eating of idol sacrifices. Because she did not repent, Christ declared that he would give her an illness and great tribulation to those who committed adultery with her. Her followers would be killed. This action will prove that He will know the hearts and minds of everyone, and will deal with them accordingly, good for good, bad for bad.

As for those who had nothing to do with Jezebel, He merely urged them to remain strong in their faith, so that in victory they would join Him (be co-heirs) in ruling over the nations of the world with an iron rod after destroying the evil ones like clay pots. He will also reward believers who heed His word to all the churches, with a share of glory with Him, like the light of a morning star.

CHAPTER 3: Christ, with the 7 spirits of God (the completeness of the Holy Spirit) controlling the 7 stars (ministers of the churches), gave John a message for the church in Sardis, a very bad church. As a materially prosperous church in an industrial area, it was judged by Christ to be spiritually dead, and told to wake up to use what little strength that remained to regain spiritual vitality to obey God as before.

Christ reminds them of the teaching they had heard, that if heeded, would keep them from sinning. If they failed to do so, He warned them of being unprepared at His 2nd coming, returning as a thief does, when least expected.

Christ acclaimed a few who were living a clean life without sin, and promised them a white raiment of righteousness (representing purity) with Him in glory, because they were worthy and victorious. Every believer can look forward to this honor as long as their names are written in God's Book of Life. Christ will testify to their qualification before God and heaven's angels. As usual, the church is urged to listen and heed His messages to all the churches.

As the holy and true Son of God, with the keys to every door in David's kingdom, Christ asks the church in Philadelphia, a very good one, to listen to his message in verses 7-13. By holding the keys, Jesus can open doors of opportunity for His churches, the door to much needed messages from ministers, doors to authority in and over the church, and through the Holy Spirit the hearts of the unsaved. By the same token, He can shut the door to heaven against the foolish wicked who reject Christianity.

In His all knowing capacity, Christ opened the mustard seed door of faith to this church, and they accepted His invitation to walk through as faithful followers. From this vantage point, they would observe how He would deal with some aberrant Jews doing the bidding of Satan, to ultimately bring them to repentance on their knees before Him and His followers, and then to know His love.

Christ promised this church a safe haven from the endtimes days of testing (trial) that will afflict the entire world, because in obedience to His encouragement, they endured the difficulties of the tribulation years. Divine grace that makes believers fruitful in times of peace, will also preserve them faithful in times of persecution, to receive Christ's glorious reward to the victorious saints.

In His time frame, He urged them to hold firmly to their faith until His coming in the near future (soon), when they would receive a crown of righteousness. By enduring and overcoming the temptation to yield to demands and threats of an antichrist domain in the latter days of Daniel's 70th week, victorious believers will be made pillars (functionaries) in Christ's millennial kingdom. They will be identified as God's servants and Christ's heirs in His new Jerusalem headquarters. The church is admonished to hear and heed His messages to all the churches.

In 14-22, Christ spoke to the church in Laodicea, a not so good one, in His capacity as a true and faithful witness and participant in God's creation agenda. He knows how weak they were in spiritual matters, without conviction, a condition that figuratively made Him want to vomit them out of his mouth. Part of their problem was self-satisfaction with material wealth, thus leaving them spiritually devoid of the real blessings of life as a fervent believer.

In the context of a city with 3 main sources of wealth, banking, wool production, and medicines, Christ admonished the church to buy His refined gold of faith, white garments of righteousness, and His eye salve for better spiritual vision. They were to do this in repentance of their lukewarm but fruitless spirituality so as to earn His love, and be spared His chastisement.

In effect, He told this church, and all like it to the end of time, to shape up, turn from sin, and victoriously walk through His door of salvation for eternal fellowship and sharing at His banquet table, which was provided by His victory on the cross. He had overcome temptations and conflicts, and was more than a conqueror. Those who suffer and endure in like manner, shall share in His glory.

The church was told to hear and heed this message to all the churches.

VIEWPOINTS: There must be a significant reason for Christ to have called for all churches to hear and heed the messages John was told to deliver to them. It seems clear that each of the 7 selected churches out of many at that time were to receive the entire book of Revelation, so that all were informed about the good and bad characteristics among them. Obviously, this was so all of them would be advised of their standing before the Lord, with a choice of shaping up or taking the end result.

Since Christ's evaluation of these representative churches for that time was meant for their own good, it appears even more conclusive that His words were intended for all Christian churches to come, up to the time of His return. It also seems logical that He intended His observations and appraisals to be both encouragement and admonition to persevere through difficult days ahead, including the tribulation of the last days, so as to reap a large harvest of true believers (the rapture) before God's Wrath Judgment falls on the wicked antichrist masses.

Some might say that His safe haven promise to the church in Philadelphia in 3:10 implied a rapture before the beginning of Daniel's 70th week of tribulation, but verses 11-12 that follow give the picture that the church should endure up to the time of His 2nd coming, which will be near the end of the 7 year tribulation time.

Since all churches then and now have this entire book of Revelation, Christ surely meant for all believers of all churches to be raptured before God's judgment falls upon the earth. He merely used the Philadephian church as an example of what all faithful believers could expect for enduring without loss of faith, obedience to His word, and God's love.

The fact that a church or churches in general are not mentioned in chapters that follow does not mean they are taken out of the picture before the beginning of apocalyptic events of the last days. The remaining chapters pertain to the unfolding of God's judgment agenda near the end of the tribulation years of Daniel's 70th week. There is no reason for the churches to be a topic of discussion in this context.

CHAPTER 4:   At this point, a revelation of what is to come from the throne of God is given to John as he is taken up to heaven in the spirit. In verses 1-3, he is invited to step through a door to heaven by Christ, with a voice of trumpet tones, to see what would happen at the end of the church age, after the world moves into Daniel's 70th week of tribulation.

He first saw the spectacular being of God, seated on a throne, which he described in the likeness of precious gems surrounded by an emerald colored rainbow. The gem description may have signified the brightness of God's glory, and the rainbow color may have related to God's promise to Noah's descendants that He would not use a flood to exact judgment on humanity as the last days unfolded.

Surrounding the throne, in verses 4-8, John saw 24 thrones, with an 'elder' seated on each throne, all dressed in white raiment and wearing a gold crown. From under God's central throne, lighting flashed and thunder pealed. In front of His throne, mounted on a crystal clear surface like a green sea, were 7 flaming torches representing His 7 spirits.

What the 24 'elders' represent is difficult to say. The title 'elders' was used in Old Testament times for synagogue leaders, from the time of Aaron when the priesthood was divided into 24 rotating duty groups (I Chron. 24). In this sense, they may have represented the faithful of the nation of Israel. Others view them as 24 special angels of God, but angels are never identified as wearing golden crowns.

From numerous existing publications that speculate on their identity, the most logical one is that they represent the redeemed of the 12 tribes of Israel as well as the redeemed which came out of Christ's Good News gospel evangelical preaching by the 12 apostles. They signify the honor, respect, and satisfaction earned with God for their faithfulness and love of Him. Their white raiment represents spiritual purity, and the crowns spoke of the glory that believers in general will have with Him.

It is beyond understanding how the 7 torches can represent 7 spirits of God and still be reconciled to the entity of the Holy Spirit. These spirits were first mentioned in 1:4 as representative of God's completeness and His all-knowing evaluation in Christ's message to the 7 churches. No feasible explanation was found in scriptures to justify 7 separate spirits comprising the Holy Spirit.

The 4 living creatures that John saw between the throne and the circle of elders, standing between God and the people, may signify the true ministers of the gospel, because of their place between God and the people. This is suggested by worshipful expressions they voiced to God on His throne.

On the other hand, their separate description as a lion, a calf, one with a man's face, and one like a flying eagle, is almost identical with the creatures described in Ezekiel 1:10-14, where they were thought to be created cherubims, a class of winged angels who functioned as guards. Another thought is that they represent the 4 portrayals of Christ as found in the New Testament Gospels of Matthew, Mark, Luke, and John, although this is a stretch of one's imagination, because they speak of the eternal nature of God in verse 8.

In 9-11, the 4 creatures gave glory, honor and thanks to God for His eternal qualities. Then the 24 elders prostrate themselves in worship with crowns placed before His throne, as they extol Him as the creator of all things, worthy of glory, honor and power forever. How great it would be if all believers of this age would constantly, in a united fashion, worship God and Jesus Christ in this grateful way.

VIEWPOINTS: Mystery prevails in this portion of Revelation, for which no plausible explanation can be given with certainty. John's symbolic descriptions were rendered in the language of his day, far remote from the perceptions of our day, in which supernatural creatures as the 4 described above could be related to weapons of war, such as helicopters or other man made inventions of technology.

Students of the word must accept their limited understanding, in faith that all will be known and understood as we become redeemed members of God's Kingdom.

CHAPTER 5: This chapter described more of what John saw in heaven around the throne of God. In verses 1-5, he saw a handwritten scroll held shut with 7 seals (secrets of the future judgment) in the hand of God. A mighty angel, believed to be Michael, asked who was qualified or authorized to break the seals to examine the scroll, since no one appeared to have that right (see Daniel 12). John grieved over this matter and wept until an elder told him to stop, forthwith revealing that Christ, the Messiah, (the Lion of the Tribe of Judah—Is. 11:1,10) would do so.

In verses 6-10, John saw a representation of Christ standing in the midst of the throne area surrounded by the 4 creatures and the 24 elders. Even though alive, Christ appeared to have been slain, but John said He had 7 horns and 7 eyes which represented the 7 spirits of God to be sent out to the 4 corners of the earth (Zech. 3:9, 4:10). To most bible scholars, the horns signify complete and perfect power to execute all the will of God, with perfect wisdom to understand it, and to do it most effectively. It is impossible to know if John actually saw the 7 horns and eyes on the body of Jesus, or if it was an illusion. He may have used this language to describe Christ's supernatural power and perception of all things.

When the Lamb, Jesus, came and received the scroll out of God's right hand, the 4 creatures and 24 elders sat down before Him, each with a small harp and a golden bowl of incense (the prayers of believers). They then worshipped Him with a song proclaiming His qualification to remove the scroll seals, and credited Him with paying the price for the redemption of believers to reign over earth with Him.

John heard the voices of millions upon millions angels around the throne in verses 11-14, plus the 4 creatures and the 24 elders, loudly proclaiming, 'Worthy is the Lamb, to receive power, riches, wisdom, strength, honor, glory, and praise.' Then he heard all creation, those in heaven and on earth, and the souls of the buried dead join in a universal praise of God and Christ. The 4 creatures repeatedly said 'Amen' as the 24 elders worshipped before the throne.

VIEWPOINTS: More unexplained mystery pervades this chapter, specifically, whether the appearance of Christ with multiple horns and eyes was factual or figurative, and the identity of those created ones in heaven who joined in praising and worshipping God and Christ. The nature of the 4 creatures also remains uncertain.

CHAPTER 6: Six of the 7 seals are opened (removed) in this part of John's vision, with plenty of 'ifs' as to the meaning of each as they pertain to the beginning of the tribulation time and God's judgment against evil. It appears that the events of the 5 seals may include a 'time of sorrows' that precedes the beginning of Daniel's 70th week (see Matt. 24:6-8), and extends into the first 3 ½ years of that tribulation time.

After John saw Christ open the 1st seal in verses 1-2, one of the 4 creatures thunderously commanded him to 'Come and See.' As if looking through a window, he saw a white horse with a man sitting on it, wearing a crown and armed with a bow, that he used to win victories. One understanding of this vision, is that it represented the early spread of Christian religion by the Apostles, crowned with Christ's commissioning, and armed with the bow of Holy Spirit conviction, to be victorious over pagan religions then, and over all evil in the end.

A contrasting view is that this is more a picture of the antichrist rising to inject deception into the Christian doctrine, to undermine Christ's salvation status, and to bring on apostasy. Since the seal removals are deemed part of God's judgment program, this identity may be more likely. Either view relates to the opening of the judgment time to come upon the wicked of the world.

John was again commanded to look out the window of the future as Christ opened the 2nd seal in verses 3-4, to see a rider on a red horse with authority given to destroy earthly peace with battles to bring death to many men with a giant sword.

This image may signify the rise of the antichrist movement which will terminate a short time of peace that the world may know, as world powers mobilize for the purpose of destroying Israel and world Christians by military force. Military engagements took place during the early time of Christianity, such as the Crusades of the middle ages, when division broke the bonds of peace.

The 3rd seal is opened by Christ in verses 5-6, and John saw a black horse with a rider carrying a pair of scales in one hand. A voice from one of the 4 creatures spoke prophetically of, 'a quart of wheat or 3 quarts of barley would cost a full day's wages, and be careful not to spoil the olive oil and wine.'

What else can this mean but that there will be famines with great food shortages and terribly inflated prices for food. The black horse may signify the spread of dark clouds of ignorance and superstition that will sweep over the Christian world to also cause a spiritual famine.

Next, in verses 6-8, as the 4th seal is removed, John saw a pale horse (yellowish-green as a corpse?) ridden by a figure named 'Death,' with an rider behind named 'Hades.' The 2 of them had power over ¼ of the earth's surface, to kill with the sword, by famines and diseases, and by wild beasts. This may mean that ¼ of the earth's population will die from these causes, brought on by strife among men and mismanagement of earthly resources. Death will claim all the bodies, of which many will not be Christians and their souls will be relegated to Hades, the pit of hell. The true believer in Christ will be raptured later.

The timing or duration of these 'time of sorrows' developments cannot be fixed. The picture seen by John is similar to what Christ predicted in Matt. 24:6-14, Mark 13: 7-13, and Luke 21:9-18.

John sees a spectacular picture in verses 9-11, as Christ removed the 5th seal, of many souls under an altar—martyrs for their faith in God's word and their witness thereof. When they cried out to Christ for vengeance upon those who had caused their death, they were given white robes of purity (redemption) and told to be patient, until the total number of believers to be martyred reached a limit set by God, as He cuts short the fierce tribulation near the end of Daniel's 70th week (see Matt. 24:22, & Mark 13:20). The opening of this seal may coincide with the beginning of the last half of Daniel's 70th week, commonly called the Great Tribulation.

As Christ removed the 6th seal, in verses 12-17, John saw a representation of a great earthquake, with the sun obliterated and the moon blood red in color, possibly caused by volcanic eruptions of ash and dust. He also saw stars (comets, asteroids, etc.) striking the earth in such large numbers as if unripe figs were blown off the tree.

Mountains and land masses were dislocated, probably causing huge clouds of dust, which combined with the volcanic ash obliterated any view of the sky. The <u>effect of all</u> <u>this was to</u> <u>frighten mankind</u>, both great and small, to hide in caves and crannies of the mountains. In great fear, they pleaded for death from the elements so they would <u>not have</u> to <u>face judgment</u> <u>from God and Christ.</u> The final word John heard was, the Day of the Lord has come, that no one can defer or stand against.

CHAPTER 7:   At this point John saw 4 angels, each standing far apart on earth at opposite directions (4 corners—the whole earth), with each <u>having control of a destructive</u> <u>wind force</u> <u>for God's judgment plan.</u> A 5th angel came up like a sunrise from the east, with a special marking to be used for the identification of God's redeemed people. This angel loudly shouted to the 4 angels, 'Don't let go of the winds yet'—they were not to harm the earth until the Seal of God has been placed <u>on the foreheads of God's servants (believers),</u> <u>from the nation</u> <u>of Israel.</u>

This delay of God's judgment action against the evil forces of the antichrist for an indeterminate time, is <u>an important event of mercy on the Lord's part.</u> He is providing a shield of protection against the conflicts ahead for Jews who will be faithful in their acceptance of Christ as the Messiah, and will endure <u>suffering through the 2nd half of</u> <u>Daniel's 70th week,</u> possibly through God's wrath judgment.

A total of 144,000 Messianic Jews are <u>to receive God's security seal,</u> 12,000 each from the 12 tribes of Israel (sons of Jacob) identified as the tribe of Judah, Reuben, Gad, Asher, Naphtali, Manasseh, Simeon, Levi, Issachar, Zebulun, Joseph, and Benjamin. The original tribe of Dan is replaced (possibly because of his idolatry) by the tribe of Manasseh, Joseph's son.

There is no way to know if the 144,000 Jews to be sealed for the remainder of the tribulation years is a fixed number, or if it represents many Messianic Jews who will serve as missionaries to all other Jews during the Great Tribulation time. Arguments that this figure represents the Christian church, composed of Jews and Gentiles, are fallacious. It is more logical to understand that the 144,000 will take up the baton of evangelizing the nation of Israel during the Day of the Lord (God's wrath judgment against antichrist nations) <u>after the</u> <u>Christian church is raptured.</u>

In verses 9-17, John saw another vast number of people, more than could be counted, standing before the throne and Christ, clothed in white garments, with palm branches in their hands, loudly praising God and Christ as the <u>providers of their salvation.</u> Angels, the 4 cherubim creatures, and the 24 elders all joined together in worship and praises before the throne of God, acknowledging Him in every way.

When an elder asked John if he knew who these people were, he responded, 'No, but you know who they are.' The elder identified them as <u>those who came out of the Great Tribulation,</u> spiritually pure and qualified to wear their white garments of righteousness. They will now serve and worship God day and night, earning His blessing of eternal life, without hunger, fear, or other problems. <u>Christ will be their everlasting leader in a life of</u> <u>eternal happiness.</u>

Who are these people, complete in body and soul, who endured to the end of the tribulation as allowed by God, and who are now under the leadership of Christ? There can be little doubt that <u>they represent the raptured church of Christ's</u> <u>children,</u> including Jews and Gentiles, who as faithful believers will endure to that time. This tells us that the rapture will take place between the opening of the 6th and 7th seal, near the end of Daniel's 70th week, <u>before God's wrath falls on the wicked of the world.</u>

VIEWPOINTS: In chapter 14:4, the 144,000 Jews are called the firstfruits unto God and the Lamb, meaning they are the <u>sealed of God pioneers who will minister to the nation of Israel</u>, and bring many of the stubborn unconverted Jews to a saving grace with Jesus as their Messiah by the end of Daniel's 70th week.

The huge number of persons that John saw in verses 9-17 cannot be the same as the those seen in chapter 6: 9-11, who were the <u>souls of martyrs crying out to God</u> for vengeance, but those in this chapter are not described as martyrs. They were pictured as complete bodies praising and worshipping God and Christ, a fitting tribute from <u>a raptured multitude of believers, including the souls seen in Ch. 6.</u>

CHAPTER 8: Now comes the removal of the 7th seal in verses 1-5, to <u>open the judgment scroll of God's wrath</u> against the wicked world. After a moment of silence, as a lull in the eye of a hurricane, John saw 7 angels (possibly angels of the 7 churches, Ch. 1:20) standing before God, with <u>each receiving a trumpet</u>. In Jewish culture, a ceremonial ram's horn called a Shophar is used to call the people of Israel together, in other words to get their attention. Revelation trumpets may be the same.

Another angel stood at an altar holding a golden container full of incense. The smoke from the burning incense rose upward to God with the prayers of His redeemed saints, until the angel filled the container with hot coals from the altar and threw them to earth. The result was great noises with thunder, lightning and a mighty earthquake.

Then in verses 6-13, the 7 angels began blowing their trumpets, one at a time, to turn <u>different pages of God's judgment agenda</u> into reality for the unbelieving world, far worse than the 6 seal troubles. As indicated by the previous chapter, the 144,000 Jews would also be present, but secure under God's seal, because He was <u>leaving the door open for unsaved Jews</u> to come to a believing realization of Christ as their long awaited Savior. Non-Jews may also be given this option.

As the 1st trumpet was sounded, bloody hail and fire, <u>destroyed 1/3 of all trees and all green grass.</u> This was preliminary warning of worse to come. The sounding of the 2nd trumpet brought <u>great volcanic activity</u> that threw a large mountain into the sea, turning the water blood red as 1/3rd of sea creatures died along with the bodies of people on 1/3 of all ships destroyed at sea. This natural disaster resembles 'tsunami' events caused by earthquakes in recent times.

Trumpet 3 caused a great star (comet, asteroid, or other heavenly body) to fall to earth as a ball of fire from atmospheric friction, which perhaps will fragment and <u>contaminate 1/3 of all fresh water</u> with bitterness like the Wormwood plant of the Middle East, causing the death of many persons who will drink such water.

As the 4th trumpet was sounded by angel 4, a 3rd of the light from the sun, moon, and stars was removed so there was complete <u>darkness for approximately 16 hours.</u> Through this time, an angel flew the heavens proclaiming in a loud voice, 'Trouble, trouble, more trouble, is coming' —when the trumpets of the remaining 3 angels are blown soon. The message here appears to be that if the earlier calamities do not affect the spiritual vacuum of the wicked, then worse will follow.

CHAPTER 9:   Angel 5 blew trumpet 5 in verses 1-6, to <u>swiftly bring a male 'star'</u> (an angel custodian) from heaven to earth, with the keys to an earthly underground prison pit for demons. As he opened the shaft leading to the pit, smoke billowed out in such volume that it darkened the sun. <u>Out of the smoke came millions of locusts</u> (demons from the pit, or a false religious movement?) with the sting of scorpions.

Evidently these creatures had understanding, as they were told not to harm grass or anything green, but <u>only wicked mankind</u>, with the 144,000 sealed Jews excluded. These creatures could only torment mankind in a manner akin to a scorpion sting, <u>for a period of 5 months</u>; they could not kill people, but their sting would make mankind long for death.

Additional description of the 'locusts' is given in verses 7-11, as <u>that of horses used</u> <u>in battle</u>, with gold crowns on their heads, and faces like men. They had long hair like a woman's, and sharp teeth like a lion. They wore iron breastplates across their 'chests' and their wings roared like many chariots charging into battle. With tails like scorpions, their sting could cripple men for up to 5 months. Their leader from the pit was named Abaddon (Hebrew), or Apollyon (Greek).

What John saw here and how he described it may be symbolic of the armaments of war in this modern age. Helicopters, unmanned flying drones, tanks, laser guns, and other technological weapons being developed continually, may be the true nature of what he saw but could not describe in language of our day. <u>Biological warfare or plagues could be</u> <u>equated to the scorpion stings.</u>

Also, the locusts could be a description of huge armies amassed from pagan lands, where false religions prevail, such as Mohammedanism (Islamism), which has historically been an enemy of Christianity, and is <u>now gathering momentum through acts of terrorism</u> against Christian nations, which they call the Great Satan.

In verses 12-21, 2 additional woes are part of John's vision. The 6th angel sounded the 6th trumpet, and a voice (Christ's) from the altar before God gave the 6th angel a command to 'Release 4 angels now restrained at the Euphrates River.' He was told that these angels had been trained for the time when <u>1/3rd of mankind was to be killed.</u> This could number in the billions of deaths of <u>those who were unbelievers</u>.

The instrument of death was a 200 million man army, mobilized from many nations. John saw it <u>as horses with heads like a lion</u>, with riders wearing colorful breastplates, and fire, smoke, and brimstone (sulfur) belching from the horses mouths, which alone would kill 1/3rd of evil mankind, again with the 144,000 secured. He said the power of the horses was in their mouths and tails, much like tanks and helicopters of today with weapons at both ends.

Those evil ones who survived these terrible judgments (plagues) <u>did not repent of their</u> <u>evil</u> but continued in demon and idol worship of all kinds, that had no real substance. They did not avoid the sins of murder, sorcery, immorality or theft. <u>God would continue His wrath</u> <u>judgment upon the unrepentant.</u>

VIEWPOINTS: No indication is given here of the part of the world where the 200 million man army would kill another 1/3rd of humanity, to total over ½ of the world's population when added to the 1/4th killed in Ch. 6:7. Deaths from the other plagues <u>could increase deaths</u> to 3/4th of the world's population. Since the 4 angels who were given control of this army were initially restrained at the river Euphrates, one could assume that the massacre would begin in the Middle East.

The composition of this military force by nation is also a point in question. Large population nations, such as Russia, China, India, and Iran could be involved. Present day hostility of Islamic nations might also contribute to this mighty army.

CHAPTER 10: This chapter ends in gastric discomfort (like an ulcer?) to John, who will keep a secret he was told to conceal. John saw a mighty angel, in verses 1-4, representative of Jesus Christ, coming from heaven to earth in a cloud with a rainbow overhead, a face radiant like the sun, and legs like columns of fire (see 1:15). The angel had a small open scroll in his hand, perhaps <u>an excerpt of the sealed scroll seen in Ch. 5.</u>

The angel planted his right foot on land and his left on the sea, as if to take control of all earth, and shouted loudly (a command to reveal the contents of the scroll?), like a lion's roar, at which <u>7 thunderous voices were also heard speaking</u>. As John prepared to write what he understood the voices saying, he heard a loud voice from heaven, perhaps Christ's, telling him not to do so, but let those words be <u>unrecorded for the moment (until after the 7th trumpet is sounded).</u>

In 5-7, the angel extended his right hand heavenward, and declared under an oath to Christ, that God's wrath judgment would no longer be delayed, but would <u>proceed as soon as the 7th angel sounded his trumpet.</u>

John heard the same voice from heaven (Christ's), telling him to take the small scroll from the angel's hand. When he asked for it, <u>the angel told him to eat it,</u> and even though it would taste sweet, it would be bitter (sour) to his stomach. He ate it, and it was sweet as honey but it turned his stomach sour. The scroll may have given details about Christ's millennial reign, a sweet event, but this was to happen after the time of judgment was over, <u>a time of great bitterness and pain.</u>

The angel then told him to prophecy to all people and nations about what would happen to them <u>as God's wrath judgment unfolded.</u>

VIEWPOINTS: Just as John was told not to record what the small scroll evidently revealed, so Daniel of the Old Testament was told not to reveal details of his vision of future events as recorded in Dan. 8:26. The prophet <u>Ezekiel was also commanded to eat a scroll</u> (also tasted sweet) about lamentations, mourning, and woe, that God's judgment will bring, as written in Ezek. 2:8-10, and 3:1-3.

The sweetness of God's word about the eternal blessings awaiting the believer who endures through much tribulation is <u>a positive we can enjoy</u>. But, the knowledge that God's judgment will wreak such a terrible toll on the lives of the unsaved (possibly including members of our own families) before their eternal hell, <u>is a bitter sour pill to swallow</u>. All the more reason to bring salvation to others.

CHAPTER 11: A complete understanding of this chapter is impossible for several reasons, but a suggested meaning will be given based on the most popular views of other bible scholars. The timing of this scenario is also a debatable issue.

In verses 1-4, John is given a measuring rod to measure a temple of God's, in an unspecified location, thought by many to be Jerusalem. This may be the temple that the antichrist will occupy about the middle of the 7 year tribulation, as stated in II Thes. 2:4; if this is so, the temple will have to come into the picture before that time, by construction or occupation of an existing structure.

John was told to measure the worship area and count the number of worshippers, an indication of God's concern for their safety, while those outside the temple would be subjected to persecution for a period of 42 months (1260 days).

The 42 months, equal to 3.5 years, will probably begin with the Great Tribulation, the last half of Daniel's 7th week, after the antichrist appears to occupy the temple, and seeks to control the Gentile nations by persecution, targeted against believers and the nation of Israel. The temple may represent Christ's church of believers who will be delivered (raptured) out of all this trouble at Christ 2nd coming.

John is told of 2 unidentified sackcloth attired witnesses who will prophesy (minister to believers) during a 42 months period, but it is not logical to relate their time to the 1st half of the tribulation years. They may arrive before the mid-point of the 7 year time, because their death must occur before that of the antichrist, near the end of God's Wrath judgment.

They are figuratively described as 2 olive trees or 2 lamp stands standing before Christ, as also spoken of in Zech. 4:12-14. Some identify them as Moses and Elijah, or Enoch, but this is questionable since the latter two became glorified of old with a special heavenly body, while the 2 witnesses are described more as mortal bodies to suffer death as humans, with a resurrection in the manner of Christ's experience. They may be two out of the 144,000 sealed Jews, or 2 Gentile believers supernaturally endowed by God to witness for the purpose of winning souls to Him. John the Baptist may be one of them. Their identity is not as important as their function.

The ability of these witnesses is given in verses 5-10, as having miraculous power similar to what Moses and Elijah had in their day. They will have a speech capability that will scorch their enemies into silence and fear, making them too cowardly to harm the witnesses, for they may call fire down from heaven to destroy their enemies (II Kings 1:10-12). They will have control over rainfall (I Kings 17:1 & 18:41:45), the ability to turn water into blood (Ex. 7:20), and to bring plagues upon earth (Ex. 8:1-12 to 12:29).

When the 42 month preaching time of the 2 witnesses is completed, God will permit the beast of the abyss (the antichrist—man of lawlessness), to strive against them until they are killed. Their bodies will be left lying in the street of a large city (Jerusalem) where Christ was crucified, which will be as sinful as Sodom in it's time.

A corrupt city population will not allow the bodies to be buried for 3.5 days, so they can celebrate their death by exchanging gifts, for their preaching was torture to them.

These ungodly celebrants will become most fearful when God gives life to the witnesses, in verses 11-14, and they stand up to rise into heaven in a cloud, on a loud command to 'Come up here.' Immediately, a severe earthquake will destroy 1/10ᵗʰ of the city and kill 7000 people. The survivors in great fear will recognize that the God of heaven had intervened, but they <u>will not accept Christ as Messiah yet.</u>

John was told that this completed the 2ⁿᵈ terrible woe but <u>another was coming soon,</u> after the 7ᵗʰ angel sounded the 7ᵗʰ trumpet.

In verses 15-19, as the 7ᵗʰ trumpet sounds, loud angelic voices in heaven, and the <u>raptured saints of Christ's church will proclaim</u> that, 'the kingdoms of the world would now be replaced by the kingdom of Christ for His eternal reign.' This will be seconded by the 24 elders who will prostrate themselves in worship before God's throne. They will praise His wrath on the wicked, judgment of the dead and living, and His rewards to His believers, prophets and apostles (ministers). This seems to signify that Christ would shortly become King for 1000 years.

A temple of God was then opened in heaven, where <u>the ark of the Lord was placed</u>, to the accompaniment of lightning, thunder, hailstorms, and an earthquake. The angels and the 24 elders knew it was time for Christ to begin His millennial reign, but the remaining evil <u>people of the world resisted by turning against God's wrath with their own anger.</u>

The opening the temple of God in heaven may be for the purpose of improved communication between heaven and earth, for prayers and praises going up, graces and blessings coming down. It also may refer to the church of God on earth for the purpose of making God's Word more available to the people, after the suppression imposed by the antichrist. As for the ark, it may serve as a token of the presence of God, with favor renewed to them in Jesus Christ, as expiation for their sins.

<u>VIEWPOINTS:</u>   The 2 witnesses may preach for a 42 month period straddling the mid-point of the tribulation years, to a time after the rapture of the Christian church, well <u>into God's wrath judgment time.</u> Since they will be translated as resurrected bodies to heaven, they need not be part of the rapture event.

The witness activity of this chapter would seem of necessity to overlap the events that will occur prior to the opening of the 7ᵗʰ seal, which seemingly will introduce the trumpet phase of God's judgment time. Also, the witnesses may minister solely to the nation of Israel, as their demise in Jerusalem suggests. This would be in keeping with God's intent to give His chosen people ample opportunity to repent of their obstinacy, and accept Jesus as their Messiah.

<u>NOTE:</u> Up to this point in Revelations, John's vision of the 7 seals and trumpets was <u>progressive in sequence towards God's final judgment day,</u> picturing the happy fate of the godly, and the sad fate of the wicked of the world. In chapter 12-15, and 17, his vision is of things <u>that may have occurred earlier relating mainly to the fate of the Christian Church and the nation of Israel.,</u> or other tribulation events.

Symbolic language is used to speak of humanity, earthly and heavenly objects, and heavenly creatures. An accurate unquestionable interpretation of them cannot be assured, because of the <u>many different but plausible viewpoints</u> expressed in existing publications on the Bible. In every case, my best effort will be to give you the most logical understanding that correlates sensibly with related scriptures.

CHAPTER 12: This chapter is loaded with symbolic meaning, about a woman threatened by a dragon, followed by a narrative of a <u>battle between good and bad angels;</u> both speak of extreme danger for the world. In his vision, John saw a woman in verses 1-6, as a 'great sign' related to God's endtimes scenario, having the brightness of the sun, the moon under her feet, and a crown of 12 stars on her head. Being pregnant, she is suffering from labor pains that precede birth of a child.

Several schools of thought exist pertaining to the identity of the woman. Some see her as the 'mother of believers' (a Catholic term) comprising the Christian church, but another view is that she represents the nation of Israel. A compromise view is that she represents the Christian Church in the 1st 5 verses of the chapter and the nation of Israel in the remaining verses.

The view favored in this commentary, is that she represents the nation of Israel, the shining initial jewel of God's choosing, in His eyes more brilliant than the moon, for which she wears a crown of stars, <u>each star representing one of the 12 tribes of Israel.</u> Mary, an Israelite virgin, gave birth to the Christ we now worship, who gave us the Good News gospel, which was <u>preached by the 12 apostles to the world.</u> Much pain was endured by early Christians to give birth to Christ's church.

A related 'sign' of a large fiery red dragon with 7 heads, each adorned with a crown, and 10 horns appeared in the sky. A swish of it's mighty tail caused 1/3rd of all stars (Satan's angels?) to fall to earth. This dragon stood before the woman in labor, with the <u>intention of eating her new born male child,</u> who was destined to rule over all nations with a rod of iron. The son was born and escaped the dragon when God took Him up to His throne in heaven.

It isn't difficult to speculate that the dragon will be blood-thirsty Satan, with great wisdom and power (7 sets of brains) <u>over 10 earthly kingdoms,</u> all of which will be alienated from God. The tail and stars falling to earth may have a tie-in with the falling stars of 8:12, or with Is. 14:12, which predicts Satan's fall from heaven (as related in verses 7-12 that follow) <u>with perhaps 1/3 of heaven's angels,</u> no longer 'stars' of heaven.

We know that Satan tried to destroy Christ while He was on earth but he failed. Christ was <u>victorious when He returned to heaven,</u> much as the child in this vision. After Christ's transfiguration, the Jewish people were persecuted and dispersed worldwide, with little safety, but this passage indicates that some will have a <u>safe haven during the last 1260 days of tribulation;</u> this surely must apply to the sealed 144,000.

Verses 7-12 tell of John's vision of a war in heaven, in which the mighty archangel (General) Michael fought with Satan and angels allied with him. How this war was fought is not revealed, but it must have been fought with unknown spiritual methods. The result will be for <u>Satan and his angels to be cast out of heaven</u> to afflict the earth full-time, probably at the mid-point of Daniel's 70th week. (The dragon's tail got them in deep trouble!) A loud voice will proclaim Christ's victory over Satan as a <u>reason for great joy in heaven,</u> but woe and trouble for those on earth who would have to endure Satan's wrath until the end of the tribulation.

In verses 13-17, a preview is given of Satan's attempt to persecute Israel, but again a manner of security will be provided by God, to at least the 144,000 sealed Jews, <u>for the Great Tribulation time of 1260 days.</u> Satan will use floods and warfare to try to destroy the Jewish people, but also the off-shoot of the nation of Israel, <u>the Gentile Christian church (descendants</u>

of the woman). His headquarters will be on some seaside beach, from which he will direct the events of chapter 13.

VIEWPOINTS: It seems logical to assume that Satan and his angels will be cast out of heaven at the mid-point of Daniel's 70ᵗʰ week, when the antichrist occupies a temple of God and proclaims himself God of the world.

Also, how Satan will attempt to destroy the nation of Israel as well as the Christian Church is unclear. The word 'floods' may relate to the massive 200 million man army described in chapter 9, for which the antichrist may be the Commander in Chief, after he is no longer restrained. Chapter 13 may be Satan's ongoing effort to destroy God's people in the last 1260 days of his time.

CHAPTER 13:   This chapter is all about John's vision of 2 beasts, one coming out of the sea, and another coming out of the earth. A indisputable identification of their symbolism is debatable, but a logical understanding based on history is possible.

In verses 1-4, John saw the 1ˢᵗ beast coming from the sea, with 7 heads and 10 horns, each horn having a crown, and a worldly (Satanic) name that was offensive to God. This image is almost identical with that of Satan (the dragon) in 12:3, except that the crowns are on the horns of this beast, instead of on the heads, as they were for the dragon.

The common belief is that the antichrist is described here, empowered by Satan of chapter 12, to wage war on God's children. His 7 heads are thought to represent 6 major historical empires of old, plus a new one for the endtimes events, that basically constitute a complete panorama of history.

In this context, the following empires, and their times, have been suggested: Egyptian, from 1600-1200 BC; Assyrian, from 900-600 BC; Babylonian, from 606-536 BC; Persian, from 536-330 BC; Greecian, from 330-146 BC; Roman, from 200 BC-400 AD, and the 7ᵗʰ, a revived Gentile Roman empire from which antichrist will rise with an unknown birth date. This empire is no doubt in formation today!

The 10 crowned horns may represent the final composition of the Gentile empire, as 10 major kingdoms or nations of power and purpose. The horn names may speak of the apostate nature of these kingdoms. John's leopard description of the beast, his legs like a bear, and a mouth like a lion may be an intimation of a great world power, similar to a vision seen by Daniel in Dan. 7:3-6.

John saw one of the heads having evidence of a mortal wound that had healed. This may be referring to a counterfeit death and resurrection of the antichrist by Satan, for the purpose of gaining undeserved respect and recognition from the naive unbelievers in Christ. They will think he is one of a kind, that no one can oppose.

In verses 5-10, this beast will receive great power from Satan for the final 42 months of Daniel's 70ᵗʰ week. With a self-deific mentality, he will be emboldened to blaspheme God, His name, His church, and the angels of heaven. He will be allowed to wage war against God's people, and exert his authority over people of every land, race, or language, without much success over God's people.

All idol worshipers, agnostics, atheists, and other unbelievers, whose name is not written in Christ's book of life, will worship the antichrist. John may have added the admonition for everyone to heed this message, lest they become a captive of the antichrist, and suffer his death. The patience and faith of the saints to endure is critical to survival for an eternal reward.

John saw the other beast rising from out of the earth in verses 11-18, having 2 horns like a sheep, and the voice of the dragon. It will serve the 1st beast, the antichrist, and influence the wicked of the earth to worship the antichrist. Satan will give him power to perform miracles, bring lighting down to earth, and otherwise deceive mankind, apparently to imitate Christ's great works while on earth, as a form of counterfeit religion. He will have power to kill those who do not worship antichrist. He can be called a false prophet!

Just as God will seal the 144,000 Jews, this beast will require all people to take an evil counterfeit mark on their right hand or their forehead, in order for them to conduct marketing, and be identified with the antichrist.

John gave a word of wisdom to those who read of this vision, to understand the number 666 that was given to this beast, a man, as insignificant and inferior to the compete number 7 of God.

CHAPTER 14:   Next in John's vision, he saw the 144,000 standing on Mount Zion around Jesus Christ, in verses 1-5, evidently after they completed their mission, and as God's judgment is nearing an end. A voice sounding like running water, thunder, and harp music will come from above, as a happy new song will be sung before God's throne, surrounded by the 4 living creatures and 24 elders of Ch. 5.

Other than the 4 living creatures and the 24 elders, as indicated in Ch. 5:9-10, only the 144,000 who are now among the redeemed will be able to sing this song, because of their undefiled (by women) spiritual character as the firstfruits from the nation of Israel.

The reference to their status as 'virgins' may reflect on the fact that they did not submit to spiritual seduction by the antichrist and his lieutenant. It is difficult to conceive of such a large number being unmarried or celibate.

In verses 6-13, 3 angels appear from heaven with special proclamations. The 1st had the Good News gospel of Jesus Christ offering the wicked of the world a last chance to accept it, with the words, **'Worship and honor God.** It is now time for you to kneel before Him, who created everything, before He judges everyone.'

A 2nd angel appeared with the announcement that 'Babylon is fallen—because her wickedness has angered God.' In this context, Babylon is the symbol of the Satanic world power and economic structure that will exist at history's end. It will be aligned with a corrupt religious system hostile to Christians, and thus be subject to total destruction in God's wrath judgment.

A 3rd angel appeared and shouted a warning to all mankind, 'If you worship the antichrist and his image, and take his mark, you will have to drink sour wine that God gives to all who make Him angry.' They will be forced to drink from His potent cup of wrath without ceasing, which will bring everlasting torment like fire.

However, saints who have faith in the Lord, who patiently endure and obey God's commandments, will <u>receive a special divine blessing</u>, whether they are martyrs or survive alive. They will find rest from their struggle, due to their good record.

John then saw a figure in verses 14-16, that he called the Son of Man, sitting on a white cloud. He wore a golden crown and carried a sharp sickle, <u>symbolic of Christ's role in rapturing the saints.</u> An angel came out of God's judgment temple with the order to <u>take up the dead in Christ and those alive.</u> Christ went into action to reap as many souls as possible, all <u>those who were true believers</u>. **This must be the rapture scenario** spoken of after the 6th seal was opened in chapter 6.

Another angel came out of God's temple with a sharp sickle, and a 2nd angel with the power of sacrifice came from an altar to <u>shout a command to proceed with a harvest of the</u> <u>fully ripe grapes of wrath (the wicked).</u> The 1st angel cut the grape vines of the antichrist with all his grapes, and threw them <u>into God's wrath winepress</u> where they were trampled until blood flowed as high as a horse's nose (bridle), for a distance of about 200 miles. Could this be the aftermath of the battle of Armaggeddon? <u>After this scene, Christ will be closer</u> to assuming <u>his kingship role.</u>

<u>VIEWPOINTS:</u>   This chapter seems to give a very clear foretelling of the proximity of the rapture with God's wrath judgment at **the very end of Daniel's 70th week**. There is no indication of a time lapse between Christ reaping His harvest of the redeemed, and the angel reaping the wicked of the antichrist, as described in verses 14-20, so one can assume <u>they may occur at the same time or with little delay.</u>

Once again, the time of the rapture is related very clearly to the time of God's wrath judgment, which can only conclude at the very end of the tribulation time. This raises the question again—How can there be a rapture before the tribulation begins?

This part of John's vision may be a preview of what is to take place before the 7 bowls of judgment are poured out as revealed in chapters to follow. It seems logical that the angel that <u>reaps the antichrist grapevines will do so after all judgments fall.</u>

CHAPTER 15:   The judgment activity is not over, and John saw another sign in heaven in verses 1-4, of 7 angels bringing the last 7 plagues (bowls of torment) on earth <u>to complete God's wrath judgment.</u> In heaven before God's throne, he also saw a platform like green glass with fire around it, which could be representative of God's victory stand for believers who will be raptured after overcoming the persecutions of the antichrist. <u>The 144,000 of the nation of Israel may be in this assembly.</u>

To the accompaniment of harps, those near the victory stand sang the song of Moses (Ex 15:1-18) to give <u>thanks for deliverance from God's wrath judgment.</u> They also sang the song of Christ for His salvation gift, and to <u>exalt God for His mighty works and fairness in judging right and wrong.</u> This implies a joint fellowship of Messianic Jews and the Gentile church of Christ for Christ's kingdom reign.

Then in 5-8, as the 7 angels with the 7 plagues came out of the temple tabernacle of heaven, they wore garments of white held shut with <u>sashes of pure gold</u> (symbols of righteousness and purity). One of 4 creatures gave each of the 7 angels a golden bowl full of God's wrath in some form. The temple was filled with the essence of God's power and glory, as smoke emanated to keep all those in heaven <u>from entering until the 7 angels</u> completed their mission, as outlined in chapter 16.

The 7 angels are God's warriors of divine justice, armed with His wrath, to <u>deliver the final judgment blows to Satan and his legions</u> of lost souls. The believers now in heaven will be most happy when the enemies of Christ are no longer in the world, and all of <u>Christ's millennial followers will begin living a new spirituality.</u>

<u>VIEWPOINTS:</u> A perfect unified congregation of saved Jews and Gentiles is pictured before the throne of God, rejoicing together over their salvation from God's wrath, and their <u>soon to be participation in Christ's millennial kingdom.</u>

Will there be any more people saved out of the last phase of the 7 bowl judgment? It is hard to say, <u>it may depend on whether or not the 144,000 sealed Jews continue their ministry</u> to the nation of Israel through this final judgment time. Up to this point, John's visions do not answer this question. We shall see!

CHAPTER 16: This is the climactic phase of God's wrath judgment. In verses 1-9, John hears God's loud voice coming from His temple, <u>ordering the 7 angels to pour the wrath of His 7 bowls</u> (vials) out onto the earth and the wicked who still live there.

The 1st angel emptied his bowl on the earth and ugly painful <u>sores like ulcers broke out on everyone</u> who had the mark of the antichrist and worshipped his image. The 2nd angel emptied his vessel on the sea, turning it blood red <u>as every living sea creature died.</u> When the 3rd angel emptied his bowl into the rivers and streams, they <u>turned to blood also.</u> The angel then proclaimed God to be the rightful judge over the wicked who were related to those who persecuted and killed His saints and prophets, and for this they deserve the blood now given for drink. An echo of this sentiment came from God's altar.

Now comes the 4th bowl, which the angel poured on the sun to intensify it's heat, which <u>scorched the evil on earth</u> to the point that they blasphemed God in anger and great pain. Their hearts will be hardened in keeping with their character.

One might wonder what ingredient is poured out of the 4 bowls or vials that produces the effect described for each bowl. The bowls may be symbolic of what God brings about in venting His wrath on wicked man, done <u>in His own supernatural way.</u> In what manner God does this is really no concern of ours. Since we are forewarned of the consequences of our sins, not confessed, regretted and forgiven, we should <u>take advantage of Christ's salvation offer</u> that is so necessary to avoid God's wrath.

In verses 10-16, the last three bowl judgments are dispensed by the angels. The 5th angel emptied his bowl on the headquarters of the antichrist to put his empire into darkness, so that the people bit their tongues in pain, <u>had painful sores and cursed God for these</u> afflictions. It did not divert them from their evil ways.

Angel 6 poured his bowl out over the great 1780 mile long Euphrates River in Iraq, <u>making it dry up to be a passable road for kings of the east,</u> believed to be the route to be taken by a huge military force from eastern Asia, mainly China, when they advance to attack Israel.

Johns sees evil spirits emanating from the mouth of Satan, the antichrist, and his false prophet (the trinity of evil), that looked like frogs. These 3 evil spirits will have much power to work miracles, which they will do to <u>influence rulers of all nations to mobilize their armies to wage war against God</u> (which will be a great victory for God's powers).

In an odd way, readers are reminded in verses 15 of Christ's statement, 'When I come, it will surprise you as thief entering your home' (Matt. 24:43-44 & Luke 12:39-40) This is His promise of blessings to the believers who are <u>ready at all times.</u> The statement about keeping clothed is related to a Roman practice of stripping a guard caught asleep on duty, another way of <u>picturing the loss an unbeliever faces</u>.

The 3 evil spirits of Satan's intelligence system will effectively <u>muster a huge army at Armageddon,</u> a site about 25 miles southwest of the Sea of Galilee. Over history, many decisive battles have been fought in this location, such as the one when King Josiah was killed in a battle with the Egyptians (II Kings 23:29-30). A final battle, which is discussed in Rev. 19:17-21, will be a victory for God's side against the forces of evil.

Finally, the last bowl will be poured out by the 7th angel into the air over Satan's domain on earth, and a voice from God will say 'It is finished,' the same words Jesus spoke on the cross. This will set off lightning flashes, great peals of thunder, and a <u>severe earthquake</u> more <u>terrific than any felt before by mankind.</u>

A great city (commonly believed to be Babylon, i.e. Baghdad?) will be split asunder by God's wrath into 3 parts, as cities are destroyed in other nations. Islands and mountains will disappear. <u>Hail stones weighing about 75 pounds will fall from the sky,</u> for which evil mankind will further blaspheme God. It is hard to imagine such havoc from hail, when golf ball size is the usual maximum.

CHAPTER 17: This chapter adds some detail on circumstances that will exist during the time <u>when the 7 bowls of God's wrath fall</u> upon the wicked of earth. In verses 1-7, one of the bowl angels invites John to witness how God will punish a shameless and immoral woman who exploits many people and nations on earth. She consorts with the rulers of nations in a manner consistent with immorality.

There is <u>wide divergence over the symbolic identification of this prostitute</u>. Some say she represents Pagan Rome, or Papal Rome, which will subdue and rule much of the world surrounding Rome with military power, coupled with false religious concepts alien and hostile to Christianity. This view seemingly implicates the Roman Catholic Church in the political and economic affairs of earth.

Others say the woman portrays a prosperous civilization totally immersed in idolatrous beliefs and practices similar to that which existed in ancient Babylon, south of Baghdad, in today's Iraq. This world system may exist in the latter days with a corrupt religion, representing all apostate religious movements, that will be totally <u>committed to the</u> <u>replacement and destruction of Christianity</u>.

A logical conclusion is that both identities are fitting to a great degree and that they can be merged to produce a totally realistic description of the political, economical, and religious system <u>that will rule the day at the end of God's time</u> for us.

Circumstances today indicate that this final world system may be controlled from a central point in the Euro-Afro-Asian part of the world, which <u>could be in or near Rome</u>. At the time of this writing, however, the United Nations, an organization which typifies the predicted Babylonian philosophy, and a proponent of a one world system, is located in New York City, but this may not be so down the road.

In his vision, John is spiritually given a view of the wilderness of the world where this harlot is seated on the back of a red beast, covered with blasphemous names, and having 7 heads and 10 horns, the antichrist described in 13:1. In regal attire as if a queen, the woman will wear a purple and scarlet gown, festooned with gold, gems, and pearls. She will hold a gold cup filled with abominations (idolatry) and the unclean things of her nature.

On her forehead, she will be identified as 'MYSTERY BABYLON, THE MOTHER OF ALL IMMORAL AND FILTHY THINGS ON EARTH.' She will be intoxicated from the blood of saints and servants (disciples, apostles, ministers, etc.), who were martyred for their faith in God and Jesus Christ. When John was puzzled over this vision, the angel said he would clarify it's meaning.

The angels' explanation is given in verses 7-13 as follows: First, the beast (the antichrist) is pictured at a time prior to the trumpet-bowl judgments, seemingly in the 1st half of the tribulation, before he will rear his ugly head at the mid-point. He will be in existence as an antichrist development but not yet recognized as the antichrist. The unbelievers on earth will marvel and be deceived at the emergence of his deceptive religious and political concepts. This calls for some common sense!

The antichrist movement will be cunning, evil and wise, as it exerts influence on the world, possibly from a city of 7 hills, a pseudonym for Rome. The beast's 7 heads are thought to represent the 7 hills of Rome, or the 7 rulers of kingdoms or empires he will control. The angel tells John that 5 of the rulers are no longer alive, a 6th was then ruling a developing antichrist system, and the 7th will come later to rule with the antichrist for a short time (1260 days), until destroyed by God.

The 10 horns represent 10 more kings, or rulers, who have not yet come into power, and they will rule for a short time, 1260 days, with the antichrist. They will be of like mind and yield all their power to the antichrist.

Under the antichrist's leadership, in verses 14-18, the 10 rulers will wage war against Christ as first implied in 16:14, but the legions of God's army will destroy the armies of the antichrist. How this will be done is not clear but the words 'those who are with Him (Christ) are the called, the chosen, and the faithful,' seems to imply that the redeemed of Christ will have a part in clearing out the wicked of the world as a prelude to Christ's millennial reign. In Chapter 19:14, armies of heaven are mentioned as following Christ, the rider on a white horse; it appears that they will be composed of angelic beings, plus the redeemed in Christ, both Jews and Gentiles.

The angel identifies the waters where the harlot sat as being the apostate people of the entire world. For some reason, the 10 subjugated world rulers, probably with the approval of the antichrist (beast), will turn against the apostate people and try to destroy them. This destruction will no doubt occur after the antichrist occupies the temple and demands that the apostate people worship him as god, rather than continue with their pagan religions. Until the rapture occurs, this could include those having a Jewish or Christian faith.

God will induce this betrayal by the antichrist forces <u>to destroy all wicked mankind</u>, and the woman, the endtimes world system called Babylon. In so doing, He will use the beast forces as <u>His instrument of judgment on the kingdom of the antichrist</u>, which will turn against all religions, including those of pagans.

CHAPTER 18:   A special glorified angel with great power then came out of heaven and loudly spoke the words in verses 1-8, about the fall of Babylon, as a continuation of the views given in 14:8 and 16:19. It will become a hell on earth for those demonic souls, rulers, and wealthy merchants <u>who indulged in spiritual fornication</u> (idolatry and apostasy) with the harlot.

Another voice will come from heaven (Christ's?), calling for God's people to stand apart from this apostate world system, which indicates that this part of John's vision <u>pertained to the last 1260 days of tribulation before the rapture</u> takes them to Christ. God was preparing to punish this evil corrupt world system for all of it's sins.

When God's judgment falls on her (antichrist's domain) she will no longer be able to say, 'I am a queen, not a widow that will suffer mourning.' In truth, <u>she will feel the power of God's judgment</u> as she suffers plagues, pestilence, famine, grief, and destruction as if burned by fire.

In 9-20, John is given insight into the initial mourning of the apostate people over the <u>fall of the Babylonian world system.</u> This includes the kings who consorted with her, and the merchants that gained wealth trading with her; they will panic when they see this economic system collapse. The entire ocean shipping industry will lament the decimation of the system as their livelihood goes out the window. A total of 28 commodities in the capitalistic marketplace will become worthless without buyers. Not only will material prosperity disappear, but so will spiritual values.

Apart from the above, a voice from heaven will encourage rejoicing by all, angels, apostles, and prophets, <u>for the retribution that God will bring on the wicked.</u> Then, in verses 21-24, a mighty angel threw a huge stone into the sea (a comet?) to show <u>how terrible the fall</u> and total <u>destruction of the Babylonian system will be.</u>

No longer will there be sounds of music, and no skilled craftsmen, machinery, illumination, or human happiness will remain for the remnant of the antichrist economy. The business community, which had been successful and prosperous, but had deceived all nations, for which all <u>will be lost because of the blood of many martyrs on their hands</u>, slain during the antichrist's reign.

VIEWPOINTS: Once again, God's Word supports the understanding that Christ will rapture His saints shortly <u>before God's wrath judgment falls</u> on the world. The voice from heaven in verse 4 admonishing God's children, those who believe in Him and Jesus as His Son, to keep themselves apart from the sins of Babylon, <u>connotes their presence on earth</u>, even though God's judgment is near. The fall of Babylon is definitely to occur near the end of the 7 year tribulation time.

CHAPTER 19:   John must have been excited at this point of his revelation vision to hear <u>how it will be when Christ returns to claim His own</u>, all those who invested their trust and faith in

Him, whether they be Jew or Gentile. In verses 1-5, he hears the loud joyous cries of millions in heaven, saying 'Hallelujah! Salvation is ours, and glory and power belong to our God.

Praises are voiced to Him (perhaps like Ps. 113) for <u>judgment rendered on the harlot Babylon,</u> who corrupted the earth with wickedness and caused the death of many saints and servants of the Lord. They repeat a Hallelujah (Praise the Lord) a 2nd time for the destructive smoke rising from the scorching the antichrist will receive. The 4 living creatures and 24 elders join them with an Amen (agreed), Hallelujah! A voice from heaven urges them to keep on voicing their praises.

John then heard the voices from the huge multitude of the redeemed in verses 6-10, like the sound of rushing water and peals of thunder, saying 'Hallelujah, for our Lord God reigns forever' They <u>expressed joy in His glory, and the event to come,</u> a joining of Christ with His 'bride,' the redeemed of the Christian church and the nation of Israel. The good works and enduring faith of all believers will become <u>their garment of beautiful white fine linen as a wedding dress.</u> They were ready too!

The angel told John to write that God would bless those who are invited to the <u>marriage supper of the Lamb,</u> His Son Jesus Christ. At this John fell at the angel's feet to worship, but the angel told him not to do so, because he was just a servant of Jesus like all the other worshippers.

The next scene described in verses 11-16, was that of Christ coming out of heaven seated on a white horse; He is called 'Faithful and True' in keeping with His righteousness in <u>judging and waging a just war against the antichrist.</u> His appearance was awesome and perhaps symbolic, for His eyes blazed like flames of fire, and He wore many crowns, signifying sovereignty and power much greater than Satan's. He had a name tag with a name no one could interpret or understand.

His robe was red from crucifixion blood, and He will be called 'The Word of God.' Following Him, also on white horses, were the <u>multitudes of heaven (angels-see Matt. 26:53), and perhaps redeemed saints,</u> all clothed in bright white linen. Symbolically, a sharp sword from Christ's mouth (representing the Word of God) attacked the masses of antichrist's domain. With a rod of iron, He will cast them into God's wrath wine press and <u>trod them to death.</u> Then John saw the name, 'KING OF KINGS, AND LORD OF LORDS' on His robe at thigh level.

Next, in verses 17-21, John sees an angel standing in bright sunlight, calling on the birds that fly high in the heavens (eagles and vultures) to <u>come down and consume all the dead bodies</u> of rulers, riders of horses (vehicles of war), soldiers of war, important and ordinary people, slaves, animals of all kinds, and everything else that died from God's wine press wrath. This must be the battle of ARMAGEDDON!

Even though the antichrist and his allied kings fought against Christ and His army, they lost the battle. The antichrist, and his lieutenant false prophet will be captured and <u>thrown into a lake of burning sulfur</u> (Gehenna, eternal hell) the eternal destiny of all unbelievers. The rest of his followers will be killed by the sword from Christ's mouth, and became <u>abundant food for the birds of the air.</u> Their souls will join Satan, and his antichrist friends at the end of the millennium reign of Christ.

VIEWPOINTS: There is plenty of mystery in this chapter. In verse 7, the phrase 'His bride (wife in some translations) has made herself ready' does not tell us in what way readiness will be accomplished, neither does it clearly identify the people involved. The best understanding is that all of the redeemed saints of the Old Testament era, and those of the <u>New Testament church age</u> will comprise the 'bride' of Christ. This will logically include the dead and the living who have their name written on the wedding invitation list, which the angels of the Lord <u>will use to carry out the rapture reaping.</u>

How Christ will strike down the antichrist nations, using the sword of His mouth (the Word of God) is beyond comprehension; <u>no doubt it will be a supernatural happening.</u> Yet, it could be speaking of God's way to turn earthly armies against each other for a type of self-destruction. What we are to understand about the symbolic casting of antichrist forces into God's wrath wine press to be trodden under is also mystery, how it will actually be done <u>to result in the predicted massive death toll</u>.

We have no clarity in this chapter on the involvement of Christ's heavenly army in crushing antichrist forces; it is easy to understand that <u>the angels may be most active in this war,</u> but it is questionable whether or not the redeemed saints will do so. It is likely, that God and Christ with supernatural power will win the victory without the involvement of redeemed mankind, which as the 'bride' of Christ will be <u>reserved for everlasting peace and blessings.</u>

CHAPTER 20:   This chapter deals with the predicted 1000 years (millennial) reign of Christ. In verses 1-6, John saw another angel coming from heaven with a key and chain (see 9:1) to seal and lock a deep pit where evil spirits will be confined in that day. This angel seized Satan, chained and threw him into the pit <u>to be confined for 1000 years under lock and key</u>—with no way to escape. But, for some reason, he would be paroled then for awhile to deceive the people of the world again.

John also saw the redeemed (raptured believers) seated on thrones amid the multitudes of martyrs from the tribulation days, along with the <u>living redeemed after the dead in Christ are raised.</u> These will be the blessed holy bride of Christ who will <u>participate with Him in His kingship</u> for 1000 years. The unsaved dead from ages past before Christ, and those since Christ's time, <u>will not be raised until after the 1000 year time</u>. They will be raised for the 'great white throne judgment.'

Verses 7-10 speak of Satan's release at the end of 1000 years to do his dirty work as before, <u>with unexpected and shameful success.</u> He will gather people from the 4 corners of the earth, from nations identified as Gog and Magog, <u>to march against the children of God</u>, those who remain loyal to Him. Most of Satan's army will likely come from those born during the millennium that <u>did not accept Christ as their divine ruler</u>, although they obeyed His laws.

Satan's forces will surround the camp and city of God's people (the new Jerusalem headquarters for Christ's reign?). Without any gain from doing so, they <u>will be destroyed by fire from heaven</u>, as if from a gigantic atomic bomb. Satan will survive to be seized again and thrown in a lake of fire and burning sulfur, <u>to join the antichrist and his false prophet</u>, where they will remain in great pain forever.

John then saw a great white throne in verses 11-15, <u>on which God was seated.</u> Before him appeared all the unsaved dead, from earthly graves and from the sea, now resurrected in some form, for His final judgment of them. The Book of Life will be opened before them, as well as other books of record on their spiritual nature and earthly behavior. Since their names will not be in the Book of Life, they will be judged according to the other records, and be relegated to the lake of fire along with Satan, his angels, and antichrist henchmen. This will be their 2nd death, irrevocable for eternity. It does not appear that any will be accepted into God's kingdom.

For those who remain true to Christ, death will be eliminated as a consequence of sin, and along with Hades, it will be cast into the lake of fire. This will be the beginning of eternity in a new purified environment with God.

CHAPTER 21: Everything will be new, heaven and earth, with no sea and with a New Jerusalem, holy as never before, beautifully adorned as a bride, as related in verses 1-8. In a loud voice, Christ declared that God will make His home with His people on this new planet, to make their lives the best ever, with no sorrow, death, suffering, pain, worries, disasters, warfare, sin, etc.—Hallelujah, nothing bad!

John was told to record God's words from His throne, 'This is the truth, everything is finished from the beginning to the end (Alpha & Omega). My water of life is freely given to all who are spiritually thirsty; this is a blessing for the victorious for I am their God and they are my people.'

A warning is also given here for the ungodly of this world to heed that they will not reap these rewards, because they will suffer a second death for their sins in the lake of fire and burning sulfur, as previously stated.

John then meets one of the 7 bowl angels in verses 9-21, who invites him to come with him to see the Lamb's bride and wife, the New Jerusalem. Carried away to a high mountain in a spiritual mode, John saw the holy city of Jerusalem coming down from God. Perhaps this was a pictorial panorama of a refurbished city that opened up to him as if newly descended from heaven. In this case, the bride is the New Jerusalem whereas in 19:7, the bride was the redeemed of Christ.

What he saw was fantastic in beauty and brilliance, reflecting the glory of God, in the mode of precious gems. Although surrounded by a strong high wall, it had 12 gates attended by 12 angels, each with the name of one of the 12 tribes of Israel. He saw 3 gates on each side of the city, facing east, west, north, and south. The names of the 12 apostles of Christ were seen on the 12 foundation stones of the wall, surrounding the city as a perfect square.

For some reason, the angel proceeded to measure the length of the city wall with a gold measuring tape. Each wall section measured out to 1500 miles, which would give a total of 2,250,000 square miles of surface area. But hold on, the construction within the walls is pictured as a skyscraper 1500 miles high. This made the city complex a cube in shape. With each floor level 15 feet above the lower one, a total of 528,000 floor levels could accommodate an enormous number of occupants.

John describes the city he saw as pure gold like clear glass, with walls of jasper, wall foundation stones made of all kinds of precious stones, as listed. Each of the 12 gates were solid pearls, and the streets appeared to be pure glassy gold.

In verses 22-27, he saw no temple because God and Christ will be present and a temple would be superfluous. Because God's and Christ's glory was so bright, <u>no sun or moon light will be necessary</u>. The occupants will have no difficulty moving around in this heavenly light, since there will be no night there. The gates will always be open to permit treasures of the new world nations<u> to be brought in to the Lord.</u>

Only people whose names will be in the Book of Life will reside in the city, because all the unsaved evil people will not be around any longer.

<u>VIEWPOINTS:</u>   It is difficult to visualize a city 1500 miles high and what kind of housing structure will be provided. Will Otis Elevator Co, provide the vertical transportation, or <u>will angelic flight be the mode of movement for everyone?</u>

The New Jerusalem may be the capital city of this new world, with the largest population of heavenly beings. While only those with their name written in the Book of Life will reside in it, the word 'nations' in<u> verse 24 implies that many other 'Book of Life' people</u> will reside elsewhere on this new earth.

<u>CHAPTER 22:</u>   In this final chapter of the most prophetic book in God's Holy Word, with all of it still ahead of mankind, John is <u>shown a crystal clear river of life,</u> in verses 1-2. It flowed from the throne of God and Jesus Christ down the middle of the New Jerusalem capital city. Many trees lined the banks of the river; they will grow and provide different kinds of ripe fruit each month of the year. These 12 fruits will sustain life and the leaves <u>will serve as medicine to keep everyone healthy.</u>

The people will be blessed, as stated in verses 3-5, because sin will plague them no more, and they <u>will enjoy worshipping God face to face,</u> as if His name was written on their foreheads. With the everlasting light of God's glory, and no night, there will be <u>no concern for sunlight or any kind of lantern light.</u>

Then John was given a reminder to record in verses 6-7, that this revelation to him was true and worthy of trust, as given by the prophets and as shown by the angels. For this reason, mankind, who would read this account before the time of the end, should remember that Christ will be coming relatively soon, and <u>God will bless all the faithful who remain</u> prepared for these future events.

Overcome with all of this awesome information, John kneeled down in verse 8-10 to worship his angel guide, but was immediately told not to do so, because the angel was a servant just like John. He told John to worship God only, and to <u>share the prophecy of this</u> book with everyone. It is now available to earth's humanity if they will but give it attention.

Verse 11 must be understood to speak of the evil sin nature of people up to the time of God's wrath judgment, and then <u>for a short time after Satan is released</u> at the end of Christ's millennial reign. After that, all will be good people, doing right as holy members of God's heavenly kingdom.

John is given fair warning again, in verses 12-14, from Christ, that <u>He will return soon to reward the deserving saints,</u> in His role as the first and last, at the beginning of creation and at the end of normal earthly time. Those wearing white garments of righteousness will be blessed by God, they will be <u>healthier than ever as they eat fruit from the trees of life,</u> and they will have ready access to the city gates.

Verse 15 is another conundrum comment, that should be understood to be speaking of the unsaved sinners before God's wrath judgment, who are unworthy to be among the saints of heaven.

In verses 16-20, Christ seems to be speaking to John to close out this vision, by identifying Himself as Jesus, and <u>the one who sent the angels to guide John</u> through all of this revelation, which is for all churches. He calls himself David's Great Descendant, a bright morning star.

As a prelude to the end times, Christ says that the Holy Spirit and His church (bride) <u>extend the invitation to all mankind</u> to 'Come' to a saving grace with Him and God. Everyone is welcome to partake of His spiritual salvation water at no cost!

Closing with this warning, Christ says that God will greatly afflict those who add to this revelation account, or take anything away from it, <u>even barring entry into heaven.</u> This book is to be heard, studied, understood, and heeded, not tampered with or modified to suits one's wishes. He ends with another, 'I am coming soon!'

John apparently responds with 'Lord Jesus, please come soon! He adds his prayer that the Lord Jesus will be kind to all people at his time and in the future, who now <u>have this prophecy and warning to be ready for His coming</u>. As the world grows colder and bolder against the God of the universe and His Son Jesus Christ, it behooves all believers to add their 'Yes Lord, please do come soon to end this mess!' The depletion of natural resources and the wasteful use of them, such as water and fuel, portend a future time when mankind may become desperate and destitute over the <u>increasingly difficult task of surviving on this earth.</u>

<u>SUMMARY:</u> One of the most striking details is the number of times that an angel or angels are engaged in carrying out the endtimes activities. The word angel, or angels, is found about 84 times in 79 verses in this book*. Since angels are heavenly servants of God and Jesus Christ, who in times past often delivered messages to humans and carried out God's will affecting mankind, it is to be expected that they will <u>play a key role in the transition of</u> this <u>world into a new remodeled world. (*New Living Translation)</u>

Angels are created beings, but when God created them is not revealed. There are <u>3 categories of angels identified in the Bible</u>: the hard-working messenger type (Gabriel), and two kinds of winged angels, cherubims and seraphims (see Ezekiel 1:4-28; 10:3-22 and Isaiah 6:2-6

Cherubims appear to function primarily as guards or attendants to the divine throne, and seraphims mostly <u>attend God's throne and voice praises</u>. Apart from all of them, the archangel Michael is one that guarded the nation of Israel and in Rev. 12:7, will command the forces of God against the forces of the dragon in a heavenly war.

Revelation tells of angels waiting on the throne of God, presiding over the corners of the earth, taking part in the cosmic reordering at the end of time, carrying out assigned tasks related to the oncoming tribulation of Daniels 70th week, and <u>pouring out God's great wrath judgment on wicked humanity at the end of it.</u>

Angels are ready for the end of time, but <u>humanity is not for the most part</u>. Every believer should share the Word of God, including Revelation, with the unsaved of this evil world. In terms of God's time, Jesus often warned that His 2nd coming would be a surprise to many who are spiritually unprepared; His reminders are repeated in Revelation up to the very last chapter.

Being prepared means to face physical death as a faithful believer in God and Jesus Christ, or to be raptured alive as such when Christ returns. Either way, we can become a guest at His wedding feast for His 'bride,' since we will be one of His redeemed saints. Our churches must heed what the Holy Spirit tells us, and as people of God, we must persevere in the hour of tribulation, knowing that our enthroned Lord will return in triumph in God's time...... Whenever that will be!

RECAP OF ENDTIMES SCENARIO

M uch speculation has arisen over the centuries since the complete Bible came into existence, about the true meaning of scriptures pertaining to God's wrap up of earthly affairs, commonly referred to as the endtimes scenario. An issue much debated is the sequence of events during a designated 7 year time of tribulation, also known as Daniel's 70th week.

Points most disputed include: 1—Will the Christian church be present on earth during the tribulation years?; 2—Will the 'rapture' of the saints take place before the tribulation begins or much later?; 3—What is meant by the 'Day of the Lord' term?; and 4—Will the Jewish people (nation of Israel) be a part of Christ's 1000 year reign?

Beginning with Old Testament prophecy, the most plausible answers to these questions will be given, based on applicable passages of scripture. Consideration will not be given to doctrinal views of any Protestant or Catholic branch of the church. God's Word should be determinate for all disputable issues apart from dogma.

Scripture references and comment follow for these 12 topics: The Ascension Factor, Passage of Time, Times of sorrows, Daniel's 70th week, Tribulation Years, Antichrist Era, Christ's 2nd Coming, Raising the Saints, God's Wrath Judgment, Christ's Millennial Reign, White Throne Judgment, and God's New Environment.

THE ASCENSION FACTOR: For this Topic, keep in mind that the word 'ascension' literally means the rising of a human body from earth to heaven. The 1st recorded scripture implying an ascension is that of Gen 5:24, where Enoch was taken up because he was highly favored by God. The 2nd instance of this took place when Elijah was taken up in a whirlwind as related in II Kings 2:11.

Psalm 68:18 can be understood to predict the ascension of Christ, and Mark 16:19, Luke 24:51, and Acts 1:2, 9 speak of the actual ascension of Christ after His resurrection from the grave.

These three instances of a supernatural removal of two humans and the divine Christ foretells the ascension that the dead and living believers in Christ will experience when Christ comes to gather His own, in a huge harvest of souls.

With Christ's departure to heaven, a new era of waiting for His 2nd coming began. Even though the disciples and the Apostle Paul spoke of His return as being around the corner, over 1950 years have elapsed since Christ's ascension. How much longer will it be? Only God knows the answer!

PASSAGE OF TIME: Any measurement of time must be joined with God's equation for time as given in Ps. 90:4 and II Peter 3:8, that with Him 'a (human?) day is like (or can become) 1000 years, and (His) thousand years is like 1 of our days.' This can mean that He can lengthen or shorten any period of time according to His agenda, and therefore human measurement is a moot point.

In John 16:16, Jesus spoke of His return taking place in a little while. Paul preached in I Cor. 7:29 that time had been shortened for the human lifespan, and so one should make the best of life, as also advised in Eph. 5:16. Finally, in Acts 1:7, Jesus told believers before His ascension, that it was not for them to know the timing of future events as ordained by God. No matter how long, we must endure in faith!

TIMES OF SORROW: Sorrow is part of life; has been so since Adam and Eve were expelled from the Garden of Eden, because of their sin. **Sorrow can be associated with sin.** We will not escape from it until we are among the redeemed with Christ, and part of God's eternal kingdom after the millennium.

David spoke of his life of sorrow in Ps. 31:9-10; he mourned over the death of Saul and Jonathan in II Samuel 1:23-26. Jeremiah spoke of his sorrow in Jer. 8:18, and how it replaces joy and gladness in 48:33. In Lamentations, we find many words about sorrow, as in 1:16, 2:11, 3:48-49, and 5:15.

Jesus felt sorrow many times, as revealed in Matt. 26:38 and John 12:27. The disciples grieved many times, as in Matt. 17:22-23, and as Jesus predicted in John 16:20, 22. Believers will suffer grief throughout their life, as indicated in II Cor. 1:4-5, and 7:9-10. The Apostle Paul suffered sorrow as written in II Cor. 2:1-4 and Phil. 2:27. Mankind will grieve as they see Christ at His 2nd coming as stated in Rev. 1:7.

Times of sorrow, travail and conflict are predicted in Matt. 24:7-8, Mark 13:7-9, and Luke 21:9-12, as a forerunner of the tribulation years to come. Such conditions have prevailed for most of the time since Christ's ascension. We have had a continuing occurrence of wars, famines, earthquakes, fires, floods, plagues, insurrections, and other stressful events, involving the loss of many lives, with much grief as an ongoing part of history since then. But the scripture indicates that these times will become increasingly difficult as we approach the terrible tribulation years.

This will give all believers an opportunity to witness, as they endure steadfastly!

DANIEL'S 70TH WEEK: The visions of Daniel as given by the angel Gabriel in Dan. 9:22-27 told him of a 490 year stretch of history, much of it in captivity, for the nation of Israel. The time was measured in weeks, with each day of the week representing 1 year, so one week is equated to 7 years, and 490 years equals 70 weeks.

Of this total, 69 weeks are interpreted to have expired as history up to the time that Jesus was crucified about 30 AD. The last week, Daniel's 70th week, interpreted to be a 7 year tribulation period predicted elsewhere, is yet to come, after time lapse of 1975 years to this date. There is no certainty as to when this tribulation period of time will start. There are predicted signs that may give mankind a clue, if one is spiritually sensitive to world events. It could be just around the corner!

Even though Daniel's vision was related to the nation of Israel, and since the Gentile nations are now tied in with God's gospel of the kingdom and His endtimes agenda, this tribulation time is applicable also to the Christian church.

In Dan. 12:1-4, his prophecy relates to the separation of those acceptable to God (Jews and Gentiles) from those who are not, (the rapture action) after a time of terrible distress, interpreted to be the Great Tribulation of 3 ½ years, the last half of Daniel's 70th week.

TRIBULATION YEARS: Otherwise known as the 7 years of Daniel's 70th week of great distress, sorrow, conflict, and apostasy, which will precede Christ's 2nd coming, and commonly referred to as the 'time of tribulation.' A preview of this time is given in Jer. 15:2-3 and 48:43-44, chiefly for the nation of Moab, a neighbor then of Israel, and a branch of the Israeli people. Most edifying is the description of the tribulation time given by Jesus in Matt. 24:5-25 and Mark 13:6-23, where He included a picture of the antichrist rising at mid-point, after the 1st half, or 3.5 years into Daniel's 70th week.

Will the Christian church be present during most of the 7 tribulation years along with the nation of Israel (all Jews, saved or unsaved)? Several N. T. scriptures imply this fate: In John 16:33, Jesus said **'in the world you will have tribulation;'** Acts 14:22 reads 'Through many tribulations we must enter the kingdom of God;' and Rom. 8:35-37 says 'tribulation will not separate us from the love of Christ.'

The exact time when the tribulation begins is not given in scriptures, and in all probability will not be known to mankind in general. The **'time of sorrows'** may lead into the 7 year tribulation time, and overlap as much as the 1st half. Keep in mind that God ordered Daniel (12:4, 8-9) to seal up his account of the tribulation vision for revelation at the end of time, in keeping with His control on secrecy.

ANTICHRIST ERA: The antichrist world system is in the making today, but the personality of the antichrist will become a reality during the 7 year tribulation time. How early he will be active in human form is hard to say, but several scriptures reveal that his public recognition will occur at the mid-point. Daniel 9:27, 11:31 and 12:11 are predictions of his appearance, where he is called the **'abomination of desolation.'**

Matt. 24:15-16 and Mark 13:14 also tell of his coming in an ungodly way. II Thes. 2:3-4 tells us that he will take his seat in God's temple for people to worship him. Most significant here is the statement that Christ will not return until there is a time of apostasy, rebellion, and worship of the antichrist. In verses 6-8 that follow, we are told antichrist types were already at work back in Paul's day but the real one will not appear until the restrainer (the archangel Michael is my choice) stands aside. Mention is also made that he will be destroyed at the end.

In I John 2:18 and 4:3, John said that many pretender antichrists appeared in his day and this meant that mankind is getting closer to the time when the real one will come to light. Verse 22 tells us the antichrist is a liar who will deny God and Christ. Then, in II John 7, we are told that he is a great deceiver who will deny that Christ came to earth as a human. Antichrist will appear before Christ's 2nd coming for the rapture of His children.

In John's vision of Rev. 6: 9, 14-15, after the angel opened the fifth seal, he saw under the altar the souls of those who had been slaughtered for the word of God and for the testimony they had given during the early part of antichrist's Great Tribulation wrath period.(during the last half of Daniel's 70th week.

CHRIST'S 2ND COMING: A question that needs answering is, '**Why is Christ coming again and when is He returning?** The New Testament clearly tells us that He is coming back to earth to redeem all believers, those of old from the grave, and those living at the time. He will come to reward His believers for their good works (according to their deeds), mainly for being good disciples in obedience to God's commands and for being good witnesses of Him, (Matt. 16:27).

He is coming to reconcile the Jews to God, those who eventually accept Christ. He is coming to establish a kingdom of believers for a millennial reign. He is coming to assist God in the final judgment before the beginning of a perfect eternity.

When Jesus was on earth, He told His followers that He would be leaving them for a time, but would return again to the earth (John 14:3, 16:16, 22) This message of the second coming is referred to as the Blessed Hope (Titus 2:13). Jesus warned His followers that they should be prepared to welcome Him back.

Jesus exhorted his followers to be watchful (ready spiritually) for His return, for it could happen anytime within the time frame that God would ordain, and that would be after much tribulation and cosmic disturbances. (See Matt. 24:29-30, 42-44, Mark 13:24-26, and Luke 21:25-28) In Phil 3:20, Paul said our citizenship is in heaven, and it is from there that we are expecting a Savior, the Lord Jesus Christ. Paul also prayed for believers to be spiritually strong and blameless at the coming of Christ with all His angels, in I Thes. 3:13.

Finally, in Matt. 24:27 and Luke 17:24, **Christ said He would come quickly** like a bolt of lightning in the east, probably middle-east Israel. He also told His disciples in Matt.

24:36, concerning the time of His return, that no one would know except His Father God. Peter wrote in II Pet. 3:8, that with the Lord 1 day is like a 1000 years and 1000 years like 1 day, to explain that God might delay Christ's return longer than humans expect or prefer, for the purpose of reaping more souls.

Paul clarified this matter in II Thes. 2:2-4, saying that Christ would not return until apostasy become a major trend, and the antichrist is revealed when he occupies a temple of God, as a pretender to that position.

Rev. 1:7 says that Christ will be seen coming with clouds; every eye will see him, even those who pierced him; and on his account all the tribes of the earth (of Israel?) will mourn over their past unbelief.

RAISING THE SAINTS: The catching up of believers by Christ at the time of His return is generally referred to as the 'rapture' a word not found in the Bible. The word is a derivative of the Latin translation of 'rapere, raptum, or rapine' meaning to seize and carry away, with an element of extreme joy or pleasure.

This is the promise believers received from Christ before He returned to heaven, for fulfillment on His 2nd coming. Yes, it will be a joyous moment to be taken out of this troubled world! As to the timing of this event, the most common view is that it will occur 'premillennial,' sometime before Christ's reign begins after Daniel's 70th week, the 7 year tribulation time.

Scripture references and comments in 2 sections above, (Tribulation Years, and the Antichrist Era,) very clearly indicate that the Christian church and the nation of Israel will be present during most of the tribulation. Matt. 16:27, 24:21-22, 31, Mark 13:19-20, 26-

27, and Luke 21:18-19, 28 collectively tell us that there will be a time of great tribulation with extreme suffering, such as has not been from the beginning of the world, after the antichrist becomes a public figure.

The prophet Joel in chapter 2:30-32 predicts a time when the heavens and earth, will be filled with blood, fire and columns of smoke. The sun will be darkened, and the moon will appear blood red, all this before the great and terrible day of the Lord comes. Those who call on the name of the Lord (believers) will be saved as the Lord has said; this will include Messianic Jews at Mount Zion and in Jerusalem that the Lord calls (including the 144,000 Jews who will be sealed). After that is completed, the Day of the Lord will come, with all His angels to judge.

If those Great Tribulation days are not cut short, no one would be physically saved; but for the sake of the elect, chosen by Christ, (Jews and Gentiles) it will be so. In I Cor. 15:51-52, Paul informs the church at Corinth of a mystery to come. It was that the dead will be raised imperishable, that living believers will not die when Christ comes for them, but both categories will be changed, as quick as the blink of an eye.

He says this will be done at the last trumpet, which should not be related to the 7th trumpet of God's wrath judgment, because the church will be spared that ordeal. The 'last trump' in this case signaled the final stage of mankind's existence on earth before Christ's 2nd coming, in the manner that trumpets were sounded in Paul's days. The trumpet was a ceremonial ram's horn used to call the people of Israel together for worship, or to marshal the Israelites against their enemies. God will provide a measure of protection to His faithful believers, both Jew and Gentile, during the tribulation up to the time of the rapture. A remnant of the nation of Israel, 144,000 will be secured under God's seal, possibly through most of His Wrath Judgment, to evangelize Jewish disbelievers to Christ.

In His Olivet Discourse, Jesus said in Matt. 24:31, that His angels would gather up his saints (elect) from the parts of the earth, the dead first, and then the living, all to have transformed bodies suitable for eternity with the Lord. This is confirmed by Paul's writing in I Cor. 15:51 and I Thes. 4:15-17. Phil 3:21 speaks of the transformation of our body to conform to the body of Christ's glory.

Rev. 3:5, 10-11 tells us that if we endure, win the victory despite much duress, that we will be clothed in white robes, since our name will be found in the book of life. Then we will also be kept from God's Wrath Judgment that will come on the whole world. At that time, Christ will come quickly, so believers should hold fast to their faith, and thus not lose their reward crowns.

Believers are to use the hope of Christ's second return as a motivation to work. Being convinced that Christ will come quickly at an unknown time, should motivate believers to serving Him to the best of their ability. Because we know not when our mortal lives will end, we should strive to live a pure and blameless life.

GOD'S WRATH JUDGMENT: This is also commonly referred to as 'The Day of the Lord,' which apparently follows immediately after Christ raptures His saints from earth near the end of the Great Tribulation time.

In Isaiah 13:6-13, we are told that the Day of the LORD will come like destruction from the Almighty, to confound humanity with heartache, pain and misery, as God's fierce <u>anger falls on them as punishment for their evil</u>. Zeph 1:14-18 adds that Day of the Lord is coming soon to bring His wrath with distress and anguish, ruin and devastation, darkness and gloom, <u>after a trumpet blast and battle cry is sounded.</u>

In Ezek. 20:33-44, God gives a promise to the nation of Israel of a future <u>restoration of their relationship to Christ</u>, and a gathering of the Jews from other lands, for a separate judgment face to face with them. This will be so they will undeniably know Him as their Messiah.

Zech. 12:8-10 tells us on that Day, the Lord will shield the inhabitants of Jerusalem, as He <u>destroys the nations that will come against Jerusalem.</u> He will have compassion on the nation of Israel and the inhabitants of Jerusalem, <u>as they recognize Him as the Messiah,</u> and grieve in repentance over their rejection of Him.

Zech. 14:3-5 says, 'On that day when He begins a battle against the antichrist nations, Christ's feet shall stand on the Mount of Olives, which shall be split in two from east to west by a very wide valley.' The wicked shall flee up the valley attempting to escape from the judgment to come on them. The Lord Jesus often stood upon the Mount of Olives when on earth.

There will be a time when the Jews of Israel and particularly Jerusalem will suffer greatly but the Lord will give encouragement of <u>better days after their enemies have been destroyed</u> (Zech. 14:8-15), and the survivors begin to worship the Lord (16-17). Luke told us in Luke 18:7-8 that God would bring justice to those believers who suffered death during the tribulation, <u>by punishing their persecutors.</u>

In Matt. 25:31-46, Jesus told of His judgment upon all the nations after coming to earth with all his angels, <u>to separate the sheep</u> (the righteous) <u>from the goats</u> (the wicked) after the Great Tribulation is over and antichrist forces are destroyed. This may occur after the saints of Christ are raptured.

In Jude 14-15 we read that the prophet Enoch said, 'the Lord is coming with ten thousands of His holy ones, to execute judgment on all, and to <u>convict everyone of all the deeds of ungodliness</u> that they have committed in such an ungodly way, and of all the harsh things that ungodly sinners have spoken against Him."

In his vision of Rev. 6:12-17, John saw the terrible cosmic disturbances associated with Christ's 2ⁿᵈ coming <u>after an angel opened the 6ᵗʰ seal,</u> and the fear that overcame the high and mighty, who could not stand against the Day of the Lord. In another vision in Rev. 7:2-3, he saw an angel telling 4 other angels not to damage the earth and sea, until the <u>144,000 Jews were sealed to endure more tribulation.</u>

Rev. 8:1-6 tells of the beginning of the trumpet and bowls judgments against the <u>wicked antichrist forces on earth</u>. Each trumpet and bowl judgment action brought devastation of a different kind on different features or areas, beginning with the earth's foliage, sea life and shipping, drinking water, the cosmos, pestilence upon mankind, death of military forces, and other plagues. During this time, Satan and his collection of evil angels <u>will be ejected from all heavenly areas, to be earthbound.</u>

After the 7ᵗʰ bowl judgment, in Rev. 16:17, a loud voice came out of God's throne room saying, "It is done!" and the <u>final devastation upon earth was over.</u> It may be that somewhere at this point, before Christ assumes His throne as King for a 1000 year reign, that the 144,000 sealed Jews, plus all Jewish converts they may have brought to a saving knowledge of Christ during the Great Tribulation and God's wrath judgment, <u>will all be</u> <u>reconciled to God to be a part of Christ's reign.</u>

In support of this thought, consider Matt. 25:31-34, 41-46, which tells of Christ carrying out a judgment call as He occupies His throne, by <u>gathering mankind before Him</u> <u>for a sheep/goat separation.</u> The sheep will inherit the kingdom prepared for them, and the <u>goats will be cast into eternal hell with Satan and his angels.</u>

CHRIST'S MILLENNIAL REIGN: Before Christ was born, an angel told Mary that He would reign over the house of Jacob forever, and of <u>His kingdom there will be no end</u> (Luke 1:32-33). It will be for 1000 years on earth and then for <u>eternity after God's White Throne Judgment</u> and the remaking of His kingdom environment.

Rev. 20:1-6 tells how Satan will be seized, bound, thrown into a pit, and securely locked in for the 1000 years, while those he had martyred for their faith in God <u>would reign</u> <u>with Christ for that time.</u> Verses 7 tells how Satan will be released to lead the weak astray again throughout the earth, and mobilize them into a military force around Jerusalem. They will be destroyed by fire from heaven.

During the millennium, Christ will reign on the earth with His saints while Satan remains bound in the bottomless pit. The <u>Jewish nation is expected to have a major role</u> in the events of the millennial period. Many bible scholars allow for symbolism in the use of the number 1,000 years for the length of this era It may not be exactly 1,000 years, based on <u>God's equation of time that an earth day can be 1000 years with Him.</u> No matter, the reign of Christ will be factual for whatever time.

It is easy to assume that the multitudes who will reside on earth with Christ during His millennial reign <u>will all be believers at the outset.</u> Whether this spiritual condition will prevail throughout is nebulous inasmuch as there is no indication in the word about <u>the spirituality of those born during the millennium.</u> A likely view is that many offspring will not fully embrace Christianity because of the large number of followers that Satan will draw to himself after his release from the pit of hell.

Rev. 20:10 reveals that Satan will be reunited with the antichrist and false prophet in the lake of fire and brimstone <u>for an eternity of torment and hell.</u> Then comes the Great White Throne Judgment by God.

WHITE THRONE JUDGMENT: Rev. 20:11-15 reveals that God will be seated on a great white throne for a final judgment of the unsaved dead, great and small, as they stand before Him with heavenly <u>ledgers opened to reveal a record of their evil.</u> They will try to flee from this horrible experience but will find <u>no place to hide.</u> From the grave, the sea, Hades, and the ash piles of cremation, they will be mustered.

This will be the last resurrection of the dead for judgment along with those who joined Satan and <u>survived their last rebellion against Christ.</u> Death and Hades will be no longer, as they will be thrown into the lake of fire, <u>along with all humans judged at this time</u> to suffer a 2<u>nd</u> death. Jesus spoke of this in Matt. 16:27 as Paul did in I Cor. 15:26. Hades is the Greek equivalent of the Hebrew term "Sheol," which refers in general to the place where souls of the dead are held until <u>resurrected for eternity in heaven or hell</u>, depending totally upon God's judgment of their deeds. Malachi 4:1-3 gives a brief foretelling of this judgment action.

GOD'S NEW ENVIRONMENT: In Rev. 21:1-7 and 22:1-5, John saw a new heaven and a new earth which <u>replaced the original model</u>. The holy city of Jerusalem will come down from heaven as a newly adorned bride. God announced that **His new home would be among humankind**, who will be His children.

There will be no more sorrow, pain, sin, or warfare. Nothing accursed will be found there any more. The angels and the <u>redeemed will be servants of God and Jesus Christ</u> and will worship before their thrones. There will be no more night; light of any kind will no longer be needed, for the Lord God will be their light, and <u>they will reign forever and ever</u> with Him. Zech. 14:6-11 also predicts this end result.

FOOTNOTE: This Recap of God's Endtimes Scenario was compiled after much effort and struggle to put together pertinent references and to understand how they are intertwined <u>to reveal the most logical understanding and timing of events to come</u>. My conclusions are based on God's Word alone, without consideration for denominational <u>church doctrine or</u> <u>wishful thinking</u> or believer preferences.

I sincerely wish that I could have arrived at an end result pleasing to everyone, including brothers and sisters in Christ from previous church affiliations, particularly those who embrace the 'pre-trib rapture concept.' Even though my view may differ from theirs, this will in no way diminish my high regard for them as friends and believers in our Lord Jesus as our mutual Savior and Benefactor for eternity. I hope <u>they will render me the</u> <u>same esteem and respect.</u>

This concludes over 6 years of effort that only God could predict. Before that time, to write a commentary on the entire Bible <u>was never a thought of mine</u>. His Holy Spirit deserves all the credit for this work, and for the <u>value it may be to students of the Bible</u>, especially the rank and file believer and church member. I hope and pray that it will be effective in strengthening the spiritual character of many.

RICHARD C. HIRSCH

NEW TESTAMENT MARTYROLOGY

What is martyrdom all about? Webster's Dictionary defines it as enduring death or intense suffering for adherence to any principle or belief. As a Greek word meaning 'witness,' it means a person who gives his life for a cause. Many were martyred in Old Testament times for their faith in God. Later, multitudes died because of their faith in Christ rather than recant, or renounce such faith. Since the time of Christ many Christians have been martyred for their faith, and will continue to be until the Lord returns to establish his millennial kingdom. The following list of some of the more prominent early Church martyrs is ample evidence of persecution to come over the centuries.

—**JESUS**: An early example of martyrdom in 30 AD, as recounted in Matthew 27, that was rendered void by His resurrection. Satan and the Jewish leaders who instigated his crucifixion gained nothing from it; it was a hollow meaningless 'victory.' But, it gave his disciples an injection of great spiritual fervor and commitment to carry the Gospel of Christ to all the world. This was God's purpose in allowing it to happen. Still, Christ's death portended centuries of such unjust deaths for Christians.

—**STEPHEN**: The 1st real martyr for the Church of Christ, he was stoned to death by the Jews about 35 AD in Jerusalem, as told in Acts 7:59. Believers had to flee Jerusalem after Stephen's death while the apostles alone remained there (Acts 8:1). He was one of the 7 early leaders of the Jerusalem Church, with power from God to work miracles and other supernatural wonders. His discourse before his death in Acts 7 is remarkable for its witnessing.

—**JAMES**: The 1st apostle to be martyred by beheading about 44 AD by order of King Herod Agrippa I of Judea, during a general persecution of Christians, as recorded in Acts 12:2. As the brother of the Apostle John, sons of Zebedee and Salome, he was told by Jesus that he would drink the same cup as He would (See Matt. 20:20-23).

—**MATTHEW**: As a tax collector called by Jesus to be an apostle (Matt. 9:9; 10:3), he contributed the important first book to the New Testament that gives evidence of his ability to accurately record factual events, as a faithful disciple of Jesus. Non-biblical accounts tell of Matthew's travel to Ethiopia where he became associated with Candace, identified with the eunuch in Acts 8:27. Supposedly, he was beheaded in that country about 60 AD.

—**JAMES**: His death occurred between 62 and 66 AD, reportedly on the order of the high priest Ananus, either by stoning (according to Flavius Josephus, first century historian of the Jews) or by being cast down from the Temple tower (per Hegesippus, early Christian writer, quoted by the third-century Christian historian Eusebius). His death is not confirmed in the New Testament. He was a brother of Jesus, and the writer of the epistle James.

—**ANDREW**: A fisherman and disciple of John the Baptist who led his brother Simon to Jesus. Under John the Baptist's witness concerning Jesus, Andrew followed Jesus to His overnight lodging and became one of His first disciples. He is believed to have been killed on an x-shaped cross (St Andrews Cross), date unknown. He is not credited with the writing of any portion of the New Testament.

—**(JOHN) MARK**: He was an early missionary and church leader in Jerusalem, and the author of the Gospel of Mark. After Barnabas and Saul completed a brief mission to

Jerusalem, they took Mark (related to Barnabas) with them to Antioch (Acts 12:25). Mark wrote his Gospel for Gentile Christians. He detailed Jewish customs, as Jesus spoke of them, for the benefit of readers unfamiliar with Judaism (Ch. 7). He is last mentioned in II Timothy 4:11, and non-biblical speculation is that he was killed in Alexandria after criticizing an idol worship ceremony,—date unknown.

—**PETER**: Among the disciples, Peter is credited with being a leader of the twelve disciples whom Jesus called. His name always occurs first in the lists of disciples (Mark 3:16; Luke 6:14; Matt. 10:2). He frequently served as the spokesman for them. Tradition holds that Peter died as a martyr in Rome, crucified upside down about 67 AD. His legacy lives on in his writing of I and II Peter in the New Testament.

—**PAUL**: As the foremost missionary and writer of the early church, Paul and his theology are important in the New Testament, not only because 13 epistles bear his name but also because of the extended biographical information on him in the Book of Acts. From the information in these two sources, he is portrayed as one of the major personalities of early Christianity. The letters of Paul as listed in the New Testament include Romans through Philemon; many believe he also wrote the book of Hebrews. He was beheaded by order of Roman emperor Nero in Rome about 66-67 AD.

—**THOMAS**: He was the 'doubting' disciple, most difficult to convince that Jesus had been resurrected, who is said to have carried the Christian gospel to Persia, Parthia, and India, where he was tortured, speared and thrown in a fiery oven by angry pagans in 70 AD. He wrote nothing for the New Testament, and is mentioned only once as part of the new Jerusalem Church, in Acts 1:13. While at first skeptical, he changed from a doubting disciple to a doubtless one.

—**LUKE**: As a non-disciple Gentile physician, believed to have been converted by the Apostle Paul, Luke became an accurate historical writer of the Gospel of Luke and the Book of Acts. His accounts of Paul's missionary journeys to the Gentiles distinguished him as a faithful servant of the Lord and a close friend of Paul. Some accounts say that he died a natural death at age 84, but others say he was hanged from an olive tree in Athens about 93 AD.

—**JOHN**: John, with brother James, was an early disciple, who became the beloved of Christ, and the author of the Gospel of John, I-II and III John, and the Book of Revelations. At one point in his life, he was thrown into a vat of boiling oil, from which he emerged unharmed. Then he was banished to the Isle of Patmos, until he was freed and moved to Ephesus, where he lived until his natural death about 98 AD. His writing of Revelations is an example of God's supernatural means of communication to the faithful.

What is the modern day trend of this kind of persecution? In the 20th Century, more Christians were martyred than in all previous centuries combined, predominantly in China, Russia, and the Muslim nations of Nigeria, Pakistan, Iran, Indonesia, and Sudan. Will it continue? The New Testament scriptures strongly indicated it will!

Consider the words of Revelations 6:9-11. The sight Apostle John beheld at the opening the fifth seal was very disturbing. He saw the souls of the martyrs under the altar; at the base of the altar in heaven, at the feet of Christ. The cause for which they suffered was their faith in the Living Word of God, and their <u>unshaken confession of that faith.</u> Yet, the Lord is a comforter of His afflicted servants, for their sacrifice is precious in His sight.

As the magnitude of persecution grows, so will <u>the number of the persecuted increase</u> <u>as martyred servants of Christ.</u> When God's time is at hand, He will send tribulation to those who trouble His Saints, and provide unbroken happiness and rest to those that were martyred for His honor and glory. God is providing a better place in His heavenly realm, for those who are faithful unto death. Many will die in His name during the tribulation years to come. The corporate prayer of Christians should be that all will endure without compromise.

ABOUT THE AUTHOR

Born in 1921 in the state of North Dakota, Richard C. Hirsch lived for 13 years as a farm boy on the plains of North Dakota. During his time there, he attended a German Lutheran Church. In 1933 he moved to Washington state with his family, where he completed his high school education in 1939. While there he attended an English speaking Baptist church. That year at age 18, he enlisted in the United States Army, Corps of Engineers, serving for 3 1/2 years to attain the rank of Staff Sergeant. Then he was selected for training to become a commissioned reserve officer as a 2nd Lieutenant in the Topographic Branch of the Corps of Engineers. He also fulfilled requirements to be certified as a regular army CWO-3 Warrant Officer in his topographic specialty.

During active duty as a commissioned officer, he served about 10 years on overseas duty assignments, 2 times for 5 years in the European Theater of Operations, 4 years in Japan and 16 months in Vietnam of the Far East Command. His assignments were generally related to the production or stocking of maps for military intelligence and combat use. After 22 years of service he retired from active duty in 1961, shortly after selection for promotion to Lieutenant Colonel. During his military time, he acquired the equivalent of a college degree at various schools, mostly by correspondence with the University of Washington, majoring in business law and accounting. In his civilian status, he spent 15 years building his own small business corporation providing bookkeeping and income tax service for the public in Kerrville, TX. He sold his corporate interest in 1985 to retire completely from an occupational status, and relocate to Fort Clark Springs, a former WW II cavalry base near Bracketville, TX.

After 5 years, in 1990, he and his wife Huguette moved to Alamogordo, New Mexico, where they lived for 12 years, enjoying membership in a local church as a Sunday School lecturer. After attending a church weekend retreat in 1995, he committed himself to honor and service God, and the Lord Jesus Christ, with a spiritual motivation to write a Bible Commentary. This objective became a reality after relocation in 2002 to the rarefied atmosphere of the Sacramento Mountains east of Cloudcroft, New Mexico.

Richard's Bible Commentary, Book 1-OT was completed in 5 years for publication in 2005, followed by a 1 year accelerated compilation of Book 2-NT for publication in 2006. In 2012, he terminated publication because of the need for some revision of narrative and typo corrections. More relocations and personal hindrances delayed republication until 2020.

Now the Hirsch's, Richard at age 98+ and Huguette 94+, living in a remote mountain village, hope to see a revived worldwide interest in these 2 books, with a subsequent growth in spirituality and obedience to God's Holy Word. They welcome sincere prayer for a productive continued availability of the books for an indefinite time span.

--